CLYMER®
MANUALS

HONDA
TRX350 RANCHER • 2000-2006

WHAT'S IN YOUR TOOLBOX?

More information available at haynes.com
Phone: 805-498-6703

J H Haynes & Co. Ltd.
Sparkford Nr Yeovil
Somerset BA22 7JJ England

Haynes North America, Inc.
2801 Townsgate Road, Suite 340
Thousand Oaks, CA 91361 USA

ISBN-10: 0-89287-997-1
ISBN-13: 978-0-89287-997-7
Library of Congress: 2005911061

Technical Illustrations: Errol McCarthy
Cover: Mark Clifford Photography at www.markclifford.com

M200-2, 11T1, 15-400

ABCDEFGHIJKLM

Common spark plug conditions

NORMAL
Symptoms: Brown to grayish-tan color and slight electrode wear. Correct heat range for engine and operating conditions.
Recommendation: When new spark plugs are installed, replace with plugs of the same heat range.

WORN
Symptoms: Rounded electrodes with a small amount of deposits on the firing end. Normal color. Causes hard starting in damp or cold weather and poor fuel economy.
Recommendation: Plugs have been left in the engine too long. Replace with new plugs of the same heat range. Follow the recommended maintenance schedule.

CARBON DEPOSITS
Symptoms: Dry sooty deposits indicate a rich mixture or weak ignition. Causes misfiring, hard starting and hesitation.
Recommendation: Make sure the plug has the correct heat range. Check for a clogged air filter or problem in the fuel system or engine management system. Also check for ignition system problems.

ASH DEPOSITS
Symptoms: Light brown deposits encrusted on the side or center electrodes or both. Derived from oil and/or fuel additives. Excessive amounts may mask the spark, causing misfiring and hesitation during acceleration.
Recommendation: If excessive deposits accumulate over a short time or low mileage, install new valve guide seals to prevent seepage of oil into the combustion chambers. Also try changing gasoline brands.

OIL DEPOSITS
Symptoms: Oily coating caused by poor oil control. Oil is leaking past worn valve guides or piston rings into the combustion chamber. Causes hard starting, misfiring and hesitation.
Recommendation: Correct the mechanical condition with necessary repairs and install new plugs.

GAP BRIDGING
Symptoms: Combustion deposits lodge between the electrodes. Heavy deposits accumulate and bridge the electrode gap. The plug ceases to fire, resulting in a dead cylinder.
Recommendation: Locate the faulty plug and remove the deposits from between the electrodes.

TOO HOT
Symptoms: Blistered, white insulator, eroded electrode and absence of deposits. Results in shortened plug life.
Recommendation: Check for the correct plug heat range, over-advanced ignition timing, lean fuel mixture, intake manifold vacuum leaks, sticking valves and insufficient engine cooling.

PREIGNITION
Symptoms: Melted electrodes. Insulators are white, but may be dirty due to misfiring or flying debris in the combustion chamber. Can lead to engine damage.
Recommendation: Check for the correct plug heat range, over-advanced ignition timing, lean fuel mixture, insufficient engine cooling and lack of lubrication.

HIGH SPEED GLAZING
Symptoms: Insulator has yellowish, glazed appearance. Indicates that combustion chamber temperatures have risen suddenly during hard acceleration. Normal deposits melt to form a conductive coating. Causes misfiring at high speeds.
Recommendation: Install new plugs. Consider using a colder plug if driving habits warrant.

DETONATION
Symptoms: Insulators may be cracked or chipped. Improper gap setting techniques can also result in a fractured insulator tip. Can lead to piston damage.
Recommendation: Make sure the fuel anti-knock values meet engine requirements. Use care when setting the gaps on new plugs. Avoid lugging the engine.

MECHANICAL DAMAGE
Symptoms: May be caused by a foreign object in the combustion chamber or the piston striking an incorrect reach (too long) plug. Causes a dead cylinder and could result in piston damage.
Recommendation: Repair the mechanical damage. Remove the foreign object from the engine and/or install the correct reach plug.

CONTENTS

QUICK REFERENCE DATA

ATV INFORMATION

MODEL:_____ YEAR:_____

VIN NUMBER:_____

ENGINE SERIAL NUMBER:_____

CARBURETOR SERIAL NUMBER OR I.D. MARK:_____

TIRE INFLATION PRESSURE

	Front and rear tires psi (kPa)
TRX350TE/TM	
Normal pressure	2.9 (20)
Minimum pressure	2.5 (17)
Maximum pressure	3.3 (23)
TRX350FE/FM	
Normal pressure	3.6 (24.8)
Minimum pressure	3.2 (22)
Maximum pressure	4.0 (27.6)

MAINTENANCE TORQUE SPECIFICATIONS

	N•m	ft.-lb.	in.-lb.
Clutch adjusting screw locknut	22	16	–
Engine oil drain bolt	18	13	–
Engine oil filter cover mounting bolts	10	–	88
Rear differential			
Drain plug	12	–	106
Oil check plug	12	–	106
Oil fill cap	12	–	106
Front differential			
Oil fill cap	12	–	106
Drain plug	12	–	106
Spark plug	18	13	–
Tie rod locknut	54	40	–
Timing hole cap	10	–	88
Valve adjuster locknut	17	12	–
Wheel nuts (front and rear)	64	47	–

RECOMMENDED LUBRICANTS AND FUEL

Engine oil	
Classification	API SG or higher
Viscosity	SAE10W-40*
Differential oil	Hypoid gear oil SAE 80
Air filter	Foam air filter oil
Brake fluid	DOT 3 or DOT 4
Steering and suspension lubricant	Multipurpose grease
Fuel	Octane rating of 86 or higher

*See text for additional information.

ENGINE OIL CAPACITY

	Liters	U.S. qt.
Oil change only	1.95	2.06
Oil and filter change	2.0	2.1
After engine disassembly	2.5	2.6

FRONT AND REAR DIFFERENTIAL OIL CAPACITY

	ml	U.S. oz.
Front differential		
Oil change	241	8.2
After disassembly	275	9.3
Rear differential		
Oil change	85	2.9
After disassembly	100	3.4

MAINTENANCE SPECIFICATIONS

Engine compression	667 kPa (97 psi) @ 450 rpm
Engine idle speed	1300-1500 rpm
Front brake lever free play	25-30 mm (1-1 1/4 in.)
Front brake lining service limit	1.0 mm (0.04 in.)
Ignition timing	Not adjustable
Rear brake lever/pedal free play	15-20 mm (5/8-3/4 in.)
Reverse lever free play	2-4 mm (1/16-5/32 in.)
Spark plug gap	0.8-0.9 mm (0.032-0.036 in.)
Spark plug type	
Standard	NGK DPR7EA-9 or Denso X22EPR-U9
Cold weather operation*	NGK DPR6EA-9 or Denso X20EPR-U9
Throttle lever free play	3-8 mm (1/8-5/16 in.)
Valve clearance	
Intake and exhaust	0.15 mm (0.006 in.)

*Below 41° F (4° C).

CHAPTER ONE

GENERAL INFORMATION

This detailed and comprehensive manual covers the 2000-2006 Honda TRX350 Rancher models.

The text provides complete information on maintenance, tune-up, repair and overhaul. Hundreds of original photographs and illustrations created during the complete disassembly of the ATV guide the reader through every job. All procedures are in step-by-step form and designed for the reader who may be working on the machine for the first time.

MANUAL ORGANIZATION

A shop manual is a tool and as in all Clymer manuals, the chapters are thumb tabbed for easy reference. Main headings are listed in the table of contents and the index. Frequently used specifications and capacities from the tables at the end of each individual chapter are listed in the *Quick Reference Data* section at the front of the manual. Specifications and capacities are provided in metric and U.S. Standard units of measure.

During some of the procedures there will be references to headings in other chapters or sections of the manual. When a specific heading is called out in a step it will be *italicized* as it appears in the manual. If a sub-heading is indicated as being "in this section" it is located within the same main heading. For example, the sub-heading *Handling Gasoline Safely* is located within the main heading *SAFETY*.

This chapter provides general information on shop safety, tools and their usage, service fundamentals and shop supplies. **Tables 1-7**, at the end of the chapter, provide general ATV and shop technical information.

WARNINGS, CAUTIONS AND NOTES

The terms WARNING, CAUTION and NOTE have specific meanings in this manual.

A WARNING emphasizes areas where injury or even death could result from negligence. Mechanical damage may also occur. WARNINGS *should be taken seriously*.

A CAUTION emphasizes areas where equipment damage could result. Disregarding a CAUTION could cause permanent mechanical damage, though injury is unlikely.

A NOTE provides additional information to make a step or procedure easier or clearer. Disregarding a NOTE could cause inconvenience but would not cause equipment damage or personal injury.

SAFETY

Professional mechanics can work for years and never sustain a serious injury or mishap. Follow these guidelines and practice common sense to safely service the ATV.

1. Do not operate the ATV in an enclosed area. The exhaust gasses contain carbon monoxide, an odorless, colorless, and tasteless poisonous gas. Carbon monoxide levels build quickly in small enclosed areas and can cause unconsciousness and death in a short time. Make sure the work area is properly ventilated or operate the ATV outside.

2. *Never* use gasoline or any extremely flammable liquid to clean parts. Refer to *Cleaning Parts* and *Handling Gasoline Safely* in this section.

3. *Never* smoke or use a torch in the vicinity of flammable liquids, such as gasoline or cleaning solvent.

4. When welding or brazing on the ATV, remove the fuel tank, carburetor and shock to a safe distance at least 50 ft. (15 m) away.

5. Use the correct type and size of tools to avoid damaging fasteners.

6. Keep tools clean and in good condition. Replace or repair worn or damaged equipment.

7. When loosening a tight fastener, be guided by what would happen if the tool slips.

8. When replacing fasteners, make sure the new fasteners are of the same size and strength as the original ones.

9. Keep the work area clean and organized.

10. Wear eye protection *anytime* the safety of eyes is in question. This includes procedures involving drilling, grinding, hammering, compressed air and chemicals.

11. Wear the correct clothing for the job. Tie up or cover long hair so it can not get caught in moving equipment.

12. Do not carry sharp tools in clothing pockets.

13. Always have an approved fire extinguisher available. Make sure it is rated for gasoline (Class B) and electrical (Class C) fires.

14. Do not use compressed air to clean clothes, the ATV or the work area. Debris may be blown into eyes or skin. *Never* direct compressed air at anyone. Do not allow children to use or play with any compressed air equipment.

15. When using compressed air to dry rotating parts, hold the part so it can not rotate. Do not allow the force of the air to spin the part. The air jet is capable of rotating parts at extreme speed. The part may be damaged or disintegrate, causing serious injury.

16. Do not inhale the dust created by brake pad and clutch wear. In most cases these particles contain asbestos. In addition, some types of insulating materials and gaskets may contain asbestos. Inhaling asbestos particles is hazardous to health.

17. Never work on the ATV while someone is working under it.

18. When placing the ATV on a lift, make sure it is secure before walking away.

Handling Gasoline Safely

Gasoline is a volatile, flammable liquid and is one of the most dangerous items in the shop. Because gasoline is used so often, many people forget that it is hazardous. Only use gasoline as fuel for gasoline internal combustion engines. Keep in mind, when working on a ATV, that gasoline is always present in the fuel tank, fuel line and carburetor. To avoid a disastrous accident when working around the fuel system, carefully observe the following precautions:

1. *Never* use gasoline to clean parts. See *Cleaning Parts* in this section.

2. When working on the fuel system, work outside or in a well-ventilated area.

3. Do not add fuel to the fuel tank or service the fuel system while the ATV is near open flames, sparks or where someone is smoking. Gasoline vapor is heavier than air, it collects in low areas and is more easily ignited than liquid gasoline.

4. Allow the engine to cool completely before working on any fuel system component.

5. When draining the carburetor, catch the fuel in a plastic container and then pour it into an approved gasoline storage device.

6. Do not store gasoline in glass containers. If the glass breaks, a serious explosion or fire may occur.

7. Immediately wipe up spilled gasoline with rags. Store the rags in a metal container with a lid until they can be properly disposed of, or place them outside in a safe place for the fuel to evaporate.

8. Do not pour water onto a gasoline fire. Water spreads the fire and makes it more difficult to put out. Use a class B, BC or ABC fire extinguisher to extinguish a gasoline fire.

9. Always turn off the engine before refueling. Do not spill fuel onto the engine or exhaust system. Do not overfill the fuel tank. Leave an air space at the top of the tank to allow room for the fuel to expand due to temperature fluctuations.

Cleaning Parts

Cleaning parts is one of the more tedious and difficult service jobs performed in the home garage. There are many types of chemical cleaners and solvents available for shop use. Most are poisonous and extremely flammable. To prevent chemical exposure, vapor buildup, fire and serious injury, observe each product warning label and note the following:

1. Read and observe the entire product label before using any chemical. Always know what type of chemical is being used and whether it is poisonous and/or flammable.

2. Do not use more than one type of cleaning solvent at a time. If mixing chemicals is called for, measure the proper amounts according to the manufacturer's instructions.

3. Work in a well-ventilated area.

4. Wear chemical-resistant gloves.

5. Wear safety glasses.

6. Wear a vapor respirator if the instructions call for it.

7. Wash hands and arms thoroughly after cleaning parts.

8. Keep chemical products away from children and pets.

9. Thoroughly clean all oil, grease and cleaner residue from any part that must be heated.

10. Use a nylon brush when cleaning parts. Metal brushes may cause a spark.

11. When using a parts washer, only use the solvent recommended by the manufacturer. Make sure the parts washer is equipped with a metal lid that will lower in case of fire.

Warning Labels

Most manufacturers attach information and warning labels to the ATV. These labels contain instructions that are important to personal safety when operating, servicing, transporting and storing the ATV. Refer to the owner's manual for the description and location of labels. Order replacement labels from the manufacturer if they are missing or damaged.

SERIAL NUMBERS

Serial numbers are stamped onto the frame and engine. Record these numbers in the *Quick Reference Data* section at the front of the manual. Have these numbers available when ordering parts.

The frame number or vehicle identification number (VIN) is stamped on the front bracket attached to the front frame down tubes (**Figure 1**).

The engine number (**Figure 2**) is stamped on a pad on the upper, lower left side of the rear crankcase.

Table 1 lists model years and serial numbers.

Record all ATV information in the *Quick Reference Data* section at the front of this manual. Have this information on hand when purchasing parts.

FASTENERS

Proper fastener selection and installation is important to ensure the ATV operates as designed and can be serviced efficiently. The choice of original equipment fasteners is not arrived at by chance. Make sure replacement fasteners meet all the same requirements as the originals.

Threaded Fasteners

Threaded fasteners secure most of the components on the ATV. Most are tightened by turning them clockwise (right-hand threads). If the normal rotation of the component would loosen the fastener, it may have left-hand threads. If a left-hand threaded fastener is used, it is noted in the text.

Two dimensions are required to match the thread size of the fastener: the number of threads in a given distance and the outside diameter of the threads.

Two systems are currently used to specify threaded fastener dimensions: the U.S. Standard system and the metric system (**Figure 3**). Pay particular attention when working with unidentified fasteners. Mismatching thread types can damage threads.

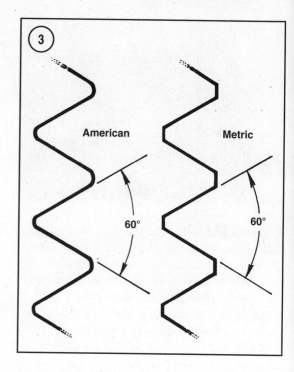

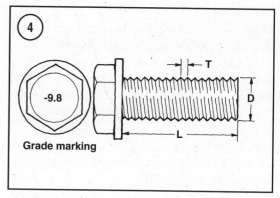

Grade marking

> *NOTE*
> *To ensure the fastener threads are not mismatched or cross-threaded, start all fasteners by hand. If a fastener is hard to start or turn, determine the cause before tightening with a tool.*

The length (L, **Figure 4**), diameter (D) and distance between thread crests (pitch) (T) classify metric screws and bolts. A typical bolt may be identified by the numbers 8—1.25 × 130. This indicates the bolt has diameter of 8 mm, the distance between thread crests is 1.25 mm and the length is 130 mm. Always measure bolt length as shown in **Figure 4** to avoid purchasing replacements of the wrong length.

If a number is located on the top of the fastener (**Figure 4**), this indicates the strength of the fastener. The higher the number, the stronger the fastener. Generally, unnumbered fasteners are the weakest.

Many bolts and studs are combined with nuts to secure particular components. To indicate the size of a nut, manufacturers specify the internal diameter and the thread pitch.

The measurement across two parallel flats on a nut or bolt head indicates the wrench size that fits the fastener.

> *WARNING*
> *Do not install fasteners with a strength classification lower than what was originally installed by the manufacturer. Doing so may cause equipment failure and/or damage.*

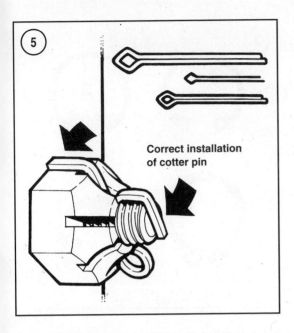

Correct installation
of cotter pin

Torque Specifications

The materials used in the manufacture of a ATV may be subjected to uneven stresses if the fasteners of the various subassemblies are not installed and tightened correctly. Fasteners that are improperly installed or that work loose can cause extensive damage. Use an accurate torque wrench when tightening fasteners, and tighten each fastener to its specified torque.

Torque specifications for specific components appear at the end of the appropriate chapters. Specifications for torque are provided in Newton-meters (N•m), foot-pounds (ft.-lb.) and inch-pounds (in.-lb.). Refer to **Table 6** for torque conversion formulas and to **Table 5** for general torque specifications. To use **Table 5**, first determine the size of the fastener as described in *Fasteners* in this chapter. Locate that size fastener in **Table 5**, and tighten the fastener to the indicated torque. Torque wrenches are described in the *Basic Tools* section of this chapter.

Self-Locking Fasteners

Several types of bolts, screws and nuts use various means to create an interference between the threads of two fasteners. The most common types are the nylon-insert nut and a dry adhesive coating on the threads of a bolt.

Self-locking fasteners offer greater holding strength than standard fasteners, which improve their resistance to vibration. Most self-locking fasteners cannot be reused. The materials used to form the lock become distorted after the initial installation and removal. Always discard and replace self-locking fasteners after their removal. Do not replace self-locking fasteners with standard fasteners.

Washers

There are two basic types of washers: flat washers and lockwashers. Flat washers are simple discs with a hole for a screw or bolt. Lockwashers are used to prevent a fastener from working loose. Washers can be used as spacers and seals, to help distribute fastener load and to prevent the fastener from damaging the component.

When replacing washers, make sure the replacements are of the same design and quality as the originals.

Cotter Pins

A cotter pin is a split metal pin inserted into a hole or slot to prevent a fastener from working loose. In certain applications, such as the rear axle on an ATV or motorcycle, the fastener must be secured in this way. For these applications, a cotter pin and castellated (slotted) nut is used.

To use a cotter pin, first make sure the pin's diameter is correct for the hole in the fastener. After correctly tightening the fastener and aligning the holes, insert the cotter pin through the hole and bend the ends over the fastener (**Figure 5**). Unless instructed to do so, never loosen a torqued fastener to align the holes. If the holes do not align, tighten the fastener just enough to achieve alignment.

Cotter pins are available in various diameters and lengths. Measure length from the bottom of the head to the tip of the shortest pin.

Snap Rings

Snap rings (**Figure 6**) are circular-shaped metal retaining clips. They secure parts and gears onto shafts, pins or rods. External type snap rings are used to retain items on shafts. Internal type snap rings secure parts within housing bores. In some applications, in addition to securing the component(s), snap rings of varying thickness also determine end play. These are usually called selective snap rings.

Two basic types of snap rings are used: machined and stamped snap rings. Machined snap rings (**Figure 7**) can be installed in either direction since both faces have sharp edges. Stamped snap rings (**Figure 8**) are manufactured with a sharp edge and a round edge. When installing a stamped snap ring in a thrust application, install the sharp edge facing away from the part producing the thrust.

E-clips are used when it is not practical to use a snap ring. Remove E-clips with a flat blade screwdriver by prying between the shaft and E-clip. To install an E-clip, center it over the shaft groove, and push or tap it into place.

Observe the following when installing snap rings:

1. Remove and install snap rings with snap ring pliers. See *Snap Ring Pliers* in this chapter.
2. In some applications, it may be necessary to replace snap rings after removing them.
3. Compress or expand snap rings only enough to install them. If overly expanded, they lose their retaining ability.
4. After installing a snap ring, make sure it seats completely.
5. Wear eye protection when removing and installing snap rings.

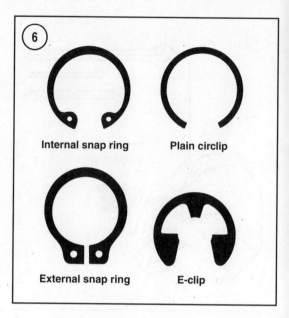

Internal snap ring   Plain circlip

External snap ring   E-clip

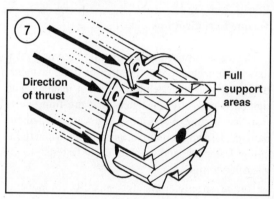

Direction of thrust   Full support areas

SHOP SUPPLIES

The following section describes the types of shop supplies most often required. Make sure to follow the manufacturer's recommendations.

Lubricants and Fluids

Periodic lubrication helps ensure a long service life for any type of equipment. Using the correct type of lubricant is as important as performing the lubrication service, although in an emergency the wrong type of lubricant is better than none.

Engine oil

Engine oil is classified by two standards: the American Petroleum Institute (API) service classi-

fication and the Society of Automotive Engineers (SAE) viscosity rating. This information is on the oil container label. Two letters indicate the API service classification. The number or sequence of numbers and letter (10W-40 for example) is the oil's viscosity rating. The API service classification and the SAE viscosity index are not indications of oil quality.

The service classification indicates that the oil meets specific lubrication standards. The first letter in the classification (*S*) indicates that the oil is for gasoline engines. The second letter indicates the standard the oil satisfies.

Always use an oil with a classification recommended by the manufacturer. Using an oil with a different classification can cause engine damage.

Viscosity is an indication of the oil's thickness. Thin oils have a lower number while thick oils have

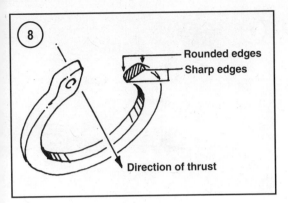

Rounded edges
Sharp edges
Direction of thrust

a higher number. Engine oils fall into the 5- to 50-weight range for single-grade oils.

Most manufacturers recommend multigrade oil. These oils perform efficiently across a wide range of operating conditions. Multigrade oils are identified by a (*W*) after the first number, which indicates the low-temperature viscosity.

Engine oils are most commonly mineral (petroleum) based; however, synthetic and semi-synthetic types are used more frequently. When selecting engine oil, follow the manufacturer's recommendation for type, classification and viscosity.

Greases

Grease is an oil to which a thickening base has been added so the end product is semi-solid. Grease is often classified by the type of thickener added, such as lithium soap. The National Lubricating Grease Institute (NLGI) grades grease. Grades range from No. 000 to No. 6, with No. 6 being the thickest. Typical multipurpose grease is NLGI No. 2. For specific applications, manufacturers may recommend water-resistant type grease or one with an additive such as molybdenum disulfide (MoS$_2$).

Brake fluid

Brake fluid is the hydraulic fluid used to transmit hydraulic pressure (force) to the wheel brakes. Brake fluid is classified by the Department of Transportation (DOT). Current designations for brake fluid are DOT 3, DOT 4 and DOT 5. This classification appears on the fluid container.

Each type of brake fluid has its own definite characteristics. Do not intermix different types of brake fluid. DOT 5 fluid is silicone-based. DOT 5 is not compatible with other fluids or in systems for which it was not designed. Mixing DOT 5 fluid with other fluids may cause brake system failure. When adding brake fluid, *only* use the fluid recommended by the ATV manufacturer.

Brake fluid will damage plastic, painted or plated surfaces. Use extreme care when working with brake fluid. Immediately wash any spills with soap and water. Rinse the area with plenty of clean water.

Hydraulic brake systems require clean and moisture-free brake fluid. Never reuse brake fluid. Brake fluid absorbs moisture, which greatly reduces its ability to perform correctly. Keep brake fluid containers and reservoirs properly sealed. Purchase brake fluid in small containers, and discard any small left-over quantities properly. Do not store a container of brake fluid with less than 1/4 of the fluid remaining. This small amount absorbs moisture very rapidly.

> **WARNING**
> *Never put a mineral-based (petroleum) oil into the brake system. Mineral oil will cause rubber parts in the system to swell and break apart, resulting in complete brake failure.*

Cleaners, Degreasers and Solvents

Many chemicals are available to remove oil, grease and other residue from the ATV. Before using cleaning solvents, consider how they will be used and disposed of, particularly if they are not water-soluble. Local ordinances may require special procedures for the disposal of various cleaning chemicals. Refer to *Safety* in this chapter for more information on their use.

Generally, degreasers are strong cleaners used to remove heavy accumulations of grease from engine and frame components.

Use brake parts cleaner to clean brake system components when contact with petroleum-based products will damage seals. Brake parts cleaner leaves no residue.

Use electrical contact cleaner to clean electrical connections and components without leaving any residue.

Carburetor cleaner is a powerful solvent used to remove fuel deposits and varnish from fuel system components. Use this cleaner carefully, as it may damage finishes.

Most solvents are designed to be used in a parts washing cabinet for individual component cleaning. For safety, use only nonflammable or high flash point solvents.

Gasket Sealant

Sealants are used in combination with a gasket or seal and are occasionally used alone. Follow the manufacturer's recommendation when using sealants. Use extreme care when choosing a sealant different from the type originally recommended. Choose sealants based on their resistance to heat, various fluids and their sealing capabilities.

One of the most common sealants is RTV, or room temperature vulcanizing sealant. This sealant cures at room temperature over a specific time period. It allows the repositioning of components without damaging gaskets.

Moisture in the air causes the RTV sealant to cure. Always install the tube cap as soon as possible after applying RTV sealant. RTV sealant has a limited shelf life and will not cure properly if the shelf life has expired. Keep partial tubes sealed, and discard them if they have surpassed the expiration date.

Applying RTV sealant

Clean all old gasket residue from the mating surfaces. Remove all gasket material from blind threaded holes; it can cause inaccurate bolt torque. Spray the mating surfaces with aerosol parts cleaner, and then wipe them with a lint-free cloth. The area must be clean for the sealant to adhere.

Apply RTV sealant in a continuous bead, 2-3 mm (0.08-0.12 in.) thick. Circle all the fastener holes unless otherwise specified. Do not allow any sealant to enter these holes. Assemble and tighten the fasteners to the specified torque within the time frame recommended by the RTV sealant manufacturer.

Gasket Remover

Aerosol gasket remover can help remove stubborn gaskets. This product can speed up the removal process and prevent damage to the mating surface that may be caused by a scraping tool. Most

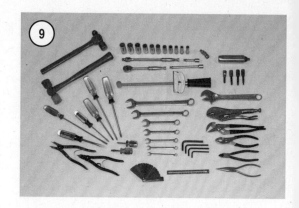

of these products are very caustic. Follow the gasket remover manufacturer's instructions for use.

Recycling

Do-it-yourself maintenance and repair comes with a responsibility to properly dispose of vehicle and shop waste products. These include: engine and transmission oils, oil filters, coolant (a petroleum product), hydraulic fluids, batteries and any cleaning chemicals. Many local and regional organizations provide collection centers for these waste products.

Threadlocking Compound

A threadlocking compound is a fluid applied to the threads of fasteners. After tightening the fastener, the fluid dries and becomes a solid filler between the threads. This makes it difficult for the fastener to work loose from vibration, or heat expansion and contraction. Some threadlocking compounds also provide a seal against fluid leaks.

Before applying threadlocking compound, remove any old compound and oil residue from both thread areas and clean them with aerosol parts cleaner. Use the compound sparingly. Excess fluid can run into adjoining parts.

Threadlocking compounds are available in different strengths. Follow the particular manufacturer's recommendations regarding compound selection. A number of manufacturers offer a wide range of threadlocking compounds for various strength, temperature and repair applications.

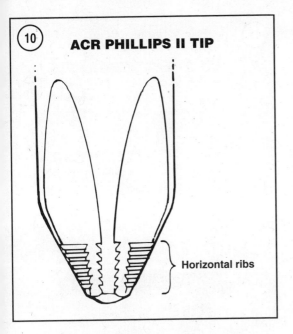

⑩ **ACR PHILLIPS II TIP**

Horizontal ribs

BASIC TOOLS

Most of the procedures in this manual can be carried out with simple hand tools and test equipment familiar to the home mechanic. Always use the correct tools for the job at hand. Keep tools organized and clean. Store them in a tool chest with related tools organized together.

Some of the procedures in this manual specify special tools. In most cases, the tool is illustrated in use. Well-equipped mechanics may be able to substitute similar tools or fabricate a suitable replacement. However, in some cases, the specialized equipment or expertise may make it impractical for the home mechanic to attempt the procedure. When necessary, such operations are identified in the text with the recommendation to have a dealership or specialist perform the task. It may be less expensive to have a professional perform these jobs, especially when considering the cost of the equipment.

Quality tools are essential. The best are constructed of high-strength alloy steel. These tools are light, easy to use and resistant to wear. Their working surface is smooth, and the tool is carefully polished. They have an easy-to-clean finish and are comfortable to use. Quality tools are a good investment.

When building a new tool kit, consider purchasing a basic tool set (**Figure 9**) from a large tool supplier. These sets contain a variety of commonly

used tools, and they provide substantial savings when compared to individually purchased tools. As one becomes more experienced and tasks become more complicated, specialized tools can be added.

Screwdrivers

Screwdrivers of various lengths and types are mandatory for the simplest tool kit. The two basic types are the slotted tip (flat blade) and the Phillips tip. These are available in sets that often include an assortment of tip sizes and shaft lengths.

As with all tools, use a screwdriver designed for the job. Make sure the size of the tip conforms to the size and shape of the fastener. Use them only for driving screws. Never use a screwdriver for prying or chiseling metal. Repair or replace worn or damaged screwdrivers. A worn tip may damage the fastener, making it difficult to remove.

Phillips-head screws are often damaged by incorrectly fitting screwdrivers. Quality Phillips screwdrivers are manufactured with their crosshead tip machined to Phillips Screw Company specifications. Poor quality or damaged Phillips screwdrivers can back out and round over the screw head, resulting in a condition known as camout. Compounding the problem of using poor quality screwdrivers are Phillips-head screws made from weak or soft materials and screws initially installed with power tools.

The best type of screwdriver to use on Phillips screws is the ACR Phillips II screwdriver, patented by the Phillips Screw Company. ACR stands for the horizontal anti-camout ribs found on the driving faces or flutes of the screwdrivers tip (**Figure 10**). ACR Phillips II screwdrivers were designed as part of a manufacturing drive system to be used with ACR Phillips II screws, but they work well on all common Phillips screws. A number of tool companies offer ACR Phillips II screwdrivers in different tip sizes and interchangeable bits to fit screwdriver bit holders.

NOTE
Another way to prevent camout and increase the grip of a Phillips screwdriver is to apply valve grinding compound or gripping agent onto the screwdriver tip. After tightening the screw, clean the screw recess to prevent engine oil contamination.

Wrenches

Box-end, open-end and combination wrenches (**Figure 11**) are available in a variety of types and sizes.

The number stamped on the wrench refers to the distance between the work areas. This must match the distance across two parallel flats on the bolt head or nut.

The box-end wrench is an excellent tool because it grips the fastener on all sides. This reduces the chance of the tool slipping. The box-end wrench is designed with either a 6- or 12-point opening. For stubborn or damaged fasteners, the 6-point provides superior holding ability by contacting the fastener across a wider area at all six edges. For general use, the 12-point works well. It allows the wrench to be removed and reinstalled without moving the handle over such a wide arc.

An open-end wrench is fast and works best in areas with limited overhead access. Because it contacts the fastener at only two points, an open-end wrench is subject to slipping under heavy force or if the tool or fastener is worn. A box-end wrench is preferred in most instances, especially when applying considerable force to a fastener.

The combination wrench has a box-end on one end and an open-end on the other. This combination makes it a very convenient tool.

Adjustable Wrenches

An adjustable wrench or Crescent wrench (**Figure 12**) fits nearly any nut or bolt head that has clear access around its entire perimeter. An adjustable wrench is best used as a backup wrench to hold a large nut or bolt while the other end is being loosened or tightened with a box-end or socket wrench.

Adjustable wrenches contact the fastener at only two points, which makes them more subject to slipping off the fastener. The fact that one jaw is adjustable and may loosen only aggravates this shortcoming. These wrenches are directional. Make certain the solid jaw is the one transmitting the force.

Socket Wrenches, Ratchets and Handles

Sockets that attach to a ratchet handle (**Figure 13**) are available with 6-point (A, **Figure 14**) or 12-point (B) openings and different drive sizes. The

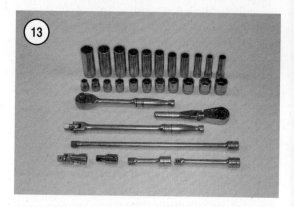

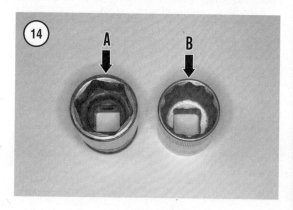

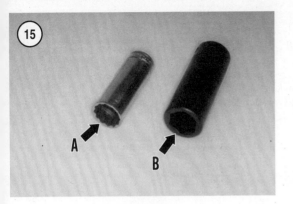

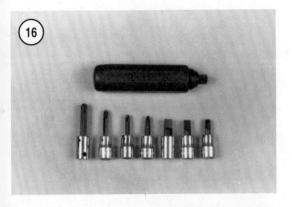

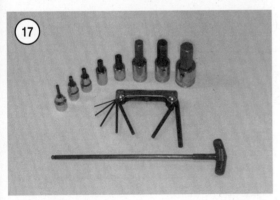

ness of a 19-mm hand socket (A, **Figure 15**) and the 19-mm impact socket (B). Use impact sockets when using an impact driver or air tools. Use hand sockets with hand-driven attachments.

> *WARNING*
> *Do not use hand sockets with air or impact tools. They may shatter and cause injury. Always wear eye protection when using any type of impact or air tool.*

Various handles are available for sockets. The speed handle is used for fast operation. Flexible ratchet heads in varying lengths allow the socket to be turned with varying force and at odd angles. Extension bars allow the socket setup to reach difficult areas. The ratchet is the most versatile wrench. It allows the user to install or remove the nut without removing the socket.

Sockets combined with any number of drivers make them undoubtedly the fastest, safest and most convenient tool for fastener removal and installation.

Impact Driver

An impact driver provides extra force for removing fasteners by converting the impact of a hammer into a turning motion. This makes it possible to remove stubborn fasteners without damaging them. Impact drivers and interchangeable bits (**Figure 16**) are available from most tool suppliers. When using a socket with an impact driver, make sure the socket is designed for impact use. Refer to *Socket Wrenches, Ratchets and Handles* in this section.

> *WARNING*
> *Do not use hand sockets with air tools or impact drivers, as they may shatter the socket and cause personal injury. Always wear eye protection when using any type of impact or air tool.*

Allen Wrenches

Allen or setscrew wrenches (**Figure 17**) are used on fasteners with hexagonal recesses in the fastener head. These wrenches are available in L-shaped bars, sockets and T-handles. A metric set is required when working on most motorcycles made by Japa-

drive size indicates the size of the square hole that accepts the ratchet handle. The number stamped on the socket is the size of the work area and must match the fastener head.

As with wrenches, a 6-point socket provides superior holding ability, while a 12-point socket needs to be moved only half as far to reposition it on the fastener.

Sockets are designated for either hand or impact use. Impact sockets are made of thicker material for more durability. Compare the size and wall thick-

nese and European manufacturers. Allen head bolts are sometimes called socket bolts.

Torque Wrenches

A torque wrench is used with a socket, torque adapter or similar extension to tighten a fastener to a measured torque. Torque wrenches come in several drive sizes (1/4, 3/8, 1/2 and 3/4) and have various methods of reading the torque value. The drive size indicates the size of the square drive that accepts the socket, adapter or extension. Common methods of reading the torque value are the deflecting beam (A, **Figure 18**), the dial indicator (B) and the audible click (C).

When choosing a torque wrench, consider the torque range, drive size and accuracy. The torque specifications in this manual provide an indication of the range required.

A torque wrench is a precision tool that must be properly cared for to remain accurate. Store torque wrenches in cases or separate padded drawers within a toolbox. Follow the manufacturer's instructions for their care and calibration.

Torque Adapters

Torque adapters extend or reduce the reach of a torque wrench. The torque adapter shown in **Figure 19** is used to tighten a fastener that cannot be reached due to the size of the torque wrench head, drive, and socket. Since a torque adapter changes the effective lever length (**Figure 20**) of a torque wrench, the torque reading on the wrench does not equal the actual torque applied to the fastener. It is necessary to recalibrate the torque setting on the wrench to compensate for the change of lever length. When a torque adapter is used at a right angle to the drive head (**Figure 19**), calibration is not required, since the effective length has not changed.

To calculate the adjusted torque reading when using a torque adapter, use the following formula and refer to **Figure 20**. The formula can be expressed as:

$$TW = \frac{TA \times L}{L + A}$$

TW is the torque setting or dial reading on the wrench. *TA* is the torque specification and the actual amount of torque that will be applied to the fastener. *A* is the amount that the adapter increases (or in

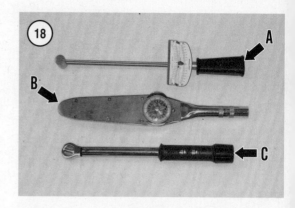

some cases reduces) the effective lever length as measured along the centerline of the torque wrench from the center of the drive to the center of the adapter box end (**Figure 20**). *L* is the lever length of the wrench as measured from the center of the drive to the center of the grip. The effective length of the torque wrench is the sum of *L* and *A*.

For example, to apply 20 ft.-lb. to a fastener, using an adapter as shown in the top example in **Figure 20**:

TA = 20 ft.-lb.

A = 3 in.

L = 14 in.

$$TW = \frac{20 \times 14}{14 + 3} = \frac{280}{17} = 16.5 \text{ ft. lb.}$$

In this example, a click-type torque wrench would be set to the recalculated torque value (TW = 16.5 ft.-lb.). When using a dial or beam-type torque wrench, tighten the fastener until the pointer aligns with 16.5 ft.-lb. In either case, although the torque wrench reads 16.5 ft.-lb., the actual torque is 20 ft.-lb.

1

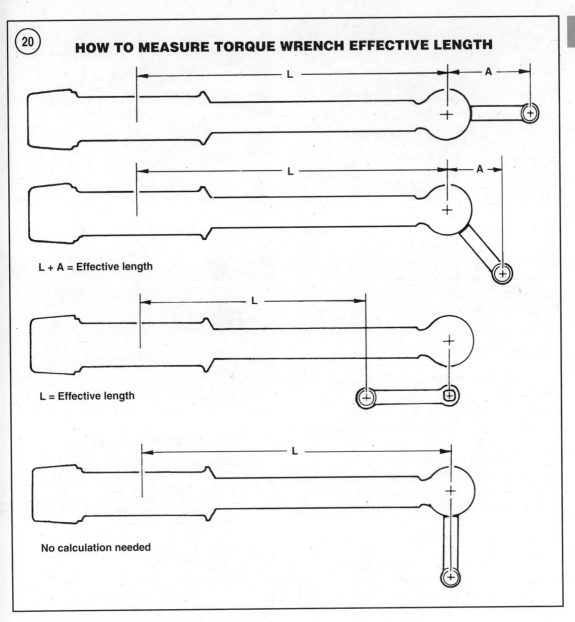

HOW TO MEASURE TORQUE WRENCH EFFECTIVE LENGTH

L + A = Effective length

L = Effective length

No calculation needed

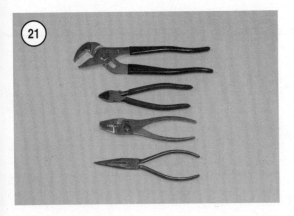

Pliers

Pliers come in a wide range of types and sizes. Pliers are useful for holding, cutting, bending and crimping. Do not use them to turn fasteners. **Figure 21** shows several types of useful pliers. Each design has a specialized function. Slip-joint pliers are general-purpose pliers used for gripping and bending. Diagonal cutting pliers cut wire and can be used to remove cotter pins. Adjustable pliers can be adjusted to hold different size objects. The jaws remain parallel so they grip around objects such as pipe or tubing.

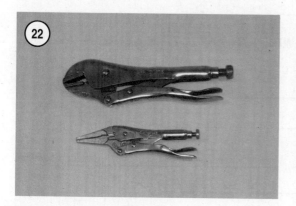

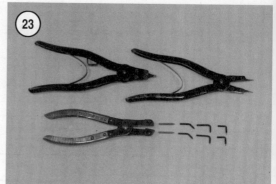

Needlenose pliers are used to hold or bend small objects. Locking pliers (**Figure 22**) are used to hold objects very tightly. They have many uses, ranging from holding two parts together to gripping the end of a broken stud. Use caution when using locking pliers. The sharp jaws will damage the objects they hold.

Snap Ring Pliers

Snap ring pliers (**Figure 23**) are specialized pliers with tips that fit into the ends of snap rings to remove and install them.

Snap ring pliers are available with a fixed action (either internal or external) or convertible (one tool works on both internal and external snap rings). They may have fixed tips or interchangeable ones of various sizes and angles. For general use, select a convertible-type pliers with interchangeable tips.

> *WARNING*
> *Always wear eye protection when using snap ring pliers. Snap rings can slip and fly off during removal and installation. Also, the snap ring plier tips may break and fly off.*

Hammers

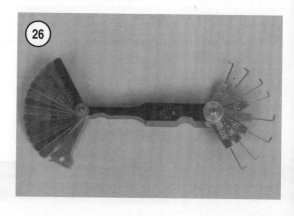

Various types of hammers (**Figure 24**) are available to fit a number of applications. A ball-peen hammer is used to strike another tool, such as a punch or chisel. Soft-faced hammers are required when a metal object must be struck without damaging it. *Never* use a metal-faced hammer on engine and suspension components. Damage will occur in most cases.

Always wear eye protection when using hammers. Make sure the hammer face is in good condition and the handle is not cracked. Select the correct

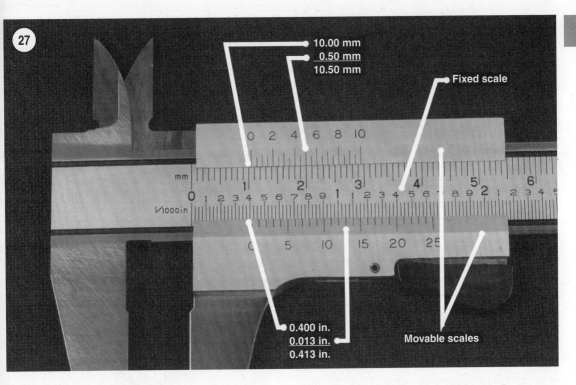

hammer for the job and make sure to strike the object squarely. Do not use the handle or the side of the hammer to strike an object.

PRECISION MEASURING TOOLS

The ability to accurately measure components is essential to successful service and repair. Equipment is manufactured to close tolerances, and obtaining consistently accurate measurements is essential to determining which components require replacement or further service.

Each type of measuring instrument (**Figure 25**) is designed to measure a dimension with a particular degree of accuracy and within a certain range. When selecting a measuring tool, make sure it is applicable to the task.

As with all tools, measuring tools provide the best results if they are cared for properly. Improper use can damage the tool and result in inaccurate results. If any measurement is questionable, verify the measurement using another tool. A standard gauge is usually provided with measuring tools to check accuracy and calibrate the tool if necessary.

Precision measurements can vary according to the experience of the person taking the measurement. Accurate results are only possible if the mechanic pos-

sesses a feel for using the tool. Heavy-handed use of measuring tools produces less accurate results than if the tool is handled properly. Grasp precision measuring tools gently between fingertips so the point at which the tool contacts the object is easily felt. This feel for the equipment produces consistently accurate measurements and reduces the risk of damaging the tool or component. Refer to the following sections for a description of various measuring tools.

Feeler Gauge

The feeler or thickness gauge (**Figure 26**) is used for measuring the distance between two surfaces.

A feeler gauge set consists of an assortment of steel strips of graduated thicknesses. Each blade is marked with its thickness. Blades can be of various lengths and angles for different procedures.

A common use for a feeler gauge is to measure piston ring end gap. Wire (round) type gauges are used to measure spark plug gap.

Calipers

Calipers (**Figure 27**) are excellent tools for obtaining inside, outside and depth measurements. Al-

DECIMAL PLACE VALUES*

0.1	Indicates 1/10 (one tenth of an inch or millimeter)
0.010	Indicates 1/100 (one one-hundreth of an inch or millimeter)
0.001	Indicates 1/1,000 (one one-thousandth of an inch or millimeter)

*This chart represents the values of figures placed to the right of the decimal point. Use it when reading decimals from one-tenth to one one-thousandth of an inch or millimeter. It is not a conversion chart (for example: 0.001 in. is not equal to 0.001 mm).

though not as precise as a micrometer, they allow reasonable precision, typically to within 0.05 mm (0.001 in.). Most calipers have a range up to 150 mm (6 in.).

Calipers are available in dial, vernier or digital versions. Dial calipers have a dial readout that is convenient to read. Vernier calipers have marked scales that must be compared to determine the measurement. The digital caliper uses an LCD display to show the measurement.

Properly maintain the measuring surfaces of the caliper. There must not be any dirt or burrs between the tool and the object being measured. Never force the caliper closed around an object. Close the caliper around the highest point so it can be removed with a slight drag. Some calipers require calibration. Always refer to the manufacturer's instructions when using a new or unfamiliar caliper.

Figure 27 shows a measurement taken with a vernier caliper. Refer to the metric scale and note that the fixed scale is graduated in centimeters, which is indicated by the whole numbers 1, 2, 3 and so on. Each centimeter is then divided into millimeters, which are indicated by the small line between the whole numbers (1 centimeter equals 10 millimeters). The movable scale is marked in increments of 0.05 (hundredths) mm. The value of a measurement equals the reading on the fixed scale plus the reading on the movable scale.

To determine the reading on the fixed scale, look for the line on the fixed scale immediately to the left of the 0-line on the movable scale. In **Figure 27**, the fixed scale reading is 1 centimeter (or 10 millimeters).

To determine the reading on the movable scale, note the one line on the movable scale that precisely aligns with a line on the fixed scale. Look closely. A number of lines will seem close, but only one lines up precisely with a line on the fixed scale. In **Figure 27**, the movable scale reading is 0.50 mm.

To calculate the measurement, add the fixed scale reading (10 mm) to the movable scale reading (0.50 mm) for a value of 10.50 mm.

Micrometers

A micrometer is an instrument designed for linear measurement using the decimal divisions of the inch or meter (**Figure 28**). While there are many types and styles of micrometers, most of the procedures in this manual call for an outside micrometer. The outside micrometer is used to measure the outside diameter of cylindrical forms and the thickness of materials.

A micrometer's size indicates the minimum and maximum size of a part that it can measure. The

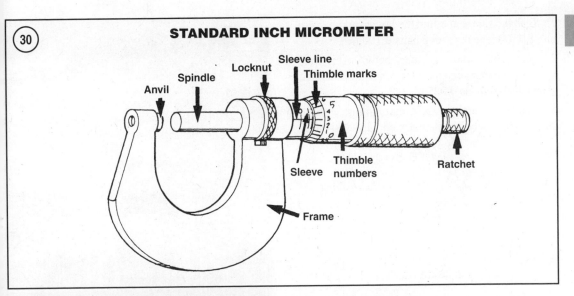

STANDARD INCH MICROMETER

③⓪

Anvil — Spindle — Locknut — Sleeve line — Thimble marks — Sleeve — Thimble numbers — Ratchet — Frame

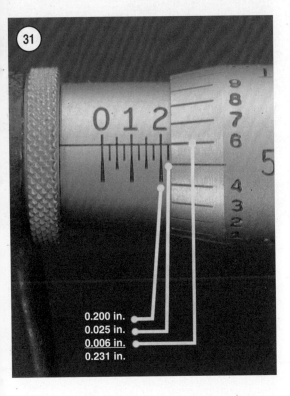

③①

0.200 in.
0.025 in.
0.006 in.
0.231 in.

usual sizes (**Figure 29**) are 0-1 in. (0-25 mm), 1-2 in. (25-50 mm), 2-3 in. (50-75 mm) and 3-4 in. (75-100 mm).

Micrometers that cover a wider range of measurement are available. These use a large frame with interchangeable anvils of various lengths. This type of micrometer offers a cost savings; however, its overall size may make it less convenient.

Reading a Micrometer

When reading a micrometer, numbers are taken from different scales and added together. The following sections describe how to read the measurements of various types of outside micrometers.

For accurate results, properly maintain the measuring surfaces of the micrometer. There must not be any dirt or burrs between the tool and the measured object. Never force the micrometer closed around an object. Close the micrometer around the highest point so it can be removed with a slight drag. **Figure 30** shows the markings and parts of a standard inch micrometer. Be familiar with these terms before using a micrometer in the following sections.

Standard inch micrometer

The standard inch micrometer is accurate to one-thousandth of an inch or 0.001. The sleeve is marked in 0.025 in. increments. Every fourth sleeve mark is numbered 1, 2, 3, 4, 5, 6, 7, 8, 9. These numbers indicate 0.100, 0.200, 0.300, and so on.

The tapered end of the thimble has 25 lines marked around it. Each mark equals 0.001 in. One complete turn of the thimble aligns its zero mark with the first mark on the sleeve or 0.025 in.

When reading a standard inch micrometer, perform the following steps while referring to **Figure 31**.

1. Read the sleeve and find the largest number visible. Each sleeve number equals 0.100 in.

2. Count the number of lines between the numbered sleeve mark and the edge of the thimble. Each sleeve mark equals 0.025 in.

3. Read the thimble mark that aligns with the sleeve line. Each thimble mark equals 0.001 in.

> *NOTE*
> *If a thimble mark does not align exactly with the sleeve line, estimate the amount between the lines. For accurate readings in ten-thousandths of an inch (0.0001 in.), use a vernier inch micrometer.*

4. Add the readings from Steps 1-3.

Metric micrometer

The standard metric micrometer is accurate to one one-hundredth of a millimeter (0.01-mm). The sleeve line is graduated in millimeter and half millimeter increments. The marks on the upper half of the sleeve line equal 1.00 mm. Every fifth mark above the sleeve line is identified with a number. The number sequence depends on the size of the micrometer. A 0-25 mm micrometer, for example, has sleeve marks numbered 0 through 25 in 5 mm increments. This numbering sequence continues with larger micrometers. On all metric micrometers, each mark on the lower half of the sleeve equals 0.50 mm.

The tapered end of the thimble has fifty lines marked around it. Each mark equals 0.01 mm. One complete turn of the thimble aligns its 0 mark with the first line on the lower half of the sleeve line or 0.50 mm.

When reading a metric micrometer, add the number of millimeters and half-millimeters on the sleeve line to the hundredths of a millimeter shown on the thimble. Perform the following steps while referring to **Figure 32**.

1. Read the upper half of the sleeve line and count the number of lines visible. Each upper line equals 1 mm.

2. See if the half-millimeter line is visible on the lower sleeve line. If so, add 0.50 to the reading in Step 1.

3. Read the thimble mark that aligns with the sleeve line. Each thimble mark equals 0.01 mm.

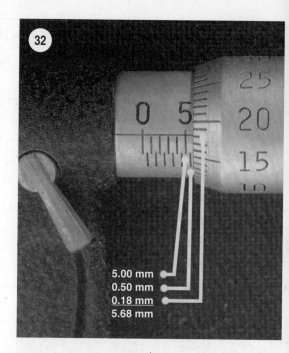

5.00 mm
0.50 mm
0.18 mm
5.68 mm

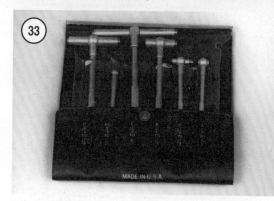

MADE IN U.S.A.

> *NOTE*
> *If a thimble mark does not align exactly with the sleeve line, estimate the amount between the lines. For accurate readings to two-thousandths of a millimeter (0.002 mm), use a metric vernier micrometer.*

4. Add the readings from Steps 1-3.

Micrometer Adjustment

Before using a micrometer, check its adjustment as follows:

1. Clean the anvil and spindle faces.

2A. To check a 0-1 in. or 0-25 mm micrometer:

a. Turn the thimble until the spindle contacts the anvil. If the micrometer has a ratchet stop, use it to ensure that the proper amount of pressure is applied.

b. The adjustment is correct if the 0 mark on the thimble aligns exactly with the 0 mark on the sleeve line. If the marks do not align, the micrometer is out of adjustment.

c. Follow the manufacturer's instructions to adjust the micrometer.

2B. To check a micrometer larger than 1 in. or 25 mm, use the standard gauge supplied by the manufacturer. A standard gauge is a steel block, disc or rod that is machined to an exact size.

a. Place the standard gauge between the spindle and anvil, and measure its outside diameter or length. If the micrometer has a ratchet stop, use it to ensure that the proper amount of pressure is applied.

b. The adjustment is correct if the 0 mark on the thimble aligns exactly with the 0 mark on the sleeve line. If the marks do not align, the micrometer is out of adjustment.

c. Follow the manufacturer's instructions to adjust the micrometer.

Micrometer Care

Micrometers are precision instruments. They must be used and maintained with great care. Note the following:

1. Store micrometers in protective cases or separate padded drawers in a toolbox.

2. Make sure the spindle and anvil faces do not contact each other or another objectw hile in storage. If they do, temperature changes and corrosion may damage the contact faces.

3. Do not clean a micrometer with compressed air. Dirt forced into the tool will cause wear.

4. Lubricate micrometers with WD-40 to prevent corrosion.

Telescoping and Small Bore Gauges

Use telescoping gauges (**Figure 33**) and small bore gauges (**Figure 34**) to measure bores. Neither gauge has a scale for direct readings. An outside micrometer must be used to determine the reading.

To use a telescoping gauge, select the correct size gauge for the bore. Compress the movable post and carefully insert the gauge into the bore. Carefully move the gauge in the bore to make sure it is centered. Tighten the knurled end of the gauge to hold the movable post in position. Remove the gauge, and measure the length of the posts with a micrometer. Telescoping gauges are typically used to measure cylinder bores.

To use a small-bore gauge, select the correct size gauge for the bore. Carefully insert the gauge into the bore. Tighten the knurled end of the gauge to carefully expand the gauge fingers to the limit within the bore. Do not overtighten the gauge, as there is no built-in release. Excessive tightening can damage the bore surface and damage the tool. Remove the gauge and measure the outside dimension (**Figure 35**). Small bore gauges are typically used to measure valve guides.

Dial Indicator

A dial indicator (A, **Figure 36**) is a gauge with a dial face and needle used to measure variations in dimensions and movements. Measuring brake rotor runout is a typical use for a dial indicator.

Dial indicators are available in various ranges and graduations. They use three basic types of mounting bases: magnetic, clamp, or screw-in stud. When purchasing a dial indicator, select the magnetic stand type (B, **Figure 36**) with a continuous dial face (**Figure 37**).

Cylinder Bore Gauge

A cylinder bore gauge is similar to a dial indicator. The gauge set shown in **Figure 38** consists of a dial indicator, handle, and different length adapters (anvils) to fit the gauge to various bore sizes. The bore gauge is used to measure bore size, taper and out-of-round. When using a bore gauge, follow the manufacturer's instructions.

Compression Gauge

A compression gauge (**Figure 39**) measures combustion chamber (cylinder) pressure, usually in psi or kg/cm^2. The gauge adapter is either inserted or screwed into the spark plug hole to obtain the reading. Disable the engine so it will not start and hold the throttle in the wide-open position when performing a compression test. An engine that does not have adequate compression cannot be properly tuned. See Chapter Three.

Spark Tester

A quick way to check the ignition system is to connect a spark tester to the end of the spark plug wire and operate the engine's kickstarter. A visible spark should jump the gap on the tester. A variety of spark testers are available from aftermarket manufacturers. Use of this tool is described in Chapter Two.

Multimeter

A multimeter (**Figure 40**) is an essential tool for electrical system diagnosis. The voltage function indicates the voltage applied or available to various electrical components. The ohmmeter function tests circuits for continuity and measures the resistance of a circuit.

Some test specifications for electrical components are based on results using a specific test meter. Results may vary if a meter not recommend by the

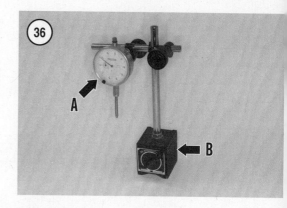

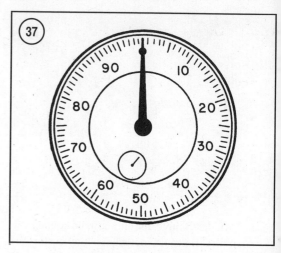

manufacturer is used. Such requirements are noted when applicable.

Ohmmeter (analog) calibration

Each time an analog ohmmeter is used or if the scale is changed, the ohmmeter must be calibrated. Digital ohmmeters do not require calibration.
1. Make sure the meter battery is in good condition.
2. Make sure the meter probes are in good condition.
3. Touch the two probes together and watch the needle. It must align with the 0 mark on the scale.
4. If necessary, rotate the set-adjust knob until the needle points directly to the 0 mark.

ELECTRICAL SYSTEM FUNDAMENTALS

A thorough study of the many types of electrical systems used in today's ATVs is beyond the scope

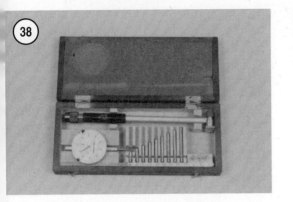

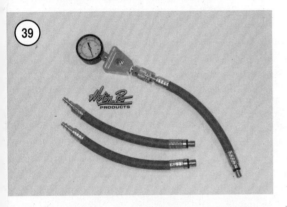

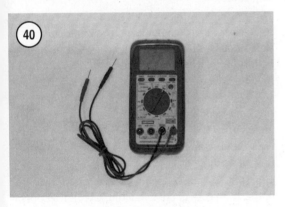

of this manual. However, an understanding of electrical basics is necessary to perform simple diagnostic tests.

Electrical Component Replacement

Most motorcycle dealerships and parts suppliers will not accept the return of any electrical part. If you cannot determine the exact cause of any electrical system malfunction, have a Honda dealership retest that specific system to verify your test results.

If you purchase a new electrical component(s), install it, and then find that the system still does not work properly, you will probably be unable to return the unit for a refund.

Consider any test results carefully before replacing a component that tests only *slightly* out of specification, especially resistance. A number of variables can affect test results dramatically. These include: the testing meter's internal circuitry, ambient temperature and conditions under which the machine has been operated.

Voltage

Voltage is the electrical potential or pressure in an electrical circuit and is expressed in volts. The more pressure (voltage) in a circuit, the more work that can be performed.

Direct current (DC) voltage means the electricity flows in one direction. All circuits powered by a battery are DC circuits.

Alternating current (AC) means that the electricity flows in one direction momentarily then switches to the opposite direction. Alternator output is an example of AC voltage. This voltage must be changed or rectified to direct current to operate in a battery powered system.

Resistance

Resistance is the opposition to the flow of electricity within a circuit or component and is measured in ohms. Resistance causes a reduction in available current and voltage.

Resistance is measured in an inactive circuit with an ohmmeter. The ohmmeter sends a small amount of current into the circuit and measures how difficult it is to push the current through the circuit.

An ohmmeter, although useful, is not always a good indicator of a circuit's actual ability under operating conditions. This is due to the low voltage (6-9 volts) that the meter uses to test the circuit. The voltage in an ignition coil secondary winding can be several thousand volts. Such high voltage can cause the coil to malfunction, yet the fault may not be detected during a resistance test.

Resistance generally increases with temperature. Perform all testing with the component or circuit at room temperature. Resistance tests performed at high temperatures may indicate high resistance readings and result in the unnecessary replacement of a component.

Amperage

Amperage is the unit of measure for the amount of current within a circuit. Current is the actual flow of electricity. The higher the current, the more work that can be performed. However, if the current flow exceeds the circuit or component capacity, the system will be damaged.

Electrical Tests

Refer to Chapter Nine for a description of various electrical tests.

BASIC SERVICE METHODS

Most of the procedures in this manual are straightforward and can be performed by anyone reasonably competent with tools. However, consider personal capabilities carefully before attempting any operation involving major disassembly.

1. Front, in this manual, refers to the front of the ATV. The front of any component is the end closest to the front of the ATV. The left and right sides refer to the position of the parts as viewed by the rider sitting on the seat facing forward. For example, the throttle control is on the right side of the handlebar.

2. Whenever servicing an engine or suspension component, secure the ATV in a safe manner.

3. Tag all similar parts for location, and mark all mated parts for position. Record the number and thickness of any shims as they are removed. Identify parts by placing them in sealed and labeled plastic bags.

4. Tag disconnected wires and connectors with masking tape and a marking pen. Do not rely on memory alone.

5. Protect finished surfaces from physical damage or corrosion. Keep gasoline and other chemicals off painted surfaces.

6. Use penetrating oil on frozen or tight bolts. Avoid using heat where possible. Heat can warp, melt or affect the temper of parts. Heat also damages the finish of paint and plastics.

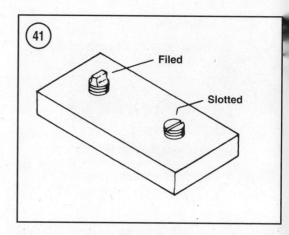

7. When a part is a press fit or requires a special tool for removal, the information or type of tool is identified in the text. Otherwise, if a part is difficult to remove or install, determine the cause before proceeding.

8. To prevent objects or debris from falling into the engine, cover all openings.

9. Read each procedure thoroughly and compare the illustrations to the actual components before starting the procedure. Perform each procedure in sequence.

10. Recommendations are occasionally made to refer service to a dealership or specialist. In these cases, the work can be performed more economically by the specialist than by the home mechanic.

11. The term *replace* means to discard a defective part and install a new part in its place. *Overhaul* means to remove, disassemble, inspect, measure, repair and/or replace parts as required to recondition an assembly.

12. Some operations require the use of a hydraulic press. If a press is not available, have these operations performed by a shop equipped with the necessary equipment. Do not use makeshift equipment that may damage the ATV.

13. Repairs are much faster and easier if the ATV is clean before starting work. Degrease the ATV with a commercial degreaser; follow the directions on the container for the best results. Clean all parts with cleaning solvent as they are removed.

> *CAUTION*
> *Do not apply a chemical degreaser to an O-ring drive chain. These chemicals will damage the O-rings.*

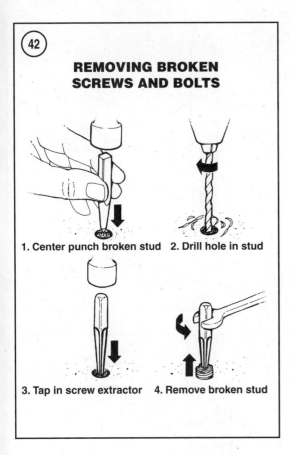

REMOVING BROKEN SCREWS AND BOLTS

1. Center punch broken stud   2. Drill hole in stud

3. Tap in screw extractor   4. Remove broken stud

Use kerosene to clean O-ring type chains.

CAUTION
Do not direct high-pressure water at steering bearings, carburetor hoses, wheel bearings, suspension and electrical components, or O-ring drive chains. The water will force the grease out of the bearings and possibly damage the seals.

14. If special tools are required, have them available before starting a procedure. When special tools are required, they will be described at the beginning of the procedure.

15. Make diagrams of similar-appearing parts. For instance, crankcase bolts are often not the same lengths. Do not rely on memory alone. It is possible that carefully laid out parts will become disturbed, making it difficult to reassemble the components correctly without a diagram.

16. Make sure all shims and washers are reinstalled in the same location and position.

17. Whenever a rotating part contacts a stationary part, look for a shim or washer.

18. Use new gaskets if there is any doubt about the condition of old ones.

19. If self-locking fasteners are used, replace them with new ones. Do not reuse a self-locking fastener. Also, do not install standard fasteners in place of self-locking ones.

20. Use grease to hold small parts in place if they tend to fall out during assembly. However, do not apply grease to electrical or brake components.

Removing Frozen Fasteners

If a fastener cannot be removed, several methods may be used to loosen it. First, apply penetrating oil such as Liquid Wrench or WD-40. Apply it liberally, and let it penetrate for 10-15 minutes. Rap the fastener several times with a small hammer. Do not hit it hard enough to cause damage. Reapply the penetrating oil if necessary.

For frozen screws, apply penetrating oil as described. Insert a screwdriver in the slot, and rap the top of the screwdriver with a hammer. This loosens the rust so the screw can be removed in the normal way. If the screw head is too damaged to use this method, grip the head with locking pliers and twist the screw out.

Avoid applying heat unless specifically instructed, as it may melt, warp or remove the temper from parts. Use a heat gun, if available.

Removing Broken Fasteners

If the head breaks off a screw or bolt, several methods are available for removing the remaining portion. If a large portion of the remainder projects out, try gripping it with locking pliers. If the projecting portion is too small, file it to fit a wrench or cut a slot in it to fit a screwdriver (**Figure 41**).

If the head breaks off flush, use a screw extractor. To do this, centerpunch the exact center of the remaining portion of the screw or bolt. Drill a small hole in the screw and tap the extractor into the hole. Back the screw out with a wrench on the extractor (**Figure 42**).

Repairing Damaged Threads

Occasionally, threads are stripped through carelessness or impact damage. Often the threads can be repaired by running a tap (for internal threads on nuts) or die (for external threads on bolts) through the threads (**Figure 43**). To clean or repair spark plug threads, use a spark plug tap.

If an internal thread is damaged, it may be necessary to install a Helicoil or some other type of thread insert. Follow the manufacturer's instructions when installing their insert.

Stud Removal/Installation

A stud removal tool is available from most tool suppliers. This tool makes the removal and installation of studs easier. If one is not available, thread two nuts onto the stud and tighten them against each other. Remove the stud by turning the lower nut (**Figure 44**).

1. Measure the height of the stud above the surface.
2. Thread the stud removal tool onto the stud and tighten it, or thread two nuts onto the stud.
3. Remove the stud by turning the stud remover or the lower nut.
4. Remove any threadlocking compound from the threaded hole. Clean the threads with an aerosol parts cleaner.
5. Install the stud removal tool onto the new stud or thread two nuts onto the stud.
6. Apply threadlocking compound to the threads of the stud.
7. Install the stud and tighten it with the stud removal tool or the top nut.
8. Install the stud to the height noted in Step 1, the height specified in the text or its torque specification.
9. Remove the stud removal tool or the two nuts.

Removing Hoses

When removing stubborn hoses, do not exert excessive force on the hose or fitting. Remove the hose clamp and carefully insert a small screwdriver or pick tool between the fitting and hose. Apply a spray lubricant under the hose and carefully twist the hose off the fitting. Use a wire brush to clean any corrosion or rubber hose material from the fitting. Clean the inside of the hose thoroughly. Never

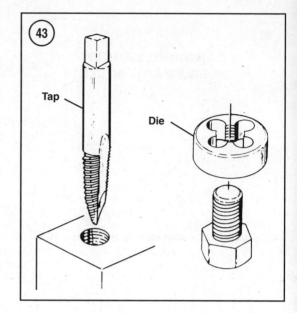

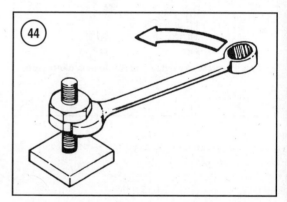

use any lubricant when installing the hose (new or old). The lubricant may allow the hose to come off the fitting, even with the clamp secure.

Bearings

Bearings are used in the engine and transmission assembly to reduce power loss, heat and noise resulting from friction. Because bearings are precision parts, they must be maintained by proper lubrication and maintenance. If a bearing is damaged, replace it immediately. When installing a new bearing, take care to prevent damaging it. Bearing replacement procedures are included in the individual chapters where applicable; however, use the following sections as a guideline.

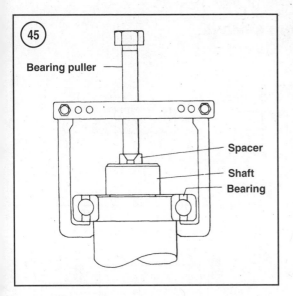

Bearing puller

Spacer
Shaft
Bearing

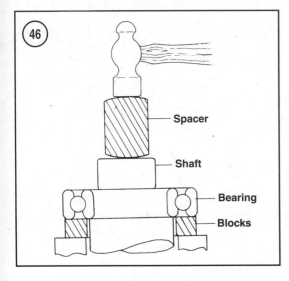

Spacer

Shaft

Bearing

Blocks

NOTE
Unless otherwise specified, install bearings with the manufacturer's mark or number facing outward.

Removal

While bearings are normally removed only when damaged, there may be times when it is necessary to remove a bearing that is in good condition. However, improper bearing removal will damage the bearing and maybe the shaft or case half. Note the following when removing bearings.

1. Before removing the bearings, note the following:

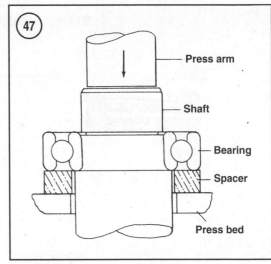

Press arm

Shaft

Bearing

Spacer

Press bed

   a. Refer to the bearing replacement procedure in the appropriate chapter for any special instructions.

   b. Remove any seals that interfere with bearing removal. Refer to *Seal Replacement* in this section.

   c. When removing more than one bearing, identify the bearings before removing them. Refer to the bearing manufacturer's numbers on the bearing.

   d. Note and record the direction in which the bearing numbers face for proper installation.

   e. Remove any set plates or bearing retainers before removing the bearings.

2. When using a puller to remove a bearing from a shaft, take care that the shaft is not damaged. Always place a piece of metal between the end of the shaft and the puller screw. In addition, place the puller arms next to the inner bearing race. See **Figure 45**.

3. When using a hammer to remove a bearing from a shaft, do not strike the hammer directly against the shaft. Instead, use a brass or aluminum spacer between the hammer and shaft (**Figure 46**) and make sure to support both bearing races with wooden blocks as shown.

4. The ideal method of bearing removal is with a hydraulic press. Note the following when using a press:

   a. Always support the inner and outer bearing races with a suitable size wooden or aluminum spacer (**Figure 47**). If only the outer race is supported, pressure applied against

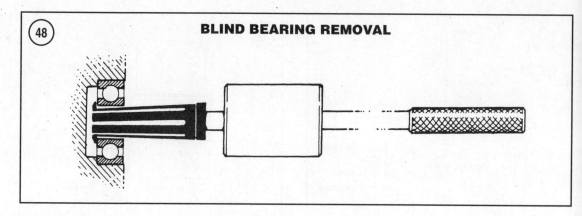

BLIND BEARING REMOVAL

(48)

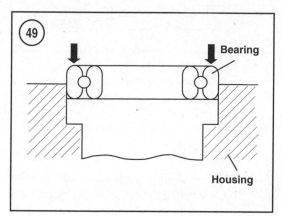

(49)

Bearing

Housing

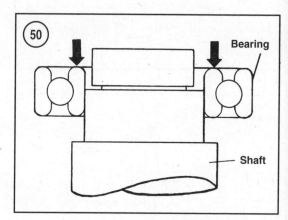

(50)

Bearing

Shaft

the balls and/or the inner race will damage them.

b. Always make sure the press arm (**Figure 47**) aligns with the center of the shaft. If the arm is not centered, it may damage the bearing and/or shaft.

c. The moment the shaft is free of the bearing, it will drop to the floor. Secure or hold the shaft to prevent it from falling.

d. When removing bearings from a housing, support the housing with 4 × 4 in. wooden blocks to prevent damage to gasket surfaces.

5. Use a blind bearing puller to remove bearings installed in blind holes (**Figure 48**).

6. When it is impossible to fit a blind bearing puller onto a bearing, first heat the case evenly with a heat gun. Then place the case on a wooden surface (bearing side down) and tap the housing from its opposite side with a plastic or rubber hammer to remove the bearing.

Installation

1. When installing a bearing into a housing, apply pressure to the *outer* bearing race (**Figure 49**). When installing a bearing onto a shaft, apply pressure to the *inner* bearing race (**Figure 50**).

2. When installing a bearing as described in Step 1, some type of driver is required. Never strike the bearing directly with a hammer or the bearing will be damaged. When installing a bearing, use a piece of pipe or a driver with a diameter that matches the bearing race. **Figure 50** shows the correct way to use a driver and hammer to install a bearing onto a shaft.

3. Step 1 describes how to install a bearing in a case half or over a shaft. However, when installing a bearing over a shaft and into a housing at the same time, a tight fit is required for both outer and inner bearing races. In this situation, install a spacer underneath the driver tool so that pressure is applied evenly across both races (**Figure 51**). If both races are not driven evenly during this procedure, the

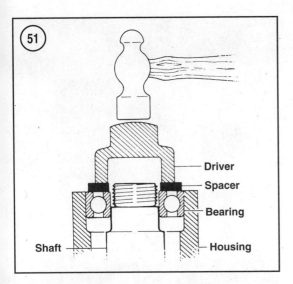

balls in the bearing will damage both bearing races when the races are forced out of alignment.

Interference fit

1. Follow this procedure when installing a bearing over a shaft. When a tight fit is required, the bearing inside diameter will be smaller than the shaft. In this case, driving the bearing onto the shaft using normal methods may cause bearing damage. Instead, heat the bearing before installation. Note the following:

    a. Refer to the bearing replacement procedure in the appropriate chapter for any special instructions.

    b. Secure the shaft so it is ready for bearing installation.

    c. Clean all residues from the bearing surface of the shaft. Remove burrs with a file or sandpaper.

    d. Fill a suitable pot or beaker with clean mineral oil. Place a thermometer rated above 120° C (248° F) in the oil. Support the thermometer so it does not rest on the bottom or side of the pot.

    e. Remove the bearing from its wrapper and secure it with a piece of heavy wire bent to hold it in the pot. Hang the bearing in the pot so it does not touch the bottom or sides of the pot.

    f. Turn the heat on and monitor the thermometer. When the oil temperature rises to approximately 120° C (248° F), remove the bearing from the pot and quickly install it. If neces-

sary, place a socket on the inner bearing race and tap the bearing into place. As the bearing chills, it will tighten on the shaft, so installation must be done quickly. Make sure the bearing is installed completely.

2. Follow this step when installing a bearing in a housing. Bearings are generally installed in a housing with a slight interference fit. Driving the bearing into the housing using normal methods may damage the housing or cause bearing damage. Instead, chill the bearing(s) and heat the housing before the bearing is installed. Note the following:

> *CAUTION*
> *Before heating the housing in this procedure, wash the housing thoroughly with detergent and water. Rinse and rewash the cases as required to remove all traces of oil and other chemical deposits.*

    a. Refer to the bearing replacement procedure in the appropriate chapter for any special instructions.

    b. Before heating the bearing housing, place the new bearing(s) in a freezer. Chilling a bearing slightly reduces its outside diameter, while the heated bearing housing assembly is slightly larger due to heat expansion. This will make bearing installation easier.

    c. Heat the housing to approximately 100° C (212° F) in an oven or on a hot plate. To accurately monitor the temperature, use temperature sticks available at welding supply stores. Heat only one housing at a time.

> *CAUTION*
> *Do not heat the housing with a propane or acetylene torch. Never bring a flame into contact with the bearing or housing. The direct heat will destroy the case hardening of the bearing and will likely warp the housing.*

    d. Remove the housing from the oven or hot plate, and hold onto the housing with heavy gloves.

> *NOTE*
> *Always install bearings with the manufacturer's mark or number facing outward unless specifically directed not to.*

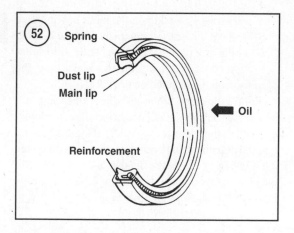

e. While the housing is still hot, install the new bearing(s) into the housing. Install the bearings by hand, if possible. If necessary, lightly tap the bearing(s) into the housing with a socket placed on the outer bearing race (**Figure 49**). Do not install new bearings by driving on the inner-bearing race. Install the bearing(s) until it seats completely.

Seal Replacement

Seals (**Figure 52**) are used to contain oil, water, grease or combustion gasses in a housing or shaft. Improper removal of a seal can damage the housing or shaft. Improper installation of the seal can damage the seal and cause leakage. Note the following:

1. Refer to the seal replacement procedure in the appropriate chapter for any special instructions.

2. Prying is generally the easiest and most effective method for removing a seal from a housing. Note the following:

   a. Record the depth or installed position to which the seal is installed.

   b. When using a screwdriver to remove a seal, place a rag underneath the screwdriver (**Figure 53**) to avoid damaging the housing.

   c. If a seal is hard to remove, do not damage the seal by using a screwdriver or similar tool. Use a seal removal tool.

3. Pack the specified grease in the seal lips before the seal is installed. If no grease is specified, use waterproof grease. If the new seal is pre-greased, do not add additional grease.

4. While seals are usually installed with the manufacturer's numbers or marks facing out, this is not always the case. In situations where double-sided seals are used, record the side of the seal that faces out. When two seals are installed back-to-back, record the side of each seal that faces out.

5. Install seals with a socket or bearing driver placed on the outer circumference of the seal as shown in **Figure 54**. Drive the seal squarely into the housing. Never install a seal by hammering on the outer side of the seal. Install the seal to its proper depth.

Table 1 ENGINE AND FRAME SERIAL NUMBERS

1

Model	Engine starting serial number	Frame starting serial number
2000		
TRX350FE	TE25E-8000001~	478TE254 YA000001~
TRX350FM	TE25E-8000001~	478TE250 YA000001~
TRX350TE	TE24E-8000001~	478TE244 YA000001~
TRX350TM	TE24E-8000001~	478TE240 YA000001~
2001		
TRX350FE	TE25E-8000001~	478TE254 1A100001~
	TE25E-8000001~	478TE254 14000001~
TRX350FM	TE25E-8000001~	478TE250 1A100001~
	TE25E-8000001~	478TE250 14000001~
TRX350TE	TE24E-8000001~	478TE244 1A100001~
TRX350TM	TE24E-8000001~	478TE240 1A100001~
2002		
TRX350FE	TE25E-8500001~	478TE254 2A200001~
	TE25E-8500001~	478TE254 24100001~
TRX350FM	TE25E-8500001~	478TE250 2A200001~
	TE25E-8500001~	478TE250 24100001~
TRX350TE	TE25E-8500001~	478TE254 2A200001~
	TE24E-8500001~	478TE244 24100001~
TRX350TM	TE24E-8500001~	478TE240 2A200001~
	TE24E-8500001~	478TE240 24100001~
2003		
TRX350FE	TE25E-8500001~	478TE254 3A300001~
	TE25E-8600001~	478TE254 34200001~
TRX350FM	TE25E-8500001~	478TE250 3A300001~
	TE25E-8600001~	478TE250 34200001~
TRX350TE	TE25E-8500001~	478TE244 3A300001~
	TE24E-8600001~	478TE244 34200001~
TRX350TM	TE24E-8500001~	478TE240 3A300001~
	TE24E-8600001~	478TE240 34200001~
2004-2006	Not available	Not available

Table 2 GENERAL DIMENSIONS

	mm	in.
Overall width		
2000-2003	1143	45.0
2004-on TE/TM	1114	43.9
2004-on FE/FM	1114	43.9
Overall length		
2000-2003	1983	78.1
2004-on TE/TM	2031	80.0
2004-on FE/FM	2031	80.0
Overall height		
2000-2003 FE/FM	1130	44.5
2000-2003 TE/TM	1119	44.1
2004-on FE/FM	1141	44.9
2004-on TE/TM	1129	44.4

(continued)

Table 2 GENERAL DIMENSIONS

	mm	in.
Wheelbase		
2000-2003 FE/FM	1246	49.1
2000-2003 TE/TM	1253	49.3
2004-on FE/FM	1246	49.1
2004-on TE/TM	1253	49.3
Front tread		
2000-2003 FE/FM	844	33.2
2000-2003 TE/TM	851	33.5
2004-on FE/FM	844	33.2
2004-on TE/TM	851	33.5
Rear tread		
2000-2003 FE/FM	860	33.9
2000-2003 TE/TM	840	33.1
2004-on FE/FM	860	33.9
2004-on TE/TM	840	33.1
Seat height		
2000-2003 FE/FM	824	32.4
2000-2003 TE/TM	812	32.0
2004-on FE/FM	819	32.3
2004-on TE/TM	812	32.0
Footpeg height		
2000-2003 FE	330	13.0
2000-2003 FM	334	13.1
2000-2003 TE	318	12.5
2000-2003 TM	323	12.7
2004-on FM	344	13.5
2004-on FE	334	13.1
2004-on TM	337	13.3
2004-on TE	327	12.9
Ground clearance		
2000-2003 FE/FM	184	7.2
2000-2003 TE/TM	186	7.3
2004-on	186	7.3

Table 3 WEIGHT SPECIFICATIONS

	kg	lb.
Dry weight		
TRX350FE		
2000-2001	242.5	534.6
2002-2003	243	536
2004-on	241	531
TRX350FM		
2000-2001	237.5	523.6
2002-2003	238	525
2004-on	238	525
TRX350TE		
2000-2001	232	511
2002-2003	232.5	512.6
2004-on	232	511
TRX350TM		
2000-2001	226	498
2002-2003	226.5	499.3
2004-on	227	500

(continued)

Table 3 WEIGHT SPECIFICATIONS (continued)

	kg	lb.
Curb weight		
TRX350FE		
2000-2001	253.5	558.9
2002-2003	254	560
2004-on	252	556
TRX350FM		
2000-2001	248.5	547.8
2002-2003	249	549
2004-on	249	549
TRX350TE		
2000-2001	243	536
2002-2003	243.5	536.8
2004-on	242	534
TRX350TM		
2000-2001	237	522
2002-2003	237.5	522
2004-on	238	525

Table 4 METRIC, INCH AND FRACTIONAL EQUIVALENTS

mm	in.	Nearest fraction	mm	in.	Nearest fraction
1	0.0394	1/32	26	1.0236	1 1/32
2	0.0787	3/32	27	1.0630	1 1/16
3	0.1181	1/8	28	1.1024	1 3/32
4	0.1575	5/32	29	1.1417	1 5/32
5	0.1969	3/16	30	1.1811	1 3/16
6	0.2362	1/4	31	1.2205	1 7/32
7	0.2756	9/32	32	1.2598	1 1/4
8	0.3150	5/16	33	1.2992	1 5/16
9	0.3543	11/32	34	1.3386	1 11/32
10	0.3937	13/32	35	1.3780	1 3/8
11	0.4331	7/16	36	1.4173	1 13/32
12	0.4724	15/32	37	1.4567	1 15/32
13	0.5118	1/2	38	1.4961	1 1/2
14	0.5512	9/16	39	1.5354	1 17/32
15	0.5906	19/32	40	1.5748	1 9/16
16	0.6299	5/8	41	1.6142	1 5/8
17	0.6693	21/32	42	1.6535	1 21/32
18	0.7087	23/32	43	1.6929	1 11/16
19	0.7480	3/4	44	1.7323	1 23/32
20	0.7874	25/32	45	1.7717	1 25/32
21	0.8268	13/16	46	1.8110	1 13/16
22	0.8661	7/8	47	1.8504	1 27/32
23	0.9055	29/32	48	1.8898	1 7/8
24	0.9449	15/16	49	1.9291	1 15/16
25	0.9843	31/32	50	1.9685	1 31/32

Table 5 GENERAL TORQUE SPECIFICATION

Fastener	N•m	in.-lb.	ft.-lb.
5 mm			
Bolt and nut	5	44	–
Screw	4	35	–
6 mm			
Bolt and nut	10	88	–
Small flange bolt (8 mm head)	10	88	–
Large flange bolt (8 mm head)	12	106	–
Large flange bolt (10 mm head)	12	106	–
Screw	9	80	–
8 mm			
Bolt and nut	22	–	16
Screw	26	–	19
10 mm			
Bolt and nut	34	–	25
Flange bolt	39	–	29
12 mm			
Bolt and nut	54	–	40

Table 6 CONVERSION FORMULAS

Multiply:	By:	To get the equivalent of:
Length		
Inches	25.4	Millimeter
Inches	2.54	Centimeter
Miles	1.609	Kilometer
Feet	0.3048	Meter
Millimeter	0.03937	Inches
Centimeter	0.3937	Inches
Kilometer	0.6214	Mile
Meter	0.0006214	Mile
Fluid volume		
U.S. quarts	0.9463	Liters
U.S. gallons	3.785	Liters
U.S. ounces	29.573529	Milliliters
Imperial gallons	4.54609	Liters
Imperial quarts	1.1365	Liters
Liters	0.2641721	U.S. gallons
Liters	1.0566882	U.S. quarts
Liters	33.814023	U.S. ounces
Liters	0.22	Imperial gallons
Liters	0.8799	Imperial quarts
Milliliters	0.033814	U.S. ounces
Milliliters	1.0	Cubic centimeters
Milliliters	0.001	Liters
Torque		
Foot-pounds	1.3558	Newton-meters
Foot-pounds	0.138255	Meters-kilograms
Inch-pounds	0.11299	Newton-meters
Newton-meters	0.7375622	Foot-pounds
Newton-meters	8.8507	Inch-pounds
Meters-kilograms	7.2330139	Foot-pounds
Volume		
Cubic inches	16.387064	Cubic centimeters
Cubic centimeters	0.0610237	Cubic inches

(continued)

Table 6 CONVERSION FORMULAS (continued)

Multiply:	By:	To get the equivalent of:
Temperature		
Fahrenheit	$(°F - 32) \times 0.556$	Centigrade
Centigrade	$(°C \times 1.8) + 32$	Fahrenheit
Weight		
Ounces	28.3495	Grams
Pounds	0.4535924	Kilograms
Grams	0.035274	Ounces
Kilograms	2.2046224	Pounds
Pressure		
Pounds per square inch	0.070307	Kilograms per square centimeter
Kilograms per square centimeter	14.223343	Pounds per square inch
Kilopascals	0.1450	Pounds per square inch
Pounds per square inch	6.895	Kilopascals
Speed		
Miles per hour	1.609344	Kilometers per hour
Kilometers per hour	0.6213712	Miles per hour

Table 7 TECHNICAL ABBREVIATIONS

ABDC	After bottom dead center
ATDC	After top dead center
BBDC	Before bottom dead center
BDC	Bottom dead center
BTDC	Before top dead center
C	Celsius (centigrade)
cc	Cubic centimeters
cid	Cubic inch displacement
CDI	Capacitor discharge ignition
cu. in.	Cubic inches
ESP	Electric Shift Program
F	Fahrenheit
ft.	Feet
ft.-lb.	Foot-pounds
gal.	Gallons
H/A	High altitude
hp	Horsepower
in.	Inches
in.-lb.	Inch-pounds
I.D.	Inside diameter
kg	Kilograms
kgm	Kilogram meters
km	Kilometer
kPa	Kilopascals
L	Liter
m	Meter
MAG	Magneto
ml	Milliliter
mm	Millimeter
N•m	Newton-meters
O.D.	Outside diameter
oz.	Ounces
psi	Pounds per square inch
PTO	Power take off
pt.	Pint
qt.	Quart
rpm	Revolutions per minute
SE	Starting enrichment

CHAPTER TWO

TROUBLESHOOTING

The troubleshooting procedures described in this chapter provide typical symptoms and logical methods for isolating the cause(s). There may be several ways to solve a problem, but only a systematic approach will be successful in avoiding wasted time and possibly unnecessary parts replacement.

Gather as much information as possible to aid in diagnosis. Never assume anything and do not overlook the obvious. Make sure there is fuel in the tank. Make sure the fuel shutoff valve is in the on position. If the motorcycle has been sitting for any length of time, fuel deposits may have gummed up the carburetor jets. Gasoline loses its volatility after standing for long periods and water condensation may have diluted the gas. Drain the old gas and fill the tank with fresh gas. Make sure the engine stop switch is in the run position. Make sure the spark plug wire is connected securely to the spark plug.

If a quick check does not reveal the problem, proceed with one of the troubleshooting procedures described in this chapter. After defining the symptoms, follow the procedure that most closely relates to the condition(s).

In most cases, expensive and complicated test equipment is not needed to determine whether repairs can be performed at home. A few simple checks could prevent an unnecessary repair charge and lost time while the motorcycle is at a dealership's service department. On the other hand, be realistic and do not attempt repairs beyond personal capabilities. Many service departments will not accept work that involves the reassembly of damaged or abused equipment; if they do, expect the cost to be high.

If the ATV does require the attention of a professional, describe symptoms and conditions accurately and fully. The more information a technician has available, the easier it will be to diagnose the problem.

Following the lubrication and maintenance schedule described in Chapter Three can reduce the need for troubleshooting by eliminating possible problems before they occur. However, even with the best of care the ATV may require troubleshooting.

OPERATING REQUIREMENTS

An engine needs three basics to run properly: correct air/fuel mixture, compression and a spark at the right time. If one basic requirement is missing, the engine will not run. Refer to **Figure 1** for four-stroke engine operating principles.

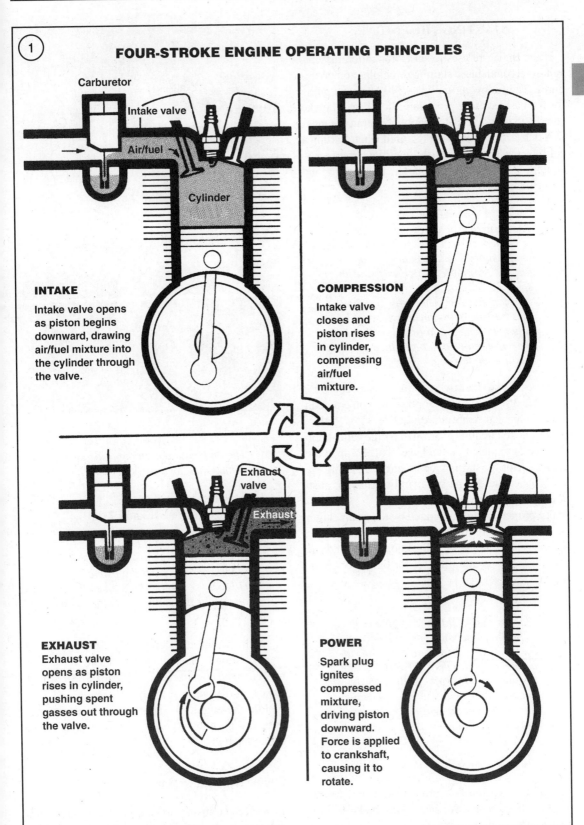

① **FOUR-STROKE ENGINE OPERATING PRINCIPLES**

2

INTAKE
Intake valve opens as piston begins downward, drawing air/fuel mixture into the cylinder through the valve.

COMPRESSION
Intake valve closes and piston rises in cylinder, compressing air/fuel mixture.

EXHAUST
Exhaust valve opens as piston rises in cylinder, pushing spent gasses out through the valve.

POWER
Spark plug ignites compressed mixture, driving piston downward. Force is applied to crankshaft, causing it to rotate.

Carburetor
Intake valve
Air/fuel
Cylinder
Exhaust valve
Exhaust

STARTING THE ENGINE

If the engine refuses to start, frustration may result in forgotten basic starting principles and procedures. The following outline will serve as a guide for the basic starting procedure. In all cases, make sure there is an adequate supply of fuel in the tank.

A rich air/fuel mixture is required when starting a cold engine. To accomplish this, the carburetor is equipped with a choke (starter jet) circuit and primer circuit.

NOTE
*The knob that actuates the starter jet is often incorrectly identified as the **choke** knob. The knob does not operate a choke plate, which is found in some carburetors to enrich the mixture for starting. The knob operates the starting enrichment valve (SE) which provides additional fuel into the carburetor bore to produce a rich mixture for starting.*

Use the choke circuit when the ambient temperature is -15° to 35° C (5° to 95° F). Use the primer circuit when the ambient temperature is below -15° C (5° F).

The choke circuit is controlled by the cable knob (**Figure 2**) mounted on the handlebar. To open the choke circuit for starting a cold engine, pull up the knob. After the engine starts and warms up, push down knob all the way.

The primer circuit is operated by the primer knob (**Figure 3**) mounted on the carburetor float bowl. To use the primer circuit, push the knob in two or three times before operating the starter button or recoil starter.

CAUTION
When trying to start the engine in the following procedure, do not operate the starter for more than 5 seconds at a time as starter damage due to overheating may result. Wait approximately 10 seconds before operating the starter button again. If necessary, use the recoil starter.

Engine is Cold

1. Shift the transmission into neutral so the neutral indicator light glows. Set the parking brake.
2. Turn the ignition switch on.

NOTE
The on position of the ignition switch is indicated by a vertical line (I).

3. Turn the fuel valve to on.
4. Pull the choke knob (**Figure 2**) up.

NOTE
*If the ambient temperature is below -15° C (5° F), push the primer knob (**Figure 3**) two or three times before operating the starter button or recoil starter.*

5. With the throttle completely closed, push the starter button or operate the recoil starter.
6. When the engine starts, push the throttle slightly to keep it running.
7. Idle the engine for approximately a minute or until the throttle responds cleanly, then push the choke knob off.

Engine is Warm or Hot

1. Shift the transmission into neutral so the neutral indicator light glows. Set the parking brake.

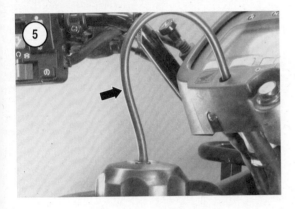

2. Turn the ignition switch on.

NOTE
The on position of the ignition switch is indicated by a vertical line (I).

3. Turn the fuel valve on.
4. Make sure the choke knob (**Figure 2**) is pushed down.
5. Open the throttle slightly and push the starter button or operate the recoil starter.

Engine is Flooded

If the engine is hard to start and there is a strong gasoline smell, the engine is probably flooded. If so, push the choke knob down (**Figure 2**). Open the throttle all the way and push the starter button or operate the recoil starter until the engine starts. If the engine is flooded badly, it may be necessary to remove the spark plug and dry its insulator, or install a new plug. When a flooded engine first starts to run, it will initially cough and run slowly as it burns the excess fuel. As the excess fuel is burned, the engine will accelerate quickly. Release the throttle at this

point. Because a flooded engine smokes badly when it first starts to run, start the engine outside and in a well-ventilated area with its muffler pointing away from all objects. Do not start a flooded engine in a garage or other closed area.

NOTE
*If the engine refuses to start, check the carburetor overflow hose attached to the fitting at the bottom of the float bowl (**Figure 4**). If fuel is running out of the hose, the float valve is stuck open or leaking, allowing the carburetor to overfill. If this problem exists, remove the carburetor and correct the problem as described in Chapter Eight.*

STARTING DIFFICULTY

If the engine cranks but is difficult to start, or will not start at all, do not drain the battery. Check for obvious problems first. Go down the following list step by step. Perform each step while remembering the three engine operating requirements described in this chapter.

If the engine still will not start, refer to the appropriate troubleshooting procedure that follows in this chapter.

1. Make sure the choke knob is in correct. See *Starting the Engine* in this chapter.
2. Make sure there is a sufficient quantity of gasoline in good condition in the fuel tank. If in doubt, drain the fuel and fill it with a fresh tank full. Check for a clogged fuel tank vent tube (**Figure 5**). Remove the tube from the filler cap, then wipe off one end and blow through it. Remove the filler cap and check for a plugged hose nozzle.

WARNING
Do not use an open flame to check in the tank. A serious explosion is certain to result.

3. Disconnect the fuel line (**Figure 6**) from the carburetor and insert the end of the hose into a clear container. Turn the fuel valve on and see if fuel flows freely. If fuel does not flow and there is a fuel filter installed in the fuel line, remove the filter and turn the fuel valve on again. If fuel flows, the filter is clogged and must be replaced. If no fuel comes out, the fuel valve may be shut off, blocked by

debris, or the fuel cap vent may be plugged. Reconnect the fuel line to the carburetor fitting.

4. If a flooded cylinder is suspected, or there is a strong smell of gasoline, open the throttle all the way and push the starter button or operate the recoil starter. If the cylinder is severely flooded (fouled or wet spark plug), remove the spark plug and dry the base and electrode thoroughly with a soft cloth. Reinstall the plug and attempt to start the engine. See *Starting the Engine* in this chapter.

5. Check the carburetor overflow hose on the bottom of the float bowl (**Figure 4**). If fuel is running from the hose, the float valve is stuck open or leaking. Turn the fuel valve off and tap the carburetor a few times. Then turn on the fuel valve. If fuel continues to run out of the hose, remove and repair the carburetor as described in Chapter Eight. Check the carburetor vent hoses to make sure they are clear. Check the end of the hoses for contamination.

NOTE
If fuel is reaching the carburetor, the fuel system could still be the problem. The jets (pilot and main) could be plugged or the air filter could·be severely restricted. However, before removing the carburetor, continue with Step 6 to make sure the ignition provides an adequate spark.

6. Make sure the engine stop switch (**Figure 7**) is operating correctly. If necessary, test the engine stop switch as described in Chapter Nine.

7. Make sure the spark plug high-tension wire and cap (**Figure 8**) is on tight. Push it on and slightly rotate it to clean the electrical connection between the spark plug and the wire connector. Hold the high-tension wire and screw the plug cap on tightly.

NOTE
If the engine still will not start, continue with the following.

8. Perform a spark test as described in this section. If there is a strong spark, perform Step 9. If there is no spark or if the spark is very weak, test the ignition system as described in *Ignition System* in this chapter.

9. Check cylinder compression as follows:
   a. Move the engine stop switch (**Figure 7**) to off.
   b. Turn the fuel valve off.
   c. Remove the spark plug and ground the spark plug shell against the cylinder head.

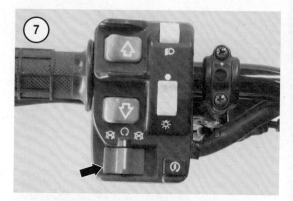

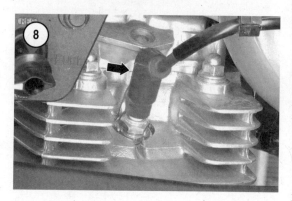

d. Place your finger tightly over the spark plug hole.

e. Operate the starter, or have an assistant operate the recoil starter. When the piston comes up on the compression stroke, pressure in the cylinder should force your finger from the spark plug hole. If so, the cylinder probably has sufficient compression to start the engine.

NOTE
A compression problem may exist even though it seems good with the previous test. Check engine compression using

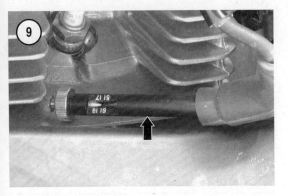

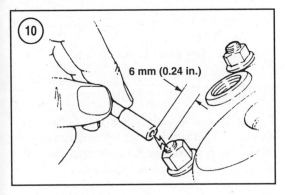

6 mm (0.24 in.)

a compression gauge as described in
Tune-Up in Chapter Three.

Spark Test

Perform the following spark test to determine if
the ignition system is producing adequate spark.
When checking spark, turn the engine stop switch
to run and the ignition switch to on.

> *CAUTION*
> *Before removing the spark plug in*
> *Step 1, clean all debris away from the*
> *plug base. Dirt that falls into the cyl-*
> *inder will cause rapid engine wear.*

1. Disconnect the plug wire and remove the spark
plug.
2. Insert the spark plug (or spark tester) into the
plug cap and touch its base against the cylinder head
to ground it (**Figure 9**). Position the plug so the
electrodes are visible. When using an adjustable
spark tester, set its air gap to 6 mm (0.24 in.).

> *CAUTION*
> *Mount the spark plug or spark tester*
> *away from the plug hole in the cylin-*

der head so that the spark from the
plug or tester cannot ignite the gasoline vapor in the cylinder.

3. Turn the engine over with the starter button or
operate the recoil starter. A fat blue spark should be
evident across the spark plug electrodes or spark
tester terminals.

> *WARNING*
> *Do not hold or touch the spark plug*
> *(or spark tester) wire or connector*
> *when making a spark check. A serious*
> *electrical shock may result.*

4. If the spark is good, check for one or more of the
following possible malfunctions:
   a. Obstructed fuel line or fuel filter (if used).
   b. Low compression or engine damage.
   c. Flooded engine.
5. If the spark is weak (white or yellow in color) or
if there is no spark, check for one or more of the following conditions:
   a. Fouled or wet spark plug. If a spark jumps
      across a spark tester but not across the origi-
      nal spark plug, the plug is fouled. Repeat the
      spark test with a new spark plug.
   b. Loose or damaged spark plug cap connection.
      Hold the spark plug wire and turn the spark
      plug cap to tighten it. Then install the spark
      plug into the cap and repeat the spark test. If
      there is still no spark, bypass the plug cap as
      described in the next step.
   c. Check for a damaged spark plug cap. Hold
      the spark plug wire and unscrew the spark
      plug cap (**Figure 8**). Hold the end of the spark
      plug wire 6 mm (0.24 in.) from the cylinder
      head as shown in **Figure 10**. Have an assis-
      tant turn the engine over and repeat the spark
      test. If there is a strong spark, the spark plug
      cap is faulty. Replace the plug cap and repeat
      the spark test.
   d. Loose or damaged spark plug wire connec-
      tions (at the coil and plug cap).
   e. Faulty ignition coil or faulty ignition coil
      ground wire connection.
   f. Faulty ICM unit or stator coil(s).
   g. On early 2000 FE and TE models, faulty
      sub-ICM unit.
   h. Sheared flywheel key.
   i. Loose flywheel nut.
   j. Loose electrical connections.

2

k. Dirty electrical connections.

> *NOTE*
> *If the engine backfires during start-*
> *ing, the ignition timing may be incor-*
> *rect. Because the ignition timing is not*
> *adjustable, incorrect ignition timing*
> *may be caused by a loose flywheel,*
> *sheared flywheel key, loose ignition*
> *pulse generator mounting screws or*
> *connector, or a damaged or defective*
> *ignition system component. Refer to*
> ***Ignition System** in this chapter.*

Engine is Difficult to Start

The following section groups the three main engine operating systems with probable causes.

Electrical system

If an ignition problem occurs, it can usually be traced to a point in the wiring harness, at the connectors or in one of the switches.

1. Spark plug:
   a. Fouled spark plug.
   b. Incorrect spark plug gap.
   c. Incorrect spark plug heat range (too cold). See Chapter Three.
   d. Worn or damaged spark plug electrodes.
   e. Damaged spark plug.
   f. Damaged spark plug cap or spark plug wire.

> *NOTE*
> *Refer to **Spark Plug Reading** in*
> *Chapter Three for additional infor-*
> *mation.*

2. Ignition coil:
   a. Loose or damaged ignition coil leads.
   b. Cracked ignition coil body (look for carbon tracks on the ignition coil).
   c. Loose or corroded ground wire.
3. Switches and wiring:
   a. Dirty or loose fitting terminals.
   b. Damaged wires or connectors (**Figure 11**).
   c. Damaged ignition switch.
   d. Damaged engine stop switch.
4. Electrical components:
   a. Damaged ignition pulse generator.
   b. Damaged ICM unit.

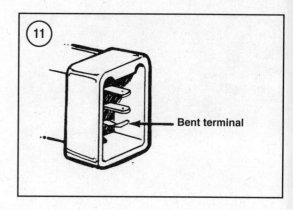

c. On early 2000 FE and TE models, damaged sub-ICM unit.
d. Sheared flywheel Woodruff key.

Fuel system

A contaminated fuel system will cause engine starting and performance related problems. It only takes a small amount of dirt in the fuel valve, fuel line or carburetor to cause a problem.

1. Air filter:
   a. Plugged air filter element.
   b. Plugged air filter housing.
   c. Leaking or damaged air filter housing-to-carburetor air boot.
2. Fuel valve:
   a. Plugged fuel hose.
   b. Plugged fuel valve filter.
3. Fuel tank:
   a. No fuel.
   b. Plugged fuel filter.
   c. Plugged fuel tank breather hose (**Figure 5**).
   d. Contaminated fuel.
4. Carburetor:
   a. Plugged or damaged choke system.
   b. Plugged main jet.
   c. Plugged pilot jet.
   d. Loose pilot jet or main jet.
   e. Plugged pilot jet air passage.
   f. Incorrect float level.
   g. Leaking or damaged float.
   h. Worn or damaged needle valve.

Engine Compression

Check engine compression as described in Chapter Three. To obtain a more accurate gauge of engine wear, perform an engine leak down test. Refer to *Cylinder Leak Down Test* in this chapter.

1. Cylinder and cylinder head:
   a. Loose spark plug.
   b. Missing spark plug gasket.
   c. Leaking cylinder head gasket.
   d. Leaking cylinder base gasket.
   e. Worn or seized piston, piston rings and/or cylinder.
   f. Loose cylinder and/or cylinder head fasteners.
   g. Cylinder head incorrectly installed and/or torqued.
   h. Warped cylinder head.
   i. Valve(s) adjusted too tight.
   j. Bent valve.
   k. Worn valve and/or seat.
   l. Worn or damaged valve guide(s).
   m. Damaged compression release cam (mounted on camshaft).
   n. Bent pushrod(s).
   o. Damaged cam follower.
2. Piston and piston rings:
   a. Worn piston rings.
   b. Damaged piston rings.
   c. Piston seizure or piston damage.
3. Crankcase and crankshaft:
   a. Seized connecting rod.
   b. Damaged crankcases.

POOR IDLE SPEED PERFORMANCE

If the engine starts, but off-idle performance is poor (engine hesitates or misfires), check the following:

1. Clogged or damaged air filter element.
2. Carburetor:
   a. Plugged pilot jet.
   b. Loose pilot jet.
   c. Damaged choke system.
   d. Incorrect throttle cable adjustment.
   e. Incorrect pilot screw adjustment.
   f. Flooded carburetor (visually check carburetor overflow hose for fuel).
   g. Vacuum piston does not slide smoothly in carburetor bore.
   h. Loose carburetor.
   i. Damaged intake tube O-ring.
3. Fuel:
   a. Water and/or alcohol in fuel.
   b. Old fuel.
4. Engine:
   a. Low engine compression.
5. Electrical system:
   a. Damaged spark plug.
   b. Damaged ignition coil.
   c. Damaged ignition pulse generator.
   d. Damaged ICM unit.
   e. On early 2000 FE and TE models, damaged sub-ICM unit.

POOR MEDIUM AND HIGH SPEED PERFORMANCE

Refer to *Engine is Difficult to Start*, then check the following:

1. Carburetor:
   a. Incorrect fuel level.
   b. Incorrect jet needle clip position.
   c. Plugged or loose main jet.
   d. Plugged fuel line.
   e. Plugged fuel valve.
   f. Plugged fuel tank vent tube.
2. Plugged air filter element.
3. Engine:
   a. Incorrect valve timing.
   b. Weak valve springs.
4. Other considerations:
   a. Overheating.
   b. Clutch slippage.
   c. Brake drag.
   d. Engine oil level too high.

ELECTRIC STARTING SYSTEM

This section describes troubleshooting procedures for the electric starting system. A fully charged battery, ohmmeter and jumper cables are required to perform many of these troubleshooting procedures.

Description

An electric starter (**Figure 12**) is used on all models. The starter is mounted horizontally at the rear of the engine.

The electric starting system requires a fully charged battery to provide the large amount of current required to operate the starter. A charge coil (mounted on the stator plate) and a voltage regulator, connected in circuit with the battery, keeps the battery charged while the engine is running. The battery can also be charged externally.

The starting circuit consists of the battery, starter, neutral/reverse switch, neutral indicator, starter relay, ignition switch and engine stop switch.

The starter relay (**Figure 13**) carries the heavy electrical current to the starter. Depressing the starter switch allows current to flow through the starter relay coil. The starter relay contacts close and allow current to flow from the battery through the starter relay to the starter.

When the ignition switch is turned on and the engine stop switch is in the run position, the starter can be operated only if the transmission is in neutral.

CAUTION
Do not operate the starter continuously for more than 5 seconds. Allow the starter to cool for at least 10 seconds between attempts to start the engine.

Preliminary Troubleshooting

Before troubleshooting the starting circuit, make sure:
1. The battery is fully charged.
2. Battery cables are the proper size and length. Replace cables that are undersize or damaged.
3. All electrical connections are clean and tight.
4. The wiring harness is in good condition, with no worn or frayed insulation or loose harness sockets.
5. The fuel system is filled with an adequate supply of fresh gasoline.

Starter Does Not Operate

If the starter does not operate, perform the following tests.

When operating the starter switch, turn the engine stop switch to run and the ignition switch to on. Make sure the transmission is in neutral.
1. Refer to Chapter Fifteen and remove the following components to access the starting circuit in this procedure.
   a. Seat.
   b. Air cleaner housing.
2. First check the 30-amp main fuse. Open the fuse holder, pull out the fuse and visually inspect it. If the fuse is blown, replace it as described in *Fuses* in

Chapter Nine. If the main fuse is good, reinstall it, then continue with Step 3.

3. Test the battery as described in *Battery* in Chapter Three. Note the following:
   a. If the battery is fully charged, perform Step 4.
   b. If necessary, clean and recharge the battery. If the battery is damaged, replace it.

4. Check for loose, corroded or damaged battery cables. Check at the battery, starter, starter relay and all cable-to-frame connections.

5. Turn the ignition switch on, then push the starter button and listen for a click sound at the starter relay switch (**Figure 13**). Note the following:
   a. If the relay clicked, perform Step 6.
   b. If the relay did not click, go to Step 7.

6. Test the battery as follows:
   a. Park the ATV on level ground and set the parking brake. Shift the transmission into neutral.
   b. Disconnect the cable from the starter (**Figure 12**).

WARNING
Because a spark will be produced in the following steps, perform this procedure away from gasoline or other volatile liquids. Make sure there is no spilled gasoline or gasoline fumes in the work area.

   c. Momentarily connect a jumper cable (thick gauge wire) from the positive battery terminal to the starter terminal. If the starter is working properly, it will turn when the jumper cable connection is made.
   d. If the starter did not turn, remove the starter and service it as described in Chapter Nine.

2

e. If the starter turned, check for a loose or damaged starter cable. If the cable is good, the starter relay (**Figure 13**) is faulty. Replace the starter relay and retest.

7. Test the following items as described in Chapter Nine:

    a. Neutral/reverse switch.

    b. Ignition switch.

    c. Diode.

8. Perform the starter relay switch voltage test as described in *Starter Relay Switch* in Chapter Nine. Note the following:

    a. If the voltmeter shows battery voltage, continue with Step 9.

    b. If there was no voltage reading, check the ignition switch and starter switch as described in Chapter Nine. If both switches are good, check the continuity of the yellow/red wire between the starter switch and the starter relay switch.

9. Perform the starter relay switch continuity test as described in *Starter Relay Switch* in Chapter Nine. Note the following:

    a. If the meter reading is correct, continue with Step 10.

    b. If the meter reading is incorrect, check for an open circuit in the yellow/red and light green/red wires. Check the wire ends for loose or damaged connectors.

10. If the starting system problem was not found after performing these steps in order, recheck the wiring system for dirty or loose-fitting terminals or damaged wires; clean and repair as required.

11. Make sure all connectors disconnected during this procedure are free of corrosion and reconnected properly.

Starter Turns Slowly

If the starter turns slowly and all engine components and systems are normal, perform the following:

1. Test the battery as described in Chapter Three.

2. Check for the following:

    a. Loose or corroded battery terminals.

    b. Loose or corroded battery ground cable.

    c. Loose starter cable.

3. Remove, disassemble and bench test the starter as described in *Starter* in Chapter Nine.

4. Check the starter for binding during operation. Disassemble the starter and check the armature shaft for bending or damage. Also, check the starter clutch as described in Chapter Five.

Starter Turns but the Engine Does Not

If the starter turns but the engine does not, perform the following:

1. Check for a damaged starter clutch (Chapter Five).

2. Check for damaged starter reduction gears (Chapter Five).

CHARGING SYSTEM

The charging system consists of the battery, alternator and a voltage regulator/rectifier. A 30-amp main fuse protects the circuit.

A malfunction in the charging system generally causes the battery to remain undercharged.

Battery Discharging

1. Check all of the connections. Make sure they are tight and free of corrosion.

2. Perform the *Charging System Current Draw Test* as described in Chapter Nine. Note the following:

    a. On FE and TE models, if the current draw exceeds 1.0 mA, perform Step 3. If the current draw is 1.0 mA or less, perform Step 4.

    b. On FM and TM models (no digital combination meter), if the current draw exceeds 0.1 mA, perform Step 3. If the current draw is 0.1 mA or less, perform Step 4.

    c. On FM and TM models (with digital combination meter), if the current draw exceeds 1.0

mA, perform Step 3. If the current draw is 1.0 mA or less, perform Step 4.

3. Disconnect the black regulator/rectifier connector, then repeat the *Charging System Current Draw Test*. Note the following:

a. If the test results are incorrect, the ignition switch may be faulty or the wiring harness is shorted; test the ignition switch as described in Chapter Nine.

b. If the test readings are correct, replace the regulator/rectifier unit and retest.

4. Perform the *Charging Voltage Test* in Chapter Nine. Note the following:

a. If the test readings are correct, perform Step 5.

b. If the test readings are incorrect, go to Step 6.

5. Test the battery with a battery tester and note the following:

NOTE
If a battery tester is not accessible, remove the battery and take it to a dealership for testing.

a. If the test readings are correct, check for an open circuit in the wiring harness and for dirty or loose-fitting terminals; clean and repair as required.

b. If the test readings are incorrect, the battery is faulty or electrical components are overloading the charging system.

6. Test the battery charging lead and ground wire as described in *Regulator/Rectifier Wiring Harness Test* in Chapter Nine. Note the following:

a. If the test readings are correct, perform Step 7.

b. If the test readings are incorrect, check for an open circuit in the wiring harness and for dirty or loose fitting terminals; clean and repair as required.

7. Test the charging coil wires at the regulator/rectifier connector as described in *Regulator/Rectifier Wiring Harness Test* in Chapter Nine. Note the following:

a. If the test readings are incorrect, replace the alternator and retest.

b. If the test readings are correct, replace the regulator/rectifier unit and retest.

Battery Overcharging

If the battery is overcharging, the regulator/rectifier unit is faulty. Replace the regulator/rectifier unit as described in Chapter Nine.

IGNITION SYSTEM

All models are equipped with a capacitor discharge ignition (CDI) system. This solid-state system uses no contact breaker point or other moving parts.

Because of the solid-state design, problems with the capacitor discharge system are rare. If a problem occurs, it generally causes a weak spark or no spark at all. An ignition system with a weak spark or no spark is relatively easy to troubleshoot. It is difficult, however, to troubleshoot an ignition system that only malfunctions when the engine is hot or under load.

Peak Voltage Testing

Honda recommends peak voltage testing (see Chapter Nine) using the Honda peak voltage adapter (part No. 07HGJ-0020100) and a digital multimeter with an impedance of 10M ohms/DVC minimum to troubleshoot the ignition system. Resistance specifications are not available. The following troubleshooting section isolates the different ignition system components and wiring using conventional equipment. If further testing is required and the special tools are not available, refer testing to a Honda dealership.

Troubleshooting

NOTE
If the problem is intermittent, perform the tests with the engine cold, then hot. Then compare the test results.

1. Perform the following ignition spark gap test as follows:

NOTE
*If an adjustable spark tester is not available, perform the spark test as described in **Spark Test** in this chapter.*

a. Disconnect the plug wire.

> *NOTE*
> *A spark tester is a useful tool to check the ignition system.* ***Figure 9*** *shows the Motion Pro Ignition System Tester. This tool is inserted in the spark plug cap and its base is grounded against the cylinder head. The tool's air gap is adjustable, which allows the spark to be seen and heard while the intensity of the spark is tested.*

b. Adjust the spark tester so the air gap distance is 6 mm (0.24 in.).

c. Insert the spark tester into the plug cap and touch its base against the cylinder head to ground it (**Figure 9**). Position the tester so the terminals are visible.

> *CAUTION*
> *If the spark plug was removed from the engine, position the spark tester away from the plug hole in the cylinder head so the spark from the tester cannot ignite the gasoline vapors in the cylinder.*

d. Turn the engine over with the starter button or operate the recoil starter. A fat blue spark should jump between the spark tester terminals.

> *WARNING*
> *Do not hold the spark tester or connector or a serious electrical shock may result.*

e. If the spark jumps the gap and is dark blue in color, the ignition system is good. If the spark does not jump the gap, hold the spark plug cable and twist the plug cap a few times to tighten it. Then recheck the spark gap. If there is still no spark or if it jumps the gap but is yellow or white, continue with Step 2.

f. Remove the spark tester from the spark plug cap.

2. Unscrew the spark plug cap (**Figure 8**) from the ignition coil plug wire and hold the end of the wire 6 mm (0.24 in.) from the cylinder head and away from the spark plug hole as shown in **Figure 10**. Have an assistant turn over the engine. A fat blue spark should pass from the end of the wire to the cylinder head. If there is no spark, perform Step 3.

3. Test the ignition coil as described in Chapter Nine. Note the following:

a. If the ignition coil is good, perform Step 4.

b. If the ignition coil fails to pass the tests described in Chapter Nine, the ignition coil is probably faulty. However, before replacing the ignition coil, take it to a dealership and have them test the spark with an ignition coil tester. Replace the ignition coil if it is faulty and retest the ignition system.

4. Test the engine stop switch as described in *Switches* in Chapter Nine. Note the following:

a. If the switch is good, perform Step 5.

b. If the switch fails to pass the test as described in Chapter Nine, the switch is faulty and must be replaced. Replace the switch and retest the ignition system.

5. Test the ignition switch as described in *Switches* in Chapter Nine. Note the following:

a. If the switch is good, perform Step 6.

b. If the switch fails to pass the test as described in Chapter Nine, the switch is faulty and must be replaced. Replace the switch and retest the ignition system.

6. Perform the pulse generator *Peak Voltage Test* as described in Chapter Nine. Note the following:

a. If the test reading is correct, perform Step 7.

b. If the test reading is incorrect, replace the pulse generator as described in Chapter Nine.

7. If a damaged component was not identified, check the ignition system wiring harness and connectors. Check for damaged wires or loose, dirty or damaged connectors. If the wiring and connectors are good, proceed to Step 8 for early FE and TE models equipped with a sub-ICM (**Figure 14**). Proceed to Step 9 for all other models.

8. On early FE and TE models equipped with a sub-ICM (**Figure 14**), disconnect both connectors from the sub-ICM. Connect the eight-terminal gray connector directly to the ICM (**Figure 15**) and perform Step 1. Note the following:

a. If a spark occurs at the spark tester, the sub-ICM is faulty.

b. If no spark occurs, reattach the connectors to the sub-ICM and proceed to Step 9.

9. If the preceeding steps do not identify a faulty component, the ICM unit (**Figure 15**) is faulty and must be replaced.

> *NOTE*
> *The ICM unit cannot be tested effectively using conventional equipment. Because ignition system problems are most often caused by an open or short circuit or poor wiring connections, replace the ICM only after determining that all other ignition system components are functioning properly. The ICM is expensive, and generally cannot be returned once purchased. Therefore, repeat the preceding tests to verify the condition of the ignition system before replacing the ICM.*

10. Install all parts previously removed. Make sure all of the connections are free of corrosion and are reconnected properly.

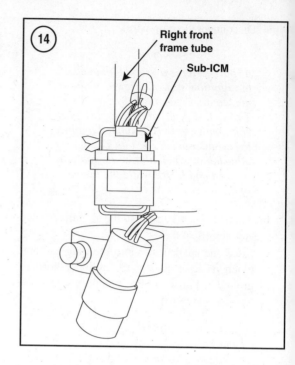

LIGHTING SYSTEM

Faulty Bulbs

If the headlight or taillight bulb(s) continually burn out, check for one or more of the following conditions:

1. Incorrect bulb type. (See Chapter Nine for the correct replacement bulb types.)
2. Damaged battery.
3. Damaged rectifier/regulator.
4. Damaged ignition switch and/or light switch.

Headlight Operates Darker than Normal

Check for one or more of the following conditions:

1. Incorrect bulb type. (See Chapter Nine for the correct replacement bulbs.)
2. Charging system problem.
3. Too many electric accessories added to the wiring harness. If one or more aftermarket electrical accessories have been connected to the wiring system, disconnect them one at a time and then start the engine and check the headlight operation. If this is the cause of the problem, contact the aftermarket manufacturer for more information.
4. Incorrect ground connection.
5. Poor main and/or light switch electrical contacts.

Headlight Inoperative

If the headlights do not come on, perform the following test.

1. Remove the headlight bulb (Chapter Nine).
   a. The headlight bulb has three terminals. Connect an ohmmeter between any two terminals. The reading should be zero ohms. Repeat the test between the remaining terminal and another terminal. The reading should be zero ohms. Replace the bulb if the ohmmeter indicates an open circuit between any two terminals.
   b. Connect an ohmmeter to one of the headlight socket terminals and to its mating electrical connector, then check for continuity. Repeat for the other wires and their terminals. Each reading should indicate continuity. If any reading does not meet specifications, replace the headlight socket if it cannot be repaired.
   c. If both sets of readings were correct, proceed to Step 2.
2. Check all of the light system connectors and wires for loose or damaged connections.
3. Check the main fuse as described in Chapter Nine.
4. Make sure the battery is fully charged. Refer to *Battery* in Chapter Three.
5. Switch a voltmeter to the 20 volt (DC) scale. In Step 6 and Step 7, connect the voltmeter leads to the wiring harness electrical connectors.

6. Connect the voltmeter positive lead to the headlight connector white lead and the voltmeter negative lead to the headlight connector green lead. Turn the ignition switch *on* and the dimmer switch to *low*. Note the voltmeter reading.

    a. If the voltmeter reads battery voltage, continue with Step 7.

    b. If the voltmeter does not read battery voltage; check the wiring harness from the ignition switch to the headlight socket for damage.

7. Turn the ignition switch *off.* Connect the voltmeter positive lead to the headlight connector blue/black lead and the voltmeter negative lead to the headlight connector green lead. Turn the ignition switch *on* and the dimmer switch to *high*. Note the voltmeter reading.

    a. If the voltmeter reads battery voltage, continue with Step 8.

    b. If the voltmeter does not read battery voltage, check the wiring harness from the ignition switch to the headlight socket for damage.

8. Turn the ignition switch *off* and disconnect the voltmeter leads.

Taillight Inoperative

If the taillight does not light, perform the following test.

1. Remove the taillight bulb (Chapter Nine) and disconnect the taillight socket connectors (**Figure 16**) from the wiring harness.

    a. Connect an ohmmeter to the bulb terminals. The reading should be zero ohms. Replace the bulb if the ohmmeter reads infinity.

    b. Connect an ohmmeter to a taillight socket terminal and to its mating electrical connector to check continuity. Repeat for the other wire. Each reading should be zero ohms. If any reading indicates an open circuit, replace the taillight socket if it cannot be repaired.

2. Check all of the light system connectors and wires for loose or damaged connections.

3. Check the main fuse as described in Chapter Nine.

4. Make sure the battery is fully charged. Refer to *Battery* in Chapter Three.

5. Switch a voltmeter to the 20-volt scale. In Step 3, connect the voltmeter leads to the taillight socket electrical connectors of the main wiring harness (**Figure 16**).

6. Connect the voltmeter positive lead to the taillight connector brown lead and the voltmeter negative lead to the taillight connector green lead. Turn the light switch to *on* and note the voltmeter reading.

    a. If the voltmeter reads battery voltage, continue with Step 7.

    b. If the voltmeter does not read battery voltage, check the wiring harness for damage.

7. Turn the light switch *off* and disconnect the voltmeter leads. If the voltmeter reads battery voltage in Step 4, the taillight wiring circuit is good.

COOLING SYSTEM

Air passing through the cylinder fins as well as air passing through the oil cooler cools the engine. At a preset temperature determined by the oil thermosensor, the cooling fan operates and draws air through the oil cooler. The oil thermosensor also triggers the oil temperature warning light.

Aside from possible leaks and damage to the oil cooler and oil lines, the oil cooler system is relatively troublefree. Refer to **Figure 17** for a troubleshooting chart that addresses the electrical components of the cooling system.

(17)

COOLING SYSTEM TROUBLESHOOTING CHART

NOTE:
Most dealerships will not accept returned electrical components. If necessary, have the dealership test the suspected component before ordering a replacement.

NOTE:
Refer to Chapter Nine and wiring diagram for location of components and connectors.

NOTE:
Be sure the neutral/reverse indicator operates properly before using the following chart.

FAN MOTOR INOPERABLE; OIL TEMPERATURE INDICATOR LIGHTS

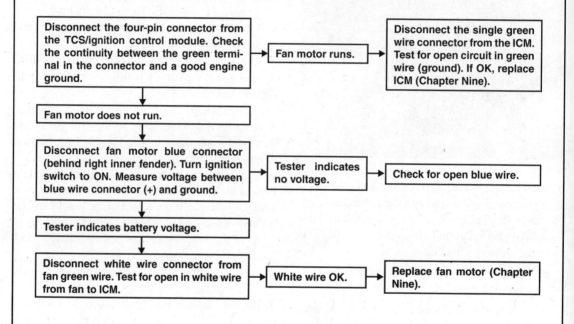

| Disconnect the four-pin connector from the TCS/ignition control module. Check the continuity between the green terminal in the connector and a good engine ground. | → Fan motor runs. → | Disconnect the single green wire connector from the ICM. Test for open circuit in green wire (ground). If OK, replace ICM (Chapter Nine). |

Fan motor does not run.

| Disconnect fan motor blue connector (behind right inner fender). Turn ignition switch to ON. Measure voltage between blue wire connector (+) and ground. | → Tester indicates no voltage. → | Check for open blue wire. |

Tester indicates battery voltage.

| Disconnect white wire connector from fan green wire. Test for open in white wire from fan to ICM. | → White wire OK. → | Replace fan motor (Chapter Nine). |

FAN MOTOR RUNS CONTINUOUSLY

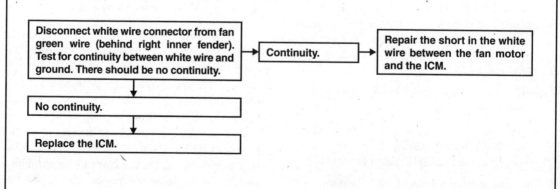

| Disconnect white wire connector from fan green wire (behind right inner fender). Test for continuity between white wire and ground. There should be no continuity. | → Continuity. → | Repair the short in the white wire between the fan motor and the ICM. |

No continuity.

Replace the ICM.

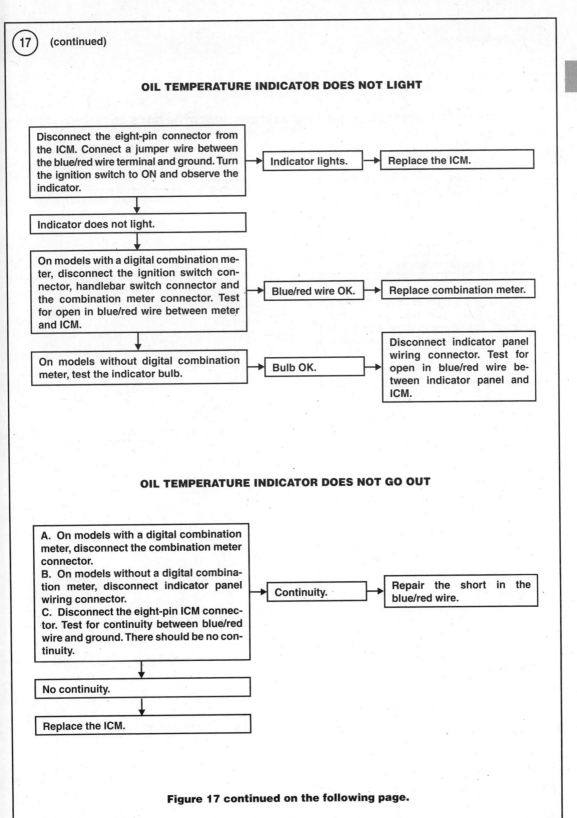

(17) (continued)

OIL TEMPERATURE INDICATOR DOES NOT LIGHT

Disconnect the eight-pin connector from the ICM. Connect a jumper wire between the blue/red wire terminal and ground. Turn the ignition switch to ON and observe the indicator. → Indicator lights. → Replace the ICM.

Indicator does not light.

On models with a digital combination meter, disconnect the ignition switch connector, handlebar switch connector and the combination meter connector. Test for open in blue/red wire between meter and ICM. → Blue/red wire OK. → Replace combination meter.

On models without digital combination meter, test the indicator bulb. → Bulb OK. → Disconnect indicator panel wiring connector. Test for open in blue/red wire between indicator panel and ICM.

OIL TEMPERATURE INDICATOR DOES NOT GO OUT

A. On models with a digital combination meter, disconnect the combination meter connector.
B. On models without a digital combination meter, disconnect indicator panel wiring connector.
C. Disconnect the eight-pin ICM connector. Test for continuity between blue/red wire and ground. There should be no continuity. → Continuity. → Repair the short in the blue/red wire.

No continuity.

Replace the ICM.

Figure 17 continued on the following page.

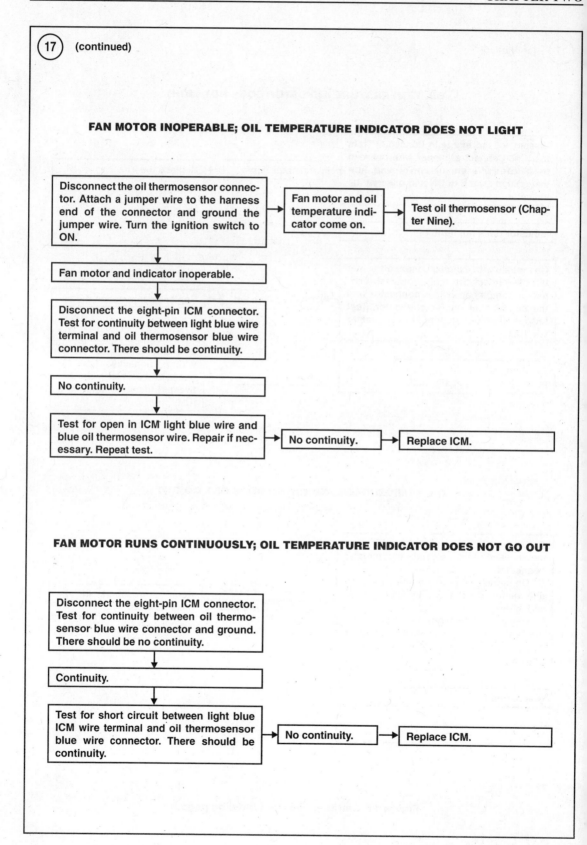

(17) (continued)

FAN MOTOR INOPERABLE; OIL TEMPERATURE INDICATOR DOES NOT LIGHT

Disconnect the oil thermosensor connector. Attach a jumper wire to the harness end of the connector and ground the jumper wire. Turn the ignition switch to ON.

→ Fan motor and oil temperature indicator come on. → Test oil thermosensor (Chapter Nine).

Fan motor and indicator inoperable.

Disconnect the eight-pin ICM connector. Test for continuity between light blue wire terminal and oil thermosensor blue wire connector. There should be continuity.

No continuity.

Test for open in ICM light blue wire and blue oil thermosensor wire. Repair if necessary. Repeat test. → No continuity. → Replace ICM.

FAN MOTOR RUNS CONTINUOUSLY; OIL TEMPERATURE INDICATOR DOES NOT GO OUT

Disconnect the eight-pin ICM connector. Test for continuity between oil thermosensor blue wire connector and ground. There should be no continuity.

Continuity.

Test for short circuit between light blue ICM wire terminal and oil thermosensor blue wire connector. There should be continuity. → No continuity. → Replace ICM.

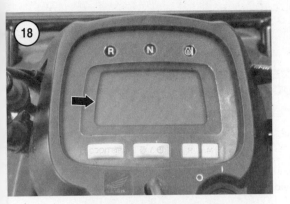

COMBINATION METER

All FE and TE models are equipped with a combination meter (**Figure 18**). FM and TM models may be equipped with a combination meter as an option. The combination meter is standard equipment on Canadian FM and TM models.

The combination meter includes a multifunction digital display that provides a speedometer, odometer, tripmeter, hourmeter and clock. A central processing unit (CPU) computer chip is contained within the combination meter.

A speed sensor (**Figure 19**) mounted on the engine provides driveshaft speed to the CPU in the combination meter.

Use the troubleshooting procedure in **Figure 20** to isolate a combination meter malfunction. Also refer to the wiring diagrams at the end of this manual for the specific model and year.

FUEL SYSTEM

Many riders automatically assume that the carburetor is at fault if the engine does not run properly.

While fuel system problems are not uncommon, carburetor adjustment is seldom the answer. In many cases, adjusting the carburetor only compounds the problem by making the engine run worse.

When troubleshooting the fuel system, start at the fuel tank and work through the system, reserving the carburetor as the final point. Most fuel system problems result from an empty fuel tank, a plugged fuel filter or fuel valve, or sour fuel. Fuel system troubleshooting is covered in *Engine Is Difficult To Start, Poor Idle Speed Performance,* and *Poor Medium and High Speed Performance* sections in this chapter.

The carburetor choke can also present problems. Check choke operation by moving the choke knob (**Figure 3**) by hand. The choke should move freely without binding or sticking in one position. If necessary, remove the choke as described in *Carburetor Disassembly* in Chapter Eight and inspect the plunger and spring for excessive wear or damage.

ENGINE OVERHEATING

Engine overheating is a serious problem because it can quickly cause engine seizure and damage. The following section groups five main systems with probable causes that can lead to engine overheating.

1. Ignition system:
   a. Incorrect spark plug gap.
   b. Incorrect spark plug heat range. (See Chapter Three.)
   c. Faulty ICM unit/incorrect ignition timing.
2. Engine compression system:
   a. Cylinder head gasket leak.
   b. Heavy carbon buildup in the combustion chamber.
3. Fuel system:
   a. Carburetor fuel level too low.
   b. Incorrect carburetor adjustment or jetting.
   c. Loose carburetor boot clamps.
   d. Leaking or damaged carburetor-to-air filter housing air boot.
   e. Incorrect air/fuel mixture.
4. Engine load:
   a. Dragging brake(s).
   b. Damaged drivetrain components.
   c. Slipping clutch.

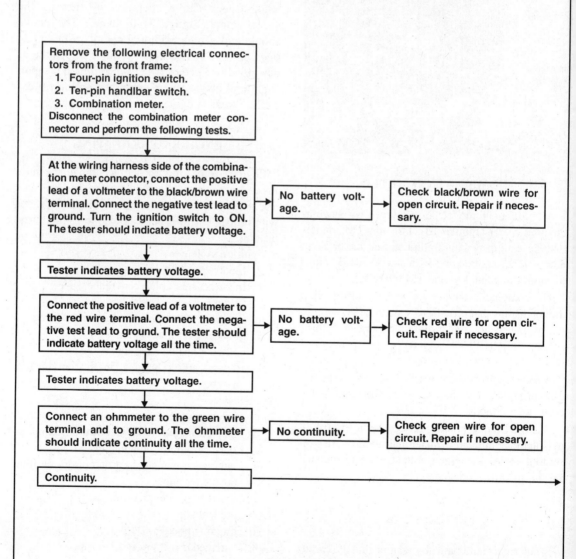

(20)

COMBINATION METER/SPEED SENSOR
TROUBLESHOOTING CHART

NOTE:
Most dealerships will not accept returned electrical components. If necessary, have the dealership test the suspected component before ordering a replacement.

NOTE:
Refer to Chapter Nine and wiring diagram for location of components and connectors.

Remove the following electrical connectors from the front frame:
1. Four-pin ignition switch.
2. Ten-pin handlbar switch.
3. Combination meter.
Disconnect the combination meter connector and perform the following tests.

↓

At the wiring harness side of the combination meter connector, connect the positive lead of a voltmeter to the black/brown wire terminal. Connect the negative test lead to ground. Turn the ignition switch to ON. The tester should indicate battery voltage. → No battery voltage. → Check black/brown wire for open circuit. Repair if necessary.

↓

Tester indicates battery voltage.

↓

Connect the positive lead of a voltmeter to the red wire terminal. Connect the negative test lead to ground. The tester should indicate battery voltage all the time. → No battery voltage. → Check red wire for open circuit. Repair if necessary.

↓

Tester indicates battery voltage.

↓

Connect an ohmmeter to the green wire terminal and to ground. The ohmmeter should indicate continuity all the time. → No continuity. → Check green wire for open circuit. Repair if necessary.

↓

Continuity. →

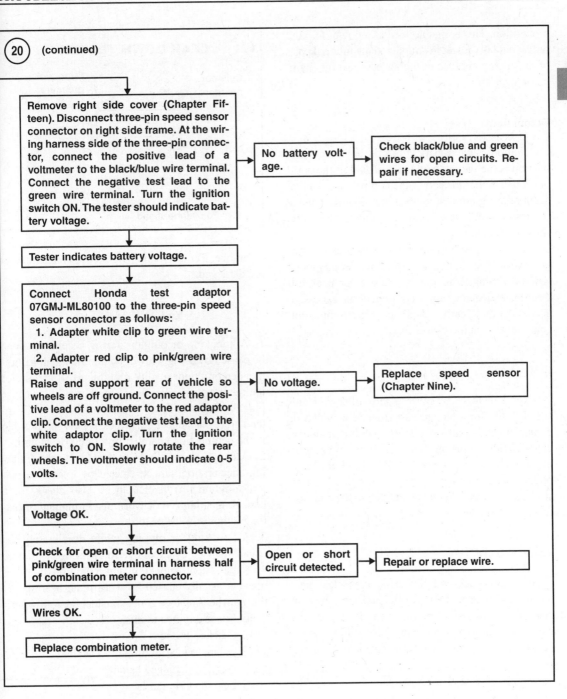

(20) (continued)

Remove right side cover (Chapter Fifteen). Disconnect three-pin speed sensor connector on right side frame. At the wiring harness side of the three-pin connector, connect the positive lead of a voltmeter to the black/blue wire terminal. Connect the negative test lead to the green wire terminal. Turn the ignition switch ON. The tester should indicate battery voltage.

→ No battery voltage. → Check black/blue and green wires for open circuits. Repair if necessary.

Tester indicates battery voltage.

Connect Honda test adaptor 07GMJ-ML80100 to the three-pin speed sensor connector as follows:
1. Adapter white clip to green wire terminal.
2. Adapter red clip to pink/green wire terminal.
Raise and support rear of vehicle so wheels are off ground. Connect the positive lead of a voltmeter to the red adaptor clip. Connect the negative test lead to the white adaptor clip. Turn the ignition switch to ON. Slowly rotate the rear wheels. The voltmeter should indicate 0-5 volts.

→ No voltage. → Replace speed sensor (Chapter Nine).

Voltage OK.

Check for open or short circuit between pink/green wire terminal in harness half of combination meter connector.

→ Open or short circuit detected. → Repair or replace wire.

Wires OK.

Replace combination meter.

d. Engine oil level too high.

5. Electric cooling system:

  a. Damaged cooling fan.

  b. Plugged or damaged oil cooler.

  c. Restricted oil cooler. Check for any cargo or foreign matter which could be restricting the air flow to the oil cooler assembly.

ENGINE

Preignition

Preignition is the premature burning of fuel and is caused by hot spots in the combustion chamber. The fuel ignites before spark ignition occurs. Glowing deposits in the combustion chamber, inadequate cooling or an overheated spark plug can all cause preignition. This is first noticed as a power loss but will eventually result in damage to the internal parts of the engine because of higher combustion chamber temperature.

Detonation

Commonly called spark knock or fuel knock, detonation is the violent explosion of fuel in the combustion chamber instead of the controlled burn that occurs during normal combustion. Severe damage can result. Use of low octane gasoline is a common cause of detonation.

Even when using a high octane gasoline, detonation can still occur. Other causes are over-advanced ignition timing, lean fuel mixture at or near full throttle, inadequate engine cooling, or the excessive accumulation of carbon deposits in the combustion chamber and on the piston crown.

Power Loss

Several factors can cause a lack of power and speed. Look for a clogged air filter or a fouled or damaged spark plug. A piston or cylinder that is galled, incorrect piston clearance, or worn or sticking piston rings may be responsible. Look for loose bolts, defective gaskets or leaking machined mating surfaces on the cylinder head, cylinder or crankcase.

Piston Seizure

This may be caused by incorrect bore clearance, piston rings with an improper end gap, compression leak, incorrect air/fuel mixture, spark plug of the wrong heat range or incorrect ignition timing. Overheating from any cause may result in piston seizure.

Piston Slap

Piston slap is an audible slapping or rattling noise resulting from excessive piston-to-cylinder clearance. If allowed to continue, piston slap will eventually cause the piston skirt to crack and shatter.

To prevent piston slap, clean the air filter element on a regular schedule. If piston slap is heard, disassemble the engine top end, measure the cylinder bore and piston diameter, and check for excessive

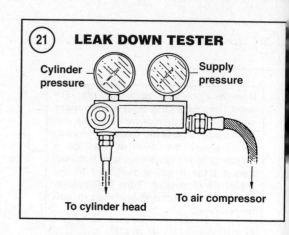

21 **LEAK DOWN TESTER**

Cylinder pressure — Supply pressure

To cylinder head — To air compressor

clearance. Replace parts that exceed wear limits or are damaged.

ENGINE NOISES

1. A knocking or pinging during acceleration can be caused by using a lower octane fuel than recommended or a poor quality fuel. Incorrect carburetor jetting or a spark plug that is too hot can also cause pinging. Refer to *Spark Plug Heat Range* in Chapter Three. Also check for excessive carbon buildup in the combustion chamber or a faulty ICM unit.
2. A slapping or rattling noises at low speed or during acceleration can be caused by excessive piston-to-cylinder wall clearance. Also check for a bent connecting rod or worn piston pin and/or piston pin holes in the piston.
3. A knocking or rapping while decelerating is usually caused by excessive rod bearing clearance.
4. A persistent knocking and vibration or other noise is usually caused by worn main bearings. If the main bearings are good, consider the following:
   a. Loose engine mounts.
   b. Cracked frame.
   c. Balancer gear improperly installed.
   d. Worn or damaged balancer gear bearings.
   e. Leaking cylinder head gasket.
   f. Exhaust pipe leak at cylinder head.
   g. Stuck piston ring.
   h. Broken piston ring.
   i. Partial engine seizure.
   j. Excessive connecting rod small end bearing clearance.
   k. Excessive connecting rod big end side clearance.
   l. Excessive crankshaft runout.

m. Worn or damaged primary drive gear.

5. A rapid on-off squeal may indicate a compression leak around the cylinder head gasket or spark plug.

CYLINDER LEAK DOWN TEST

A cylinder leak down test can determine if an engine problem is caused by leaking valves, a blown head gasket, or broken, worn or stuck piston rings. Perform a cylinder leak down test by applying compressed air to the cylinder and then measuring the percent of leakage. A cylinder leak down tester and an air compressor are required to perform this test (**Figure 21**). Follow the tester manufacturer's directions along with the following information when performing a cylinder leak down test.

1. Start and run the engine until it reaches normal operating temperature. Then turn the engine off.
2. Remove the air filter assembly as described in Chapter Three. Open and secure the throttle in the wide-open position.
3. Remove the spark plug.
4. Position the piston at TDC on the compression stroke. See *Valve Clearance Check and Adjustment* in Chapter Three.

NOTE
The engine may turn when air pressure is applied to the cylinder. To prevent this from happening, shift the transmission into fifth gear and set the parking brake.

5. Connect the cylinder leak down tester into the spark plug hole (**Figure 22**).
6. Make a cylinder leak down test following the tester manufacturer's instructions. Listen for air leaking while noting the following:
    a. Air leaking through the exhaust pipe indicates a leaking exhaust valve.
    b. Air leaking through the carburetor indicates a leaking intake valve.
    c. Air leaking through the crankcase breather tube indicates worn piston rings.
7. A cylinder with 10% or more cylinder leakage requires further service.
8. Remove the tester and reinstall the spark plug.

CLUTCH

All clutch service, except adjustment, requires partial engine disassembly to identify and fix the problem. Refer to Chapter Six.

The TRX350 uses two clutch assemblies: centrifugal (A, **Figure 23**) and change (B).

Clutch Slipping

1. Clutch wear or damage:
    a. Incorrect clutch adjustment.
    b. Worn clutch shoe (centrifugal clutch).
    c. Loose, weak or damaged clutch spring (change and centrifugal clutch).
    d. Worn friction plates (change clutch).
    e. Warped steel plates (change clutch).
    f. Worn clutch center and/or clutch outer (change clutch).
    g. Incorrectly assembled clutch.
2. Engine oil:
    a. Low oil level.
    b. Oil additives.
    c. Low viscosity oil.

Clutch Dragging

1. Clutch wear or damage:

a. Incorrect clutch adjustment.
b. Damaged or incorrectly assembled clutch lever assembly.
c. Warped steel plates.
d. Swollen friction plates.
e. Warped pressure plate.
f. Incorrect clutch spring tension.
g. Incorrectly assembled clutch.
h. Loose clutch nut.
i. Incorrect clutch mechanism adjustment (change clutch).
2. Engine oil:
a. Oil level too high.
b. High viscosity oil.

Rough Clutch Operation

1. Damaged clutch outer slots (change clutch).
2. Damaged clutch center splines (change clutch).
3. Incorrect engine idle speed.

Transmission is Hard to Shift

1. Clutch wear or damage:
a. Incorrect clutch adjustment.
b. Damaged clutch lifter mechanism.
2. Damaged shift drum shifter plate.

TRANSMISSION

Transmission symptoms can be difficult to distinguish from clutch symptoms. Make sure the clutch is not causing the problem before working on the transmission.

Transmission gears on FM and TM models are manually shifted using a conventional foot lever. On FE and TE models, the transmission gears are shifted using an electric motor that rotates the shift shaft through a set of reduction gears. (Refer to Chapter Nine).

Faulty Electric Shifting (2000-2002 FE and TE Models)

Before following a troubleshooting procedure, determine if the shifting problem is due to the electric shifting system or internal shift components. Install the emergency manual shift lever (**Figure 24**). With the ignition switch *off*, attempt to shift the gears.

CAUTION
Only use the manual shift lever for emergency or troubleshooting purposes. Continued use may cause internal damage to the master shift arm. Do not operate the manual shift lever while operating the ATV. The lever must be hand-operated and never operated using a foot.

NOTE
It may be necessary to move the ATV backward or forward to engage gears while using the manual shift lever.

NOTE
If the electric shift will not operate after the manual shift lever was used, turn the ignition switch off and on to recycle the ECU.

If the gears shift, follow the electric shift troubleshooting procedure. If the gears cannot be shifted using the manual lever, refer to the possible causes in the following sections.

The electric control unit (ECU) controls the shift mechanism. Refer to Chapter Nine. The ECU can detect faults and will enter a *failure mode* if a problem exists. In the failure mode, the electric system is disabled and will not function. The ECU on 2000-2002 models does not display a trouble code or provide a means to identify a problem. The ECU leaves the failure mode and resets automatically when the ignition switch is turned off, but will return to the failure mode if the problem persists when the ignition switch is turned back on.

Refer to the chart in **Figure 25** when troubleshooting electric shifting related transmission problems. Note the following:

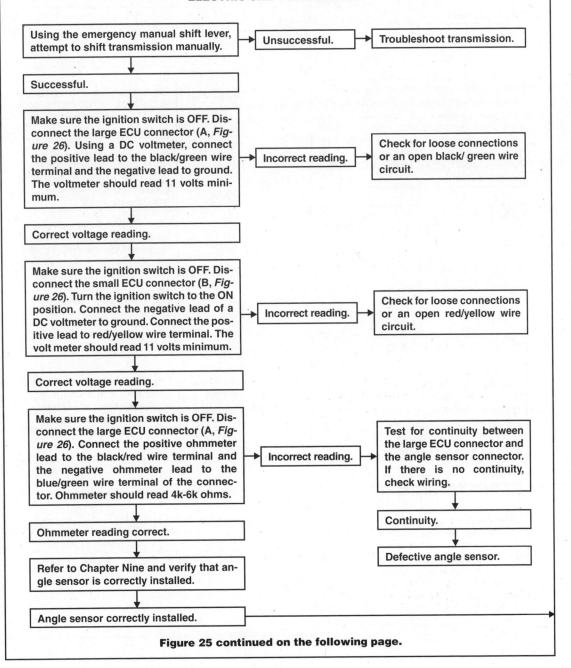

(25)

ELECTRIC SHIFT TROUBLESHOOTING CHART (2000-2002)

*Before replacing the ECU, take the vehicle to a Honda dealership or other qualified repair shop for further testing. Most parts suppliers will not accept the return of electrical components. Confirm that the ECU is faulty before purchasing a replacement.

2

ELECTRIC SHIFT INOPERABLE

Using the emergency manual shift lever, attempt to shift transmission manually. → Unsuccessful. → Troubleshoot transmission.

Successful.

Make sure the ignition switch is OFF. Disconnect the large ECU connector (A, *Figure 26*). Using a DC voltmeter, connect the positive lead to the black/green wire terminal and the negative lead to ground. The voltmeter should read 11 volts minimum. → Incorrect reading. → Check for loose connections or an open black/ green wire circuit.

Correct voltage reading.

Make sure the ignition switch is OFF. Disconnect the small ECU connector (B, *Figure 26*). Turn the ignition switch to the ON position. Connect the negative lead of a DC voltmeter to ground. Connect the positive lead to red/yellow wire terminal. The volt meter should read 11 volts minimum. → Incorrect reading. → Check for loose connections or an open red/yellow wire circuit.

Correct voltage reading.

Make sure the ignition switch is OFF. Disconnect the large ECU connector (A, *Figure 26*). Connect the positive ohmmeter lead to the black/red wire terminal and the negative ohmmeter lead to the blue/green wire terminal of the connector. Ohmmeter should read 4k-6k ohms. → Incorrect reading. → Test for continuity between the large ECU connector and the angle sensor connector. If there is no continuity, check wiring.

Ohmmeter reading correct.

Continuity.

Defective angle sensor.

Refer to Chapter Nine and verify that angle sensor is correctly installed.

Angle sensor correctly installed.

Figure 25 continued on the following page.

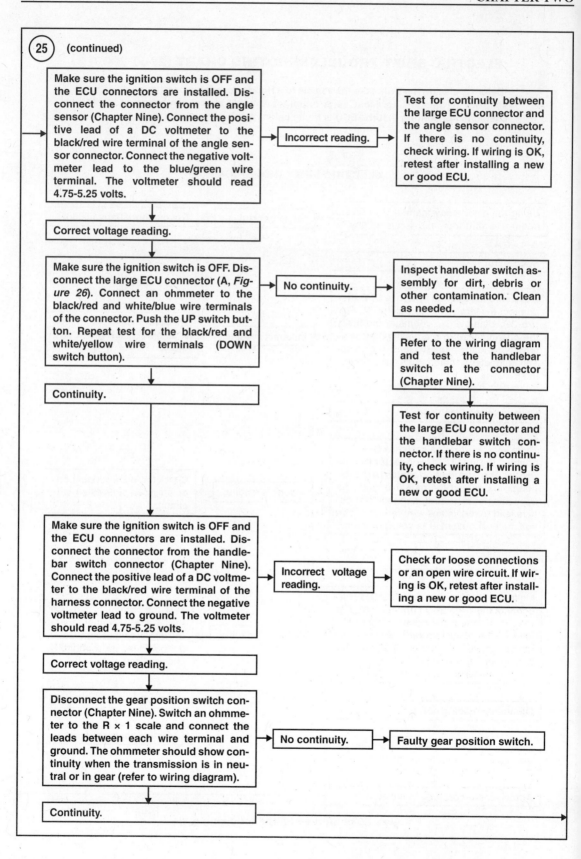

(25)   (continued)

Make sure the ignition switch is OFF and the ECU connectors are installed. Disconnect the connector from the angle sensor (Chapter Nine). Connect the positive lead of a DC voltmeter to the black/red wire terminal of the angle sensor connector. Connect the negative voltmeter lead to the blue/green wire terminal. The voltmeter should read 4.75-5.25 volts.

→ Incorrect reading. →

Test for continuity between the large ECU connector and the angle sensor connector. If there is no continuity, check wiring. If wiring is OK, retest after installing a new or good ECU.

Correct voltage reading.

Make sure the ignition switch is OFF. Disconnect the large ECU connector (A, *Figure 26*). Connect an ohmmeter to the black/red and white/blue wire terminals of the connector. Push the UP switch button. Repeat test for the black/red and white/yellow wire terminals (DOWN switch button).

→ No continuity. →

Inspect handlebar switch assembly for dirt, debris or other contamination. Clean as needed.

Refer to the wiring diagram and test the handlebar switch at the connector (Chapter Nine).

Continuity.

Test for continuity between the large ECU connector and the handlebar switch connector. If there is no continuity, check wiring. If wiring is OK, retest after installing a new or good ECU.

Make sure the ignition switch is OFF and the ECU connectors are installed. Disconnect the connector from the handlebar switch connector (Chapter Nine). Connect the positive lead of a DC voltmeter to the black/red wire terminal of the harness connector. Connect the negative voltmeter lead to ground. The voltmeter should read 4.75-5.25 volts.

→ Incorrect voltage reading. →

Check for loose connections or an open wire circuit. If wiring is OK, retest after installing a new or good ECU.

Correct voltage reading.

Disconnect the gear position switch connector (Chapter Nine). Switch an ohmmeter to the R × 1 scale and connect the leads between each wire terminal and ground. The ohmmeter should show continuity when the transmission is in neutral or in gear (refer to wiring diagram).

→ No continuity. →

Faulty gear position switch.

Continuity.

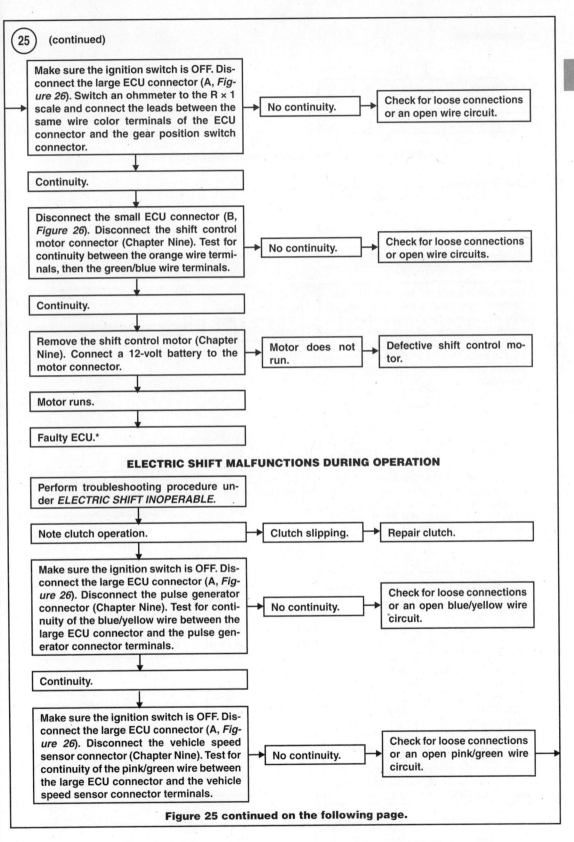

(25) (continued)

Make sure the ignition switch is OFF. Disconnect the large ECU connector (A, *Figure 26*). Switch an ohmmeter to the R × 1 scale and connect the leads between the same wire color terminals of the ECU connector and the gear position switch connector. → No continuity. → Check for loose connections or an open wire circuit.

Continuity.

Disconnect the small ECU connector (B, *Figure 26*). Disconnect the shift control motor connector (Chapter Nine). Test for continuity between the orange wire terminals, then the green/blue wire terminals. → No continuity. → Check for loose connections or open wire circuits.

Continuity.

Remove the shift control motor (Chapter Nine). Connect a 12-volt battery to the motor connector. → Motor does not run. → Defective shift control motor.

Motor runs.

Faulty ECU.*

ELECTRIC SHIFT MALFUNCTIONS DURING OPERATION

Perform troubleshooting procedure under *ELECTRIC SHIFT INOPERABLE.*

Note clutch operation. → Clutch slipping. → Repair clutch.

Make sure the ignition switch is OFF. Disconnect the large ECU connector (A, *Figure 26*). Disconnect the pulse generator connector (Chapter Nine). Test for continuity of the blue/yellow wire between the large ECU connector and the pulse generator connector terminals. → No continuity. → Check for loose connections or an open blue/yellow wire circuit.

Continuity.

Make sure the ignition switch is OFF. Disconnect the large ECU connector (A, *Figure 26*). Disconnect the vehicle speed sensor connector (Chapter Nine). Test for continuity of the pink/green wire between the large ECU connector and the vehicle speed sensor connector terminals. → No continuity. → Check for loose connections or an open pink/green wire circuit. →

Figure 25 continued on the following page.

2

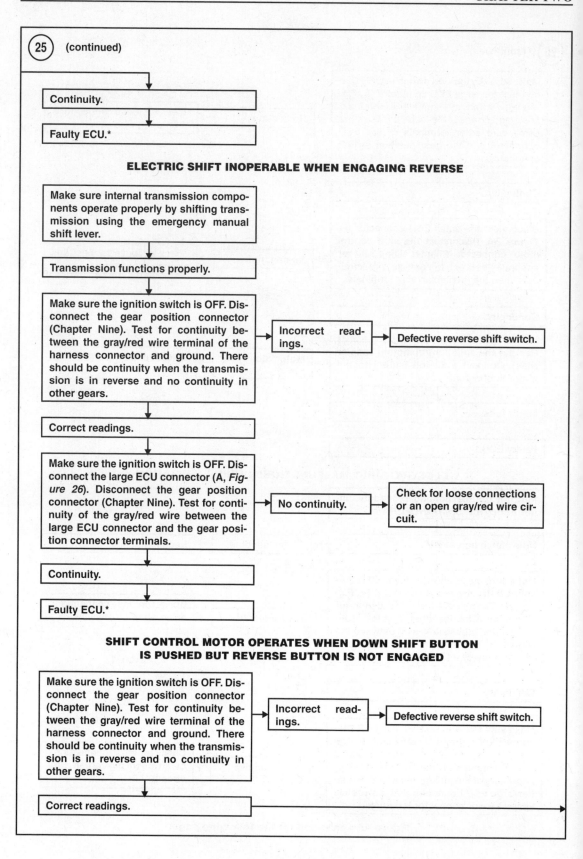

25 (continued)

Continuity.

Faulty ECU.*

ELECTRIC SHIFT INOPERABLE WHEN ENGAGING REVERSE

Make sure internal transmission components operate properly by shifting transmission using the emergency manual
shift lever.

Transmission functions properly.

Make sure the ignition switch is OFF. Disconnect the gear position connector
(Chapter Nine). Test for continuity between the gray/red wire terminal of the
harness connector and ground. There
should be continuity when the transmission is in reverse and no continuity in
other gears.
→ Incorrect read-
ings. → Defective reverse shift switch.

Correct readings.

Make sure the ignition switch is OFF. Disconnect the large ECU connector (A, *Figure 26*). Disconnect the gear position
connector (Chapter Nine). Test for continuity of the gray/red wire between the
large ECU connector and the gear position connector terminals.
→ No continuity. → Check for loose connections
or an open gray/red wire cir-
cuit.

Continuity.

Faulty ECU.*

SHIFT CONTROL MOTOR OPERATES WHEN DOWN SHIFT BUTTON
IS PUSHED BUT REVERSE BUTTON IS NOT ENGAGED

Make sure the ignition switch is OFF. Disconnect the gear position connector
(Chapter Nine). Test for continuity between the gray/red wire terminal of the
harness connector and ground. There
should be continuity when the transmission is in reverse and no continuity in
other gears.
→ Incorrect read-
ings. → Defective reverse shift switch.

Correct readings.

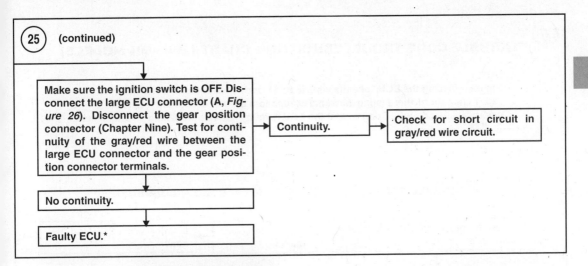

25 (continued)

Make sure the ignition switch is OFF. Disconnect the large ECU connector (A, *Figure 26*). Disconnect the gear position connector (Chapter Nine). Test for continuity of the gray/red wire between the large ECU connector and the gear position connector terminals. → Continuity. → Check for short circuit in gray/red wire circuit.

No continuity.

Faulty ECU.*

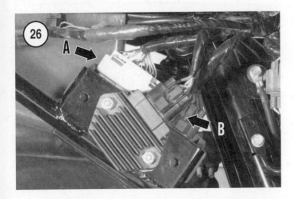

1. The ignition switch must be *off* unless directed otherwise.
2. The battery must be fully charged and in good condition.
3. The clutch must be properly adjusted.
4. The fuses must be good.

If the shifting problem is not caused by the electric shifting system, refer to the *Faulty Mechanical Shifting* section.

Faulty Electric Shifting (2003-On FE and TE Models)

Before following a troubleshooting procedure, determine if the shifting problem is due to the electric shifting system or internal shift components. Install the emergency manual shift lever (**Figure 24**). With the ignition switch *off*, attempt to shift the gears.

CAUTION
Only use the manual shift lever for emergency or troubleshooting pur-

poses. Continued use may cause internal damage to the master shift arm. Do not operate the manual shift lever while operating the ATV. The lever must be hand-operated and never operated using a foot.

NOTE
It may be necessary to move the ATV backward or forward to engage gears while using the manual shift lever.

NOTE
If the electric shift will not operate after the manual shift lever was used, turn the ignition switch off and on to recycle the ECU.

If the gears shift, follow the electric shift troubleshooting procedure. If the gears cannot be shifted using the manual lever, refer to the possible causes in the following sections.

The electric control unit (ECU) controls the shift mechanism. (Refer to Chapter Nine). The ECU can detect faults and will enter a *failure mode* if a problem exists. In the failure mode, the electric system is disabled and will not function. The ECU on 2003 models provides a trouble code if it detects a problem. The ECU leaves the failure mode and resets automatically when the ignition switch is turned off, but will return to the failure mode if the problem persists when the ignition switch is turned back *on*.

Refer to the chart in **Figure 27** when troubleshooting electric shifting related transmission problems. Note the following:

TROUBLE CODE TROUBLESHOOTING CHART (2003-ON MODELS)

NOTE:
Before replacing the ECU, take the vehicle to a Honda dealership or other qualified repair shop for further testing. Most parts suppliers will not accept the return of electrical components. Confirm that the ECU is faulty before purchasing a replacement.

TROUBLE CODE 1: ECU (WRITING AND RECORDING CIRCUIT)

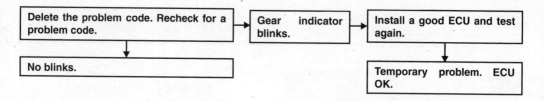

TROUBLE CODE 2: ELECTRIC SHIFT SWITCH SYSTEM (UP AND DOWN)

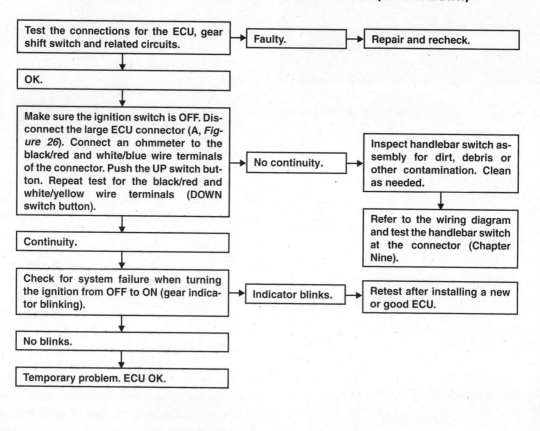

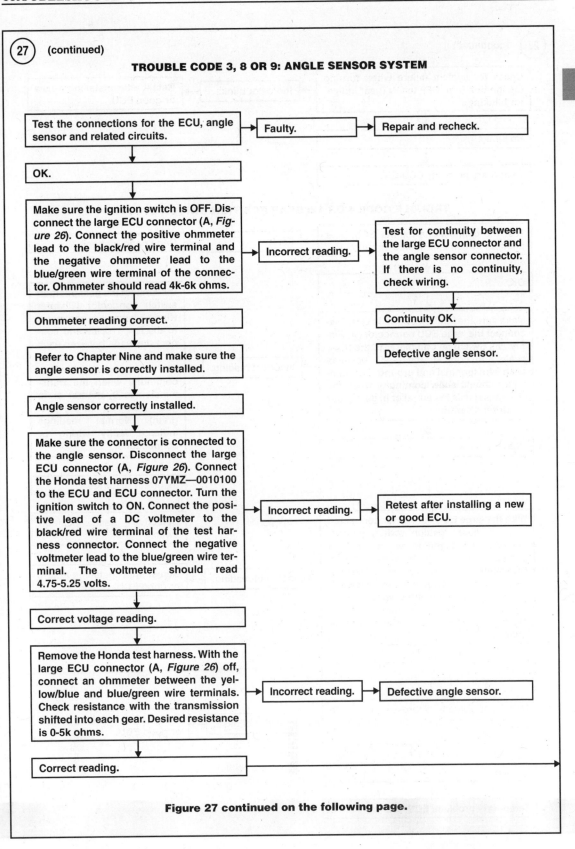

27 (continued)

TROUBLE CODE 3, 8 OR 9: ANGLE SENSOR SYSTEM

Test the connections for the ECU, angle sensor and related circuits. → Faulty. → Repair and recheck.

↓

OK.

↓

Make sure the ignition switch is OFF. Disconnect the large ECU connector (A, *Figure 26*). Connect the positive ohmmeter lead to the black/red wire terminal and the negative ohmmeter lead to the blue/green wire terminal of the connector. Ohmmeter should read 4k-6k ohms. → Incorrect reading. → Test for continuity between the large ECU connector and the angle sensor connector. If there is no continuity, check wiring.

↓

Ohmmeter reading correct.

Continuity OK.

↓

Refer to Chapter Nine and make sure the angle sensor is correctly installed.

Defective angle sensor.

↓

Angle sensor correctly installed.

↓

Make sure the connector is connected to the angle sensor. Disconnect the large ECU connector (A, *Figure 26*). Connect the Honda test harness 07YMZ—0010100 to the ECU and ECU connector. Turn the ignition switch to ON. Connect the positive lead of a DC voltmeter to the black/red wire terminal of the test harness connector. Connect the negative voltmeter lead to the blue/green wire terminal. The voltmeter should read 4.75-5.25 volts. → Incorrect reading. → Retest after installing a new or good ECU.

↓

Correct voltage reading.

↓

Remove the Honda test harness. With the large ECU connector (A, *Figure 26*) off, connect an ohmmeter between the yellow/blue and blue/green wire terminals. Check resistance with the transmission shifted into each gear. Desired resistance is 0-5k ohms. → Incorrect reading. → Defective angle sensor.

↓

Correct reading.

Figure 27 continued on the following page.

2

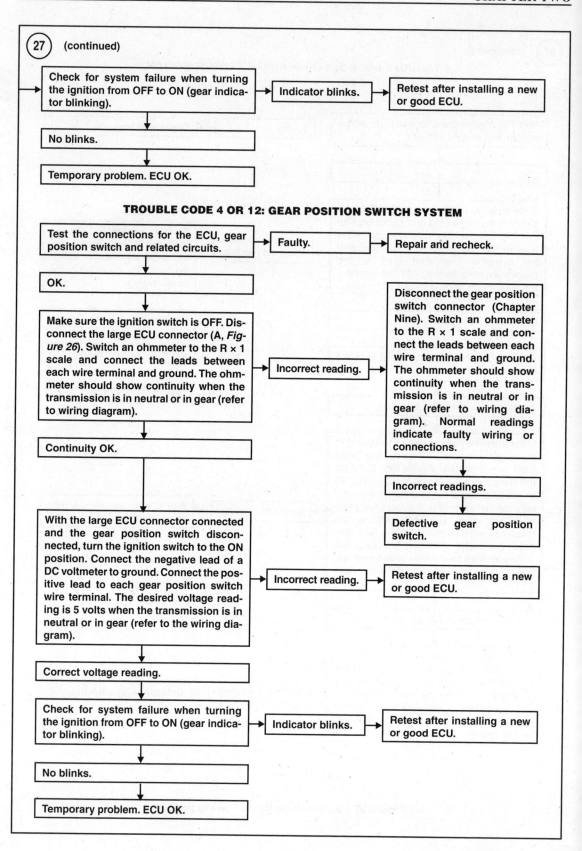

(27) (continued)

Check for system failure when turning the ignition from OFF to ON (gear indicator blinking). → Indicator blinks. → Retest after installing a new or good ECU.

No blinks.

Temporary problem. ECU OK.

TROUBLE CODE 4 OR 12: GEAR POSITION SWITCH SYSTEM

Test the connections for the ECU, gear position switch and related circuits. → Faulty. → Repair and recheck.

OK.

Make sure the ignition switch is OFF. Disconnect the large ECU connector (A, *Figure 26*). Switch an ohmmeter to the R × 1 scale and connect the leads between each wire terminal and ground. The ohmmeter should show continuity when the transmission is in neutral or in gear (refer to wiring diagram). → Incorrect reading. → Disconnect the gear position switch connector (Chapter Nine). Switch an ohmmeter to the R × 1 scale and connect the leads between each wire terminal and ground. The ohmmeter should show continuity when the transmission is in neutral or in gear (refer to wiring diagram). Normal readings indicate faulty wiring or connections.

Continuity OK.

Incorrect readings.

With the large ECU connector connected and the gear position switch disconnected, turn the ignition switch to the ON position. Connect the negative lead of a DC voltmeter to ground. Connect the positive lead to each gear position switch wire terminal. The desired voltage reading is 5 volts when the transmission is in neutral or in gear (refer to the wiring diagram). → Incorrect reading. → Retest after installing a new or good ECU.

Defective gear position switch.

Correct voltage reading.

Check for system failure when turning the ignition from OFF to ON (gear indicator blinking). → Indicator blinks. → Retest after installing a new or good ECU.

No blinks.

Temporary problem. ECU OK.

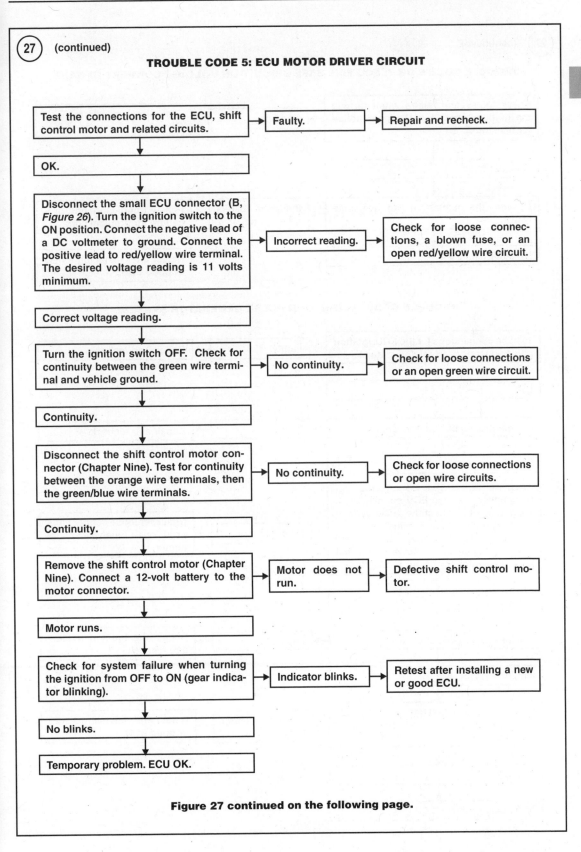

(27) (continued)

TROUBLE CODE 5: ECU MOTOR DRIVER CIRCUIT

Test the connections for the ECU, shift control motor and related circuits.	→ Faulty. →	Repair and recheck.

OK.

Disconnect the small ECU connector (B, *Figure 26*). Turn the ignition switch to the ON position. Connect the negative lead of a DC voltmeter to ground. Connect the positive lead to red/yellow wire terminal. The desired voltage reading is 11 volts minimum.	→ Incorrect reading. →	Check for loose connections, a blown fuse, or an open red/yellow wire circuit.

Correct voltage reading.

Turn the ignition switch OFF. Check for continuity between the green wire terminal and vehicle ground.	→ No continuity. →	Check for loose connections or an open green wire circuit.

Continuity.

Disconnect the shift control motor connector (Chapter Nine). Test for continuity between the orange wire terminals, then the green/blue wire terminals.	→ No continuity. →	Check for loose connections or open wire circuits.

Continuity.

Remove the shift control motor (Chapter Nine). Connect a 12-volt battery to the motor connector.	→ Motor does not run. →	Defective shift control motor.

Motor runs.

Check for system failure when turning the ignition from OFF to ON (gear indicator blinking).	→ Indicator blinks. →	Retest after installing a new or good ECU.

No blinks.

Temporary problem. ECU OK.

Figure 27 continued on the following page.

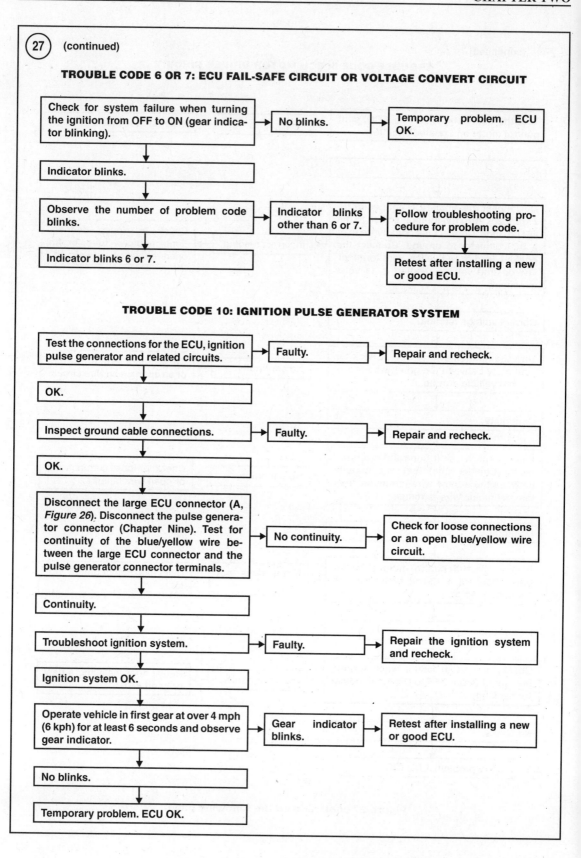

27 (continued)

TROUBLE CODE 6 OR 7: ECU FAIL-SAFE CIRCUIT OR VOLTAGE CONVERT CIRCUIT

Check for system failure when turning the ignition from OFF to ON (gear indicator blinking). → No blinks. → Temporary problem. ECU OK.

Indicator blinks.

Observe the number of problem code blinks. → Indicator blinks other than 6 or 7. → Follow troubleshooting procedure for problem code.

Indicator blinks 6 or 7.

Retest after installing a new or good ECU.

TROUBLE CODE 10: IGNITION PULSE GENERATOR SYSTEM

Test the connections for the ECU, ignition pulse generator and related circuits. → Faulty. → Repair and recheck.

OK.

Inspect ground cable connections. → Faulty. → Repair and recheck.

OK.

Disconnect the large ECU connector (A, *Figure 26*). Disconnect the pulse generator connector (Chapter Nine). Test for continuity of the blue/yellow wire between the large ECU connector and the pulse generator connector terminals. → No continuity. → Check for loose connections or an open blue/yellow wire circuit.

Continuity.

Troubleshoot ignition system. → Faulty. → Repair the ignition system and recheck.

Ignition system OK.

Operate vehicle in first gear at over 4 mph (6 kph) for at least 6 seconds and observe gear indicator. → Gear indicator blinks. → Retest after installing a new or good ECU.

No blinks.

Temporary problem. ECU OK.

2

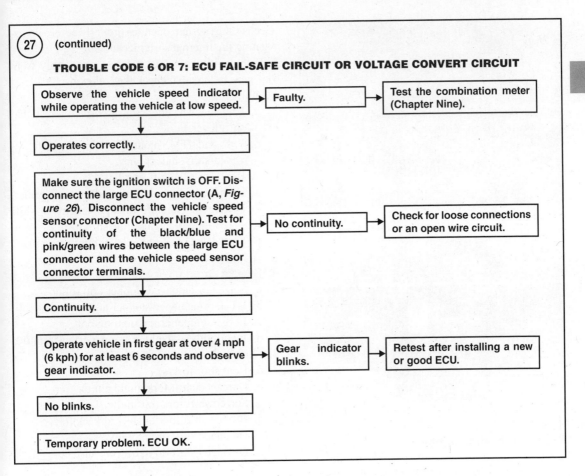

(27) (continued)

TROUBLE CODE 6 OR 7: ECU FAIL-SAFE CIRCUIT OR VOLTAGE CONVERT CIRCUIT

Observe the vehicle speed indicator while operating the vehicle at low speed. → Faulty. → Test the combination meter (Chapter Nine).

Operates correctly.

Make sure the ignition switch is OFF. Disconnect the large ECU connector (A, *Figure 26*). Disconnect the vehicle speed sensor connector (Chapter Nine). Test for continuity of the black/blue and pink/green wires between the large ECU connector and the vehicle speed sensor connector terminals. → No continuity. → Check for loose connections or an open wire circuit.

Continuity.

Operate vehicle in first gear at over 4 mph (6 kph) for at least 6 seconds and observe gear indicator. → Gear indicator blinks. → Retest after installing a new or good ECU.

No blinks.

Temporary problem. ECU OK.

1. The ignition switch must be *off* unless directed otherwise.
2. The battery must be fully charged and in good condition.
3. The clutch must be properly adjusted.
4. The fuses must be good.

If the shifting problem is not caused by the electric shifting system, refer to the *Faulty Mechanical Shifting* section.

Trouble codes

If a problem exists that the ECU can detect, the ECU will display a trouble code by blinking the gear indicator N on the combination meter (**Figure 28**). The number of blinks corresponds to the trouble code number.

Proceed as follows to obtain the ECU trouble code:
1. Make sure the ignition switch is *off*.
2. Make sure the transmission is in neutral.

3. Set the parking brake.
4. Simultaneously push the *up* and *down* shift buttons (**Figure 29**). Continue to hold the buttons while performing Step 5.
5. Turn the ignition switch *on*.
6. Release the shift buttons before the N appears in the gear indicator window on the combination meter.
7. Push in both shift buttons again for more than 3 seconds, then release. The trouble code should appear.
8. Count the number of blinks and refer to **Table 1**. Note that more than one trouble code may be displayed. The most recent trouble code is displayed first.
9. To delete a trouble code, perform the steps to display the code. While the code is blinking, push in both shift buttons.

NOTE
The gear indicator must function properly for the ECU to display a trouble code. Troubleshoot the gear indicator if it does not function properly.

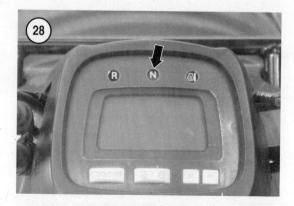

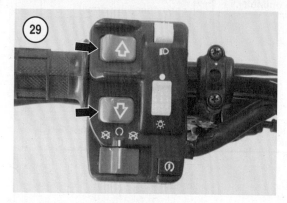

Faulty Mechanical Shifting

The following sections outline possible causes of mechanical problems. When using the emergency manual shift lever on FE and TE models, be aware of the following:

> *CAUTION*
> *Only use the manual shift lever for emergency or troubleshooting purposes. Continued use may cause internal damage to the master shift arm. Do not operate the manual shift lever while operating the ATV. The lever must be hand-operated and never operated using a foot.*

> *NOTE*
> *It may be necessary to move the ATV backward or forward to engage gears while using the manual shift lever.*

Difficult shifting

The following problems apply to all models except as noted. On FE and TE models, make sure the

electric shift system operates properly before investigating the internal shift mechanism.

If the shift shaft does not move smoothly from one gear to the next, check the following.

1. Shift shaft:
   a. FM and TM models—Incorrectly installed shift lever.
   b. FM and TM models—Stripped shift lever-to-shift shaft splines.
   c. Bent sub-gearshift spindle.
   d. Damaged sub-gearshift spindle return spring.
   e. Damaged gearshift linkage assembly shift shaft where it engages the shift drum.
   f. Shift drum positioning lever binding on pivot bolt.
2. Stopper arm:
   a. Seized or damaged stopper arm roller.
   b. Weak or damaged stopper arm spring.
   c. Loose stopper arm mounting bolt.
   d. Incorrectly assembled stopper arm assembly.
3. Shift drum and shift forks:
   a. Bent shift fork(s).
   b. Damaged shift fork guide pin(s).
   c. Seized shift fork (on shaft).
   d. Broken shift fork or shift fork shaft.
   e. Damaged shift drum groove(s).
   f. Damaged shift drum bearing surfaces.

Gears pop out of mesh

If the transmission shifts into gear, but then slips or pops out, check the following:

1. Gearshift linkage:
   a. Incorrectly assembled sub-gearshift spindle and gearshift A arm assembly.
   b. Stopper arm fails to move or set properly.
2. Shift drum:
   a. Incorrect thrust play.
   b. Worn or damaged shift drum groove(s).
3. Bent shift fork(s).
4. Transmission:
   a. Worn or damaged gear dogs.
   b. Excessive gear thrust play.
   c. Worn or damaged transmission shaft circlips or thrust washers.

Transmission overshifts

If the transmission overshifts when shifting up or down, check for a weak or broken shift lever return spring or a weak or broken stopper arm and spring assembly.

Transmission fails to shift into reverse

If the transmission fails to shift into or operate in reverse properly, check the following possible causes. On FE and TE models, make sure the electric shift system operates properly before investigating the internal shift mechanism.

1. Incorrect reverse cable adjustment.

2. Loose or damaged reverse stopper arm.

3. Damaged reverse stopper shaft.

DRIVETRAIN

Noise is usually the first indication of a drivetrain problem. It is not always easy to diagnose the trouble by determining the source of the noise and the operating conditions that produce it.

Some clues as to the cause of the trouble may be gained by noting: whether the noise is a hum, growl or knock; whether it is produced when the ATV is accelerating under load or coasting; and whether it is heard when the vehicle is going straight or making a turn.

Drivetrain service procedures are covered in Chapter Eleven (front) and Chapter Twelve (rear).

> *CAUTION*
> *Improperly diagnosed noises can lead to rapid and excessive drivetrain wear and damage. If you are not familiar with the operation and repair of the front and rear final drive assemblies, refer troubleshooting to a qualified Honda dealership.*

Oil Inspection

Drain the gearcase oil (Chapter Three) into a clean container. Rub the drained oil between two fingers and check for the presence of metallic particles. Also check the drain bolt for metal particles. While a small amount of particles in the oil is normal, an abnormal amount of debris is an indication of bearing or gear damage.

Front Differential

Consistent noise while cruising

1. Low oil level.
2. Gear oil contamination.
3. Chipped or damaged gear teeth.
4. Worn or damaged ring gear bearing.
5. Worn or damaged ring gear.
6. Worn pinion gear or shaft side washers.
7. Worn or damaged ring gear and drive pinion.
8. Incorrect ring gear and drive pinion tooth contact.

Consistent gear noises during coasting

1. Damaged or chipped gears.
2. Gear oil contamination.
3. Incorrect ring gear and drive pinion tooth contact.

Gear noise during normal operation

1. Low oil level.
2. Gear oil contamination.
3. Chipped or damaged gear teeth.
4. Incorrect ring gear and drive pinion tooth contact.

Overheating

1. Low oil level.
2. Insufficient ring gear and drive pinion gear backlash.

Oil leak

1. Oil level too high.
2. Plugged breathe hole or tube.
3. Damaged oil seal(s).
4. Loose cover mounting bolts.
5. Housing damage.

Abnormal noises during starting or acceleration

1. Worn or damaged cone spring or shim.
2. Excessive pinion gear backlash.
3. Worn differential splines.
4. Excessive ring gear and drive pinion backlash.
5. Loose fasteners.

Abnormal noises when turning

1. Worn or damaged cone spring or shim.
2. Damaged driveshaft splines.
3. Worn or damaged cams or face cams.
4. Worn or damaged ring gear bearing.

Rear Differential
Excessive Noise

1. Low oil level.
2. Excessive ring gear and pinion gear backlash.
3. Worn or damaged drive pinion and splines.
4. Damaged driven flange and wheel hub.
5. Worn or damaged driven flange and ring gear shaft.

HANDLING

Poor handling will reduce overall performance and may cause loss of control and a crash. If the handling is poor, check the following items:
1. If the handlebars are hard to turn, check for the following:
  a. Low tire pressure.
  b. Incorrect throttle cable routing.
  c. Damaged steering shaft bushing and/or bearing.
  d. Bent steering shaft or frame.
  e. Steering shaft nut too tight.
2. If there is excessive handlebar shake or vibration, check for the following:
  a. Loose or damaged handlebar clamps.
  b. Incorrect handlebar clamp installation.
  c. Bent or cracked handlebar.
  d. Worn wheel bearing(s).
  e. Excessively worn or damaged tire(s).
  f. Damaged rim(s).
  g. Loose, missing or broken engine mount bolts and mounts.
  h. Cracked frame, especially at the steering head.
  i. Incorrect tire pressure.
  j. Damaged shock absorber damper rod.
  k. Leaking shock absorber damper housing.
  l. Sagged shock spring(s).
  m. Loose or damaged shock mount bolts.
3. If the rear suspension is too soft, check for the following:
  a. Damaged shock absorber damper rod.

  b. Leaking shock absorber damper housing.
  c. Sagged shock spring.
  d. Loose or damaged shock mount bolts.
4. If the rear suspension is too hard, check for the following:
  a. Rear tire pressure too high.
  b. Incorrect shock absorber adjustment.
  c. Damaged shock absorber damper rod.
  d. Leaking shock absorber damper housing.
  e. Sagged shock spring.
  f. Loose or damaged shock mount bolts.
5. Check the following on the frame:
  a. Damaged frame.
  b. Cracked or broken engine mount brackets.
6. If the wheel is wobbling, check for the following:
  a. Loose wheel nuts.
  b. Loose or incorrectly installed wheel hub.
  c. Excessive wheel bearing play.
  d. Loose wheel bearing.
  e. Bent wheel rim.
  f. Bent frame or other suspension component.
7. If the ATV pulls to one side, check for the following:
  a. Incorrect tire pressure.
  b. Incorrect tie rod adjustment.
  c. Bent or loose tie rod.
  d. Incorrect wheel alignment.
  e. Bent frame or other suspension component.

FRAME NOISE

Noises traced to the frame or suspension are usually caused by loose, worn or damaged parts. Various noises that are related to the frame are listed below.
1. The most common drum brake noise is a screeching sound during braking. Drum brake noises can be caused by:
  a. Glazed brake lining or drum surface.
  b. Excessively worn brake linings drums.
  c. Warped brake drum.
2. Front or rear shock absorber noise can be caused by:
  a. Loose shock absorber mounting bolts.
  b. Cracked or broken shock spring.
  c. Damaged shock absorber.
3. Some other frame associated noises can be caused by:
  a. Cracked or broken frame.
  b. Broken swing arm or shock linkage.

c. Loose engine mounting bolts.

d. Damaged steering shaft bearings.

e. Loose mounting bracket.

BRAKES

The front and rear brakes are critical to riding performance and safety. Inspect the brakes frequently and repair any problem immediately. When replacing or refilling the front brake fluid, use only DOT 3 or DOT 4 brake fluid from a sealed container. See Chapter Thirteen for additional information on brake fluid selection and drum brake service.

Front Drum Brake

If the front drum brakes are not working properly, check for one or more of the following conditions.

1. Incorrect front brake adjustment.
2. Air in brake line.
3. Brake fluid level too low.
4. Loose brake hose banjo bolts. Brake fluid is leaking out.
5. Loose or damaged brake hose or line.
6. Worn or damaged brake drum.
7. Worn or damaged brake linings.
8. Oil on brake drum or brake lining surfaces.
9. Worn or damaged wheel cylinder(s).

10. Weak or damaged brake return springs.

Rear Drum Brake

If the rear drum brake is not working properly, check for one or more of the following conditions.

1. Incorrect rear brake adjustment.
2. Incorrect brake cam lever position.
3. Worn or damaged brake drum.
4. Worn or damaged brake linings.
5. Oil on brake drum or brake lining surfaces.
6. Worn or damaged wheel cylinder(s).
7. Weak or damaged brake return springs.

Water Entering the Front Brake Drum(s)

1. Damaged waterproof seal.
2. Incorrectly installed waterproof seal.
3. Loose or unsealed wheel cylinder assembly.
4. Damaged hub O-ring.
5. Loose front axle nut.
6. Damaged brake panel O-ring.
7. Damaged wheel hub dust seal.
8. Damaged brake drum dust seal.
9. Damaged brake drum.
10. Damaged steering knuckle axle seal.
11. Loose brake panel mounting bolt(s).
12. Incorrect breather tube routing.

Table 1 ELECTRIC SHIFT TROUBLE CODES (2003-ON FE AND TE MODELS)

Number of gear indicator blinks	Faulty system	Probable faulty component
1	ECU (writing and recording circuit)	ECU
2	ES shift switch system (up and down)	Shift switch or related wire harness or ECU
3	Angle sensor system	Angle sensor, related wiring or ECU
4	Gear position switch system	Gear position switch, related wiring or ECU
5	ECU motor driver circuit	ECU
6	ECU fail-safe relay circuit	ECU
7	ECU voltage convert circuit	ECU
8	Angle sensor system	Angle sensor, shift control motor, related wiring or ECU
9	Angle sensor system	Angle sensor, related wiring or ECU
10	Ignition pulse generator system	Ignition pulse generator, related wiring or ECU
11	Vehicle speed sensor system	Vehicle speed sensor, related wiring or ECU
12	Gear position switch system	Gear position switch, related wiring or ECU

CHAPTER THREE

LUBRICATION, MAINTENANCE
AND TUNE-UP

This chapter includes lubrication, maintenance and tune-up procedures required for the Honda models covered in this book.

Table 1 lists the recommended maintenance and lubrication schedule.

Table 2 lists tire inflation specifications.

Table 3 lists maintenance and tune-up torque specifications.

Table 4 lists battery capacity.

Table 5 lists recommended lubricants and fuel.

Table 6 lists engine oil capacity.

Table 7 lists front and rear differential oil capacity.

Table 8 lists toe-in/out specifications.

Table 9 lists maintenance specifications.

Tables 1-9 are located at the end of this chapter.

PRE-RIDE CHECK LIST

Perform the following checks before the first ride of the day. All of these checks are described in this chapter. If a component requires service, refer to the appropriate section.

1. Inspect all fuel lines and fittings for leaks.

2. Make sure the fuel tank is full of fresh gasoline.

3. Make sure the engine oil level is correct.

4. Check the throttle operation for proper operation in all steering positions. Open the throttle all the way and release it. The throttle should close quickly with no binding or roughness.

5. Make sure the brake levers operate properly with no binding. Replace any broken lever. Check the lever housings for damage.

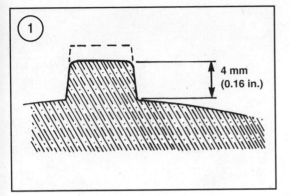

6. Check the brake fluid level in the front master cylinder reservoir. Add DOT 4 brake fluid if necessary.
7. Check the parking brake operation and adjust it if necessary.
8. Inspect the front and rear suspension. Make sure they have a good solid feel with no looseness. Turn the handlebar from side to side to check steering play. Service the steering assembly if excessive play is noted. Make sure the handlebar cables do not bind.
9. Check the drive shaft boots for damage.
10. Check the front and rear differential oil level. Top it off if necessary.
11. Check tire pressure (**Table 2**).
12. Check the exhaust system for looseness or damage.
13. Check for missing or damaged skid plates.
14. Check the tightness of all fasteners, especially engine, steering and suspension mounting hardware.
15. Make sure the headlight and taillight work.
16. Make sure all switches work properly.
17. Check the air filter drain tube for contamination.
18. When carrying cargo, make sure it is properly secured.
19. Start the engine, then stop it with the engine stop switch. If the engine stop switch does not work properly, test the switch as described in *Switches* in Chapter Nine.

MAINTENANCE SCHEDULE

Table 1 provides the maintenance schedule for all models. Strict adherence to these recommendations will help ensure long vehicle service. Perform the services more often when operating the vehicle commercially and in dusty or other harsh conditions.

Most of the services in **Table 1** are described in this chapter. However, some procedures which require more than minor disassembly or adjustment are covered in the appropriate chapter and are so indicated.

TIRES AND WHEELS

Tire Pressure

Check and adjust tire pressure to maintain the smoothness of the tire, good traction and handling, and to get the maximum life from the tire. A simple, accurate gauge can be purchased for a few dollars and should be carried in the vehicle's tool box. The correct tire pressures are listed in **Table 2**. Check tire pressure when the tires are cold.

> *WARNING*
> *Always inflate both tire sets (front and rear) to the correct air pressure. If the vehicle is run with unequal air pressures, the vehicle may run toward one side, causing poor handling.*

> *CAUTION*
> *Do not overinflate the tires as they can be permanently distorted and damaged.*

Tire Inspection

The tires take a lot of punishment due to the variety of terrain they are subjected to. Inspect them daily for excessive wear, cuts, abrasions or punctures. If a nail or other object is found in the tire, mark its location with a light crayon before removing it. Service the tire as described in Chapter Ten.

To gauge tire wear, inspect the height of the tread knobs. If the average tread knob height measures 4 mm (0.16 in.) or less (**Figure 1**), replace the tire as described in Chapter Ten.

> *WARNING*
> *Do not ride the vehicle with damaged or excessively worn tires. Tires in these conditions can cause loss of control. Replace damaged or severely worn tires immediately.*

Rim Inspection

Inspect the wheel rims for damage. Rim damage may be sufficient to cause an air leak or knock the wheel out of alignment. Improper wheel alignment can cause vibration and result in an unsafe riding condition.

Make sure the wheel nuts (**Figure 2**) are tightened securely on each wheel. Tighten the wheel nuts in a crossing pattern to 64 N•m (47 ft.-lb.).

BATTERY

Many electrical system troubles can be traced to battery neglect. Inspect and clean the battery at periodic intervals.

Safety Precautions

When working with batteries, use extreme care to avoid spilling or splashing the electrolyte. This solution contains sulfuric acid, which can ruin clothing and cause serious chemical burns. If the electrolyte is spilled or splashed on clothing or skin, immediately neutralize the affected area with a solution of baking soda and water. Then flush the area with an abundance of clean water. While the TRX350 uses a sealed battery, it vents gasses and electrolyte can leak through cracks in the battery case.

> *WARNING*
> *Battery electrolyte is extremely harmful when splashed into eyes or onto an open sore. Always wear safety glasses and appropriate work clothes when working with batteries. If the electrolyte gets into someone's eyes, flush them thoroughly with clean water and get prompt medical attention.*

When charging a battery, highly explosive hydrogen gas forms in each cell. Some of this gas escapes through filler cap openings and can form an explosive atmosphere in and around the battery. This condition can persist for several hours. Sparks, an open flame or a lighted cigarette can ignite the gas, causing an internal battery explosion and possible serious personal injury.

When servicing the battery, note the following precautions to prevent an explosion or personal injury.

1. Do not smoke or permit any open flame near any battery being charged or near a recently charged battery.

2. Do not disconnect live circuits at battery terminals because a spark usually occurs when a live circuit is broken.

3. Take care when connecting or disconnecting any battery charger. Make sure its power switch is off before making or breaking connections. Poor connections are a common cause of electrical arcs that cause explosions.

4. Keep all children and pets away from charging equipment and batteries.

5. Do not try to open the maintenance-free battery.

Removal/Installation

On all models covered in this manual, the negative terminal of the battery is grounded. When removing the battery, disconnect the negative cable first, then the positive cable. This sequence reduces

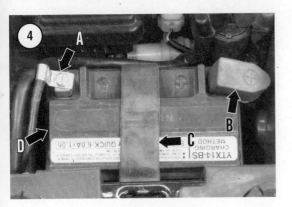

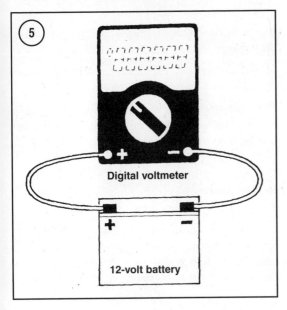

Digital voltmeter

12-volt battery

6. Push back the red terminal cover (B, **Figure 4**), then disconnect the positive battery cable from the battery.

7. Detach the rubber battery strap (C, **Figure 4**), then remove the battery (D).

8. Service the battery as described in this section.

9. Install the battery into the battery box with its terminals facing in the direction shown in **Figure 4**.

10. Attach the battery retaining strap.

11. Coat the battery terminals with a thin layer of dielectric grease. This will help to retard corrosion and decomposition of the terminals.

12. Attach the positive battery cable to the battery, then place the red terminal cover over the positive terminal (B, **Figure 4**).

13. Attach the negative battery cable (A, **Figure 4**) to the battery.

14. Install the cover (B, **Figure 3**) and plastic screws (A).

15. Install the seat (Chapter Fifteen).

Inspection

For a preliminary test, connect a digital voltmeter to the battery negative and positive terminals (**Figure 5**) and measure battery voltage. A fully charged battery will read between 13.0-13.2 volts. If the voltmeter reads 12.3 volts or less, the battery is under charged. If necessary, charge the battery as described in this chapter.

A bench type battery tester can be used to accurately test the maintenance-free battery. When using a battery tester, follow the manufacturer's instructions and test results. For best results, make sure the tester's cables are in working order and clamp tightly onto the battery terminals.

NOTE
A battery tester suitable for testing motorcycle batteries can be ordered through a dealership from K&L Supply Co. in Santa Clara, California.

Charging

Always follow the manufacturer's instructions when using a battery charger.

CAUTION
Never connect a battery charger to the battery with the battery leads still

the chance of a tool shorting to ground when disconnecting the positive cable.

WARNING
When performing the following procedures, protect eyes, skin and clothing. If electrolyte gets into someone's eyes, flush them thoroughly with clean water and get prompt medical attention.

1. Read the information listed in *Safety Precautions* in this section, then continue with Step 2.

2. Make sure the ignition switch is turned off.

3. Remove the seat (Chapter Fifteen).

4. Remove the plastic screws (A, **Figure 3**), then remove the electrical compartment cover (B).

5. Disconnect the negative battery cable (A, **Figure 4**) from the battery.

connected. Always remove the battery from the vehicle before charging it.

1. Remove the battery as described in this chapter.
2. Connect the positive charger lead to the positive battery terminal and the negative charger lead to the negative battery terminal.

> *CAUTION*
> *Do not exceed the recommended charging amperage rate or charging time on the label attached to the battery (**Figure 6**).*

> *CAUTION*
> *Do not charge the battery with a high rate charger. The high current forced into the battery will overheat the battery and damage the battery plates.*

3. Set the charger to 12 volts. If the charger output is variable, select a low setting. Use the following charging amperage and length of charging time:
   a. Standard charge: 1.4 amps at 5 to 10 hours.
   b. Quick charge: 6.0 amps at 1 hour.
4. Turn the charger on.
5. After charging the battery at the rate specified on the battery, turn off the charger and disconnect the charger leads.
6. Connect a digital voltmeter to the battery terminals (**Figure 5**) and measure battery voltage. A fully charged battery will read 13.0-13.2 volts.
7. If the battery voltage remains stable for one hour, the battery is charged.
8. Clean the battery cable connectors, battery terminals and case. Coat the terminals with a thin layer of dielectric grease. This will help to retard corrosion and decomposition of the battery terminals.
9. Reinstall the battery as described in this chapter.

Cables

To ensure good electrical contact between the battery and the electrical cables, keep the cables clean and free of corrosion.
1. If the electrical cable terminals are badly corroded, disconnect them from the battery as described in *Removal/Installation* in this section.
2. Thoroughly clean each connector with a wire brush and then with a water and baking soda solution. Wipe dry with a clean cloth.

3. After cleaning, apply a thin layer of dielectric grease to the battery terminals before reattaching the cables.

4. If disconnected, reconnect the battery cables as described in *Removal/Installation* in this section.

5. Coat the terminals with a thin layer of dielectric grease. This will help to retard corrosion and decomposition of the battery terminals.

Replacement

Always replace the sealed maintenance-free battery with another maintenance-free battery. The charging system is designed to operate with this type of battery in the system.

Before installing a new battery, make sure it is fully charged. Failure to do so will prevent the battery from ever obtaining a complete charge.

> *NOTE*
> *Because a maintenance-free battery requires a higher voltage charging system, do not replace a maintenance-free battery with a standard battery. Always replace the battery with the correct type and designated capacity. Refer to the battery capacity specifications in **Table 4** when purchasing a new battery.*

> *NOTE*
> *Recycle the old battery. The lead plates and the plastic case can be recycled. Most motorcycle dealerships will accept an old battery in trade after the purchase of a new one.*

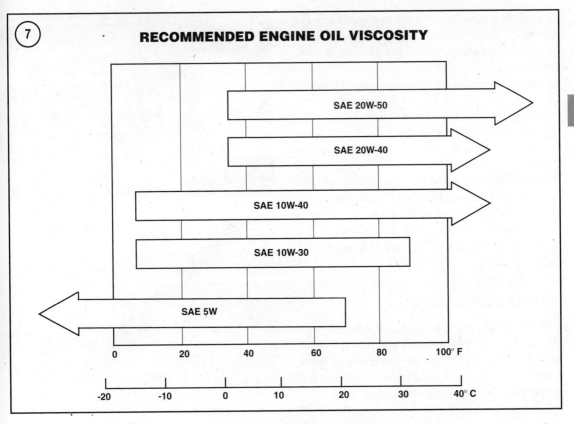

RECOMMENDED ENGINE OIL VISCOSITY

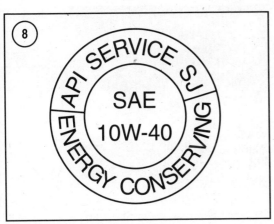

PERIODIC LUBRICATION

Refer to **Table 1** for lubrication service intervals.

Engine Oil and Filter

Engine oil type

Honda recommends the use of Honda GN4 four-stroke oil or an equivalent 10W-40 engine oil with an API service classification of SG or higher. The service classification is stamped or printed on the can or label on plastic bottles. Try to use the same brand of oil at each oil change. Do not use oils with graphite or molybdenum additives as these can cause clutch slippage and other clutch related problems. Refer to **Figure 7** for the correct oil weight recommended to use in anticipated ambient temperatures (not engine oil temperature).

> *CAUTION*
> ***Do not** use oils labeled **Energy Conserving** in the service designation circles on the oil container (**Figure 8**). Energy conserving oils contain additives which may damage motorcycle clutch components.*

Engine oil level check

Check the engine oil level with the dipstick cap mounted on the right side of the engine.

1. Park the ATV on level ground and set the parking brake.

2. Start the engine and let it run approximately 2-3 minutes.

3. Shut off the engine and let the oil drain into the crankcase for a few minutes.

4. Unscrew and remove the dipstick cap (**Figure 9**) and wipe the dipstick clean. Reinsert it into the threads in the hole; do not screw it in. Remove the dipstick and check the oil level.

5. The level is correct when it is between the two dipstick lines (**Figure 10**).

6. If necessary, remove the filler cap on the left side of the engine (**Figure 11**) and add the recommended type oil (**Table 5**) to correct the level.

7. Replace the dipstick O-ring if it is damaged.

8. Install the dipstick/oil fill cap (**Figure 9**) and tighten it securely.

Engine oil and filter change

Table 1 lists the recommended oil and filter change intervals. This assumes that the ATV operates in moderate climates. If it operates in dusty conditions, the oil will get dirty more quickly and will require more frequent oil changes.

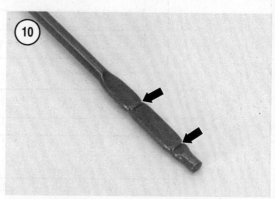

> *NOTE*
> *Never dispose of engine oil in the trash, on the ground or down a storm drain. Many service stations and oil retailers will accept use oil and filters for recycling. Do not combine other fluids with engine oil to be recycled. To locate a recycler, contact the American Petroleum Institute (API) at www.recycleoil.org.*

> *NOTE*
> *Running the engine heats the oil, which enables the oil to flow more freely and carry contaminates and sludge out with it when drained.*

1. Park the ATV on level ground and apply the parking brake.

2. Start the engine and let it warm to normal operating temperature. Then shut the engine off.

3. Place a clean drain pan underneath the engine.

4. Remove the drain plug (**Figure 12**) located in the bottom of the engine and allow the oil to drain.

5. Remove the dipstick cap (**Figure 9**) to help speed up the flow of oil.

6. Allow the oil to drain completely.

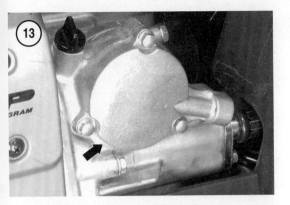

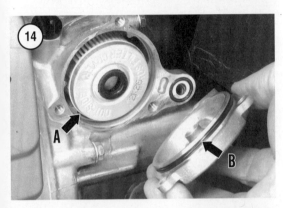

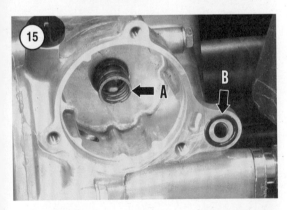

3

7. To replace the oil filter, perform the following:
   a. Remove the engine oil filter cover mounting bolts and cover (**Figure 13**).
   b. Remove and discard the oil filter (A, **Figure 14**).
   c. Remove the O-ring (B, **Figure 14**) from the oil filter cover groove.
   d. Remove the spring (A, **Figure 15**) from the engine.
   e. Remove the O-ring (B, **Figure 15**) from the engine.
   f. Clean the spring and the filter cover in solvent and dry them thoroughly.
   g. Replace any cracked or damaged O-rings.
   h. Lubricate each O-ring with engine oil.
   i. Install the O-ring into the engine groove (B, **Figure 15**).
   j. Install the O-ring into the filter cover groove (B, **Figure 14**).
   k. Install the spring (A, **Figure 15**).

CAUTION
Installing the oil filter backwards will re-strict oil flow and cause engine damage.

   l. Install the new oil filter with the outside mark (**Figure 16**) facing out.
   m. Install the engine oil filter cover (**Figure 13**) and tighten the mounting bolts to 10 N•m (88 in.-lb.).

8. Replace the drain plug gasket if it is damaged or if it was leaking. Install the drain plug (**Figure 12**) and gasket and tighten to 18 N•m (13 ft.-lb.).

9. Insert a funnel into the oil fill hole and fill the engine with the correct weight and quantity oil; see *Engine Oil Type* in this section. Refer to **Table 6** for engine oil capacity.

CAUTION
*Honda lists three different engine oil ca-pacities (**Table 6**), each specified for the type of service being performed. Be sure to install the correct oil capacity.*

10. Screw in the dipstick cap (**Figure 9**) securely.
11. Start the engine and run it at idle speed.
12. Turn the engine off and check the drain bolt and oil filter cover for leaks.
13. Check the oil level and adjust it if necessary.

WARNING
Prolonged contact with used oil may cause skin cancer. Wash your hands

with soap and water after handling or coming in contact with motor oil.

Oil screen

Two oil screens (**Figure 17**) are located inside the engine. Because the engine must be disassembled to service the oil screens, servicing them is not part of the engine periodic maintenance schedule. However, service the oil screens when troubleshooting a lubrication system problem or when internal engine damage occurs.

Front Differential Gearcase

Recommended gearcase oil

Honda recommends Honda shaft drive oil or an equivalent SAE 80 hypoid gear oil (**Table 5**).

Oil level check

1. Park the ATV on a level surface and set the parking brake.
2. Wipe the area around the oil fill cap clean and unscrew the oil fill plug (**Figure 18**).
3. The oil level should be level with the bottom thread of the fill plug hole. If the oil level is low, add hypoid gear oil (**Table 5**) until the level is correct.
4. Inspect the oil fill plug O-ring and replace it if it is damaged.
5. Install the oil fill cap and tighten it to 12 N•m (106 in.-lb.).

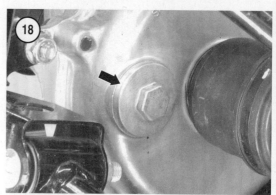

Oil change

The recommended oil change interval is listed in **Table 1**.

Discard old oil as described in *Engine Oil and Filter Change* in this chapter.

> *NOTE*
> *A short ride heats the front differential gearcase oil, which enables the oil to flow more freely and carry more contaminates and sludge when drained.*

1. Ride the ATV until normal operating temperature is reached, then park the ATV on a level surface and set the parking brake. Turn the engine off.

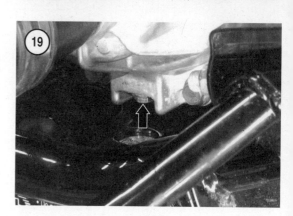

> *NOTE*
> *Skid plate removal is not necessary for access to drain plug.*

2. Place a drain pan underneath the drain plug (**Figure 19**).

3. Remove the oil fill plug (**Figure 18**).

4. Remove the drain plug (**Figure 19**) and allow the oil to drain.

5. Replace the drain plug gasket if it is leaking or damaged.

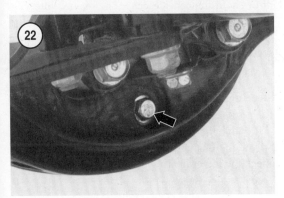

11. Test ride the ATV and check for leaks. After the test ride, recheck the oil level and adjust it if necessary.

Rear Differential Gearcase

Recommended gearcase oil

Honda recommends Honda shaft drive oil or an equivalent SAE 80 hypoid gear oil (**Table 5**).

Oil level check

1. Park the ATV on a level surface and set the parking brake.
2. Wipe the area around the oil check plug (**Figure 20**) and remove it. Oil should immediately start to flow out of the check hole. If oil flows out of the hole, the oil level is correct. Reinstall the oil check plug and tighten it to 12 N•m (106 in.-lb.). If oil did not flow out of the hole, continue with Step 3.
3. Remove the oil fill cap (**Figure 21**) and slowly add hypoid gear oil (**Table 5**) until oil starts to flow out of the check hole. Reinstall the oil check plug and tighten it to 12 N•m (106 ft.-lb.).
4. Install the oil fill cap (**Figure 21**) and tighten it to 12 N•m (106 in.-lb.).

Oil change

The recommended oil change interval is listed in **Table 1**.

Discard old oil as described in the *Engine Oil and Filter Change* in this chapter.

> *NOTE*
> *A short ride heats the rear gearcase oil, which enables the oil to flow more freely and carry more contaminates and sludge out when drained.*

1. Ride the ATV until it reaches normal operating temperature, then park the ATV on a level surface and set the parking brake. Turn the engine off.
2. Place a drain pan underneath the drain plug (**Figure 22**). Unscrew the drain plug and remove it. Allow the oil to drain out.
3. Wipe the area around the oil fill cap clean and unscrew the oil fill cap (**Figure 21**).
4. Inspect the drain plug washer and replace it if it is leaking or damaged.

6. Install the drain plug and gasket, and tighten to 12 N•m (106 in.-lb.).
7. Insert a funnel into the oil fill plug hole and pour in the recommended type (**Table 5**) and quantity (**Table 7**) of gear oil.
8. Remove the funnel and check the oil level. It should come up to the bottom thread of the fill plug hole. Add additional oil if necessary.
9. Inspect the oil fill plug O-ring and replace it if it is damaged.
10. Install the oil fill plug (**Figure 18**) and tighten to 12 N•m (106 in.-lb.).

5. When the oil stops draining, install the drain plug and gasket and tighten to 12 N•m (106 in.-lb.).

6. Insert a funnel into the oil fill cap hole and add the recommended type (**Table 5**) and quantity (**Table 7**) gear oil.

7. Inspect the oil fill cap O-ring and replace it if it is damaged.

8. Install the oil fill cap (**Figure 21**) and tighten it to 12 N•m (106 in.-lb.).

9. Test ride the ATV and check for leaks.

Control Cables

Clean and lubricate the throttle, brake, choke and reverse cables at the intervals indicated in **Table 1**. Also, check the cables for kinks, excessive wear, damage or fraying that could cause the cables to fail or stick.

The best method of control cable lubrication involves the use of a cable lubricator and a can of cable lube or a general lubricant. Do not use chain lube as a cable lubricant.

1. Disconnect the cable to be lubricated. Note the following:

   a. To service the throttle cable, refer to *Throttle Housing and Cable* in Chapter Eight.

   b. To service the brake cables, refer to *Rear Brake Pedal and Cable* and *Rear Brake Lever/Parking Brake Cable* in Chapter Thirteen.

   c. To service the choke cable, refer to *Choke Cable Replacement* in Chapter Eight.

   d. To service the reverse cable, refer to *Reverse Selector Cable Replacement* in Chapter Seven.

2. Attach a cable lubricator to the end of the cable following its manufacturer's instructions (**Figure 23**).

3. Inject cable lubricant into the cable until it begins to flow out of the other end of the cable.

NOTE
Place a shop cloth at the end of the cable to catch the oil as it runs out.

4. Disconnect the lubricator.

5. Apply a light coat of grease to the cable ends before reconnecting them. Reconnect the cable and adjust it as described in this chapter.

6. Reverse Step 1 to reconnect the cables.

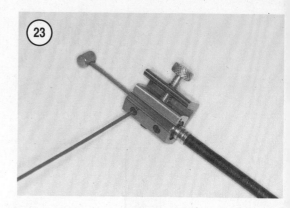

7. After lubricating the throttle cable, operate the throttle lever at the handlebar. It should open and close smoothly with no binding.

8. After lubricating the brake cable(s), check brake operation.

UNSCHEDULED LUBRICATION

The services listed in this section are not included in **Table 1** (maintenance and lubrication schedule). However, lubricate these items throughout the service year. The service intervals depend on ATV use. Use a water-resistant bearing grease when grease is specified in the following sections.

Steering Shaft

Remove the steering shaft (Chapter Ten) and lubricate the bushing with grease. At the same time, check the lower bearing and seals for damage.

Front Upper and Lower Control Arms

Remove the upper and lower control arm pivot bolts and lubricate the bolts and bushings with grease. Refer to Chapter Ten for service.

Front Wheel Bearing Seals

Lubricate the front wheel bearing seals with grease. If the front wheel bearings are not sealed, lubricate them as well. Refer to Chapter Ten for service.

**Rear Shock Absorber
Mounting Bolt**

Remove the front (Chapter Ten) and rear (Chapter Twelve) shock absorbers and lubricate the mounting bolts with grease.

PERIODIC MAINTENANCE

Periodic maintenance intervals are listed in **Table 1**.

Air Box Drain Tube

Inspect the drain tube (**Figure 24**) mounted on the bottom of the air box. If the hose is filled with water, dirt and other debris, clean and re-oil the air filter. Clean the air box and drain the drain tube at the same time.

Air Filter

A clogged air filter will decrease the efficiency and life of the engine. Never run the engine without an air filter properly installed. Dust that enters the engine can cause severe engine wear and clog carburetor jets and passages.

Refer to **Figure 25**.

Removal and installation

1. Remove the seat (Chapter Fifteen).
2. Release the air box cover retaining clips and remove the cover (**Figure 26**).
3. Loosen the air filter hose clamp (A, **Figure 27**) and remove the air filter assembly (B).

4. Disassemble, clean and oil the air filter as described in the following procedure.
5. Check the air box and carburetor boot for dirt or other contamination.
6. Wipe the inside of the air box with a clean rag. If more extensive cleaning is required, remove and clean the air box (Chapter Eight).
7. Cover the air box opening with a clean shop rag.
8. Inspect all fittings, hoses and connections from the air box to the carburetor.
9. Inspect the crankcase breather foam filter (**Figure 28**). If it is dirty, clean the filter using soapy water and let it dry. When installing the filter, do not push it too far into the opening.
10. Assemble the air filter.
11. Install the air filter into the air box. Tighten the air filter hose clamp (A, **Figure 27**) securely.
12. Install the air box cover (**Figure 26**) and secure with the retaining clips.
13. Install the seat (Chapter Fifteen).

Air filter cleaning and re-oiling

Service the air filter element in a well-ventilated area, away from all sparks and flames.

1. Remove the hose clamp (A, **Figure 29**), then remove the element core (B) from the filter element (C).

> *WARNING*
> *Do not clean the filter element with gasoline.*

2. Clean the filter element with a filter solvent to remove oil and dirt.
3. Inspect the filter element. Replace it if it is torn or broken in any area.
4. Fill a clean pan with liquid detergent and warm water.
5. Submerge the filter element in the cleaning solution and gently work the cleaner into the filter pores. Soak and gently squeeze the filter element to clean it.

> *CAUTION*
> *Do not wring or twist the filter element when cleaning it. This could damage the filter pores or tear the filter loose at a seam. This would allow unfiltered air to enter the engine and cause severe and rapid wear.*

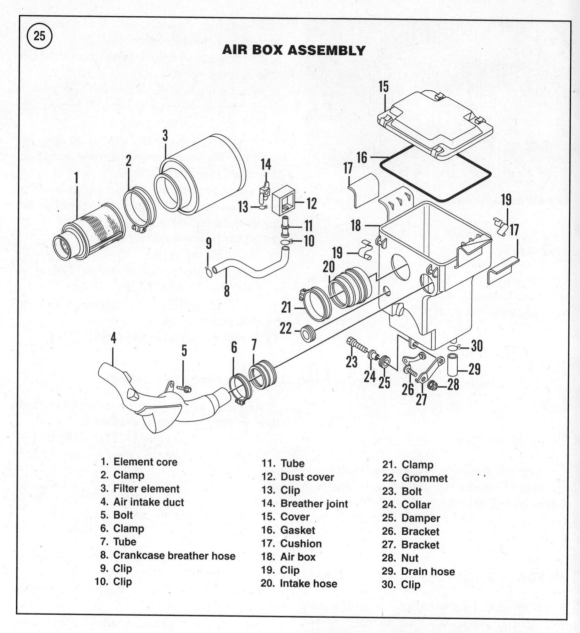

AIR BOX ASSEMBLY

1. Element core
2. Clamp
3. Filter element
4. Air intake duct
5. Bolt
6. Clamp
7. Tube
8. Crankcase breather hose
9. Clip
10. Clip

11. Tube
12. Dust cover
13. Clip
14. Breather joint
15. Cover
16. Gasket
17. Cushion
18. Air box
19. Clip
20. Intake hose

21. Clamp
22. Grommet
23. Bolt
24. Collar
25. Damper
26. Bracket
27. Bracket
28. Nut
29. Drain hose
30. Clip

6. Rinse the filter element under warm water while soaking and gently squeezing it.

7. Repeat Step 6 and Step 7 until there is no dirt being rinsed from the filter element.

8. After cleaning the element, inspect it again carefully. If it is torn or broken in any area, replace it. Do not run the engine with a damaged filter element.

9. Set the filter element aside and allow it to dry thoroughly.

10. Clean and dry the element core. Check the element core for damage and replace it if necessary.

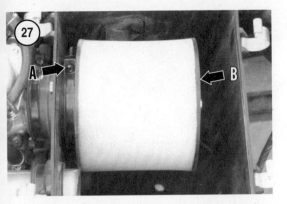

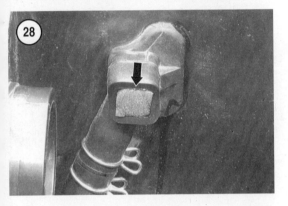

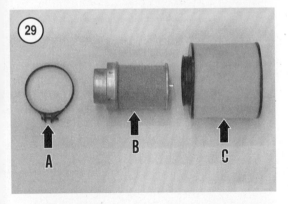

CAUTION
Make sure the filter element is completely dry before oiling it.

11. Properly oiling an air filter element is a messy but important job. Wear a pair of disposable rubber gloves when performing this procedure. Oil the filter as follows:

    a. Purchase a box of gallon size storage bags. The bags can be used when cleaning the filter as well as for storing engine and carburetor parts during disassembly service procedures.

    b. Place the filter element into a storage bag.

    c. Pour foam filter oil onto the filter to soak it.

    d. Gently squeeze and release the filter to soak filter oil into the filter's pores. Repeat until all of the filter's pores are saturated with oil.

    e. Remove the filter element from the bag and check the pores for uneven oiling. This is indicated by light or dark areas on the filter element. If necessary, soak the filter element and squeeze it again.

    f. When the filter oiling is even, squeeze the filter element a final time.

    g. Pour the leftover filter oil from the bag back into the bottle for reuse.

    h. Dispose of the plastic bag.

12. Install the filter element onto the element core. Install the clamp (A, **Figure 29**).

13. Install the filter assembly as described in this section.

Fuel Line Inspection

WARNING
Some fuel may spill during the procedure in this section. Because gasoline is extremely flammable, perform the following procedure away from all open flames (including appliance pilot lights) and sparks. Do not smoke or allow someone who is smoking in the work area. Always work in a well-ventilated area. Wipe up any spills immediately.

Inspect the fuel line (**Figure 30**) for leaks, cracks, hardness, age deterioration or other damage. Make sure each end of the hose is secured with a hose clamp. Check the carburetor overflow and vent hose ends for contamination.

> *WARNING*
> *A damaged or deteriorated fuel line presents a very dangerous fire hazard to both the rider and machine.*

Fuel Tank Vent Hose

Check the fuel tank vent hose (**Figure 31**) for proper routing and make sure it is not kinked. Check the end of the hose for contamination.

Front Brake Lining Check

1. Remove the rubber inspection cap (**Figure 32**) from the front wheel and brake drum.
2. Move the ATV in either direction until the inspection hole aligns with one of the brake linings.

> *NOTE*
> *Figure 33 shows a brake shoe with the brake drum removed for clarity. It is not necessary to remove the brake drum for this procedure.*

3. Measure the lining thickness (**Figure 33**). The standard lining thickness is 4.0 mm (0.16 in.). The service limit is 1.0 mm (0.04 in.). If the lining thickness appears thin or excessively worn, remove the brake drum (Chapter Thirteen) to inspect and measure the lining thickness.
4. Repeat Step 3 for the other three front brake linings.
5. Install the rubber inspection cap (**Figure 32**).

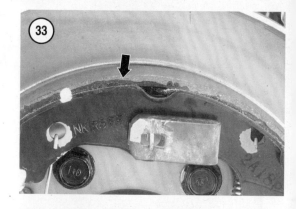

Rear Brake Lining Check

Apply the rear brake fully. If the indicator plate (A, **Figure 34**) aligns with the fixed index mark on the brake panel (B), replace both rear brake shoes (Chapter Thirteen).

Front Brake Adjustment

1. Perform the *Front Brake Lining Check* in this section. If the brake lining thickness is within specifications, continue with Step 2.
2. Apply the front brake lever and measure the amount of free play travel until the front brakes start

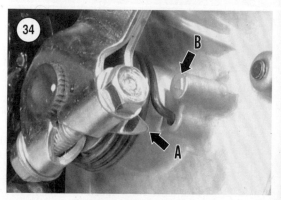

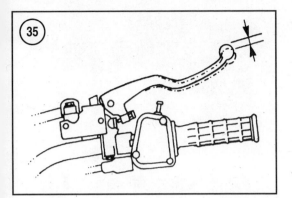

to engage (**Figure 35**). The correct front brake lever free play measurement is 25-30 mm (1-1 1/4 in.). If the brake linings contact the brake drum too early or too late, continue with Step 3 to adjust the front brakes.

NOTE
Contamination inside the brake drum can cause the brakes to engage too soon. If inspection reveals dirt or other debris inside the drum, remove the brake drum and inspect the drum

surface and brake linings as described in Chapter Thirteen.

3. Support the ATV with the front wheels off the ground.
4. Remove the rubber plug (**Figure 32**) from one of the brake drums.
5. Turn the wheel to align the hole with one of the brake adjusters (**Figure 36**).

NOTE
Each wheel is equipped with two brake adjusters. It does not matter which adjuster is adjusted first.

6. Insert a slotted screwdriver into the hole (**Figure 37**) and rotate the adjuster in the direction of the arrow cast on the wheel cylinder (**Figure 36**) until the drum is locked and can no longer move. From this position, rotate the adjuster in the opposite direction three clicks. Apply the front brake lever several times.
7. Rotate the wheel and make sure the brake is not dragging on the drum.

NOTE
A build-up of rust and dirt in the brake drum can cause the brake linings to drag.

8. Turn the wheel to align the hole with the other brake adjuster and repeat Steps 6 and 7.
9. Repeat Steps 4-8 for the opposite front wheel.
10. After adjusting the brakes on both front wheels, recheck the brake lever free play (Step 2). It should be within specification.

NOTE
If the free play is excessive after adjusting the brakes, there is probably air in the brake line. Bleed the front brakes (Chapter Thirteen), then recheck the brake lever free play.

11. Install the rubber plug (**Figure 32**) into each brake drum.
12. Install the front wheels (Chapter Ten).
13. Lower the ATV so all four wheels are on the ground.

WARNING
Do not ride the ATV until the brakes are working properly.

Rear Brake Adjustment

1. Before adjusting the rear brake, check the brake pedal, brake cables and adjusters for loose or damaged connections. Replace or repair any damage before continuing with Step 2.

2. Lubricate the rear brake cables as described in this chapter.

3. Release the parking brake if it is set.

4. Perform the *Rear Brake Lining Check* in this section. If the brake lining thickness is within specifications, continue with Step 5.

5. Apply the rear brake lever and measure the amount of free play travel until the rear brake starts to engage (**Figure 38**). The correct rear brake lever free play is 15-20 mm (5/8-3/4 in.). Note the following:

    a. If the brake linings contact the brake drum too early or too late, perform Step 6.

    b. If the free play travel is within specification, go to Step 7.

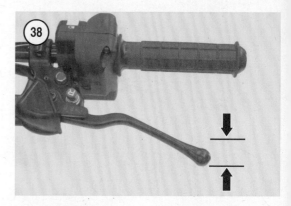

> *NOTE*
> *Contamination inside the brake drum can cause the brakes to apply too soon. If inspection reveals dirt or other debris inside the drum, remove the brake drum and inspect the drum surface and brake linings as described in Chapter Thirteen.*

6. Turn the *lower* adjusting nut (A, **Figure 39**) in or out to achieve the correct amount of free play.

> *NOTE*
> *Make sure the cutout relief in the adjust nut is properly seated on the collar.*

7. At the brake pedal, apply the rear brake and check the pedal free play. With the pedal in the rest position, apply the brake pedal and check the distance it travels until the rear brake is applied (**Figure 40**). The correct brake pedal free play is 15-20 mm (5/8-3/4 in.). If it is out of adjustment, turn the upper adjusting nut (B, **Figure 39**) in or out to achieve the correct amount of free play.

> *NOTE*
> *Make sure the cutout relief in the adjusting nut is properly seated on the collar.*

8. Support the ATV with the rear wheels off the ground.

9. Rotate the rear wheels and make sure the brake is not dragging. If the brake is dragging, repeat this procedure until there is no drag.

> *NOTE*
> *Brake drag can also be caused by dirt and other contamination in the brake drum and on the brake linings. If necessary, remove the brake drum*

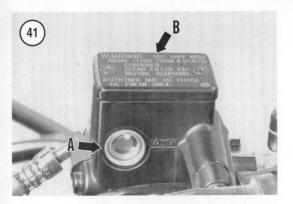

(Chapter Thirteen) and check the brake drum and linings.

10. Lower the ATV so all four wheels are on the ground.

Brake Fluid Level Check

1. Turn the handlebar so the master cylinder is level.

2. Check the brake fluid level through the master cylinder inspection window (A, **Figure 41**). The level should be above the LOWER level line. If necessary, add brake fluid as follows:

NOTE
If the brake fluid is low, check the front brake lining wear as described in this chapter.

3. Clean any dirt from the cover and master cylinder.

4. Remove the two cover screws, cover and diaphragm (B, **Figure 41**).

5. Add new DOT 4 brake fluid to raise the brake fluid level to the casting mark (**Figure 42**) in the reservoir.

WARNING
Use brake fluid clearly marked DOT 4. Others may cause brake failure. Do not intermix different brands or types of brake fluid as they may not be compatible. Do not intermix a silicone based (DOT 5) brake fluid as it can cause brake component damage leading to brake system failure.

CAUTION
Be careful when handling brake fluid. Do not spill it on painted or plastic surfaces as it will damage the surface. Immediately wash the area with soap and water and thoroughly rinse it off.

6. Reinstall the diaphragm and cover (B, **Figure 41**). Install the screws and tighten them securely.

Brake Fluid Change

Every time the master cylinder top cover is removed, a small amount of dirt and moisture can enter the brake fluid. The same thing happens if a leak occurs or if any part of the hydraulic system is loosened or disconnected. Dirt can clog the system and cause wear and brake failure. Water in the brake fluid will cause corrosion inside the hydraulic system, impairing the hydraulic action and reducing the brake's stopping ability.

To maintain peak performance, change the brake fluid every 2 years or whenever rebuilding or replacing the master cylinder or a wheel cylinder. To change brake fluid, follow the brake bleeding procedure in Chapter Thirteen.

WARNING
Use brake fluid clearly marked DOT 4. Others may cause brake failure. Do not intermix different brands or types of brake fluid as they may not be compatible. Do not intermix a silicone based (DOT 5) brake fluid as it can cause brake component damage leading to brake system failure.

Brake Hoses

Inspect the brake hoses for cracks, cuts, bulges, deterioration and leaks. Check the metal brake lines for cracks and leaks. Refer to Chapter Thirteen for service procedures.

Clutch Adjustment

Adjust the clutch at the interval specified in **Table 1**.

This adjustment pertains only to the change (manual) clutch. The centrifugal clutch requires no adjustment. Since there is no clutch cable, the mechanism is the only component that requires adjustment. This adjustment takes up slack caused by clutch component wear.

1. Loosen the clutch adjusting screw locknut (A, **Figure 43**).

2. Turn the adjusting screw (B, **Figure 43**) counterclockwise until resistance is felt, then stop.

3. From this point, turn the adjusting screw (B, **Figure 43**) clockwise 1/4 of a turn, then stop.

> *NOTE*
> *Make sure the adjusting screw does not move when tightening the locknut in Step 4.*

4. Hold the adjusting screw and tighten the locknut (A, **Figure 43**) to 22 N•m (13 ft.-lb.).

5. Test ride the ATV to make sure the clutch is operating correctly. Readjust if necessary.

> *NOTE*
> *If the clutch adjustment is difficult, the friction plates may be worn. Remove the clutch cover and inspect the friction plates as described in Chapter Six.*

Throttle Cable Adjustment

1. Before adjusting the throttle cable, operate the throttle lever and make sure it opens and closes properly with the handlebar turned in different positions. If it does not, check the throttle cable for damage or improper routing. Check the throttle lever for damage. Replace or repair any damage before continuing with Step 2.

2. Lubricate the throttle cable as described in this chapter.

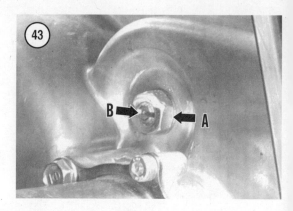

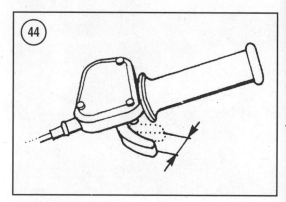

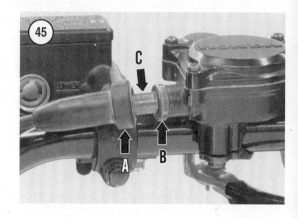

3. Operate the throttle lever and measure the amount of free play travel (**Figure 44**) until the cable play is taken up and the carburetor lever starts to move. The correct throttle lever free play measurement is 3-8 mm (1/8-5/16 in.). If the free play is out of specification, continue with Step 4.

4. At the upper throttle cable adjuster on the handlebar, slide the rubber boot (A, **Figure 45**) off the adjuster and loosen the cable adjuster locknut (B). Turn the adjuster (C, **Figure 45**) in or out until the free play is correct. Hold the adjuster and tighten

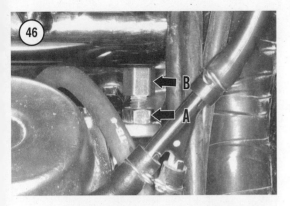

3

9. If the throttle cable cannot be adjusted properly, the cable has stretched excessively and must be replaced as described in Chapter Eight.

10. Make sure the throttle lever moves freely from its fully closed to fully open positions and is within the specification.

11. Apply the parking brake.

12. Start the engine and allow it to idle in neutral. Turn the handlebar from side to side. If the engine speed increases as the handlebar is being turned, the throttle cable is routed incorrectly or there is not enough cable free play. Readjust the throttle cable, or if necessary, replace the throttle cable as described in Chapter Eight.

NOTE
A damaged throttle cable will prevent
the engine from idling properly.

Choke Cable Inspection

There is no choke cable adjustment. Inspect the choke cable as described in this procedure.

1. Operate the choke knob (**Figure 47**). Make sure the lever moves smoothly and the cable is working properly.

2. If necessary, lubricate the choke cable as described in this chapter.

3. Visually inspect the choke cable for cracks or other damage. If necessary, replace the choke cable as described in Chapter Eight.

Reverse Lock System
Check and Adjustment

1. Check the reverse selector cable for loose or damaged cable ends. Check the reverse lever for damage. Repair or replace any damaged parts.

2. If necessary, lubricate the reverse selector cable as described in this chapter.

3. Push the reverse selector knob (**Figure 48**) in while squeezing the rear brake lever, then measure the reverse lever free play (**Figure 48**). The correct amount of free play is 2-4 mm (1/16-5/32 in.).

the locknut securely. Recheck the throttle lever free play while noting the following:

   a. If the proper amount of free play cannot be achieved at the throttle end of the cable, continue with Step 5.

   b. If the free play measurement is correct, slide the rubber boot (A, **Figure 45**) over the adjuster, then go to Step 11.

5. Loosen the upper cable adjuster locknut and loosen the adjuster (C, **Figure 45**) to obtain as much throttle cable free play as possible.

6. Remove the seat (Chapter Fifteen).

7. Slide the rubber boot off the lower cable adjuster and loosen the cable adjuster locknut (A, **Figure 46**). Turn the adjuster (B, **Figure 46**) to remove some of the cable free play, then tighten the locknut (A).

8. Repeat Step 4 to adjust the throttle lever free play. If necessary, readjust the lower (B, **Figure 46**) and upper (C, **Figure 45**) cable adjusters until the free play is correct. Then tighten both cable adjuster locknuts securely. Slide the rubber boots over the cable adjusters.

4. To adjust, loosen the reverse selector cable locknut (A, **Figure 49**) and turn the adjuster (B) in or out to obtain the correct amount of free play. Tighten the locknut and recheck the free play.

5. Start the engine and then shift the transmission into reverse following normal operating procedures. Make sure the transmission shifts into and out of reverse correctly.

Spark Arrestor

Clean the spark arrestor at the interval indicated in **Table 1** or sooner if a considerable amount of slow riding is done.

> *WARNING*
> *To avoid burnt hands, do not perform this cleaning operation when the exhaust system is hot. Work in a well-ventilated area (outside the garage or work area) that is free of any fire hazards. Be sure to wear safety glasses or goggles.*

1. Remove the bolt (**Figure 50**) from the base of the muffler.

2. Wear heavy gloves, such as welding gloves, and block the muffler opening with several shop cloths (**Figure 51**) that are free of all chemicals.

3. Have an assistant start the engine. Open and close the throttle several times to blow out accumulated carbon in the tail section of the muffler. Continue until carbon stops coming out of the muffler opening.

4. Turn the engine off and let the muffler cool.

5. Install the bolt (**Figure 50**) and tighten it securely.

Steering Shaft and
Front Suspension Inspection

Inspect the steering system and front suspension at the interval indicated in **Table 1**. If any of the following front suspension and steering fasteners are loose, refer to Chapter Ten for the correct service procedures and tightening torques.

1. Park the ATV on level ground and set the parking brake.

2. Visually inspect all components of the steering system. Repair or replace damaged components as described in Chapter Ten.

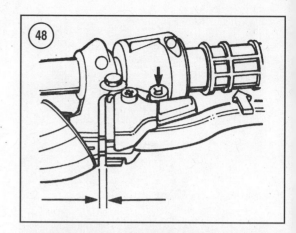

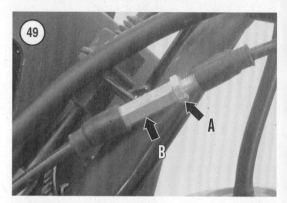

3. Check the shock absorbers as described in this section.

4. Remove the combination meter cover or handlebar cover, as equipped, (Chapter Fifteen). Make sure the handlebar holder bolts are tight. Reinstall the combination meter cover or handlebar cover.

5. Make sure the front axle nuts are tight and all cotter pins are in place.

6. Make sure the cotter pins are in place on all steering components. If any cotter pin is missing,

check the nut for looseness. Torque the nut and install a new cotter pin as described in Chapter Ten.

7. Check the steering shaft play as follows:

 a. Support the ATV with the front wheels off the ground.

 b. To check steering shaft radial play, move the handlebar from side to side (without attempting to move the wheels). If radial play is excessive, the upper steering bushing is probably worn or the bushing holder mounting bolts (**Figure 52**) are loose. Replace the upper bushing or tighten the bushing holder bolts as necessary.

 c. To check steering shaft thrust play, lift up and then push down on the handlebar. If there is excessive thrust play, check the lower steering shaft nut (**Figure 53**) for looseness. If the nut is tightened properly, check the lower steering shaft bearing for excessive wear or damage.

 d. If necessary, service the steering shaft as described in Chapter Ten.

 e. Lower the ATV so all four tires are on the ground.

8. Check the steering knuckle and tie rod ends as follows:

 a. Turn the handlebar quickly from side to side. If there is appreciable looseness between the handlebar and tires, check the tie rod ends for excessive wear or damage.

 b. Service the steering knuckle and tie rods as described in Chapter Ten.

> *NOTE*
> *If any cotter pins were removed in this section, install new cotter pins during reassembly.*

Shock Absorber Inspection

1. Check the front and rear shock absorbers for oil leaks, a bent damper rod or other damage.

2. If necessary, replace the shock absorbers as described in Chapter Ten (front) or Chapter Twelve (rear).

Front Axle Joint Boot Inspection

At the interval specified in **Table 1**, inspect the front axle joint boots (**Figure 54**) for tearing or other damage. Replace damaged boots as described in Chapter Eleven.

Toe Adjustment

Toe-in is a condition where the front of the tires are closer together than the back (**Figure 55**). If the wheels are toed-out, the front of the tires are farther apart than the rear of the tires. Check the toe-in/out adjustment at the interval specified in **Table 1**, after servicing the front suspension or when replacing the tie rods.

Adjust toe-in/out by changing the length of the tie rods.

1. Inflate all four tires to the recommended pressure in **Table 2**.
2. Park the ATV on level ground and set the parking brake. Then raise and support the front of the vehicle so both front tires just clear the ground.
3. Turn the handlebar so the wheels are facing straight ahead.
4. Using a tape measure, carefully measure the distance between the center of both front tires as shown in A, **Figure 55**. Mark the tires with a piece of chalk at these points. Record the measurement.
5. Rotate each tire exactly 180° and measure the distance between the center of both front tires at B, **Figure 55**. Record the measurement.
6. Subtract the measurement in Step 4 from Step 5 as shown in **Figure 55**. Refer to the specification in **Table 8**. If the toe-in/out measurement is incorrect, continue with Step 7. If the measurement is correct, go to Step 10.
7. Loosen the locknut (A, **Figure 56**) at each end of both tie rods.
8. Use a wrench on the flat portion (B, **Figure 56**) of the tie rods and slowly turn both tie rods the same amount until the toe-in measurement is correct.

> *WARNING*
> *If the tie rods are not adjusted equally, the handlebar will not be centered while traveling straight ahead. This condition may cause loss of control. If necessary, refer adjustment to a Honda dealership or qualified shop.*

> *NOTE*
> *Turn both tie rods the same number of turns. This ensures the tie rod length*

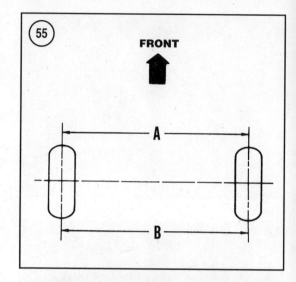

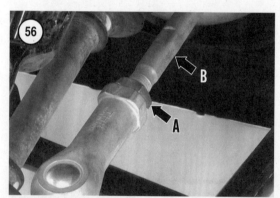

*will remain the same on each side. To check the lengths of the tie rods, refer to **Tie Rods** in Chapter Ten.*

9. When the toe-in/out adjustment is correct, hold each tie rod in place and tighten the locknuts to 54 N•m (40 ft.-lb.).

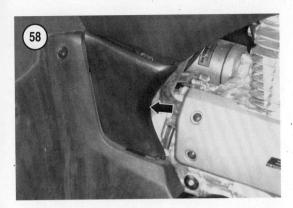

10. Lower the ATV so both front wheels are on the ground.
11. Start the engine and test ride it slowly on level ground. Steer straight ahead and make sure the handlebar does not turn toward the left- or right-side.

Rear Suspension Check

1. Support the ATV so the rear wheels are off the ground.
2. Try to move the rear axle (**Figure 57**) sideways while checking for excessive play at the swing arm bearings.
3. If there is any play, check the swing arm pivot bolts for looseness (Chapter Twelve). If they are tightened properly, the swing arm bearings may require replacement. See Chapter Twelve.
4. Lower the ATV so all four tires are on the ground.

Skid Plates

Check the front, middle and rear skid plates for damage and loose mounting bolts. Repair or replace damaged skid plates. Replace missing or damaged mounting bolts. Tighten the mounting bolts securely.

Fasteners

Constant vibration can loosen many of the fasteners on the ATV. Check the tightness of all fasteners, especially those on:
1. Engine mounting hardware.
2. Cylinder head bracket bolts.
3. Engine crankcase covers.
4. Handlebar.
5. Gearshift lever.
6. Brake pedal and lever.
7. Exhaust system.
8. Steering and suspension components.

ENGINE TUNE-UP

A tune-up is general adjustment and maintenance to ensure peak engine performance.

The following section discuss each phase of a proper tune-up which should be performed in the order given. Unless otherwise specified, the engine should be thoroughly cool before any tune-up procedure is started.

Have the new parts on hand before beginning.

Camshaft Chain Adjustment

The engine is equipped with an automatic camshaft chain tensioner. No adjustment is required.

Valve Clearance Check and Adjustment

Check and adjust the valve clearance while the engine is cold (below 35° C [95° F]).
1. Park the ATV on level ground and set the parking brake.
2. Remove the recoil starter cover (**Figure 58**).
3. Remove the fuel tank and the engine heat guard (Chapter Eight).
4. Remove the bolts and the cylinder head cover (**Figure 59**) and gasket.
5. Remove the O-ring (**Figure 60**).
6. Remove the spark plug. This will make it easier to turn the engine with the recoil starter and align the timing marks.

7. Remove the timing hole cap (**Figure 61**).

8. The engine must be set to top dead center (TDC) on its compression stroke for checking and adjusting the valve clearance. Perform the following:

a. Pull the recoil starter handle slowly and align the T mark on the flywheel with the index mark on the rear crankcase cover (**Figure 62**).

b. Move both rocker arms by hand. When the engine is set at TDC on its compression stroke, both rocker arms will have some side clearance, indicating that the intake and exhaust valves are closed. If the rocker arms are tight (indicating that the valves are open), turn the crankshaft 360° and realign the T mark as described in substep a. The engine should now be set at TDC on its compression stroke.

9. Check the clearance of both the intake valve and exhaust valve by inserting a flat feeler gauge between the rocker arm pad and the valve stem (A, **Figure 63**). See **Table 9** for the intake and exhaust valve clearances. When the clearance is correct, there will be a slight resistance on the feeler gauge when it is inserted and withdrawn.

10. Adjust the valve clearance as follows:

a. Loosen the locknut (B, **Figure 63**) and turn the adjuster (C) in or out until the clearance is correct. There should be a slight resistance felt when the feeler gauge is drawn from between the adjuster and valve tip.

b. Hold the adjuster to prevent it from turning and tighten the locknut securely as shown in **Figure 64**.

c. Recheck the clearance to make sure the adjuster did not move when the locknut was tightened. If necessary, readjust the valve clearance.

11. Install the spark plug and spark plug cap. Tighten the spark plug to 18 N•m (13 ft.-lb.).

12. Inspect the O-ring for cracks or other damage and replace it if necessary.

13. Lubricate the O-ring with oil and install it into the rocker arm holder groove (**Figure 60**).

14. Remove all gasket residue from the cylinder head cover and cylinder head gasket surfaces. Replace the cylinder head cover gasket if it is leaking or damaged.

15. Install the cylinder head cover gasket.

16. Clean the cylinder head cover and oil passages with solvent and compressed air.

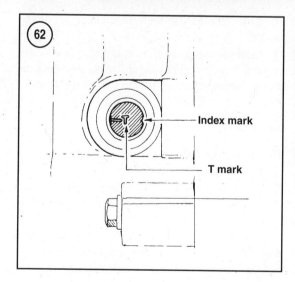

17. Install the cylinder head cover (**Figure 59**) and tighten the mounting bolts securely.

18. Install the timing hole cap and O-ring, and tighten to 10 N•m (88 in.-lb.).

19. Install the engine heat guard and fuel tank (Chapter Eight).

20. Install the recoil starter cover (**Figure 58**).

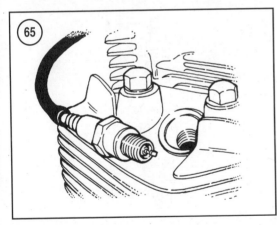

Cylinder Compression

A cylinder compression test is one of the quickest ways to check the condition of the rings, head gasket, piston and cylinder. It is a good idea to check compression during each tune-up, and compare it with the reading obtained at the next tune-up. This will help spot any developing problems.

1. Warm the engine to normal operating temperature.

2. Remove the spark plug. Insert the plug into the plug cap and ground the plug against the cylinder head (**Figure 65**).

3. Install a compression gauge into the cylinder head spark plug hole. Make sure the gauge is seated properly against the hole.

4. Turn the engine stop switch off.

> *NOTE*
> *The battery must be fully charged when the engine is cranked over with the starter or a false compression reading may be obtained. Because the engine must be turning at least 450 rpm when the compression test is made, do not use the recoil starter to turn the engine over.*

5. Hold the throttle wide open and crank the engine with the starter for several revolutions until the gauge stabilizes at its highest reading. Record the pressure reading and compare it to the specification in **Table 9**. Press the gauge button to release pressure from the gauge.

6. If the reading is higher than normal, there may be a buildup of carbon deposits in the combustion chamber or on the piston crown. This condition can cause detonation and overheating. Service the piston as described in Chapter Four.

7. Low compression readings indicate a leaking cylinder head gasket, a leaking valve or worn, stuck or broken piston rings. To determine which, pour about a teaspoon of engine oil through the spark plug hole onto the top of the piston. Crank the engine once to distribute the oil, then make another compression test and record the reading. If the compression increases significantly, the valves are good but the rings are worn or damaged. If compression does not increase, the valves or the cylinder head gasket is leaking. A valve could be hanging open or a piece of carbon could be on the valve seat.

> *NOTE*
> *If worn, stuck or broken piston rings are suspected, disconnect the crankcase breather tube (**Figure 66**) while the engine is running. If there is smoke inside the tube, check for a stuck or damaged piston ring(s).*

8. Remove the compression tester. Install the spark plug and reconnect the spark plug cap.

> *NOTE*
> *If the compression is low, the engine cannot be tuned to maximum performance.*

Spark Plug Removal

1. Grasp the spark plug lead as near the plug as possible and pull it off the plug. If it is stuck to the plug, twist it slightly to break it loose.

> *CAUTION*
> *Whenever the spark plug is removed, dirt around it can fall into the plug hole. This can cause expensive engine damage.*

2. Blow away any dirt that has collected around the spark plug.
3. Remove the spark plug (**Figure 67**) with a spark plug socket.

> *NOTE*
> *If the plug is difficult to remove, apply penetrating oil, like WD-40 or Liquid Wrench, around the base of the plug and let it soak about 10-20 minutes.*

4. Inspect the plug carefully. Look for a broken center porcelain, excessively eroded electrodes and excessive carbon or oil fouling.

Spark Plug Gap and Installation

Carefully adjust the electrode gap on a new spark plug to ensure a reliable, consistent spark. Use a spark plug gapping tool and a wire feeler gauge.
1. Remove the terminal nut from the end of the plug (A, **Figure 68**).
2. Insert a wire feeler gauge between the center and side electrode of the plug (**Figure 69**). The correct gap is listed in **Table 9**. If the gap is correct, a slight drag will be felt while the wire is pulled through. If there is no drag, or the gauge will not pass through, bend the side electrode with a gaping tool (**Figure 70**) to set the proper gap.
3. Apply an antiseize compound to the plug threads before installing the spark plug. Do not use engine oil on the plug threads.

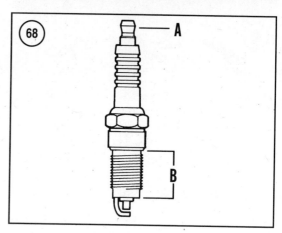

4. Screw the spark plug in by hand until it seats. Very little effort should be required. If force is necessary, the plug may be cross-threaded. Unscrew it and try again.

5. Use a spark plug wrench and tighten the new spark plug to 18 N•m (13 ft.-lb.). If a torque wrench is not available, tighten the plug an additional 1/4 to 1/2 turn after the gasket has made contact with the head. When installing a used spark plug, only tighten an additional 1/4 turn. Do not overtighten.

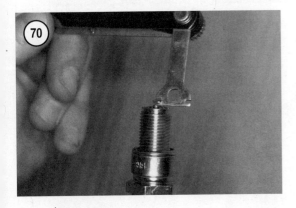

Spark Plug Heat Range

Spark plugs are available in various heat ranges that are either hotter or colder than the original plug. However, in most cases the heat range of the spark plug originally installed by the manufacturer (**Table 9**) will perform adequately under most conditions.

Select plugs with a heat range designed for the anticipated load and operating conditions. A plug with an incorrect head range can foul, overheat and cause piston damage. Do not change the spark plug heat range to compensate for adverse engine or carburetor conditions.

In general, use a hot plug for low speeds and low temperatures. Use a cold plug for high speeds, high loads and high temperatures. The plug should operate hot enough to burn off unwanted deposits but not so hot that it becomes damaged or causes preignition. Determine if plug heat range is correct by examining the insulator as described in *Spark Plug Reading* in this section.

When replacing plugs, make sure the reach or thread length (B, **Figure 68**) is correct. The thread length of any replacement spark plug must be the same as the original, which matches the length of

the threads in the cylinder head. A longer than standard plug could interfere with the piston and cause engine damage. A shorter plug provides poor ignition.

Spark Plug Reading

Reading the spark plug can provide information about engine performance. Reading a plug that has been in use indicates spark plug operation, air/fuel mixture composition and engine conditions (such as oil consumption and pistons). Before checking the spark plug, operate the ATV under a medium load for approximately 6 miles (10 km). Avoid prolonged idling before shutting off the engine. Remove the spark plug as described in this section. Examine the plug, and compare it to those shown in **Figure 71**, typical. Refer to the following sections to determine the operating conditions.

When reading the plugs to evaluate carburetor jetting, start with a new plug and operate the ATV at the load that corresponds to the jetting information desired. For example, if the main jet is in question, operate the ATV at full throttle; shut the engine off and coast to a stop.

Normal condition

If the plug has a light tan- or gray-colored deposit and no abnormal gap wear or erosion, the engine, carburetion and ignition condition are good. The plug in use is of the proper heat range and may be serviced and returned to use.

Carbon fouled

Soft, dry, sooty deposits covering the entire firing end of the plug are evidence of incomplete combustion. Even though the firing end of the plug is dry, the plug's insulation decreases. An electrical path is formed that lowers the voltage from the ignition system. Engine misfiring is a sign of carbon fouling. Carbon fouling can be caused by one or more of the following:

1. Too rich fuel mixture.
2. Spark plug heat range too cold.
3. Clogged air filter.
4. Retarded ignition timing.
5. Ignition component failure.
6. Low engine compression.

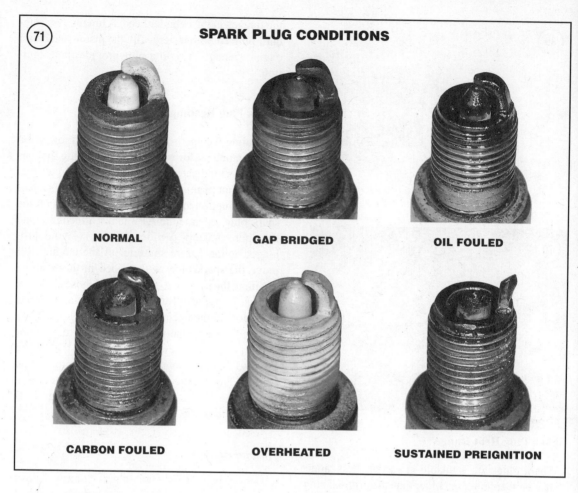

SPARK PLUG CONDITIONS

NORMAL   GAP BRIDGED   OIL FOULED

CARBON FOULED   OVERHEATED   SUSTAINED PREIGNITION

7. Prolonged idling.

Oil fouled

An oil fouled plug has a black insulator tip, a damp oily film over the firing end and a carbon layer over the entire nose. The electrodes are not worn. Common causes for this condition are:

1. Incorrect carburetor jetting.

2. Low idle speed or prolonged idling.

3. Ignition component failure.

4. Spark plug heat range too cold.

5. Engine still being broken in.

An oil fouled spark plug may be cleaned in an emergency, but it is better to replace it. It is important to correct the cause of fouling before the engine is returned to service.

Gap bridging

Plugs with this condition exhibit gaps shorted out by combustion deposits between the electrodes. If this condition is encountered, check for an improper oil type or excessive carbon in the combustion chamber. Be sure to locate and correct the cause of this condition.

Overheating

Badly worn electrodes and premature gap wear, along with a gray or white blistered porcelain insulator surface are signs of overheating. The most common cause for this condition is using a spark plug of the wrong heat range (too hot). If a hotter spark plug has not been installed, but the plug is overheated, consider the following causes:

1. Lean fuel mixture.

2. Ignition timing too advanced.

3. Engine lubrication system malfunction.

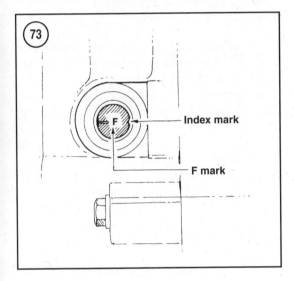

Index mark

F mark

4. Engine vacuum leak.

5. Improper spark plug installation (too tight).

6. No spark plug gasket.

Worn out

Corrosive gases formed by combustion and high voltage sparks have eroded the electrodes. Spark plugs in this condition require more voltage to fire under hard acceleration. Replace with a new spark plug.

Preignition

If the electrodes are melted, preignition is probably the cause. Check for carburetor mounting or intake manifold leaks and over-advanced ignition timing. It is also possible that a plug of the wrong heat range (too hot) is being used. Find the cause of the preignition before returning the engine into service.

Ignition Timing

All models are equipped with a capacitor discharge ignition system (CDI). Ignition timing is not adjustable. Check the ignition timing to make sure all components within the ignition system are working correctly. If the ignition timing is incorrect, troubleshoot the ignition system as described in Chapter Two. Incorrect ignition timing can cause a drastic loss of engine performance and efficiency. It may also cause overheating.

Before starting this procedure, check all electrical connections related to the ignition system. Make sure all connections are tight and free from corrosion, and all ground connections are clean and tight.

1. Start the engine and let it warm approximately 2-3 minutes.

2. Park the ATV on level ground and apply the parking brake. Shut off the engine.

3. Remove the timing hole cap and O-ring (**Figure 72**).

4. Connect a portable tachometer following its manufacturer's instructions.

5. Connect a timing light following its manufacturer's instructions.

6. Restart the engine and let it run at the idle speed indicated in **Table 9**. Adjust the idle speed if necessary as described in this chapter.

7. Aim the timing light at the timing hole and pull the trigger. The F mark on the flywheel should align with the index mark on the rear crankcase cover as shown in **Figure 73**. If the ignition timing is incorrect, troubleshoot the ignition system as described in Chapter Two.

8. Turn the ignition switch off and disconnect the timing light and portable tachometer.

9. Install the timing hole cap and O-ring, and tighten to 10 N•m (88 in.-lb.).

Pilot Screw Adjustment

The pilot screw does not require adjustment unless the carburetor has been overhauled or a new pilot screw was installed. To adjust the pilot screw under these conditions, refer to *Carburetor Adjustments* in Chapter Eight.

Idle Speed Adjustment

1. Start the engine and let it warm up approximately 10 minutes.
2. Park the ATV on level ground, apply the parking brake and shut off the engine.
3. Connect a portable tachometer to the engine following the manufacturer's instructions.
4. Restart the engine and turn the idle adjust screw (**Figure 74**) to set the idle speed. See **Table 9** for the idle speed specification.
5. Open and close the throttle a couple of times and check for variation in idle speed. Readjust if necessary.

> *WARNING*
> *With the engine idling, move the handlebar from side to side. If idle speed increases during this movement, the throttle cable needs adjusting or may be incorrectly routed through the frame. Correct this problem immediately. Do not ride the vehicle in this unsafe condition.*

6. Turn the engine off and disconnect the portable tachometer.
7. Install the right lower side cover (Chapter Fifteen).

STORAGE

Several months of inactivity can cause a general deterioration of the ATV. This is especially true in extreme climates. This section describes procedures on how to prepare the ATV for storage.

Selecting a Storage Area

The most likely place to store the ATV is in a home garage or workshop. If a home garage or suitable building is not available, facilities suitable for long-term vehicle storage are readily available for rent or lease in most areas. When selecting a building, consider the following points.

1. The storage area must be dry. Heating is not necessary, but the building should be well insulated to minimize extreme temperature variation.
2. Buildings with large window areas should be avoided, or such windows should be masked if direct sunlight can fall on the ATV.

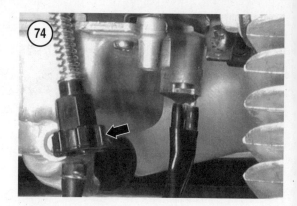

Preparing ATV for Storage

Careful preparation will minimize deterioration and make it easier to restore the ATV to service later. Use the following procedure.

1. Wash the ATV completely. Be sure to remove all dirt in all the hard to reach areas. Completely dry all parts.
2. Run the engine long enough to warm the engine oil. Drain the oil, regardless of the time since the last oil change. Refill with the normal quantity and type of oil as described in this chapter.
3. Drain all gasoline from the fuel tank, fuel hose, and the carburetor. Make sure the fuel tank filler cap is tightened securely and the vent hose is connected properly.
4. Clean and lubricate the control cables as described in this chapter.
5. Remove the spark plug and add about one tablespoon of engine oil into the cylinder. Then turn the engine over the recoil starter to distribute the oil to the cylinder wall and piston. Reinstall the spark plug and connect the spark plug cap.
6. Tape or tie a plastic bag over the end of the muffler to prevent the entry of moisture.
7. Inflate the tires to the correct pressure and move the ATV to the storage area. Support the ATV with all four wheels off the ground.
8. Remove the battery and charge it as described in this chapter. Then store the battery in a safe area away from freezing or excessively warm temperatures. Inspect and charge the battery once a month.
9. Clean the battery terminals, then lubricate them with dielectric grease.
10. When storing the ATV in a humid or salt-air area, spray all exposed metal surfaces with a light film of oil. Do not spray the seat, tires or any rubber part.

11. Cover the ATV with a tarp, blanket or heavy plastic drop cloth. Place this cover over the ATV mainly as a dust cover; do not wrap it tightly, especially any plastic material, as it may trap moisture and cause rust to form. Leave room for air to circulate around the ATV.

Returning ATV to Service

1. Before removing the ATV from the storage area, check air pressure in the tires and inflate the tires to the correct pressure.

2. Remove the plug from the end of the muffler.

3. When the ATV is brought to the work area, refill the fuel tank with fresh gasoline.

4. Charge and install the battery.

5. Check the operation of the engine stop switch. Oxidation of the switch contacts during storage may make it inoperative.

6. Check the brakes and throttle controls before riding the ATV.

7. The remainder of service required depends on length of non-use and operating conditions. Refer to the maintenance and lubrication schedule and determine which areas require service.

Table 1 MAINTENANCE AND LUBRICATION SCHEDULE

Initial maintenance: 100 miles (150 km) or 20 hours, whichever comes first
Inspect valve clearance
Replace engine oil and filter
Check engine Idle speed
Inspect brake fluid level**
Inspect brake system
Inspect reverse lock system
Inspect clutch system
Check for loose or missing fasteners
Inspect wheels and tires
Regular maintenance: 600 miles (1000 km) or 100 hours, whichever comes first
Clean air filter*
Drain air filter housing drain tube*
Inspect spark plug
Inspect valve clearance
Replace engine oil and filter
Check engine idle speed
Clean spark arrester
Inspect drive shaft boots (TRX350FE/FM)
Inspect brake system/lubricate cables
Inspect reverse lock system/lubricate cable
Inspect clutch system
Check for loose or missing fasteners
Check engine guard and skid plates
Inspect wheels and tires
Inspect front and rear suspension
(continued)

Table 1 MAINTENANCE AND LUBRICATION SCHEDULE (continued)

Regular maintenance: 1200 miles (2000 km) or 200 hours, whichever comes first
  Inspect/lubricate throttle
  Check fuel line
  Inspect/lubricate choke cable
  Drain air filter housing drain tube
  Inspect spark plug
  Inspect valve clearance
  Replace engine oil and filter
  Check engine idle speed
  Clean spark arrestor
  Inspect brake fluid level*
  Inspect brake shoe wear*
  Inspect brake system/lubricate cables
  Inspect drive shaft boots (TRX350FE/FM)
  Inspect reverse lock system/lubricate cables
  Inspect clutch system
  Check for loose or missing fasteners
  Check engine guard and skid plates
  Inspect wheels and tires
  Inspect front and rear suspension
  Inspect steering shaft bearing holder
  Inspect steering system/check toe adjustment
  Change front gearcase oil (TRX350FE/FM)**
  Change rear gearcase oil**

*Inspect more frequently when operating in wet or muddy conditions or when riding in sand, snow or in dusty areas.
**Replace every two years.

Table 2 TIRE INFLATION PRESSURE

	Front and rear tires psi (kPa)
TRX350TE/TM	
Normal pressure	2.9 (20)
Minimum pressure	2.5 (17)
Maximum pressure	3.3 (23)
TRX350FE/FM	
Normal pressure	3.6 (24.8)
Minimum pressure	3.2 (22)
Maximum pressure	4.0 (27.6)

Table 3 MAINTENANCE TORQUE SPECIFICATIONS

	N•m	ft.-lb.	in.-lb.
Clutch adjusting			
screw locknut	22	16	–
Engine oil drain bolt	18	13	–
Engine oil filter cover			
mounting bolts	10	–	88
Rear differential			
Drain plug	12	–	106
Oil check plug	12	–	106
Oil fill cap	12	–	106
(continued)			

Table 3 MAINTENANCE TORQUE SPECIFICATIONS (continued)

	N•m	ft.-lb.	in.-lb.
Front differential			
Oil fill cap	12	–	106
Drain plug	12	–	106
Spark plug	18	13	–
Tie rod locknut	54	40	–
Timing hole cap	10	–	88
Valve adjuster locknut	17	12	–
Wheel nuts (front and rear)	64	47	–

Table 4 BATTERY CAPACITY

Battery type	Maintenance-free
Capacity	12 volt, 12 amp hour

Table 5 RECOMMENDED LUBRICANTS AND FUEL

Engine oil	
Classification	API SG or higher
Viscosity	SAE10W-40*
Differential oil	Hypoid gear oil SAE 80
Air filter	Foam air filter oil
Brake fluid	DOT 4
Steering and suspension lubricant	Multipurpose grease
Fuel	Octane rating of 86 or higher

*See text for additional information.

Table 6 ENGINE OIL CAPACITY

	Liters	U.S. qt.
Oil change only	1.95	2.06
Oil and filter change	2.0	2.1
After engine disassembly	2.5	2.6

Table 7 FRONT AND REAR DIFFERENTIAL OIL CAPACITY

	ml	U.S. oz.
Front differential		
Oil change	241	8.2
After disassembly	275	9.3
Rear differential		
Oil change	85	2.9
After disassembly	100	3.4

Table 8 TOE-IN/OUT SPECIFICATIONS

Toe-in/out (TE/TM)	From 18 mm (0.71 in.) toe-in to 12 mm (0.47 in.) toe-out
Toe-out (FE/FM)	3-33 mm (0.12-1.30 in.)

Table 9 MAINTENANCE SPECIFICATIONS

Engine compression	667 kPa (97 psi) @ 450 rpm
Engine idle speed	1300-1500 rpm
Front brake lever free play	25-30 mm (1-1 1/4 in.)
Front brake lining service limit	1.0 mm (0.04 in.)
Ignition timing	Not adjustable
Rear brake lever/pedal free play	15-20 mm (5/8-3/4 in.)
Reverse lever free play	2-4 mm (1/16-5/32 in.)
Spark plug gap	0.8-0.9 mm (0.032-0.036 in.)
Spark plug type	
Standard	NGK DPR7EA-9 or Denso X22EPR-U9
Cold weather operation*	NGK DPR6EA-9 or Denso X20EPR-U9
Throttle lever free play	3-8 mm (1/8-5/16 in.)
Valve clearance	
Intake and exhaust	0.15 mm (0.006 in.)

*Below 41° F (4° C).

CHAPTER FOUR

ENGINE TOP END

This chapter provides complete service and over-haul procedures, including information for disassembly, removal, inspection, service and reassembly of the engine top end components. These include the rocker arms, cylinder head, valves, cylinder block, piston, piston rings and camshaft. Exhaust system service is also covered. Before starting any work, read the service tips in Chapter One.

Table 1 lists general engine specifications and **Table 2** lists engine service specifications. **Tables 1-3** are located at the end of the chapter.

The TRX350 is equipped with an overhead valve pushrod engine. The camshaft is mounted in the crankcase and is driven off the crankshaft by a short cam chain. The camshaft operates followers which move the pushrods against the rocker arms.

CLEANLINESS

Repairs go much faster and easier if the engine is clean before beginning work. This is important when servicing the engine top end. Clean the engine and surrounding area before working on the engine top end.

EXHAUST SYSTEM

Refer to **Figure 1**.

Removal/Installation

> *WARNING*
> *Do not remove the exhaust pipe or muffler while they are hot.*

1. Remove the side cover and rear fender (Chapter Fifteen).
2. Loosen the exhaust pipe flange nuts.
3. Remove the muffler as follows:
   a. Loosen the muffler clamp bolts (**Figure 2**).
   b. Remove the muffler mounting nuts (**Figure 3**).
   c. Remove the muffler and gasket (13, **Figure 1**).

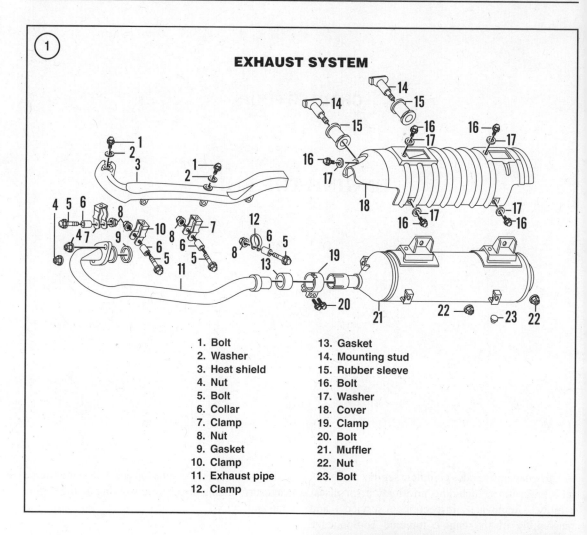

EXHAUST SYSTEM

1. Bolt
2. Washer
3. Heat shield
4. Nut
5. Bolt
6. Collar
7. Clamp
8. Nut
9. Gasket
10. Clamp
11. Exhaust pipe
12. Clamp
13. Gasket
14. Mounting stud
15. Rubber sleeve
16. Bolt
17. Washer
18. Cover
19. Clamp
20. Bolt
21. Muffler
22. Nut
23. Bolt

4. Remove the exhaust pipe as follows:

   a. Remove the exhaust pipe mounting nuts (A, **Figure 4**) from the cylinder head.

   b. On FM/TM models, remove the rear fender brace retaining bolt (**Figure 5**) and move the brace out of the way.

   c. Remove the exhaust pipe (B, **Figure 4**) and gasket (**Figure 6**).

5. Refer to **Figure 1** to replace the heat shield. Tighten the heat shield mounting bolts to 22 N•m (16 ft.-lb.).

6. Install the exhaust pipe and muffler by reversing the preceding removal steps, plus the following:

   a. Install new gaskets (**Figure 6** and 13, **Figure 1**).

   b. Loosely install all of the exhaust pipe nuts and bolts. Tighten the exhaust pipe mounting

nuts and the muffler mounting bolts in the following order.

   c. Tighten the exhaust pipe mounting nuts (A, **Figure 4**) securely.

   d. Tighten the muffler clamp bolts (**Figure 2**) to 23 N•m (17 ft.-lb.).

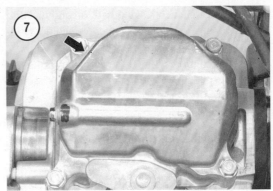

4

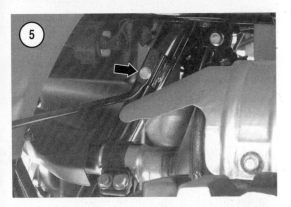

e. Tighten the muffler mounting nuts (**Figure 3**) securely.

f. Start the engine and check for exhaust leaks.

CYLINDER HEAD COVER

Removal/Installation

1. Remove the seat (Chapter Fifteen).

2. Disconnect the negative battery cable from the battery.

3. Remove the fuel tank and heat guard (Chapter Eight).

4. Remove the bolts, cylinder head cover (**Figure 7**) and gasket.

5. Remove the O-ring (**Figure 8**).

6. Clean and dry the cylinder head cover. Flush the cylinder head cover oil passages and holes (**Figure 9**) with compressed air.

7. Install the cylinder head cover by reversing the preceding removal steps, plus the following:

a. Replace the cylinder head cover gasket if it is leaking or damaged.

b. Lubricate a new O-ring with oil and install it into the groove in the rocker arm holder (**Figure 8**).

c. Tighten the cylinder head cover bolts securely in two or three steps and in a crisscross pattern.

ROCKER ARMS, PUSHRODS AND CYLINDER HEAD

The rocker arms, pushrods and cylinder head (**Figure 10**) can be removed with the engine mounted in the frame. Some of the following photographs show the engine removed from the frame for clarity.

Cylinder Head Removal

NOTE
Perform Steps 1-6 if the engine is mounted in the frame.

1. Remove the fuel tank and heat guard (Chapter Eight).

2. Remove the exhaust pipe as described in this chapter.

3. Remove the carburetor (Chapter Eight).

4. Remove the upper engine hanger bolts, bracket bolts and engine hanger (A, **Figure 11**).

5. Remove the bolts, intake manifold and O-ring (B, **Figure 11**).

6. Remove the cylinder head cover as described in this chapter.

7. Remove the timing hole cap (**Figure 12**) and O-ring.

8. Remove the spark plug and ground it against the cylinder head.

9. Position the engine at TDC on its compression stroke as follows:

a. Slowly pull the recoil starter and align the flywheel T mark with the index mark on the rear crankcase cover (**Figure 13**).

b. Make sure the piston is at TDC on its compression stroke by moving both rocker arms by hand; both rocker arms should have some free play. If both rocker arms are tight, turn the crankshaft one full turn and realign the flywheel T mark with the index mark. Make sure both rocker arms are loose.

10. Remove the cylinder head 6 mm bolts (**Figure 14**).

11. Loosen the cylinder head acorn nuts (A, **Figure 15**) and rocker arm holder bolt (B) in two or three steps following a crisscross pattern. Remove the fasteners and washers.

12. Remove the rocker arm assembly (C, **Figure 15**).

13. Remove the two dowel pins (A, **Figure 16**).

NOTE
*Identify the two pushrods (**Figure 17**) so they can be installed in their original positions.*

14. Remove the two pushrods (B, **Figure 16**).

15. Remove the cylinder head. If the head is stuck, tap the head with a plastic mallet to break it loose.

16. Remove the cylinder head gasket and dowel pins (**Figure 18**).

Rocker Arm Holder Disassembly/Inspection/Reassembly

Refer to **Table 2** when measuring the rocker arm components in this section. Replace worn or damaged parts.

NOTE
Before removing the rocker arms in Step 1, mark the position of both rocker arms so they can be installed in their original position.

1. Remove the bolt (A, **Figure 19**), rocker arm shaft (B) and both rocker arms (C).

2. Clean and dry the rocker arm holder assembly. Flush all oil passages with compressed air.

⑩ **CYLINDER HEAD**

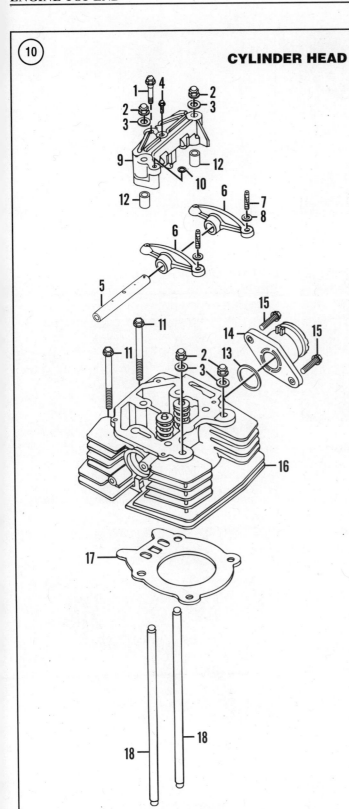

4

1. Bolt
2. Acorn nut
3. Washer
4. Bolt
5. Rocker shaft
6. Rocker arm
7. Adjuster
8. Nut
9. Rocker shaft holder
10. O-ring
11. Bolt
12. Dowel pin
13. O-ring
14. Intake tube
15. Bolt
16. Cylinder head
17. Head gasket
18. Pushrod

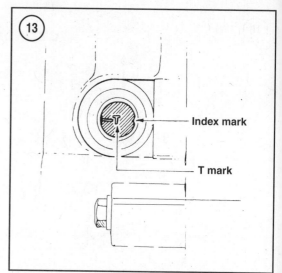

Index mark

T mark

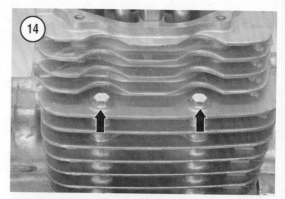

3. Inspect the push rod socket on the rocker arm (**Figure 20**). Check for cracks, uneven wear or signs of heat damage.

4. Inspect the valve adjuster pads (**Figure 20**) for flat spots, cracks or other damage. Inspect the locknuts for damage or rounded hex corners.

5. Inspect the rocker arm shaft (**Figure 20**) for scoring, cracks or other damage, and replace it if necessary.

6. Measure the rocker arm bore inside diameter (**Figure 20**) with a snap gauge. Measure the snap gauge with a micrometer. If it is within specification, record the dimension and continue with Step 7.

7. Measure the rocker arm shaft outside diameter (**Figure 20**) where both rocker arms ride. If it is within specification, record the dimension and perform Step 8.

8. Calculate the rocker arm-to-rocker arm shaft clearance as follows:

    a. Subtract the rocker arm shaft outside diameter (Step 7) from the rocker arm bore inside diameter (Step 6) to determine rocker arm-to-shaft clearance.

    b. Replace the rocker arms and/or the rocker arm shaft if the clearance is out of specification.

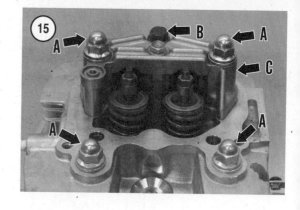

9. Lubricate the rocker arm bores and rocker arm shaft with engine oil.

NOTE
When using the original rocker arms, install them in their original mounting positions.

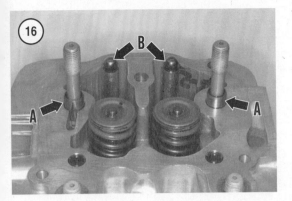

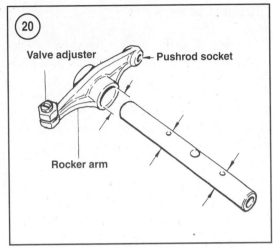

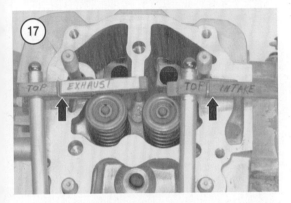

10. Install the rocker arms (C, **Figure 19**) into the rocker arm holder, then install the rocker arm shaft (B) with the screwdriver slot end facing out.

11. Turn the rocker arm shaft to align the hole in the rocker arm shaft with the bolt hole in the rocker arm holder. Install the rocker arm shaft mounting bolt (A, **Figure 19**) and tighten it to 7 N•m (62 in.-lb.).

12. Make sure both rocker arms pivot smoothly on the rocker arm shaft.

Pushrod Inspection

   Replace the pushrods (18, **Figure 10**) if they are excessively worn or damaged.

> *CAUTION*
> *While both pushrods are identical (same part number), used pushrods must be reinstalled in their original mounting positions. When cleaning and inspecting the pushrods, do not remove the identification marks made during removal.*

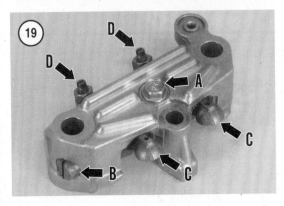

1. Clean and dry the pushrods.

2. Roll each pushrod on a flat surface and check for bending.

3. Check the pushrod ends for uneven wear, cracks or signs of heat damage (discoloration).

Cylinder Head Inspection

1. Remove all gasket residue from the cylinder head gasket surfaces. Do not scratch the gasket surface.

2. Without removing the valves, remove all carbon deposits from the combustion chamber (A, **Figure 21**). Use a fine wire brush dipped in solvent or make a scraper from hardwood. Take care not to damage the head, valves or spark plug threads.

> *CAUTION*
> *Do not clean the combustion chamber after removing the valves. The valve seat surfaces may be damaged, which may cause poor valve seating.*

3. Examine the spark plug threads in the cylinder head for damage. If damage is minor or if the threads are dirty or clogged with carbon, use a spark plug thread tap to clean the threads following the manufacturer's instructions. If thread damage is excessive, restore the threads with a steel thread insert.

> *CAUTION*
> *Aluminum spark plug hole threads can be damaged by galling, cross-threading and overtightening. To prevent galling, apply an anti-seize compound on the plug threads before installation and do not overtighten.*

> *NOTE*
> *When using a tap to clean spark plug threads, coat the tap with an aluminum tap cutting fluid or kerosene.*

4. After cleaning the combustion chamber, valve ports and spark plug thread hole, clean the entire head in solvent.

> *CAUTION*
> *If the cylinder head was bead-blasted, clean the head first with solvent, and then with hot soapy water. Residue grit that seats in small crevices and other areas can be hard to dislodge. Also, chase each exposed thread with a tap to remove grit trapped between the threads. Residue grit left in the engine will cause premature piston, ring and bearing wear.*

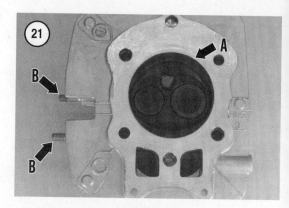

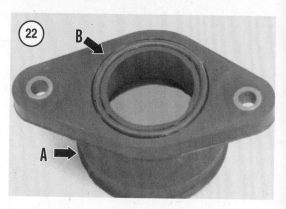

5. Examine the piston crown. The crown should not be worn or damaged. If the crown appears pecked or spongy-looking, also check the spark plug, valves and combustion chamber for aluminum deposits. If these deposits are found, the cylinder is suffering from excessive heat caused by a lean fuel mixture or preignition.

6. Inspect the intake tube (A, **Figure 22**) for cracks or other damage that would allow unfiltered air to enter the engine. Replace the intake tube O-ring (B, **Figure 22**) if it is excessively worn or damaged.

> *NOTE*
> *If the engine is installed in the frame, do not install the intake manifold until after the cylinder head is installed on the engine.*

7. Check the exhaust pipe studs (B, **Figure 21**) for damage. Replace the studs as described in Chapter One.

8. Inspect the combustion chamber (A, **Figure 21**) and exhaust port for cracks.

9. Place a straightedge across the gasket surface between the bolt holes (**Figure 23**). Measure warp

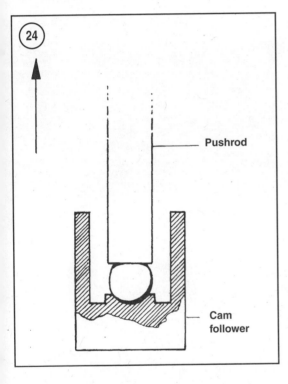

Pushrod

Cam follower

by inserting a feeler gauge between the straight-edge and cylinder head at each location. Measure warp between each set of bolt holes. **Table 2** specifies the maximum allowable warp. Warp or nicks in the cylinder head surface could cause an air leak and overheating. If the cylinder is warped, resurface or replace the cylinder head. Consult with a Honda dealership or a machine shop for this type of work.

10. Check the acorn nuts for thread damage. Discard the washers as new washers must be installed during installation.

11. To service the valves, refer to *Valves and Valve Components* in this chapter.

Cylinder Head Installation

1. Clean the cylinder head and cylinder mating surfaces of all gasket residue.

2. Install the two dowel pins (**Figure 18**) and a new cylinder head gasket. Note that the head gasket only fits properly in one direction.

3. Install the cylinder head. Be sure to seat the two dowel pins (**Figure 18**) and head gasket against the cylinder.

4. Lubricate the pushrod ends with engine oil, then install both pushrods (B, **Figure 16**) by seating them into the center of the cam follower grooves as shown in **Figure 24**.

> *NOTE*
> *When installing the original pushrods, make sure to install them in their original operating positions. Refer to the marks (**Figure 17**) made during removal.*

5. Install the two rocker arm holder dowel pins (A, **Figure 16**).

6. Loosen the two valve adjuster locknuts and loosen the adjusters (D, **Figure 19**).

7. If the engine was rotated after the pushrods and rocker arm holder were removed, reposition the engine at TDC by slowly pulling the recoil starter and aligning the flywheel T mark with the index mark on the rear crankcase cover (**Figure 13**).

> *CAUTION*
> *The engine must remain at TDC while the pushrods, rocker arm holder and cylinder head nuts are installed and tightened.*

8. Lubricate the rocker arm contact surfaces (**Figure 25**) with engine oil. Install the rocker arm holder (A, **Figure 26**) onto the crankcase studs. Push the rocker arm holder in place while positioning the two rocker arms onto the pushrod ends.

9. Lubricate the cylinder acorn head nuts, and the rocker holder bolt (B, **Figure 26**) with engine oil, then install them. Using a crossing pattern, tighten the cylinder acorn head nuts (C, **Figure 26**) to 39 N•m (29 ft.-lb.) and the rocker arm holder bolt to 30 N•m (22 ft.-lb.). Tighten them in 2-3 steps.

10. Install the 6 mm bolts (**Figure 27**) and tighten them to 12 N•m (106 in.-lb.).

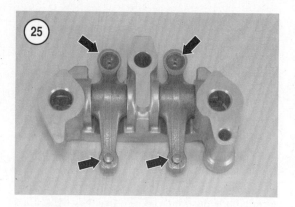

11. Adjust the valve clearance as decribed in Chapter Three.

12. Reverse Steps 1-9 in the *Cylinder Head Removal* section to complete installation.

13. Tighten the upper engine hanger bolt to 54 N•m (40 ft.-lb.) and the upper engine hanger bracket bolts to 32 N•m (24 ft.-lb.).

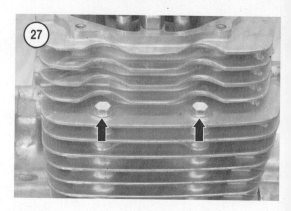

VALVES AND
VALVE COMPONENTS

A complete valve job, consisting of reconditioning the valve seats and replacing the valve guides, requires specialized tools and experience. This section describes service procedures on checking the valve components for wear and how to determine what type of service is required. Refer all valve service work requiring machine work and guide replacement to a Honda dealership.

Special Tools

A valve spring compressor is required to remove and install the valves. This tool compresses the valve springs so the valve keepers can be released from the valve stem. Do not attempt to remove or install the valves without a valve spring compressor. Because of the limited working area found in the typical ATV and motorcycle cylinder head, most automotive type valve spring compressors will not work. Instead, rent or purchase a valve spring compressor designed for ATV and motorcycle applications.

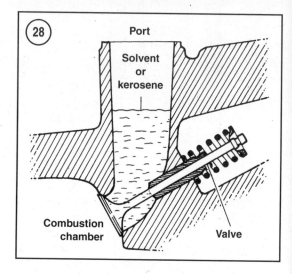

Solvent Test

For proper engine operation, the valves must seat tightly against their seats. Any condition that prevents the valves from seating properly can cause valve burning and reduced engine performance. Before removing the valves from the cylinder head, perform the following solvent test to check valve seating.

VALVE COMPONENTS

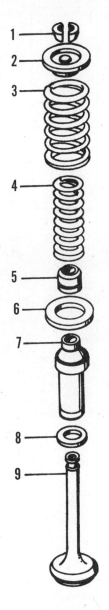

1. Valve keepers
2. Valve spring retainer
3. Outer valve spring
4. Inner valve spring
5. Valve stem seal
6. Spring seat
7. Valve guide
8. O-ring
9. Valve

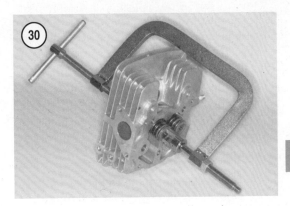

4

1. Remove the cylinder head as described in this chapter.

2. Support the cylinder so the exhaust port faces up and pour solvent or kerosene into the port (**Figure 28**). Then check the combustion chamber for fluid leaking past the exhaust valve seat.

3. Repeat Step 2 for the intake port and intake valve and seat.

4. If there is fluid leaking around a valve seat, the valve is not seating properly on its seat. The following conditions can cause poor valve seating:

    a. A bent valve stem.

    b. A worn or damaged valve seat (in the cylinder head).

    c. A worn or damaged valve face.

    d. A crack in the combustion chamber.

Removal

A valve spring compressor is required to remove and install the valves.

Refer to **Figure 29** for this procedure.

1. Remove the cylinder head as described in this chapter.

2. Install a valve spring compressor squarely over the valve spring seat with the other end of tool placed against valve head (**Figure 30**). Position the compressor head so the valve keepers can be reached and removed in Step 3.

NOTE
When compressing the valve springs in Step 3, do not compress them any more than necessary.

WARNING
Wear safety glasses or goggles when performing Step 3.

3. Tighten the valve spring compressor to remove all tension from the upper spring seat and valve keepers. Then remove the valve keepers (1, **Figure 29**) with pliers or a magnet.

4. Slowly loosen the valve spring compressor and remove it from the head.

5. Remove the valve spring retainer and both valve springs.

CAUTION
*Remove any burrs from the valve stem groove (**Figure 31**) before removing the valve; otherwise, the valve guide can be damaged as the valve stem passes through it.*

6. Remove the valve from the cylinder head.

7. Pull the valve stem seal (A, **Figure 32**) off the valve guide and discard it.

8. Remove the spring seat (B, **Figure 32**).

CAUTION
Keep all parts of each valve assembly together. Do not mix components from the different valves or excessive wear may result.

9. Repeat Steps 2-8 to remove the remaining valve.

Inspection

When measuring the valve components (**Figure 29**) in this section, compare the actual measurements to the specifications in **Table 2**. Replace parts that are out of specification or show damage as described in this section.

Refer to the troubleshooting chart in **Figure 33** when inspecting and troubleshooting the valves in this section.

1. Clean the valves in solvent. Do not gouge or damage the valve seating surface.

2. Inspect the contact surface (**Figure 34**) of each valve for burning. Minor roughness and pitting can be removed by lapping the valve as described in this section. Excessive unevenness in the contact surface is an indication that the valve is not serviceable.

3. Inspect the valve stems for wear and roughness. Measure the valve stem diameter for wear (**Figure 35**).

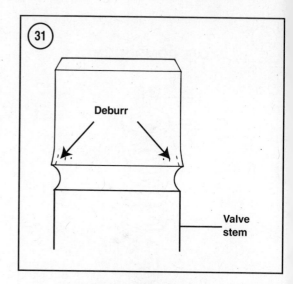

Deburr

Valve stem

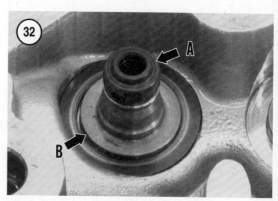

4. Remove all carbon and varnish from the valve guides with a stiff spiral wire brush before measuring wear.

NOTE
If the required measuring tools are not available, proceed to Step 7.

5. Measure each valve guide at its top, center and bottom inside diameter with a small bore gauge. Then measure the small hole gauge with a micrometer to determine the valve guide inside diameter.

6. Subtract the measurement made in Step 3 from the measurement made in Step 5. The difference is the valve stem-to-guide clearance. Replace any guide or valve that is not within tolerance. Refer valve guide replacement to a dealership.

7. If a small bore gauge is not available, insert each valve in its guide. Hold the valve just slightly off its seat and rock it sideways (**Figure 36**). If the valve rocks more than slightly, the guide is probably

(33)

VALVE TROUBLESHOOTING

Valve deposits

Check:
- Worn valve guide
- Carbon buildup from incorrect tuning
- Carbon buildup from incorrect carburetor adjustment
- Dirty or gummed fuel
- Dirty engine oil

Valve sticking

Check:
- Worn valve guide
- Bent valve stem
- Deposits collected on valve stem
- Valve burning or overheating

Valve burning

Check:
- Valve sticking
- Cylinder head warped
- Valve seat distorted
- Valve clearance incorrect
- Incorrect valve spring
- Valve spring worn
- Worn valve seat
- Carbon buildup in engine
- Engine ignition and/or carburetor adjustments incorrect

Valve seat/face wear

Check:
- Valve burning
- Incorrect valve clearance
- Abrasive material on valve face and seat

Valve damage

Check:
- Valve burning
- Incorrectly installed or serviced valve guides
- Incorrect valve clearance
- Incorrect valve, spring seat and retainer assembly
- Detonation caused by incorrect ignition and/or carburetor adjustments

4

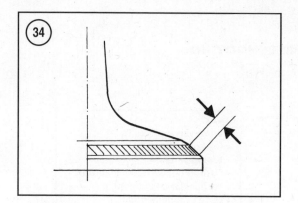

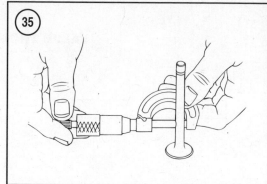

worn. However, as a final check, take the cylinder head to a dealership and have the valve guides measured.

8. Check the inner and outer valve springs as follows:

    a. Check each valve spring for visual damage.

    b. Use a square and check each spring for distortion or tilt (**Figure 37**). Distortion should be minimal.

    c. Measure the valve spring free length with a vernier caliper (**Figure 38**).

    d. Replace worn or damaged springs as a set.

9. Check the valve spring seats and valve keepers for cracks or other damage.

10. Inspect the valve seats (**Figure 39**) for burning, pitting, cracks, excessive wear or other damage. If worn or burned, have them reconditioned by a machine shop. Seats and valves in near-perfect condition can be reconditioned by lapping them with fine carborundum paste. Check as follows:

    a. Clean the valve seat and valve mating areas with contact cleaner.

    b. Coat the valve seat with machinist's blue.

    c. Install the valve into its guide and rotate it against its seat with a valve lapping tool. See *Lapping* in this section.

    d. Lift the valve out of the guide and measure the seat width (**Figure 40**) with a vernier caliper.

    e. The seat width for intake and exhaust valves should be within the specifications listed in **Table 2** all the way around the seat. If the seat width exceeds the service limit, have a dealership machine the seats.

    f. Remove all machinist's blue residue from the seats and valves.

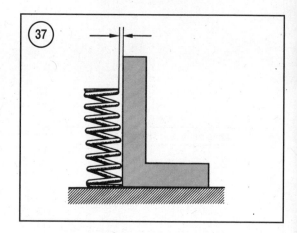

Guide Replacement

Refer valve guide replacement to a Honda dealership. Otherwise, a 5.5 mm valve guide reamer is required.

Seat Reconditioning

The valve seats are an integral part of the cylinder head and cannot be replaced separately. Valve seat

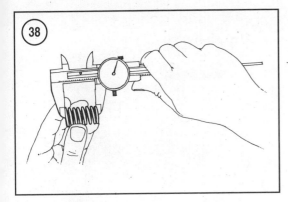

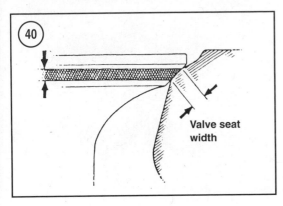

Valve seat width

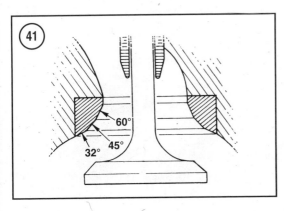

wear and damage can be repaired by cutting the seats. Refer this service to a Honda dealership. If the necessary tools and expertise are available, refer to **Figure 41** for the valve seat angles required. Refer to **Table 2** for valve seat width dimensions.

Lapping

Lapping the valves restores the valve seal without machining, if the amount of wear or distortion is not too great.

This procedure should only be performed after determining that the valve seat width and outside diameter are within specifications. See *Inspection* in this section.

1. Smear a light coat of fine grade valve lapping compound on the valve face seating surface.
2. Insert the valve into the head.
3. Wet the suction cup of the lapping stick and stick it onto the head of the valve. Lap the valve to the seat by spinning the lapping stick in both directions. Every 5 to 10 seconds, rotate the valve 180° in the valve seat. Continue this action until the mating surfaces on the valve and seat are smooth and equal in size.
4. Closely examine the valve seat in the cylinder head. It should be smooth and even with a smooth, polished seating ring.
5. Thoroughly clean the valves and cylinder head in solvent, then with hot, soapy water, to remove all lapping compound. Any compound left on the valves or the cylinder head will contaminate the engine oil and cause excessive wear and damage. After drying the cylinder head, lubricate the valve guides with engine oil to prevent rust.
6. After installing the valves into the cylinder, test the valve seat seal as described in *Solvent Test* in this section. If fluid leaks past the seat, remove the valve assembly and repeat the lapping procedure until there is no leaking. When there is no leaking, remove both valve sets and reclean the cylinder head assembly as described in Step 5.

Installation

1. Clean and dry all parts. If the valve seats were machined or lapped, or the valve guides replaced, thoroughly clean the valves and cylinder head in solvent, then with hot, soapy water, to remove all lapping and grinding compound. Any abrasive resi-

due left on the valves or in the cylinder head will contaminate the engine oil and cause excessive wear and damage. After drying the cylinder head, lubricate the valve guides with engine oil to prevent rust.

2. Install the spring seat (B, **Figure 32**).

3. Install new valve seals as follows:

> *NOTE*
> *New valve seals must be installed whenever the valves are removed.*

    a. Lubricate the inside of each new valve seal with molybdenum disulfide paste.

    b. Install the new valve seal over the valve guide and seat it into place (A, **Figure 32**).

4. Coat a valve stem with molybdenum disulfide paste and install it into its correct guide.

> *NOTE*
> *Install both valve springs so the end with the coils closest together (**Figure 42**) faces toward the cylinder head.*

5. Install the inner and outer valve springs.

6. Install the valve spring retainer.

> *WARNING*
> *Wear safety glasses or goggles when performing Step 7.*

7. Install the valve spring compressor (**Figure 30**). Push down on the upper valve seat and compress the springs, then install the valve keepers (**Figure 43**). Release tension from the compressor and make sure the keepers seat evenly around the end of the valve. Tap the end of the valve stem (**Figure 44**) with a soft-faced hammer to ensure the keepers are properly seated.

8. Repeat Steps 2-7 for the opposite valve.

9. After installing the cylinder head and rocker arm holder onto the engine, adjust the valve clearance. See Chapter Three.

CYLINDER

The alloy cylinder has a pressed-in cast iron cylinder liner. Oversize piston and ring sizes are available through Honda dealerships and aftermarket piston suppliers.

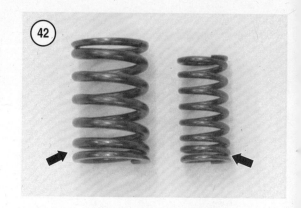

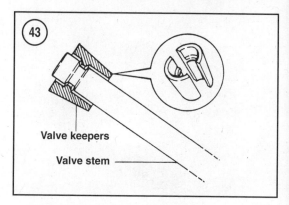

Valve keepers

Valve stem

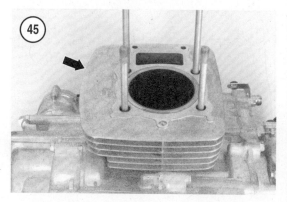

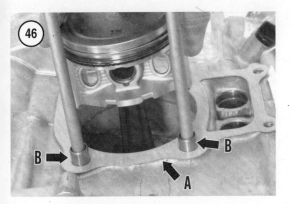

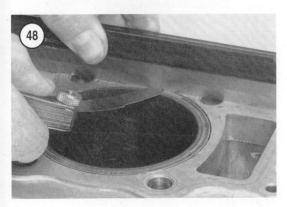

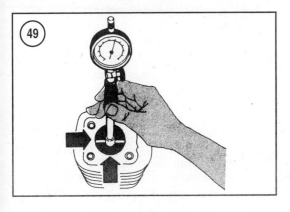

The cylinder and piston can be serviced with the engine mounted in the frame. Because of the engine's mounting position in the frame, the following photographs are shown with the engine removed for clarity.

Removal

1. Remove the pushrods and cylinder head as described in this chapter.
2. Loosen the cylinder by tapping around the perimeter with a rubber or plastic mallet.
3. Pull the cylinder (**Figure 45**) straight up and off the crankcase. Remove and discard the base gasket (A, **Figure 46**).
4. If necessary, remove the piston as described in *Piston and Piston Rings* in this chapter.
5. If necessary, remove the cam followers as described in *Camshaft* in this chapter.
6. If necessary, remove the two dowel pins (B, **Figure 46**).
7. Cover the crankcase opening to prevent objects from falling into the crankcase.

Inspection

Refer to **Table 2** when measuring the cylinder in this section.
1. Remove all gasket residue from the top and bottom cylinder gasket surfaces.
2. Wash the cylinder (**Figure 47**) in solvent. Dry it with compressed air.
3. Check the dowel pin holes for cracks or other damage.
4. Check the cylinder for warp with a feeler gauge and straightedge as shown in **Figure 48**. Check at several places on the cylinder and compare it to **Table 2**. If it is out of specification, refer service to a Honda dealership.

> *NOTE*
> *Unless the precision measuring equipment and expertise are available, have the cylinder bore measured by a Honda dealership or machine shop.*

5. Measure the cylinder bore with a bore gauge or inside micrometer (**Figure 49**) at the points shown in **Figure 50**. Measure in 3 axes: aligned with the piston pin and at 90° to the pin. Use the maximum

bore dimension to determine cylinder wear. Average the other measurements to determine taper and out-of-round. If any dimension is out of specification (**Table 2**), the cylinder must be rebored and a new piston and ring assembly must be installed. Refer this service to a Honda dealership.

NOTE
*To determine piston clearance, refer to **Piston and Piston Rings** in this chapter.*

6. If the cylinder is not worn past the service limit, check the bore for scratches or gouges. The bore still may require boring and reconditioning.

CAUTION
The soap and water described in Step 7 is the only solution that can wash the fine grit residue out of the cylinder crevices. Solvent and kerosene cannot do this. Grit residue left in the cylinder will act like a grinding compound and cause rapid and premature wear to the contact surfaces of the piston rings, cylinder bore and piston.

7. After servicing the cylinder, wash the bore in hot soapy water. This is the only way to clean the cylinder wall of the fine grit material left from the bore or honing job. After washing the cylinder wall, run a clean white cloth through it. The cylinder must be free of all grit and other residue. If the rag is dirty, rewash the cylinder wall again and recheck it with the white cloth. Repeat until the cloth comes out clean. When the cylinder is clean, lubricate it with engine oil to prevent the cylinder liner from rusting.

Installation

1. Make sure the top and bottom cylinder surfaces are clean of all gasket residue.

2. If the cam followers were removed, install them as described in *Camshaft* in this chapter.

3. If the pistons and rings were removed, install them as described in *Piston and Piston Rings* in this chapter.

CAUTION
Be sure to install and secure the piston pin circlips.

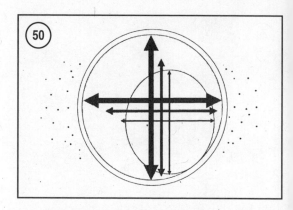

4. Install the two dowel pins into the crankcase (B, **Figure 46**).

5. Apply a non-hardening liquid gasket sealer to the seams of the crankcase mating surfaces shown in **Figure 51**.

CAUTION
Do not get any of the sealer on the piston skirt or cam followers. Otherwise, engine damage may occur.

6. Install a new base gasket onto the crankcase (A, **Figure 46**). Make sure all holes align.

7. Install a piston holding fixture (**Figure 52**) under the piston.

8. Lubricate the cylinder wall, piston and rings with engine oil.

9. Stagger the piston rings around the piston as shown in **Figure 53**.

NOTE
It is easier to install the cylinder over the piston by first compressing the rings with a ring compressor. As the cylinder is installed over the piston, the rings pass into the cylinder com-

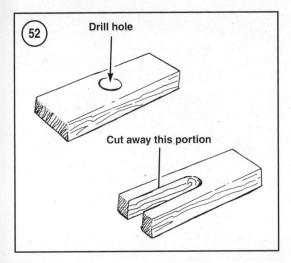

Drill hole

Cut away this portion

52

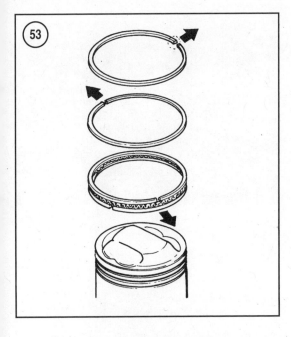

53

pressed and then expand out once they are free of the ring compressor. A hose clamp works well for this. Before using a ring compressor or hose clamp, lubricate its ring contact side with engine oil. When using a ring compressor or hose clamp, do not overtighten. The tool should be able to slide freely as the cylinder pushes against it.

10A. Compress the rings with a ring compressor or appropriate size hose clamp. Then align the cylinder with the piston and carefully slide it down past the rings. When all of the rings are installed in the

cylinder, hold the cylinder block and remove the ring compressor or hose clamp.

10B. When not using a ring compressor or hose clamp, align the cylinder with the piston and install the cylinder; compress each ring with your fingers as the ring enters the cylinder.

11. Remove the piston holding fixture and slide the cylinder all the way down.

12. While holding the cylinder down with one hand, operate the recoil starter. The piston must move up and down in the bore with no binding or roughness.

NOTE
If the piston does not move smoothly, one of the piston rings may have slipped out of its groove when the cylinder was installed. Lift the cylinder and piston up together so there is space underneath the piston. Install a clean rag underneath the piston to catch any pieces from a broken piston ring, then remove the cylinder.

13. Install the cylinder head and pushrods as described in this chapter.

PISTON AND PISTON RINGS

The piston is made of an aluminum alloy. The piston pin is made of steel and is a precision fit in the piston. The piston pin is held in place by a clip at each end.

Refer to **Figure 54**.

Piston Removal/Installation

1. Remove the cylinder as described in this chapter.

2. Block off the crankcase below the piston to prevent the piston pin circlips from falling into the crankcase.

3. Before removing the piston, hold the rod and rock the piston (**Figure 55**). Any rocking motion (do not confuse with the normal sliding motion) indicates wear on the piston pin, rod bore, pin bore, or a combination of all three.

WARNING
Wear safety glasses or goggles when removing the circlips in Step 4.

4

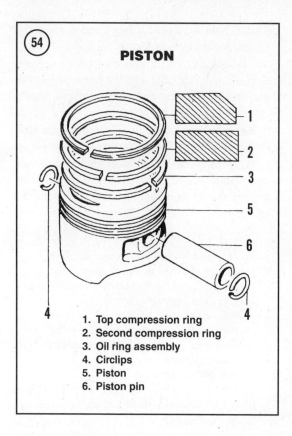

PISTON

1. Top compression ring
2. Second compression ring
3. Oil ring assembly
4. Circlips
5. Piston
6. Piston pin

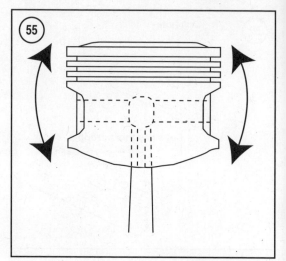

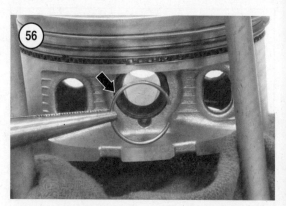

4. Remove the circlips from the piston pin bore grooves (**Figure 56**).

> *NOTE*
> *Discard the piston circlips. Install new circlips during reassembly.*

5. Push the piston pin (A, **Figure 57**) out of the piston by hand. If the pin is tight, use a homemade tool (**Figure 58**) to remove it. Do not drive the piston pin out as the force may damage the piston pin, connecting rod or piston.

6. Lift the piston (B, **Figure 57**) off the connecting rod.

7. Inspect the piston as described in this chapter.

Piston Inspection

1. Remove the piston rings as described in this chapter.

2. Clean the carbon from the piston crown (**Figure 59**) with a soft scraper. Large carbon accumulations reduce piston cooling and result in detonation and piston damage.

> *CAUTION*
> *Do not wire brush the piston skirt.*

3. After cleaning the piston, examine the crown. The crown must show no signs of wear or damage. If the crown appears pecked or spongy-looking, also check the spark plug, valves and combustion

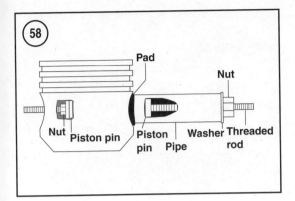

Pad

Nut

Nut Piston pin Piston Washer Threaded
pin Pipe rod

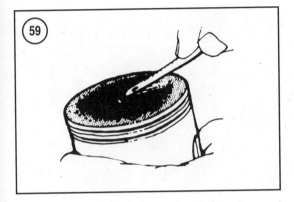

chamber for aluminum deposits. If these deposits are found, the engine is overheating.

4. Examine each ring groove (**Figure 60**) for burrs, dented edges or other damage. Pay particular attention to the top compression ring groove as it usually wears more than the others. Because the oil rings are bathed in oil, their rings and grooves wear less than compression rings and their grooves. If there is evidence of oil ring groove wear or if the oil ring is tight and difficult to remove, the piston skirt may have collapsed due to excessive heat. Replace the piston.

5. Check the piston oil control holes for carbon or oil sludge buildup. Clean the holes with wire.

6. Inspect the piston skirt (**Figure 61**) for cracks or other damage. If the piston shows signs of partial seizure (bits of aluminum on the piston skirt), replace the piston.

NOTE
If the piston skirt is worn or scuffed unevenly from side-to-side, the connecting rod may be bent or twisted.

7. Check the piston circlip grooves for wear, cracks or other damage. If a circlip groove is worn, replace the piston.

8. Measure piston-to-cylinder clearance as described under *Piston Clearance* in this chapter.

Piston Pin Inspection

Refer to **Table 2** when measuring the piston pin components in this section. Replace parts that are out of specification or show damage.

1. Clean and dry the piston pin.

2. Inspect the piston pin for chrome flaking, cracks or signs of heat damage.

3. Lubricate the piston pin and install it in the piston. Slowly rotate the piston pin and check for excessive play as shown in **Figure 62**. Determine piston pin clearance by performing the following steps.

4. Measure the piston pin bore diameter (**Figure 63**) in the piston. If it is within specification, record the dimension and continue with Step 5.

5. Measure the piston pin outside diameter. If it is within specification, record the dimension and continue with Step 6.

6. Subtract the measurement made in Step 5 from the measurement made in Step 4 to determine the piston-to-piston pin clearance. Replace the piston and/or piston pin if the clearance is excessive.

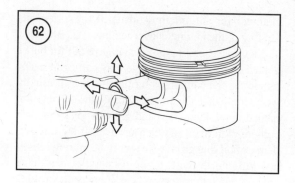

Connecting Rod Small End Inspection

1. Inspect the connecting rod small end (**Figure 64**) for cracks or signs of heat damage.
2. Measure the connecting rod bore diameter with a snap gauge (**Figure 65**). Then measure the snap gauge with a micrometer and check against the dimension in **Table 2**. If the bore wear is excessive, replace the crankshaft assembly. The connecting rod cannot be replaced separately.

Piston Clearance

Unless precision measuring equipment and expertise are available, have this procedure performed by a Honda dealership or machine shop.
1. Make sure the piston and cylinder walls are clean and dry.
2. Measure the cylinder bore with a bore gauge or inside micrometer (**Figure 49**) at the points shown in **Figure 50**. Measure the bore with the gauge aligned with the piston pin and 90° to the pin. This measurement determines the cylinder bore diameter. Write down the bore diameter measurement.
3. Measure the piston diameter with a micrometer at a right angle to the piston pin bore (**Figure 66**). Measure 15 mm (0.6 in.) from the bottom edge of the piston skirt (**Figure 66**). Write down the piston diameter measurement.
4. Subtract the piston diameter from the largest bore diameter; the difference is piston-to-cylinder clearance. If the clearance exceeds the service limit in **Table 2**, the cylinder must be bored and a new piston/ring assembly must be installed.

Piston Installation

1. Install the piston rings onto the piston as described in this chapter.

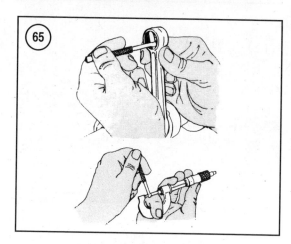

2. Coat the connecting rod bore, piston pin and piston with engine oil.
3. Slide the piston pin into the piston until its end is flush with the piston pin boss as shown in **Figure 67**.
4. Place the piston over the connecting rod so the IN mark (**Figure 68**) on the piston crown faces toward the intake side of the engine.
5. Align the piston pin with the hole in the connecting rod. Push the piston pin (A, **Figure 57**) through

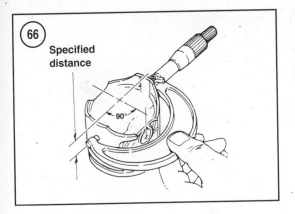

Specified distance

90°

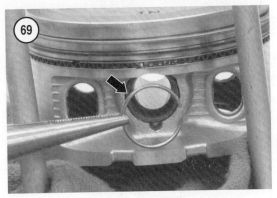

4

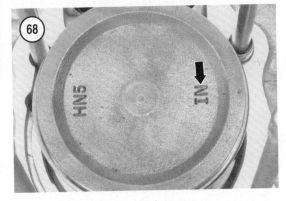

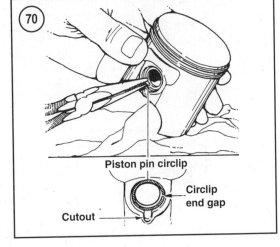

Piston pin circlip

Circlip end gap

Cutout

pletely. Turn the circlips so that their end gaps do not align with the cutout in the piston (**Figure 70**).

8. Install the cylinder as described in this chapter.

Piston Ring Inspection and Removal

A three-ring type piston and ring assembly is used (**Figure 71**). The top and second rings are compression rings. The lower ring is an oil control ring assembly consisting of two ring rails and an expander spacer.

1. Measure the side clearance of each compression ring in its groove with a flat feeler gauge (**Figure 72**) and compare the measurement with the specifications in **Table 2**. If the clearance is greater than specified, replace the rings. If the clearance is still excessive with the new rings, replace the piston.

WARNING
The edges of all piston rings are very sharp. Be careful when handling them to avoid cut fingers.

the connecting rod and into the other side of the piston and center it in the piston.

6. Cover the crankcase opening with clean rags.

WARNING
Wear safety glasses or goggles when installing the piston pin circlips in Step 7.

7. Install new piston pin circlips (**Figure 69**) in both ends of the piston pin bore (**Figure 70**). Make sure the circlips seat in the piston clip grooves com-

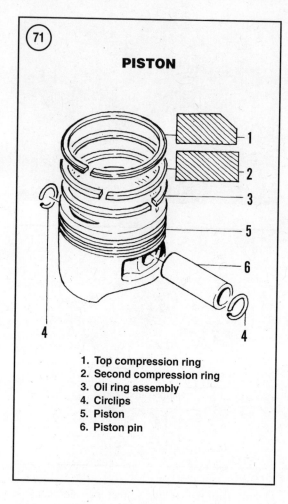

PISTON

1. Top compression ring
2. Second compression ring
3. Oil ring assembly
4. Circlips
5. Piston
6. Piston pin

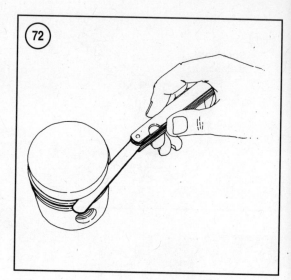

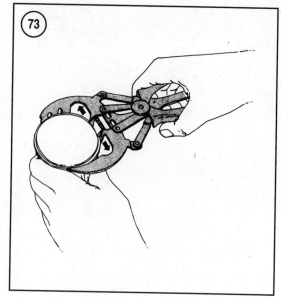

NOTE
Store the rings in order of removal.

2. Remove the compression rings with a ring expander tool (**Figure 73**) or spread the ring ends with your thumbs and lift the rings out of their grooves and up over the piston (**Figure 74**).

3. Remove the oil ring assembly (**Figure 75**) by first removing the upper (A, **Figure 76**) and then the lower ring rails. Then remove the expander spacer (B, **Figure 76**).

NOTE
When cleaning the piston ring grooves in Step 4, use the same type of ring that operates in the groove. Using a ring that is dissimilar to the groove will damage the groove.

4. Using a broken piston ring, remove carbon and oil residue from the piston ring grooves (**Figure 77**).

CAUTION
Do not remove aluminum material from the ring grooves as this will increase ring side clearance.

5. Inspect the ring grooves for burrs, nicks or broken or cracked lands. Replace the piston if necessary.

6. Check the end gap of each ring. To check, insert the ring into the bottom of the cylinder bore and square it with the cylinder wall by tapping it with the piston (**Figure 78**). Measure the end gap with a feeler gauge (**Figure 78**). Compare the end gap dimension with **Table 2**. Replace the

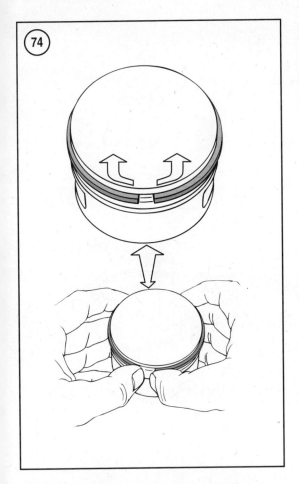

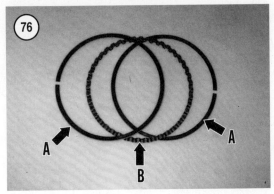

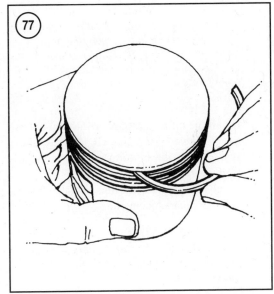

*ring rail end gaps only. Do not measure the expander spacer (B, **Figure** 76).*

7. Roll each ring around its piston groove (**Figure 79**) to check for binding. Repair minor binding with a fine-cut file.

Piston Ring Installation

1. Hone or deglaze the cylinder before installing new piston rings. This machining process will help the new rings seat in the cylinder. If necessary, refer this job to a Honda dealership or motorcycle repair shop. After honing, measure the end gap of each ring and compare it to the dimensions in **Table 2**.

rings if the gap is too large. If the gap on the new ring is smaller than specified, hold a fine-cut file in a vise. File the ends of the ring to enlarge the gap.

NOTE
When measuring the oil control ring end gap, measure the upper and lower

2. Clean the piston and rings with hot soapy water, then dry them with compressed air.

3. If the cylinder was honed, clean the cylinder as described under *Cylinder* in this chapter.

4. Clean the piston and rings in solvent. Dry them with compressed air.

> *NOTE*
> *The top and second compression rings are different. Refer to **Figure 71** to identify the rings.*

5. Install the piston rings as follows:

> *NOTE*
> *Install the piston rings—first the bottom, then the middle, then the top ring—by spreading the ring ends with your thumbs or a ring expander tool, then slip the rings over the top of the piston.*

a. Install the oil ring assembly into the bottom ring groove. First install the expander spacer, then the bottom and top ring rails (**Figure 75**).

b. Install the compression rings with their manufacturer's marks facing up.

> *NOTE*
> *On OEM pistons, the top compression ring is thinner than the second compression ring.*

c. Install the second compression ring.
d. Install the top compression ring.

6. Position the end gaps around the piston as shown in **Figure 71**. Make sure the piston rings rotate freely.

CAMSHAFT

The camshaft and chain tensioner assembly can be removed with the engine mounted in the frame. Because of the engine's position in the frame, the following illustrations show the engine removed for clarity.

Refer to **Figure 80**.

Camshaft Removal

1. Remove the cylinder as described in this chapter.

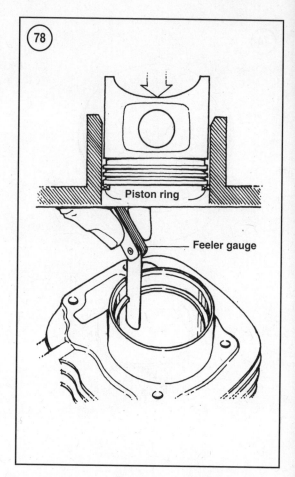

Piston ring

Feeler gauge

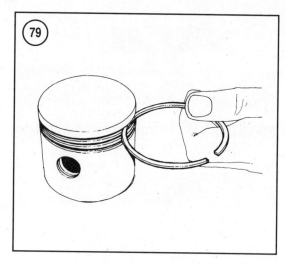

2. Remove the flywheel and starter driven gear (Chapter Five).

3. Remove the two bolts (A, **Figure 81**) and the cam chain tensioner assembly (B).

4

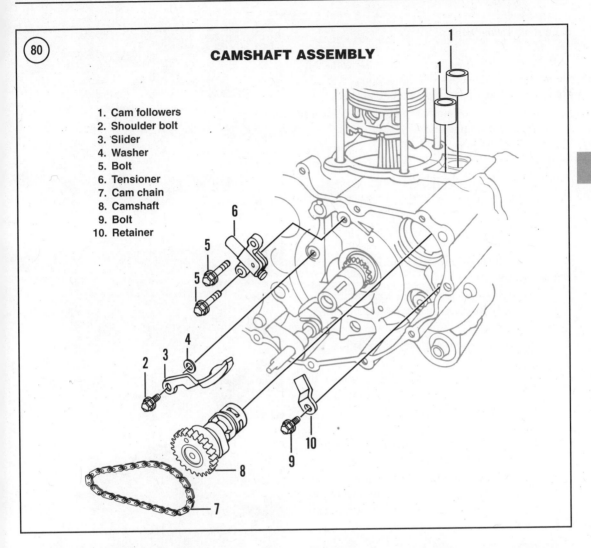

CAMSHAFT ASSEMBLY

1. Cam followers
2. Shoulder bolt
3. Slider
4. Washer
5. Bolt
6. Tensioner
7. Cam chain
8. Camshaft
9. Bolt
10. Retainer

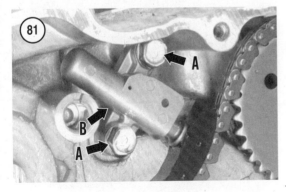

NOTE
*Mark the two cam followers (**Figure 82**) so they can be installed in their original positions.*

4. Remove the cam followers (**Figure 82**).

5. Remove the cam chain slider pivot bolt (A, **Figure 83**), slider (B) and washer.

6. Remove the bolt (A, **Figure 84**) and the camshaft bearing retainer (B).

7. Remove the camshaft and cam chain (**Figure 85**).

Camshaft Inspection

Refer to **Table 2** when measuring the camshaft components (**Figure 80**) in this section. Replace parts that are out of specification or damaged.

1. Clean and dry the camshaft assembly. Lubricate the bearing with engine oil.

2. Make sure the camshaft bearings (A, **Figure 86**) fit tightly on the camshaft. If either bearing is loose, replace the camshaft assembly.

3. Turn the camshaft bearings (A, **Figure 86**) by hand. The bearings must turn without roughness, catching, binding or excessive play. If either bearing is damaged, replace the camshaft assembly.

4. Examine the cam lobes (B, **Figure 86**) for scoring or other damage.

5. Measure each cam lobe height with a micrometer (**Figure 87**). Replace the camshaft if either lobe is out of specification.

6. Check the decompressor cam operation as follows:

    a. Press on the decompressor cam as shown in **Figure 88**. The decompressor cam should move and lock above the exhaust base.

    b. Press on the opposite side of the decompressor cam. The decompressor lobe should move below the exhaust base.

7. If the camshaft, bearings or decompressor cam fail to operate properly or are excessively worn, replace the camshaft assembly. The bearings and decompressor cam are not available separately.

Cam Follower Inspection

Refer to **Table 2** when measuring the cam followers and cam follower bores in this section. Replace parts that are out of specification or damaged.

CAUTION
The cam followers must not be interchanged when they are cleaned in Step 1. Each cam follower should be installed in its original operating position.

1. Clean and dry the cam followers.

2. Inspect the cam followers (**Figure 89**) for scoring, cracks or other damage.

3. Inspect the cam follower bores in the crankcase for scoring, severe wear or other damage.

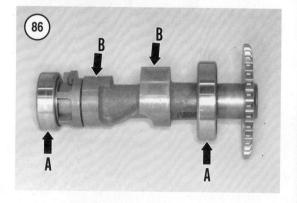

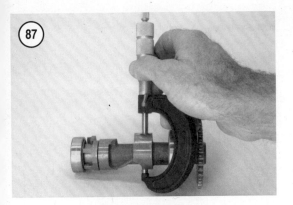

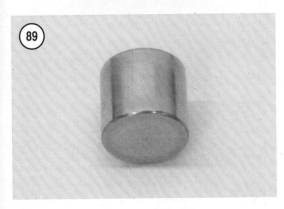

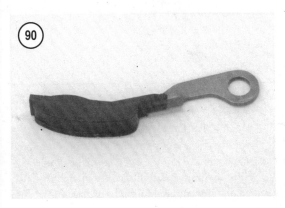

4. Measure the cam follower outside diameter. Record the dimension. Replace the cam follower if it is out of specification.

5. Measure the cam follower bore inside diameter. Record the dimension. Replace the crankcase half if the bore is out of specification.

NOTE
The front and rear crankcase halves can be replaced separately. See Chapter Five.

6. If the cam followers and cam follower bore inside diameters are within specifications, determine the cam follower-to-bore clearance as follows:

   a. Subtract the dimension in Step 5 from the dimension in Step 4. The result is cam follower-to-bore operating clearance. Repeat for both cam followers.

   b. If it is out of specification, replace the cam follower and then remeasure it. If the operating clearance is still out of specification, replace the crankcase half.

Camshaft Chain and Sprocket Inspection

1. Inspect the sprockets on the camshaft and crankshaft for broken or chipped teeth. Also, check the teeth for cracks or other damage. If the drive sprocket on the crankshaft is damaged, replace the crankshaft assembly; see Chapter Five.

2. Inspect the cam chain for severe wear, loose or damaged pins, cracks, or other damage. Replace it if it is damaged.

**Cam Chain Tensioner
Slipper Surface Inspection**

1. Examine the slipper surfaces on the tensioner slider (**Figure 90**) for excessive wear or damage. Replace it if necessary.

2. Remove all threadlock residue from the cam chain tensioner arm mounting bolt and crankcase bolt threads.

Cam Chain Tensioner

The adjustable cam chain tensioner (**Figure 91**) is a sealed unit. Do not attempt to disassemble it.

The plunger is spring-loaded. Ratcheting action allows the plunger to extend, but not retract.

1. Inspect the tensioner rod and housing for damage.

2. Check tensioner operation as follows. Attempt to push in the plunger; it should not move inward. Push in the ratchet stopper (A, **Figure 91**), then push in the plunger (B). The plunger should move freely in and out of the tensioner body. With the ratchet stopper released, the plunger should extend fully.

3. Lock the plunger in the retracted position as follows:

    a. Push in the ratchet stopper.

    b. Push in the plunger fully.

    c. Insert a paper clip or other piece of wire into the tensioner body hole (**Figure 92**) to hold the plunger in the retracted position.

Camshaft Installation

1. Rotate the crankshaft so the flywheel keyway points up in a direction that is parallel with the cylinder studs (**Figure 93**).

2. Apply molybdenum disulfide grease to the camshaft lobes.

3. Lubricate the camshaft bearings with engine oil.

> *NOTE*
> *Make sure the crankshaft does not rotate during Step 4.*

4. Install the camshaft chain onto the camshaft sprocket.

> *NOTE*
> *On 2002-on models, there are two punch marks on the camshaft sprocket. In Step 5 use the punch mark near the 350 number (A, **Figure 94**).*

5. Install the camshaft and chain so the sprocket tooth nearest the punch mark (B, **Figure 94**) aligns with the triangle cast in the crankcase (C).

6. Apply medium strength threadlock onto the camshaft retainer bolt. Install the retainer (B, **Figure 84**) and bolt (A). Tighten the bolt to 12 N•m (106 in.-lb.).

7. Install the tensioner slider (A, **Figure 95**), bolt (B) and washer (C). Apply medium strength threadlock onto the tensioner slider mounting bolt.

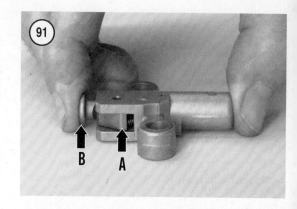

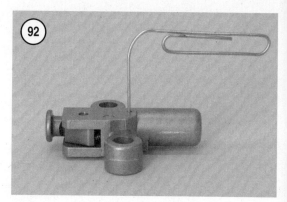

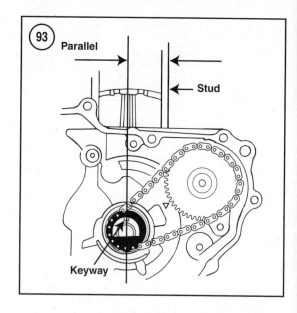

Make sure the slider pivots freely on the bolt shoulder. Tighten the bolt to 12 N•m (106 in.-lb.).

8. Lock the tensioner plunger in the fully retracted position as described in *Cam Chain Tensioner*.

9. Apply medium strength threadlock onto the two cam chain tensioner mounting bolts. Install the cam

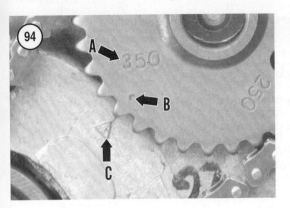

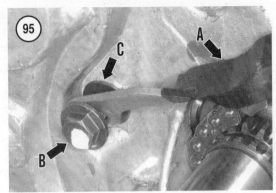

chain tensioner (B, **Figure 81**) and tighten the mounting bolts (A) securely.

10. Remove the locking pin from the tensioner so the plunger extends against the slider.

> *CAUTION*
> *Improper cam timing can cause severe engine damage. Before completing engine assembly, make sure the timing marks align as described in this section.*

11. Lubricate the cam followers with engine oil.

> *CAUTION*
> *The original cam followers must not be interchanged when they are installed in Step 12.*

12. Install each cam follower (**Figure 82**) in its original operating position. Refer to the marks made during removal. Install each cam follower with its open side facing up.

13. Install the starter driven gear and flywheel as described in Chapter Five.

14. Install the cylinder as described in this chapter.

Table 1 GENERAL ENGINE SPECIFICATIONS

Engine	Four-stroke, overhead valve pushrod engine
Displacement	329 cc (20.08 cu.-in)
Compression ratio	8.8:1
Cooling system	Air cooled
Valve timing	
Intake valve opens	8° BTDC
Intake valve closes	38° ABDC
Exhaust valve opens	40° BBDC
Exhaust valve closes	7° ATDC

Table 2 ENGINE SERVICE SPECIFICATIONS

	New mm (in.)	Service limit mm (in.)
Cylinder head warp	–	0.10 (0.004)
Cam lobe height		
Intake and exhaust	35.2995-35.4595 (1.38974-1.39604)	35.13 (1.383)
Cam follower outside diameter	22.467-22.482 (0.8845-0.8851)	22.46 (0.884)
Cam follower bore diameter	22.510-22.526 (0.8862-0.8868)	22.54 (0.887)
Cam follower-to-bore clearance	0.028-0.059 (0.0011-0.0023)	0.07 (0.003)
Rocker arm bore Inside diameter	12.000-12.018 (0.4724-0.4731)	12.05 (0.474)
Rocker arm shaft outside diameter	11.966-11.984 (0.4711-0.4718)	11.92 (0.469)
Rocker arm-to-shaft clearance	0.016-0.052 (0.0006-0.0020)	0.08 (0.003)
(continued)		

Table 2 ENGINE SERVICE SPECIFICATIONS (continued)

	New mm (in.)	Service limit mm (in.)
Valve clearance	0.15 (0.006)	–
Valve stem diameter		
Intake	5.475-5.490 (0.2156-0.2161)	5.45 (0.215)
Exhaust	5.455-5.470 (0.2148-0.2154)	5.43 (0.214)
Valve guide inside diameter	5.500-5.512 (0.2165-0.2170)	5.525 (0.2177)
Valve stem-to-guide clearance		
Intake	0.010-0.037 (0.0004-0.0015)	0.12 (0.005)
Exhaust	0.030-0.057 (0.0012-0.0022)	0.14 (0.006)
Valve seat width	1.2 (0.05)	–
Valve spring free length		
Inner	36.95 (1.455)	36.94 (1.454)
Outer	41.67 (1.640)	40.42 (1.591)
Cylinder bore diameter		
(standard bore)	78.500-78.510 (3.0905-3.0910)	78.60 (3.094)
Cylinder out of round	–	0.10 (0.004)
Cylinder taper	–	0.10 (0.004)
Cylinder warp	–	0.10 (0.004)
Piston diameter (standard piston)	78.465-78.485 (3.0892-3.0900)	78.43 (3.088)
Piston measuring point	See text	–
Piston-to-cylinder clearance	0.015-0.045 (0.0006-0.0018)	0.10 (0.004)
Piston pin bore diameter	17.002-17.008 (0.6694-0.6696)	17.04 (0.671)
Piston pin outside diameter	16.994-17.000 (0.6691-0.6693)	17.96 (0.668)
Piston-to-piston pin clearance	0.002-0.014 (0.0001-0.0006)	0.12 (0.005)
Piston ring side clearance		
Top compression ring	0.03-0.06 (0.001-0.002)	0.09 (0.004)
Second compression ring	0.015-0.045 (0.0006-0.0018)	0.09 (0.004)
Piston ring end gap		
Top compression ring	0.15-0.30 (0.006-0.012)	0.5 (0.020)
Second compression ring	0.30-0.45 (0.012-0.018)	0.6 (0.024)
Oil ring (side rails)	0.20-0.70 (0.008-0.028)	–
Connecting small end inside diameter	17.016-17.034 (0.6699-0.6706)	17.10 (0.673)
Connecting rod-to-piston pin clearance	0.016-0.040 (0.0006-0.0016)	0.06 (0.002)

Table 3 ENGINE TORQUE SPECIFICATIONS

	N•m	in.-lb.	ft.-lb.
Camshaft retainer bolt	12	106	–
Cam chain tensioner mounting bolt	12	106	–
Cylinder head acorn nuts	39	–	29
Cylinder head 6 mm bolts	12	106	–
Exhaust system			
Muffler clamp bolts	23	–	17
Heat shield bolts	22	–	16
Rocker arm holder bolt	30	–	22
Rocker arm shaft mounting bolt	7	62	–
Upper engine hanger bolt	54	–	40
Upper engine hanger bracket bolt	32	–	24

CHAPTER FIVE

ENGINE LOWER END

This chapter describes service procedures for the following lower end components:

1. Recoil starter.
2. Alternator cover.
3. Flywheel and starter clutch.
4. Gearshift linkage.
5. Reverse shaft assembly.
6. Oil pump.
7. Relief valve.
8. Oil strainer screen.
9. Crankcase and crankshaft.
10. Transmission shifting check.

One of the most important aspects of a successful engine overhaul is preparation. Before removing the engine and disassembling the crankcase, degrease the engine and frame. Have all the necessary hand and special tools available. Make sure the work area is clean and well lit. Identify and store individual parts and assemblies in appropriate storage containers.

Throughout the text there is frequent mention of the front and rear sides of the engine. This refers to the engine as it sits in the vehicle's frame, not as it sits on the workbench. Likewise, the references to the left and right sides of the engine refer to the engine as it is mounted in the frame.

Table 1 lists general engine specifications and **Table 3** lists oil pump service specifications. **Table 4** lists crankshaft service specifications. **Table 5** lists engine torque specifications. **Tables 1-4** are located at the end of this chapter.

SERVICING ENGINE IN FRAME

Many engine components may be serviced with the engine mounted in the frame. The following components can be serviced with the engine mounted in the frame:

1. Cylinder head.
2. Cylinder and piston.
3. Clutch.
4. Recoil starter.
5. Oil pump
6. Carburetor.

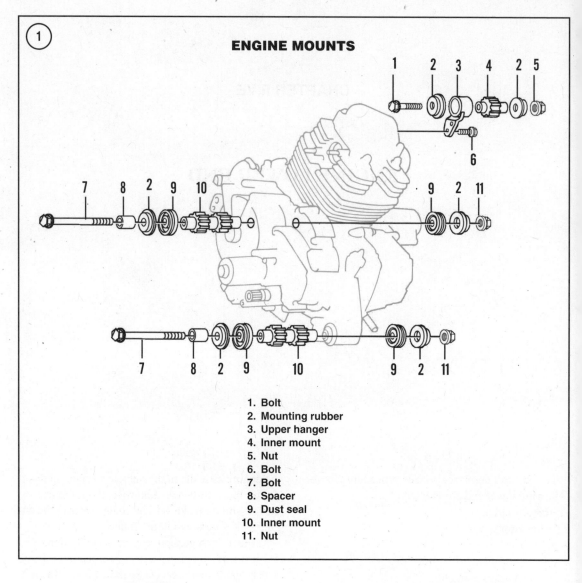

ENGINE MOUNTS

1. Bolt
2. Mounting rubber
3. Upper hanger
4. Inner mount
5. Nut
6. Bolt
7. Bolt
8. Spacer
9. Dust seal
10. Inner mount
11. Nut

ENGINE

Refer to **Figure 1** when removing and installing the engine in the frame.

Removal/Installation

1. Park the vehicle on a level surface and set the parking brake.

2. Before disassembling the engine, perform a compression test (Chapter Three) and leak down test (Chapter Two). Record the readings for future use.

3. Remove the seat (Chapter Fifteen).

4. Disconnect the negative battery cable from the battery (Chapter Three).

5. Drain the engine oil (Chapter Three).

6. Remove the fuel tank and heat guard (Chapter Eight).

7. Remove the fuel valve panel (**Figure 2**).

8. On FM and TM models, remove the clamp bolt (A, **Figure 3**), then remove the gearshift lever (B).

9. On FE and TE models, remove the center mud guards (Chapter Fifteen).

10. On FM and TM models, remove the rear mud guards (Chapter Fifteen).

11. Remove the front mud guards (Chapter Fifteen).

12. Remove the self-tapping screw under the front fender on both sides (**Figure 4**).

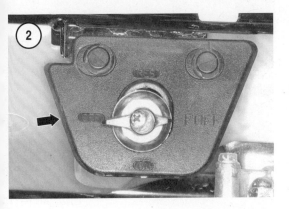

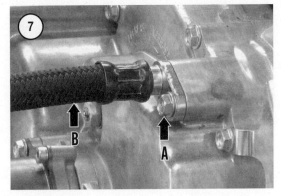

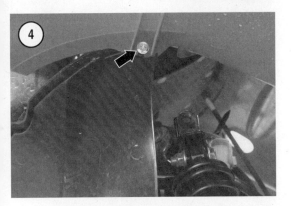

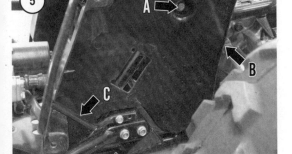

13. Remove the inner fender mounting bolt (A, **Figure 5**) and remove each inner fender (B).

14. Remove the mud guard brace mounting bolt (C, **Figure 5**) and remove the guard braces.

15. Remove the carburetor (Chapter Eight).

16. Remove the exhaust system (Chapter Four).

17. Remove the engine covers on both sides (**Figure 6**).

18. Disconnect the oil cooler hoses from the engine as follows:

    a. Remove the retaining bolt (A, **Figure 7**), then detach the oil hose (B) from each side of the engine. Cover the hose ends to prevent oil leaks and contamination.

    b. Remove the oil hose O-ring (**Figure 8**).

19. Remove the retaining nut (A, **Figure 9**) and disconnect the cable (B) from the starter.

20. Remove the bolt and disconnect the two ground cables (C, **Figure 9**) from the engine.

NOTE
Refer to Chapter Nine to identify and disconnect the electrical connectors in Step 21.

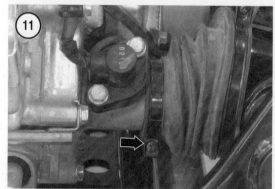

21. Disconnect the following electrical connectors:
   a. Speed sensor connector.
   b. Alternator/pulse generator connector.
   c. Neutral/reverse switch connector.
   d. Oil thermosensor connector.

22. Remove the brake pedal as described in Chapter Thirteen.

23. Remove the reverse control cable bracket mounting bolt (**Figure 10**), then disconnect the reverse control cable from the lever mounted on the engine.

24. On FE and TE models, remove the electric shift (ESP) reduction gears as described in Chapter Six.

25. Loosen the rear driveshaft boot clamp screw (**Figure 11**).

> *NOTE*
> *The right axle was removed for clarity in* ***Figure 12***. *It is not necessary to remove the axles in order to move the front differential forward.*

26. On FE and FM models, proceed as follows:
   a. Remove the lower front differential mounting bolt (**Figure 12**).

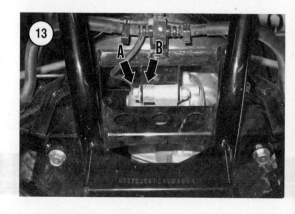

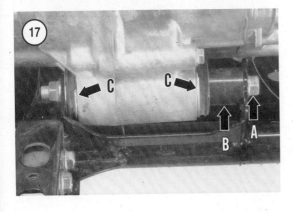

5

    b. Remove the upper front differential mounting bolt (A, **Figure 13**) and spacer (B).

    c. Remove the front differential front mounting bracket bolts (**Figure 14**).

    d. Push the front differential forward, then push the front driveshaft forward so it disconnects from the engine output shaft (**Figure 15**).

27. Disconnect the spark plug wire.

28. Remove the engine upper hanger bolt (A, **Figure 16**).

29. Remove the engine upper hanger bracket bolts (B, **Figure 16**) and the upper hanger assembly.

30. Support the engine with just enough force to remove weight from the lower engine hanger mounting bolts while removing them in the following steps. Be sure to protect the frame and engine cases.

31. Remove the lower engine hanger bolt (A, **Figure 17**) and spacer (B) on both sides.

NOTE
Table 1 *lists the approximate weight of an assembled engine. Two people may be required to safely remove the engine from the frame.*

32. Move the engine forward to disconnect the universal joint from the rear driveshaft. Tip the engine to the right to lower the cylinder head, then remove the engine from the left side of the frame. Support the engine on a workbench.

33. Install the engine in the frame by reversing the preceding steps while noting the following:

    a. Install a new O-ring onto the front engine output shaft (**Figure 18**).

    b. Lubricate the universal joint, engine and driveshaft splines with molybdenum disulfide grease.

c. Make sure the splines on the engine rear output shaft and the rear driveshaft universal joint fit properly. Cocking will prevent the engine from sitting correctly in the frame.

d. Replace damaged engine mount fasteners.

e. Apply an antiseize compound to the shoulders on each engine mount bolt. This will help to prevent rust and corrosion.

f. Install the lower rubber mounting dampers so the larger diameter side faces the engine (C, **Figure 17**).

g. Install the upper hanger rubber mounting dampers so the wide side faces the bracket.

h. Install the spacer on each lower hanger bolt so the spacer is in front of the engine (B, **Figure 17**). Tighten the lower engine hanger bracket bolts (A, **Figure 17**) to 54 N•m (40 ft.-lb.).

i. Tighten the upper engine hanger bracket bolts (B, **Figure 16**) to 54 N•m (40 ft.-lb.).

j. Tighten the upper engine hanger bolt (A, **Figure 16**) to 32 N•m (24 ft.-lb.).

k. On FE and FM models, tighten the front differential mounting bracket bolts (**Figure 14**) to 22 N•m (16 ft.-lb.).

l. On FE and FM models, tighten the front differential lower mounting bolt to 44 N•m (33 ft.-lb.).

m. On FE and FM models, install the spacer on the front differential upper mounting bolt as shown in B, **Figure 13**. Tighten the mounting bolt to 44 N•m (33 ft.-lb.).

n. Check the electrical connectors for corrosion. Pack the connectors with dielectric grease before reconnecting them.

o. Fill the engine with the recommended type and quantity of oil; refer to Chapter Three.

p. Check throttle operation (Chapter Three).

q. Check the reverse selector cable adjustment (Chapter Three).

r. Check brake pedal free play (Chapter Three).

RECOIL STARTER

The recoil starter can be removed and installed with the engine mounted in the frame. The following procedures are shown with the engine removed for clarity.

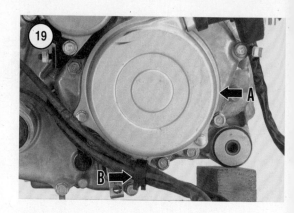

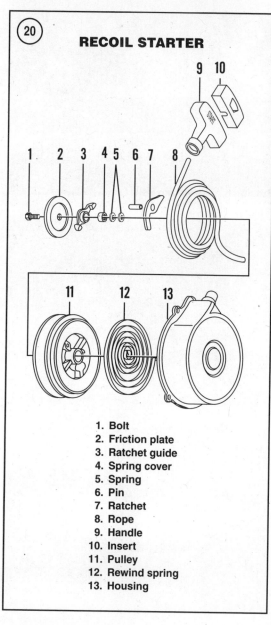

RECOIL STARTER

1. Bolt
2. Friction plate
3. Ratchet guide
4. Spring cover
5. Spring
6. Pin
7. Ratchet
8. Rope
9. Handle
10. Insert
11. Pulley
12. Rewind spring
13. Housing

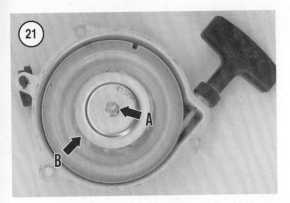

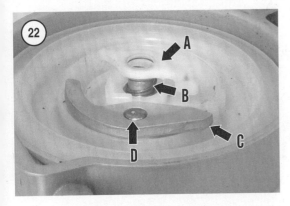

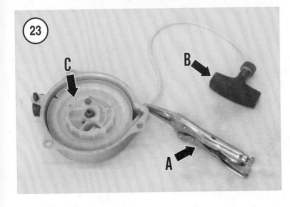

Removal/Installation

1. If the engine is mounted in the frame, remove any wires or cables from the guides mounted on the recoil starter assembly.

2. Remove the three bolts and the recoil starter assembly (A, **Figure 19**).

3. Install the recoil starter assembly by reversing removal while noting the following:

    a. Install the cable guide in the hole shown at B, **Figure 19**.

    b. Tighten the recoil starter assembly mounting bolts securely.

    c. Pull the recoil starter handle to check operation.

Disassembly

Refer to **Figure 20** for this procedure.

> *WARNING*
> *The rewind spring is under pressure and may jump out when the starter is serviced in the following steps. The spring is not very strong, but it may cause eye injury and is sharp enough to cut fingers and hands. Safety glasses must be worn when disassembling the starter.*

1. Remove the starter housing as described in this chapter.

2. Remove the bolt (A, **Figure 21**) and ratchet cover (B).

3. Remove the friction plate (A, **Figure 22**), spring seat and spring (B).

4. Remove the ratchet (C, **Figure 22**) and pivot pin (D).

5. Pull out the starter rope, then grip the rope with locking pliers (A, **Figure 23**) to prevent retraction back into the starter.

6. Untie the starter rope and remove the starter handle (B, **Figure 23**), then release the starter rope slowly and allow the drive pulley to unwind. Remove the drive pulley (C, **Figure 23**) and starter rope assembly.

7. Remove the starter rope from the drive pulley.

8. If necessary, remove the rewind spring from the housing as follows:

    a. Place the starter housing on the floor with the spring side facing down.

    b. Tap on the top of the housing with a plastic hammer while holding the housing firmly against the floor. The spring should fall out and unwind inside the housing.

Inspection

Replace worn or damaged parts as described in this section.

1. Clean and dry all parts. Do not clean the drive pulley, rope or ratchet cover in solvent.

5

2. Examine the starter shaft in the starter housing. Replace the starter housing if the starter shaft is severely worn or damaged.

3. Examine the drive pulley for severe wear or damage.

4. Examine the ratchet, pivot pin, guide and ratchet spring (**Figure 24**) for damage.

5. Examine the rewind spring for cracks or damaged ends.

6. Examine the starter rope for tearing, fraying or other damage.

7. Examine the ratchet cover for damage.

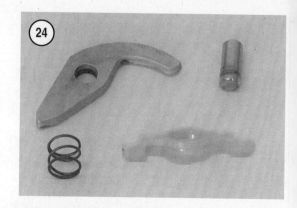

Assembly

1. If the rewind spring was removed, install it into the starter housing as follows:

> *WARNING*
> *Significant force is applied to the rewind spring when it is installed it in the following steps. Safety glasses and gloves must be worn when installing the rewind spring and assembling the starter assembly.*

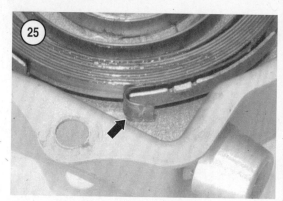

a. Before installing the rewind spring, wipe some grease onto a clean rag, then slide the spring against the rag to lubricate it with grease. Wipe off any excess grease.

b. Lubricate the starter housing shaft with the same type of grease.

c. Hook the outer end of the rewind spring onto the spring guide as shown in **Figure 25**.

d. Wind the rewind spring counterclockwise—working from the outside of the spring—into the starter housing (**Figure 26**).

2. Before installing the rope, check the rope ends for fraying. Apply heat with a heat gun (**Figure 27**) to defray loose rope ends. Do not overheat.

3. Install the rope as follows:

a. Tie a knot in one end of the rope (**Figure 28**).

b. Insert the rope through the hole in the drive pulley. Pull the rope tight so the knot enters the raised shoulder on the pulley.

c. With the ratchet side of the drive pulley facing up, wind the rope counterclockwise around the drive pulley as shown in **Figure 29**.

4. Grease the drive pulley shaft bore.

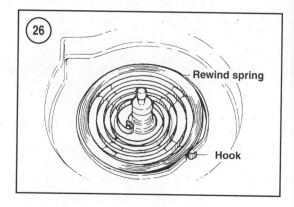

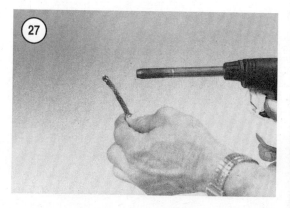

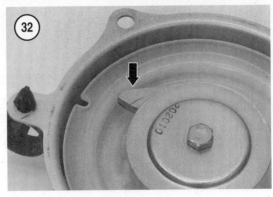

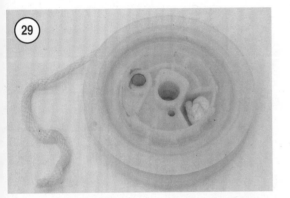

5. Install the drive pulley into the starter housing as follows:

    a. Align the hook in the bottom of the drive pulley with the end of the rewind spring and install the drive pulley into the housing.

    b. Rotate the drive pulley slightly counterclockwise until it drops into place, indicating that the hook in the drive pulley engages the rewind spring end.

6. Pull the rope end up into the drive pulley notch (**Figure 30**).

7. Rotate the drive pulley four turns counterclockwise and hold it in this position; do not let go of the drive pulley.

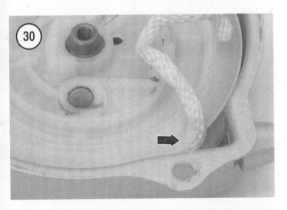

8. Feed the rope through the starter housing rope hole and secure it in place with a pair of locking pliers (A, **Figure 23**). Then slip the rope out of the drive pulley notch.

9. Install the starter handle onto the rope. Tie a knot in the end of the rope.

10. Remove the locking pliers and allow the drive pulley to unwind in the housing while pulling the rope into the housing.

11. Lubricate, then install the pivot pin (D, **Figure 22**) and ratchet (C) onto the pulley.

12. Install the spring (B, **Figure 22**), spring seat and ratchet guide (A). Note that the spring seat fits into the bottom of the ratchet guide (**Figure 31**).

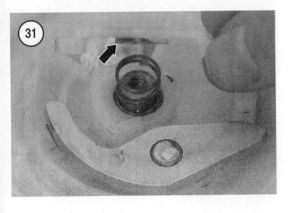

13. Install the friction plate (B, **Figure 21**). Lubricate the bolt threads with oil, then install the bolt (A).

14. Pull the starter handle and make sure the ratchet extends as shown in **Figure 32**. If the ratchet does not extend, remove the friction plate and reassemble the parts.

DRIVEN PULLEY

Removal/Installation

1. Remove the recoil starter assembly as described in this chapter.

2. Loosen and remove the driven pulley bolt (A, **Figure 33**). To prevent pulley rotation, insert a screwdriver or other tool between the flanges as shown in **Figure 34**.

3. Remove the driven pulley (B, **Figure 33**).

4. Inspect the driven pulley for cracks or other damage. Replace it if necessary.

5. Inspect the O-ring (A, **Figure 35**) on the bolt and replace it if it is damaged.

6. Install the driven pulley by reversing the preceding removal steps while noting the following:

   a. Apply engine oil to the driven pulley shaft and the seal in the alternator cover.

   b. Align the master spline on the end of the driven pulley (B, **Figure 35**) with the corresponding spline in the flywheel, then install the driven pulley.

   c. Lubricate the O-ring with engine oil and install it onto the driven pulley bolt.

   d. Secure the driven pulley with the same tool used during removal.

   e. Apply engine oil to the bolt threads and seating surface, then install the driven pulley bolt and tighten it to 108 N•m (80 ft.-lb.).

ALTERNATOR COVER

The stator coil assembly and ignition pulse generator are mounted onto the alternator cover.

Removal/Installation

1. Remove the engine as described in this chapter.

> *NOTE*
> *The starter gears may fall out of the rear crankcase cover when the alternator cover is removed in Step 2.*

2. Remove the bolts and the alternator cover (A, **Figure 36**).

3. Remove the gasket and, if necessary, the dowel pins (A, **Figure 37**).

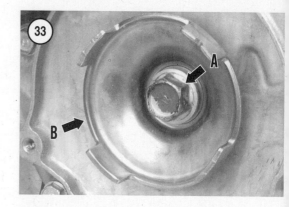

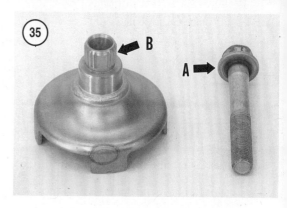

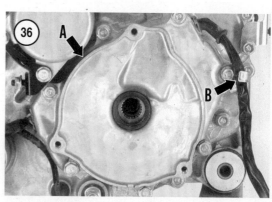

NOTE
The alternator cover will be pulled with considerable magnetic force toward the engine during installation. Make sure no wires or other objects can be trapped while installing the cover.

4. Install the alternator cover by reversing the preceding removal steps while noting the following:

    a. Apply Yamabond No. 4 (or an equivalent) onto the grommets in the crankcase cover (B, **Figure 37**) and in the alternator cover (A, **Figure 38**).

    b. Install and tighten the alternator cover mounting bolts securely. Note the position of the wire clamp (B, **Figure 36**).

Alternator Cover Oil Seal Inspection/Replacement

1. Inspect the alternator cover oil seal (**Figure 39**) for oil leaks, wear or damage.

2. Replace the alternator cover oil seal as follows:

    a. Pry the oil seal out of the cover with a wide-blade screwdriver. Pad the bottom of the screwdriver to prevent it from damaging the alternator cover.

    b. Pack the lips of the new oil seal with grease.

    c. Press in the oil seal with its flat side (**Figure 39**) facing out.

Disassembly/Reassembly

Remove the stator coil, ignition pulse generator or neutral/reverse switch assembly as follows:

1. Disconnect the connector from the top of the ignition pulse generator (A, **Figure 40**).

2. Remove the ignition pulse generator (A, **Figure 40**) and wire clamp (B) mounting bolts. Remove the ignition pulse generator.

3. Remove the stator mounting bolts (B, **Figure 38**), then remove the stator assembly.

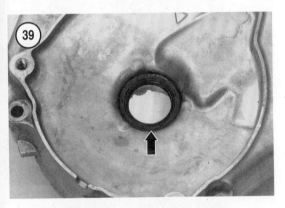

NOTE
There are two replacement stators available (ND and Mitsuba) for 2003 models. Make sure the outside diameter of the replacement matches the original.

4. Install by reversing the preceding removal steps while noting the following:

    a. Tighten the stator mounting bolts (B, **Figure 38**) to 10 N•m (88 in.-lb.).

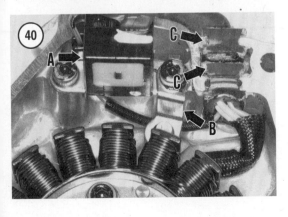

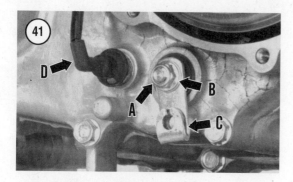

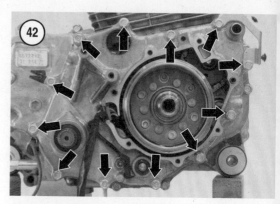

b. Remove all threadlock residue from the ignition pulse generator mounting bolt threads.

c. Apply a medium strength threadlock onto the ignition pulse generator mounting bolts. Install and tighten the bolts to 6 N•m (53 in.-lb.).

d. Make sure the ignition pulse generator wire is routed under the wire clamp (B, **Figure 40**) and ignition pulse generator.

e. Apply Yamabond No. 4 (or an equivalent) onto the grommets (C, **Figure 40**) and make sure they are properly seated in the notches in the alternator cover.

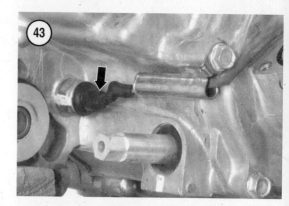

REAR CRANKCASE COVER

The rear crankcase cover houses the following components:

1. Gearshift spindle and gearshift arm A.
2. Final drive shaft seal.
3. Reverse spindle seal.
4. Neutral/reverse switch.
5. Vehicle speed sensor.

Removal/Installation

The rear crankcase cover can be removed with the flywheel installed on the engine.

1. Remove the alternator cover as described in this chapter.
2. Remove the starter motor (Chapter Nine).
3. Remove the speed sensor (Chapter Nine).
4. Remove the retaining nut (A, **Figure 41**), washer (B) and reverse selector arm (C).
5. Disconnect the neutral/reverse switch wire connector (D, **Figure 41**).
6. Remove the rear cover bolts (**Figure 42**).
7. Disconnect the thermosensor wire (**Figure 43**).
8. Remove the rear crankcase cover.

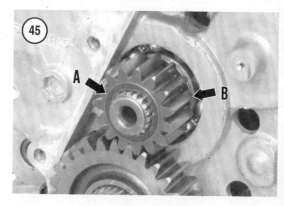

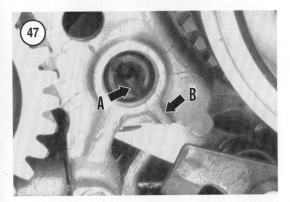

9. Remove the reduction gear shaft (A, **Figure 44**) and gear (B).

10. Do not lose the washer (A, **Figure 45**) on the final drive gear (B).

11. If necessary, remove the two dowel pins (**Figure 46**).

10. Remove all gasket material from the rear crankcase cover and engine mating surfaces.

11. Inspect the rear crankcase cover assembly as described in this section.

12. Install the rear crankcase cover assembly by reversing the preceding removal steps while noting the following:

    a. Pack all of the oil seal lips with grease.

    b. The transmission must be in neutral, which is indicated by the position of the slot on the shift drum (A, **Figure 47**). The slot must be aligned with the boss (B) on the crankcase.

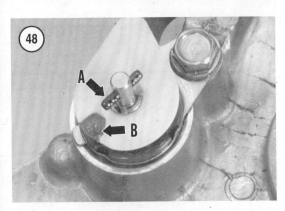

    c. The long end of the neutral/reverse switch pin (A, **Figure 48**) must align with the N mark (B), which positions the switch in neutral.

    d. Make sure the washer (A, **Figure 45**) is installed on the final drive gear (B).

    e. Thoroughly clean the mating surfaces of the crankcase and crankcase cover. Apply a bead of Yamabond No. 4 or equivalent to the rear crankcase cover mating surface as shown in **Figure 49**.

    f. Install the engine side cover bracket on the upper crankcase cover bolts (A, **Figure 50**).

    g. Install the speed sensor wire guide on the left crankcase cover bolt (B, **Figure 50**).

    h. Tighten the rear crankcase cover mounting bolts in a crossing pattern and in two or three steps. Tighten all cover bolts to 12 N•m (106 in.-lb.).

    i. Install the reverse control lever (C, **Figure 41**) with the slotted side facing out. Tighten the retaining nut securely.

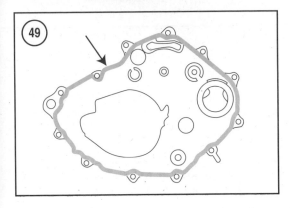

Inspection

1. Service the starter reduction assembly as described in *Flywheel and Starter Clutch* in this chapter.

2. Service the neutral/reverse switch as described in Chapter Nine.

3. Clean and dry the rear crankcase cover.

4. Inspect the final driveshaft (A, **Figure 51**) and reverse spindle (B) oil seals for leaks or damage. When replacing the oil seals, note the following:

   a. Remove the oil seal by prying it out of the cover with a wide-blade screwdriver.

   b. Check the oil seal mounting bore for cracks or other damage.

   c. Pack the lip of the new oil seal with grease.

   d. Install both oil seals with their flat side facing out (A and B, **Figure 51**).

FLYWHEEL AND STARTER CLUTCH

This section describes service to the starter reduction gears, flywheel and starter clutch assembly.

Refer to **Figure 52** when performing the following procedures.

Flywheel Puller

A flywheel puller is required to remove the flywheel from the crankshaft. Use Honda flywheel puller part No. 07725-00400000 (**Figure 53**).

Flywheel Removal

1. Remove the rear crankcase cover as described in this chapter.

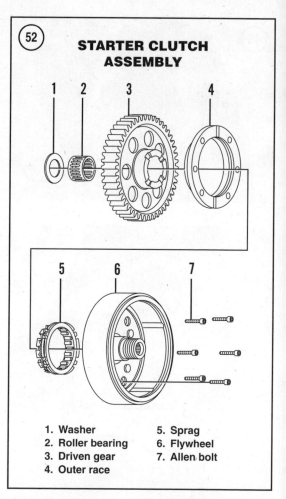

STARTER CLUTCH ASSEMBLY

1. Washer	5. Sprag
2. Roller bearing	6. Flywheel
3. Driven gear	7. Allen bolt
4. Outer race	

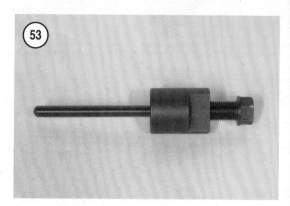

2. Remove the starter reduction gear shaft (A, **Figure 54**) and gear (B) if they were not previously removed.

NOTE
Apply grease to the puller bolt threads and the tip of the puller stem.

3. Install the flywheel puller into the flywheel.

> **CAUTION**
> *Do not try to remove the flywheel without a puller. Any attempt to do so will ultimately lead to some form of damage to the crankshaft and flywheel.*

> **CAUTION**
> *If normal flywheel removal attempts fail, do not force the puller. Excessive force will strip the flywheel threads, causing expensive damage. Take the engine to a dealership and have them remove the flywheel.*

4. Hold the flywheel and gradually tighten the flywheel puller (**Figure 55**) until the flywheel pops off the crankshaft taper.

5. Remove the puller from the flywheel.

6. Remove the flywheel and the starter clutch assembly (**Figure 56**).

7. Remove the roller bearing (A, **Figure 57**) and washer (B).

8. If necessary, remove the Woodruff key (C, **Figure 57**) from the crankshaft keyway.

9. Inspect the flywheel, starter clutch and starter reduction gear assembly as described in this section.

**Starter Clutch
Removal/Inspection/Installation**

Refer to **Figure 52** when servicing the starter clutch assembly.

1. Check the one-way clutch operation as follows:
   a. Place the flywheel and starter clutch on the workbench so the driven gear faces up as shown in **Figure 58**.

b. Hold the flywheel and try to turn the driven gear clockwise and then counterclockwise. The driven gear should only turn clockwise as viewed in **Figure 58**.

c. If the driven gear turns counterclockwise, the one-way clutch is damaged and must be replaced as described later in this procedure.

2. Remove the driven gear from the one-way clutch assembly.

3. Inspect the driven gear (**Figure 59**) for the following conditions:

a. Worn or damaged gear teeth.

b. Worn or damaged bearing shoulder.

c. Measure the outside diameter of the bearing surface and refer to **Table 2**.

4. Inspect the one-way clutch (**Figure 60**) for the following conditions:

a. Severely worn or damaged one-way clutch rollers.

b. Loose one-way clutch Torx bolts.

5. Replace the one-way clutch (**Figure 60**) as follows:

a. Secure the flywheel with a strap or band wrench.

b. Using an impact driver, remove the one-way clutch mounting bolts (**Figure 61**).

c. Separate the clutch outer race (A, **Figure 62**) and the sprag clutch (B).

d. Install the sprag clutch into the outer race so the flange on the sprag fits into the recess in the outer race as shown in **Figure 63**.

e. Apply a medium strength threadlock to the threads of each mounting bolt.

f. Install the one-way clutch mounting bolts finger-tight, then tighten them to 23 N•m (17 ft.-lb.).

6. Inspect the roller bearing (2, **Figure 52**). The rollers should be smooth and polished with no flat spots, cracks or other damage. Inspect the bearing cage for cracks or other damage. Replace the bearing if necessary.

7. Inspect the washer (1, **Figure 52**) for cracks, scoring or other damage.

Flywheel Inspection

1. Clean and dry the flywheel (**Figure 56**).

2. Check the flywheel for cracks or breaks.

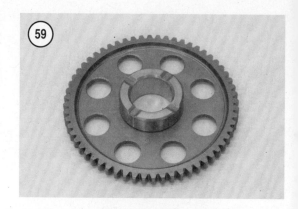

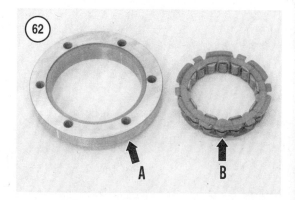

A   B

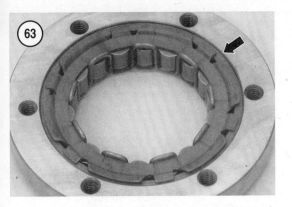

WARNING
Replace a cracked or chipped fly-
wheel. A damaged flywheel can fly
apart at high rpm, throwing metal
fragments into the engine. Do not
attempt to repair a damaged fly-
wheel.

3. Check the flywheel tapered bore and the crank-shaft taper for damage.

4. Replace damaged parts as required.

Starter Reduction Assembly Inspection

Replace parts that show damage as described in this section.

1. Clean and dry the gear and shaft (**Figure 64**).

2. Inspect the reduction gears for the following conditions:
    a. Excessively worn or damaged gear teeth.
    b. Excessively worn or damaged bearing sur-faces.

3. Inspect the reduction shaft for excessive wear or damage.

Flywheel Installation

1. Apply engine oil to the one-way clutch rollers and the driven gear shoulder.

2. To install the driven gear:
    a. Place the flywheel on the workbench so the one-way clutch faces up.
    b. Rotate the driven gear clockwise and slide it into the one-way clutch (**Figure 58**).

3. Apply engine oil onto the washer and needle bearing before installing them onto the crankshaft.

4. Install the washer (B, **Figure 57**) and the roller bearing (A) onto the crankshaft.

5. Install the Woodruff key (C, **Figure 57**) into the crankshaft keyway if it was removed.

6. Align the keyway in the flywheel with the Woodruff key in the crankshaft and install the fly-wheel (A, **Figure 65**).

NOTE
Performing Step 7 will seat the fly-
wheel on the crankshaft taper. If the
flywheel is not secured in this manner,
magnetic force will pull the flywheel
off the crankshaft when the stator coil
(alternator cover assembly) is in-
stalled.

7. Secure the flywheel to the crankshaft as follows:
    a. Temporarily install the recoil starter pulley (B, **Figure 65**) and the mounting bolt.
    b. Hold the flywheel and tighten the mounting bolt sufficiently to seat the flywheel on the taper.
    c. Remove the mounting bolt and the recoil starter pulley (B, **Figure 65**).

8. Install the reduction gear (B, **Figure 54**), then insert the shaft (A).

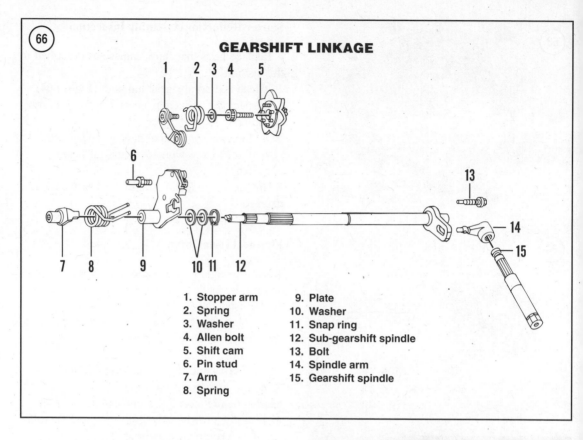

GEARSHIFT LINKAGE

1. Stopper arm
2. Spring
3. Washer
4. Allen bolt
5. Shift cam
6. Pin stud
7. Arm
8. Spring
9. Plate
10. Washer
11. Snap ring
12. Sub-gearshift spindle
13. Bolt
14. Spindle arm
15. Gearshift spindle

9. Install the rear crankcase cover as described in this chapter.

GEARSHIFT LINKAGE

The transmission gears are shifted manually on FM and TM models using a typical foot-operated gearshift lever. On FE and TE models, gears shifting is accomplished using the Electric Shift Program (ESP), which is described in Chapter Nine. FE and TE models are equipped with essentially the same gearshift components as the FM and TM models. On FM and TM models, the gearshift lever is attached to the gearshift spindle. On FE and TE models, the gearshift lever is absent and the gearshift spindle has a hex end so it may be used for emergency shifting purposes.

The gearshift linkage assembly is mounted on the front side of the engine, behind the clutch cover. While the linkage is accessible without removing the engine, servicing the gearshift spindle assembly will require engine removal.

Refer to **Figure 66** when servicing the gearshift linkage assembly in the following sections.

Removal

1. If the engine is installed in the frame, remove the gearshift pedal.

2. Remove the clutch cover (Chapter Six).

3. Remove the centrifugal clutch and change clutch assemblies (Chapter Six).

4. When servicing the gearshift spindle assembly, remove the rear crankcase cover as described in this chapter.

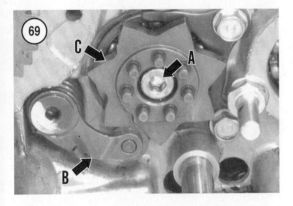

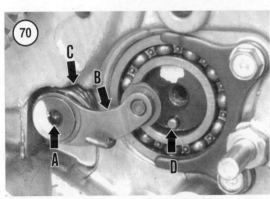

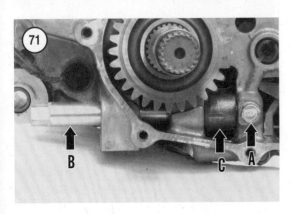

5. Remove the oil transfer pipe retaining bracket (A, **Figure 67**). Remove the retaining bolt (B, **Figure 67**), then remove the oil pipe (C).

6. Remove the gearshift plate assembly (A, **Figure 68**).

7. Remove the shift cam retaining bolt (A, **Figure 69**).

8. Pry or force the stopper arm (B, **Figure 69**) away from the shift cam (C) using a screwdriver, then remove the shift cam.

9. Remove the bolt (A, **Figure 70**), stopper arm (B), washer and return spring (C).

10. Remove the gearshift spindle retaining bolt (A, **Figure 71**) on the rear crankcase.

11. Withdraw the gearshift spindle (B, **Figure 71**), then remove the spindle arm (C).

> *NOTE*
> *The engine crankcase must be disassembled as described in this chapter for access to the sub-gearshift spindle (B, Figure 68).*

Inspection

Refer to **Figure 66** when inspecting the gearshift linkage assembly. Replace excessively worn or damaged parts as described in this section.

1. Clean and dry all parts.

2. Inspect the sub-gearshift spindle (B, **Figure 68**) for damaged splines and straightness. If necessary, disassemble the crankcase to remove the sub-gearshift spindle.

4. Inspect the drum shifter for wear, cracks or other damage.

5. Inspect the stopper arm assembly for:

   a. Damaged stopper arm.

   b. Worn or damaged roller.

   c. Weak or damaged return spring.

6. Inspect the gearshift plate assembly (**Figure 72**) for:

   a. Damaged gearshift arm.

   b. Weak or damaged return spring.

7. Inspect the gearshift spindle dust seal and needle bearings (installed in the front crankcase cover) for damage. Note the following:

   a. To replace the oil seal, refer to *Seals* in Chapter One. Install the oil seal with the closed side facing out.

   b. To replace the needle bearings, first remove the bearing with a blind bearing remover.

5

Then inspect the bearing mounting bores for cracks or other damage. Press in the new bearings.

8. Inspect the splines on the gearshift spindle and spindle arm (**Figure 73**).

9. If necessary, replace the gearshift spindle oil seal (**Figure 74**). Install the oil seal so the flat side is out.

Installation

1. If the gearshift spindle assembly was removed, install it as follows:

   a. Pack the oil seal lip (**Figure 74**) with a water-proof grease.

   b. Note the master splines on the spindle (A, **Figure 75**) and spindle arm and the end groove (B) on the spindle. Insert the gearshift spindle partway into the crankcase.

   c. Install the spindle arm so the arm is on the left side (**Figure 76**). The arm must engage the slot in the sub-gearshift arm.

   d. Align the punch mark on the spindle (A, **Figure 77**) with the casting indentation (B) on the spindle arm. This should align the master splines. Insert the spindle fully into the arm.

   e. Apply medium strength threadlock to the retaining bolt threads. Make sure the spindle is fully inserted, then install the retaining bolt (A, **Figure 71**) so the pin on the bolt end fits into the retaining groove on the end of the spindle.

   f. Tighten the retaining bolt securely.

2. Install the stopper arm assembly as follows:

   a. Install the bolt through the stopper arm (roller side), then install the washer onto the bolt (A, **Figure 78**).

   b. Hook the return spring (B, **Figure 78**) onto the stopper arm.

   c. Apply medium strength threadlock to the bolt threads, then install the stopper arm assembly as shown in **Figure 70**. Make sure the return spring is hooked onto the stopper arm as shown in **Figure 70**. Tighten the stopper arm bolt (A, **Figure 70**) to 12 N•m (106 ft.-lb.).

   d. Push the stopper arm down and release it. It should move under spring pressure with no binding.

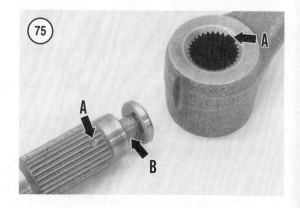

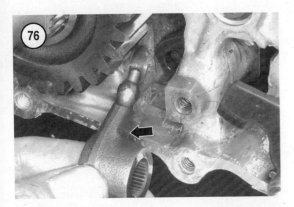

5

NOTE
If the stopper arm does not move, the bolt is not centered through the stopper arm, washer or spring. Loosen the bolt and reinstall it.

3. Install the dowel pin (D, **Figure 70**) into the shift drum hole if it was removed.

4. Pry the stopper arm away from the shift drum, then install the drum shifter cam (C, **Figure 69**) onto the dowel pin and shift drum. Release the stopper arm.

5. Apply medium strength threadlock to the cam bolt threads and install it (A, **Figure 69**). Tighten the bolt to 23 N•m (17 ft.-lb.).

6. Install the gearshift plate assembly (A, **Figure 68**). Align the master splines on the plate hub and sub-gearshift spindle. Fit the spring ends around the crankcase stud (C, **Figure 68**).

7. Install new O-rings onto the oil transfer pipe (**Figure 79**). Lubricate the O-rings with engine oil, then install the oil pipe (C, **Figure 67**), bolt (B) and bracket (A).

8. Install the rear crankcase cover as described in this chapter.

9. Install the change clutch and centrifugal clutch assemblies (Chapter Six).

10. Install the clutch cover (Chapter Six).

11. Install the engine as described in this chapter.

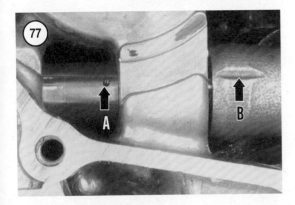

REVERSE SHAFT ASSEMBLY

The reverse shaft assembly consists of the reverse control lever and shaft assembly mounted on the back side of the engine.

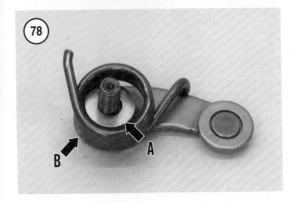

Removal/Inspection/Installation

1. Remove the engine from the frame as described in this chapter.

2. Remove the rear crankcase cover as described in this chapter.

3. On FM and TM models, remove the washer from the reverse shaft.

NOTE
*FE and TE models are shown in **Figure 80**. FM and TM models are similar.*

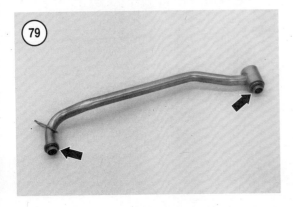

4. Hold down the reverse arm (A, **Figure 80**) with a screwdriver, then remove the reverse shaft (B) assembly.

5. On FE and TE models, the reverse shaft assembly is only available as a unit assembly. Inspect the reverse shaft assembly (**Figure 81**) for:

    a. Weak or damaged spring.

    b. Damaged reverse shaft.

6. On FM and TM models, inspect the reverse shaft assembly (**Figure 82**) for:

    a. Weak or damaged spring.

    b. Damaged reverse shaft.

    c. Damaged circlip groove.

7. Install the reverse shaft assembly by reversing the preceding removal steps while noting the following:

    a. When installing the reverse shaft (B, **Figure 80**), insert the end of the reverse arm (A) into the shift drum groove.

    b. Position the bottom leg of the spring against the crankcase bottom (**Figure 83**), then push the lower spring end inward so the spring end is flat against the crankcase.

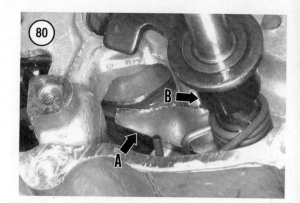

OIL PUMP

The oil pipes and oil pump assemblies are mounted on the front side of the engine. The oil pump consists of two stages. One side of the pump transfers oil from the bottom of the crankcase to an oil chamber in the crankcase. The remaining side of the pump forces oil from the oil chamber to the engine components.

The oil pump can be removed with the engine mounted in the frame. The following illustrations depict the engine removed for clarity.

Refer to **Figure 84**.

Removal/Installation

1. Remove the front crankcase cover as described in this chapter.

> *NOTE*
> *Clutch removal is not necessary, but the clutch was removed in the following illustrations for clarity.*

2. Remove the oil transfer pipe retaining bracket (A, **Figure 85**). Remove the retaining bolt (B), then remove the oil pipe (C).

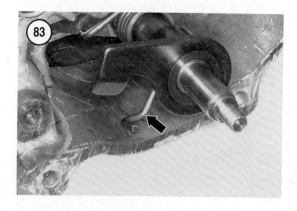

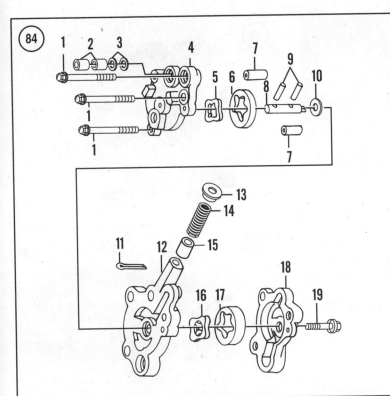

OIL PUMP

1. Bolt
2. Hollow dowel pin
3. Rubber seal
4. Body
5. Inner rotor
6. Outer rotor
7. Dowel pin
8. Pump shaft
9. Pin
10. Washer
11. Cotter pin
12. Body
13. Spring seat
14. Spring
15. Relief valve
16. Inner rotor
17. Outer rotor
18. Base
19. Bolt

5

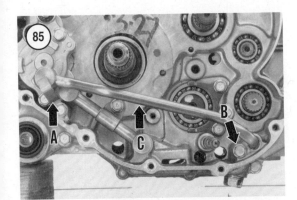

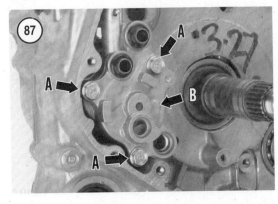

3. Remove the oil scavenge pipe retaining bolt (A, **Figure 86**), then remove the oil pipe (B).

4. Remove the oil pump retaining bolts (A, **Figure 87**), then remove the oil pump (B).

NOTE
If the oil pump is not going to be serviced, store it in a plastic bag.

5. Service the oil pump as described in this section.

6. Install the oil pump by reversing the preceding removal steps while noting the following:

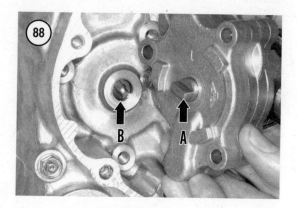

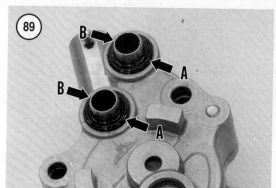

a. Align the shoulder on the end of the pump shaft (A, **Figure 88**) with the slot in the end of the balancer shaft (B) and install the oil pump.
b. Install and tighten the oil pump mounting bolts securely (A, **Figure 87**).
c. Install new rubber O-rings (**Figure 79**) on both oil pipes.

Disassembly

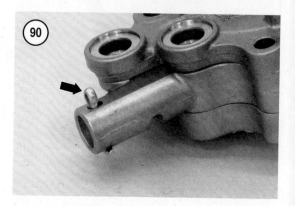

1. Remove the rubber seals (A, **Figure 89**) and hollow dowel pins (B) if they were not previously removed.
2. Remove the cotter pin (**Figure 90**), then remove the spring seat (A, **Figure 91**), spring (B) and relief valve (C).
3. Remove the bolt (A, **Figure 92**) and pump base (B).

> *NOTE*
> *If the rotors are not marked, mark them so they can be installed in their original positions.*

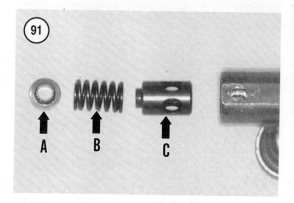

4. Remove the inner and outer rotors. See **Figure 93**.
5. Remove the drive pin (A, **Figure 94**) and thrust washer (B).
6. Remove the spacer from the pump body.
7. Remove the pump shaft (A, **Figure 95**), drive pin, dowel pins (B) and rotors (C) from the pump body.

Cleaning and Inspection

An excessively worn or damaged oil pump will not maintain oil pressure and should be repaired or replaced before it causes engine damage. Inspect

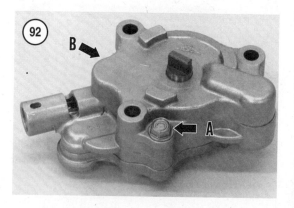

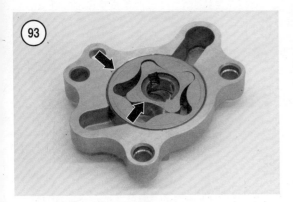

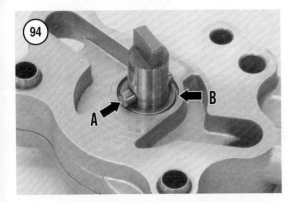

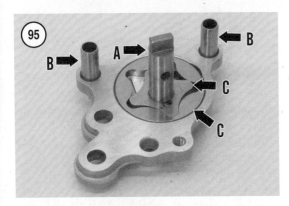

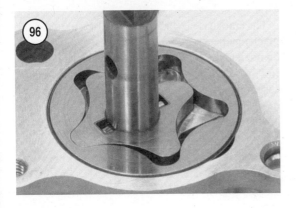

5

the oil pump carefully when troubleshooting a lubrication or oil pressure problem.

Refer to **Table 3** when measuring the oil pump components in this section. Replace parts that are out of specification or show damage as described in this section.

1. Clean and dry all parts. Place the parts on a clean, lint-free cloth.

2. Check the pump shaft for scoring, cracks or signs of heat discoloration.

3. Check the oil pump base, body and spacer for:
   a. Warped or cracked mating surfaces.
   b. Rotor bore damage.

4. Check the oil pump rotors for:
   a. Cracked or damaged outer surface.
   b. Worn or scored inner mating surfaces.

5. If the oil pump base, body, spacer and all rotors are in good condition, check the operating clearances as described in Steps 6-7.

NOTE
The pump rotors are sold separately. The pump base, body, spacer and pump shaft are available only as a new pump unit.

6. Install the respective inner and outer rotors and pump shaft into the pump body (**Figure 96**).

7. Using a flat feeler gauge, measure the clearance between the outer rotor and the oil pump body (**Figure 97**) and check it against the body clearance in **Table 3**. If it is out of specification, replace the outer rotor and remeasure it. If it is still out of specification, replace the oil pump assembly.

8. Using a flat feeler gauge, measure the clearance between the inner rotor tip and the outer rotor (**Figure 98**) and check it against the tip clearance in **Ta-**

ble 3. If it is out of specification, replace the inner and outer rotors.

9. Using a flat feeler gauge and straightedge, measure the clearance between the body surface and rotors (**Figure 99**) and check it against the side clearance in **Table 3**. If it is out of specification, replace the oil pump assembly.

Reassembly

1. If necessary, reclean the parts as described in the previous section. Lubricate the rotors, base, body and spacer with engine oil when installing them in the following steps.

2. Install the outer and inner rotors (C, **Figure 95**) into the pump body. When installing the original rotors, install them with their original side facing up as identified during disassembly.

3. Install the pump shaft (A, **Figure 95**) and drive pin into the inner rotor. The flat end of the shaft must be out.

4. Install the dowel pins (B, **Figure 95**) into the pump body.

5. Install the spacer onto the pump body.

6. Install the thrust washer (B, **Figure 94**) and drive pin (A).

7. Install the inner and outer rotors into the pump base (**Figure 93**). When installing the original rotors, install them with their original side facing up as identified during disassembly.

8. Mate the pump base with the body/spacer assembly. Make sure the pump shaft drive pin aligns with the slot in the inner rotor.

> *NOTE*
> *Be sure there are no gaps between the mating surfaces of the pump base, spacer and body. If a gap exists, disassemble the pump and find the cause.*

9. Install and tighten the bolt (A, **Figure 92**).

10. Turn the pump shaft. If there is any roughness or binding, disassemble the oil pump and check it for damage.

11. Lubricate the relief valve and spring with engine oil. Install the relief valve (C, **Figure 91**) so the stepped end is toward the spring. Install the spring (B, **Figure 91**) and spring seat (A). Push in the spring seat and install the cotter pin (**Figure 90**). Bend the cotter pin ends around the pump.

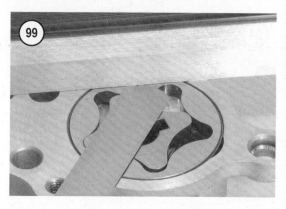

12. Store the oil pump in a plastic bag until installation.

OIL STRAINER SCREENS

Two oil strainer screens are installed inside the crankcase. Service the oil strainer screens whenever splitting the crankcase. Refer to *Crankcase and Crankshaft* in this chapter.

CRANKCASE AND CRANKSHAFT

The crankcase is made in two halves of thin-wall, precision diecast aluminum alloy. To avoid damage, do not hammer or pry on any of the interior or exterior projected walls. A liquid gasket seals the crankcase halves while dowel pins align the crankcase halves when they are bolted together. The crankcase halves can be replaced separately.

The crankshaft assembly consists of two full-circle flywheels pressed together on a crankpin. Two ball bearings in the crankcase support the crankshaft assembly.

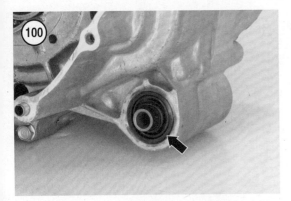

To install the crankshaft into the crankcase, a number of Honda crankshaft installation tools or their equivalents will be required. These tools and part numbers are called out during the crankshaft installation procedure in this chapter.

Crankcase Disassembly

This procedure describes disassembly of the crankcase halves and removal of the transmission and internal shift mechanism. Crankshaft removal is covered in a separate procedure.

Chapter Seven describes transmission and internal shift mechanism service procedures.

1. Remove all exterior engine assemblies as described in this chapter and other related chapters:
   a. Cylinder head (Chapter Four).
   b. Cylinder and piston (Chapter Four).
   c. Recoil starter (this chapter).
   d. Flywheel and starter clutch (this chapter).
   e. Starter motor (Chapter Nine).
   f. Clutch and primary drive gears (Chapter Six).
   g. Gearshift linkage (this chapter).
   h. Oil pump (this chapter).
2. Remove the engine dampers and bushings (**Figure 100**).
3. Remove the washer (A, **Figure 101**), drive gear (B) and driven gear (C) if they were not previously removed.

NOTE
To prevent loss and to ensure proper bolt location during assembly, draw the crankcase outline on cardboard, then punch holes to correspond with bolt locations. Insert the bolts in their appropriate locations after removing them.

4. Loosen and remove the rear crankcase bolts (**Figure 102**) in a crossing pattern. Install them in the cardboard.
5. Turn around the engine so the front side (clutch side) is accessible.
6. Loosen and remove the front crankcase mounting bolts (**Figure 103**) in a crossing pattern. Install them in the cardboard.

CAUTION
Perform this operation over and close to the work bench as the crankcase

The following procedure is a complete, step-by-step major lower end overhaul. When servicing only the transmission, the crankcase may be disassembled and reassembled without removing the crankshaft.

References to the front and rear side of the engine, as used in the text, refer to the engine as it sits in the frame, not as it sits on a workbench.

Special Tools

A press is required to remove the crankshaft from the crankcase.

halves may easily separate. Do not hammer on the crankcase halves.

> **CAUTION**
> *Do not pry between the crankcase mating surfaces when separating the crankcase halves. Doing so may cause an oil leak.*

7. Position the crankcase on wooden blocks so the crankshaft is vertical and the front side is up.

8. Tap on the front crankcase half using a soft-faced hammer while lifting it off the engine. Tap the transmission shafts if they bind with the crankcase and prevent disassembly.

9. If necessary, remove the dowel pins (**Figure 104**).

> **NOTE**
> *Steps 10-14 describe removal of the transmission assembly.*

10. Remove the washer (A, **Figure 105**) and sub-gearshift spindle (B).

11. Remove the output shaft (A, **Figure 106**) and washer (B).

12. Remove the shift fork assembly as follows:

   a. Remove the shift fork shaft (A, **Figure 107**) and shift drum (B).

   b. Remove the three shift forks (C, **Figure 107**).

13. Remove the shaft (A, **Figure 108**) and the reverse idler gear assembly (B).

14. Remove the mainshaft and countershaft assemblies (**Figure 109**) at the same time. See **Figure 110**.

15. If necessary, remove the crankshaft and balancer shaft as described in the following section.

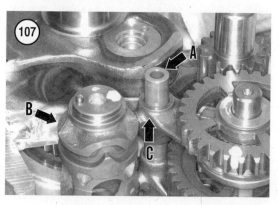

5

Crankshaft/Balancer Shaft Removal

Remove the crankshaft (A, **Figure 111**) and balancer shaft (B) as follows:

1. Support the rear crankcase in a press.

> *CAUTION*
> *When the rear crankcase is being supported in the press, make sure there is adequate room to press the crankshaft out without the connecting rod hitting against the press bed. If this happens, a connecting rod may be bent. Check the setup carefully before applying pressure to the crankshaft.*

> *CAUTION*
> *Catch the crankshaft and balancer shaft once the crankshaft is free of the rear crankcase half. Otherwise, these parts can fall to the floor, causing severe damage.*

2. Center the crankshaft under the press ram (**Figure 112**) and press the crankshaft out of the crankcase.

3. Remove the crankshaft and balancer shaft from the crankcase half.

4. Remove the rear crankcase from the press.

Crankcase Inspection

1. Remove all gasket residue from the crankcase mating surfaces.

> *CAUTION*
> *When drying the crankcase bearings in Step 3, do not allow the inner bearing races to spin. The bearings are not lubricated and damage may result.*

When drying the bearings with compressed air, do not allow the air jet to spin the bearing. The air jet can rotate the bearings at excessive speeds. This could cause a bearing to fly apart, causing personal injury.

2. Clean both crankcase halves and all crankcase bearings with solvent. Thoroughly dry them with compressed air.

3. Flush all crankcase oil passages with compressed air.

4. Lightly oil all of the crankcase bearings with engine oil before checking the bearings in Step 5.

5. Check the bearings for roughness, pitting, galling and play by rotating them slowly by hand. Replace any bearing that turns roughly or has excessive play (**Figure 113**).

6. Replace any worn or damaged bearings as described in *Crankcase Bearing Replacement* in this section.

NOTE
Always replace the opposing bearing at the same time.

7. Carefully inspect the cases for cracks and fractures, especially in the lower areas where they are vulnerable to rock damage.

8. Check the areas around the stiffening ribs, around bearing bosses and threaded holes for damage. Refer crankcase repair to a shop specializing in the repair of precision aluminum castings.

9. Check the threaded holes in both crankcase halves for thread damage, dirt or oil buildup. If necessary, clean or repair the threads with the correct size metric tap. Coat the tap threads with kerosene or an aluminum tap fluid before use.

10. Check the gearshift stopper pin (**Figure 114**) for looseness or damage. During installation, apply a threadlock to the bolt threads and tighten them to 22 N•m (16 ft.-lb.).

Crankcase Stud Replacement

The crankcase studs are different lengths. When replacing the studs, measure their length prior to removal.

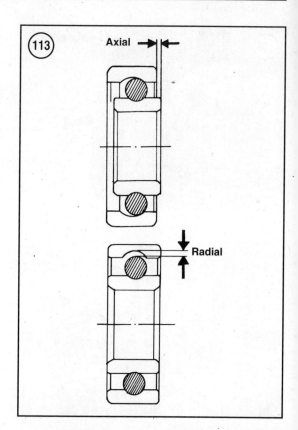

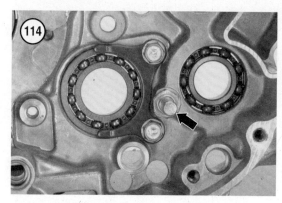

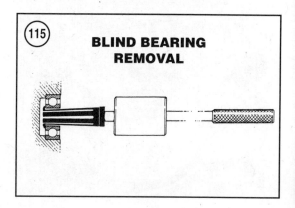

BLIND BEARING REMOVAL

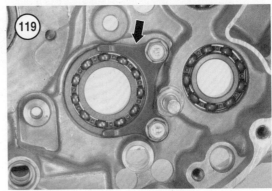

5

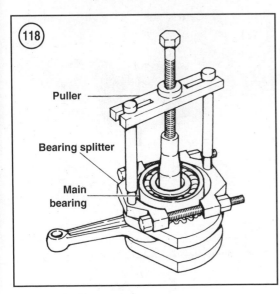

Puller

Bearing splitter

Main
bearing

Crankcase Bearing Replacement

When replacing bearings in the following steps, note the following:

1. Because of the number of bearings used in the front and rear crankcase halves, identify the bear-

ings before removing them. Identify each bearing by referring to its size code marks.

2. Before removing the bearings, note and record the direction in which the bearings size codes face for proper reinstallation.

3. Replace the bearings as described in *Bearing Replacement* in Chapter One. Use a blind bearing remover to remove bearings installed in blind holes (**Figure 115**).

4. Refer to **Figure 116** to identify the bearings installed in the front crankcase half.

    a. Crankshaft (A).

    b. Balancer shaft (B).

    c. Countershaft (C).

    d. Mainshaft (D).

    e. Shift drum (E).

    f. Final driveshaft (F).

5. Refer to **Figure 117** to identify the bearings installed in the rear crankcase half.

    a. Crankshaft (A).

    b. Balancer shaft (B).

    c. Countershaft (C).

    d. Mainshaft (D).

    e. Shift drum (E).

    f. Final driveshaft (F).

6. If the rear crankshaft bearing remained on the crankshaft, remove the bearing with a bearing splitter and bearing puller as shown in **Figure 118**. Press a new bearing into the rear crankcase half. Do not install the bearing onto the crankshaft.

7. On a bearing so equipped, remove the bolts (**Figure 119**, typical) securing the bearing retainer plate and remove the retainer plate. If bearing replacement is not required, check the retaining screws for tightness.

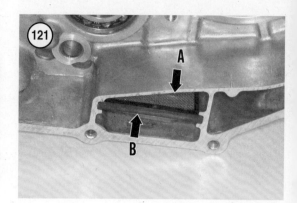

Oil Strainer Screens

Two oil strainer screens are installed inside the crankcase. Both screens are located in the front crankcase half (**Figure 120** and A, **Figure 121**). A strainer plate is located below the bottom strainer (B, **Figure 121**).

When the engine is disassembled, remove and clean the strainer screens and the strainer plate using solvent.

The strainer screens are tapered (**Figure 122**). Install the screen by inserting the thin edge first. Install the strainer plate so the hole is toward the crankcase mating surface (**Figure 123**).

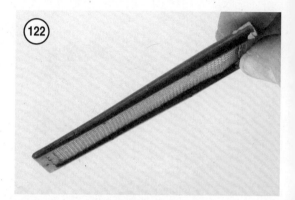

Crankshaft Inspection

Handle the crankshaft carefully while performing the following cleaning and inspection procedures. Individual crankshaft components are not available separately. If the crankshaft is excessively worn or damaged, or if any measurement is out of specification, replace the crankshaft as an assembly.

1. Clean the crankshaft thoroughly with solvent. Clean the crankshaft oil passageway with compressed air. Dry the crankshaft with compressed air, then lubricate all bearing surfaces with a light coat of engine oil.

2. Check the crankshaft journals for scratches, heat discoloration or other defects.

3. Check the flywheel taper, threads and keyway for damage.

4. Check the connecting rod big end for signs of damage, including bearing or thrust washer damage.

5. Check the connecting rod small end for signs of excessive heat (blue coloration) or other damage.

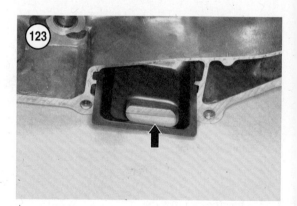

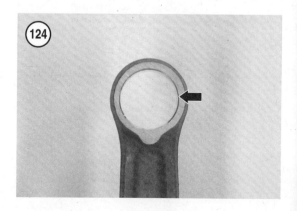

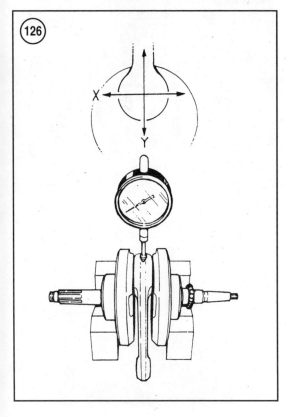

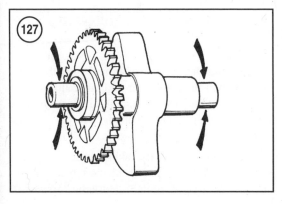

6. Measure the connecting rod small end inside diameter (**Figure 124**) with a snap gauge or an inside micrometer and check the measurement against the dimension in **Table 4**.

7. Slide the connecting rod to one side and check the connecting rod side clearance with a flat feeler gauge (**Figure 125**) and check it against the dimension in **Table 4**.

8. Place the crankshaft on a set of V-blocks or between lathe centers and measure runout with a dial indicator at the points listed in **Table 4**. If the runout exceeds the service limit in **Table 4**, take the crankshaft to a Honda dealership for service or replacement.

9. Place the crankshaft on a set of V-blocks and measure the connecting rod big end radial clearance with a dial indicator. Measure it in the two directions shown in **Figure 126** and compare the measurements to the dimension in **Table 4**.

Balancer Shaft Inspection

1. Inspect the balancer shaft bearing journals (**Figure 127**) for deep scoring, excessive wear, heat discoloration or cracks.

2. Examine the oil pump drive slot in the end of the balancer shaft for cracks or excessive wear.

3. Replace the balancer shaft if necessary.

Final Drive Shaft and Gear Inspection

1. Inspect the final drive shaft (**Figure 128**) for:
   a. Worn or damaged splines.
   b. Worn or damaged bearing surfaces.
   c. Bent shaft.

2. Inspect the final drive shaft gear (**Figure 128**) for:

a. Missing, broken or chipped teeth.

b. Cracked or scored gear bore.

3. Replace the final drive shaft and gear if necessary.

Transmission Inspection

Refer to Chapter Seven for all disassembly, inspection and reassembly procedures.

Crankshaft and
Balancer Shaft Installation

Use the following Honda tools (or equivalents) to install the crankshaft and balancer shaft into the rear crankcase.

1. Threaded adapter (part No. 07931-KF00200): A, **Figure 129**.

2. Shaft puller (part No. 07931-ME4010B USA only or 07965-VM00200): B, **Figure 129**.

3. Threaded adapter (part No. 07931-HB3020A): C, **Figure 129**.

4. Assembly collar (part No. 07965-VM00100): D, **Figure 129**.

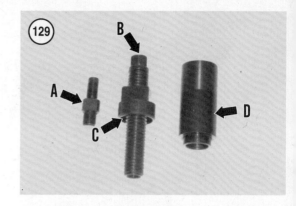

NOTE
Before ordering these tools, confirm the tool part numbers with a Honda dealership.

1. Place the rear crankcase on wooden blocks with its inside surface facing up.

2. Lubricate the crankshaft and balancer shaft bearings with oil.

3. Align the timing marks on the crankshaft and balancer shaft (**Figure 130**) and install both parts into the rear crankcase. Recheck the timing mark alignment.

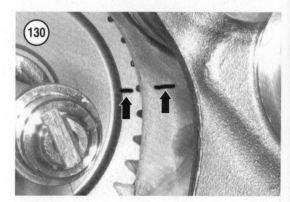

4. Install the threaded adapter into the end of the crankshaft (**Figure 131**, typical).

5. Install the crankshaft puller assembly (**Figure 132**) over the end of the crankshaft and thread it into the threaded adapter. Center the tool assembly on the main bearing inner race.

connecting rod and crankcase damage.

CAUTION
When installing the crankshaft in Step 6, position the connecting rod at its TDC or BDC position. Otherwise, the connecting rod may contact the side of the crankcase, causing expensive

6. Hold the threaded adapter and turn the shaft puller to pull the crankshaft into the main bearing. When installing the crankshaft, frequently make sure it is going straight into the bearing and not binding to one side.

7. Continue to turn the shaft puller until the crankshaft bottoms against the main bearing. Remove the crankshaft tools and turn the crankshaft.

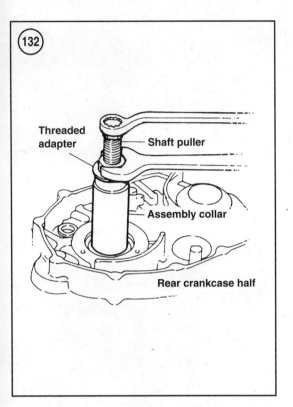

Threaded adapter — Shaft puller

Assembly collar

Rear crankcase half

The crankshaft must turn with no binding or roughness.

8. Make sure the index marks on the crankshaft and balancer shaft align as shown in **Figure 130**. The drive slot in the end of the balancer shaft should align with the mark on the crankshaft counter-weight (**Figure 133**).

> *CAUTION*
> *Severe engine damage will occur if the crankshaft and balancer shaft index marks do not align.*

Crankcase Assembly

1. Install the crankshaft and balancer shaft into the rear crankcase as described in this chapter.
2. Lightly oil all of the crankcase bearings.
3. Check the assembly of the following components as described in Chapter Seven. Make sure all washers and snap rings are properly installed in their correct position. Set each assembly aside until reassembly:
   a. Mainshaft (**Figure 134**).
   b. Countershaft (**Figure 135**).

> *NOTE*
> *Do not install the countershaft first gear bushing, first gear and copper washer at this time. They will be installed during the following steps.*

   c. Reverse idler gear assembly (**Figure 136**).
4. Place the rear crankcase half on two wooden blocks.
5. Make sure both crankcase mating surfaces are clean and dry.
6. Install the mainshaft and countershaft as follows:

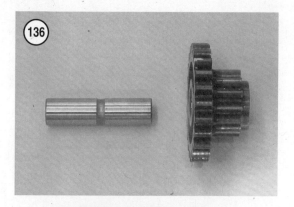

a. Make sure the washer (**Figure 137**) is installed on the mainshaft.

b. Make sure the washer (**Figure 138**) is installed on the countershaft.

c. Mesh the countershaft and mainshaft together as shown in **Figure 139**.

d. Install the countershaft (A, **Figure 140**) and mainshaft (B) into the rear crankcase half. Make sure the outer washers did not fall off the mainshaft and countershaft.

NOTE
To identify the shift forks when installing them in Step 7, refer to the letter mark(s) on each shift fork: F (front), C (center) and RR (rear). See ***Figure 141***.

7. Install the shift forks (**Figure 142**) and shift drum assembly as follows:

a. Install each shift fork with the letter mark facing up.

b. Install the RR (rear) shift fork into the mainshaft third gear groove (A, **Figure 143**).

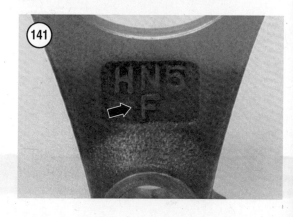

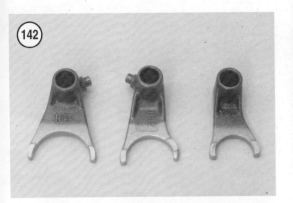

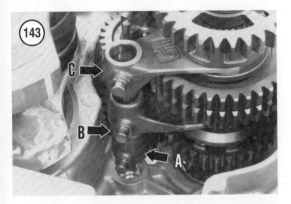

c. Install the C (center) shift fork into the countershaft fourth gear groove (B, **Figure 143**).

d. Install the F (front) shift fork into the reverse counter shifter groove (C, **Figure 143**).

e. Install the shift drum (**Figure 144**) into the crankcase.

f. Engage the RR shift fork pin into the bottom shift drum groove.

g. Engage the C shift fork pin into the middle shift drum groove.

h. Engage the F shift fork pin into the upper shift drum groove.

8. Install the shift fork shaft (**Figure 145**) through the three shift forks. Make sure each shift fork is still engaged with its respective gear and its pin is in the correct shift drum groove.

9. Install the reverse idler gear and shaft (**Figure 146**).

10. Spin the transmission shafts and shift through the gears using the shift drum. Make sure it shifts into each gear correctly.

11. After making sure the transmission shifts into all of the gears correctly, shift the transmission assembly into neutral.

12. Install the washer (A, **Figure 147**) and output shaft (B).

13. Install the sub-gearshift spindle (A, **Figure 148**) and washer (B).

14. Make sure the oil screens are installed as described in *Oil Strainer Screens*.

15. Install the two dowel pins (**Figure 149**) if they were removed.

16. Lubricate all of the shafts and gears with engine oil.

17. Thoroughly clean the mating surfaces of the crankcases halves. Apply a bead of Yamabond No.

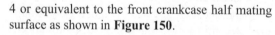

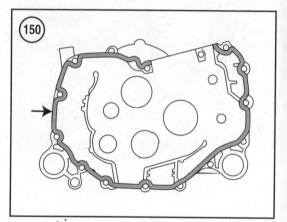

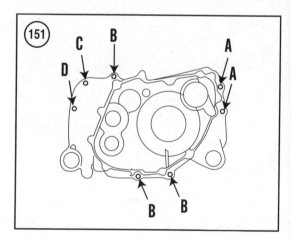

4 or equivalent to the front crankcase half mating surface as shown in **Figure 150**.

18. Align the front crankcase half with the shafts and crankshaft, and install it onto the rear crankcase half. Push the crankcase down squarely into place until it engages the dowel pins and then seats completely against the rear crankcase half.

CAUTION
When the shafts align properly, the front crankcase can be installed without the use of force. If the crankcase halves do not fit together completely, do not pull them together with the crankcase bolts. Remove the front crankcase half and investigate the cause of the interference. If the transmission or reverse assemblies were disassembled, make sure a gear was not installed incorrectly. If the crankshaft was removed, make sure it is installed and seated properly in the rear crankcase main bearing.

19. Turn all of the exposed shafts, crankshaft and shift drum. Each component must turn freely with no binding. If everything turns properly, continue with Step 20.

20. Refer to the cardboard guides made during disassembly, or use **Figure 151** and **Figure 152** as follows:

    a. A = M6 × 75.

    b. B = M6 × 40.

    c. C = M6 × 105.

    d. D = M6 × 115.

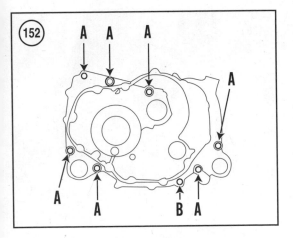

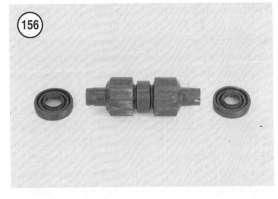

disassemble the engine as needed and correct the problem.

24. Perform *Transmission Shifting Check* in this chapter.

25. Install the drive gear (B, **Figure 155**) and driven gear (C). Install the drive gear so the splined end is out. Install the washer (A, **Figure 155**) next to the drive gear.

26. Inspect the engine mounting dust seal and bushing (**Figure 156**) sets for severe wear or damage.

27. Install the bushing sets so the outer dust seal lips face out as shown in **Figure 157**.

28. Install all exterior engine assemblies as described in this chapter and other related chapters.

21. Install the front crankcase mounting bolts. Be sure to install the engine cover bracket (**Figure 153**). Tighten the crankcase mounting bolts in a crossing pattern to 12 N•m (106 in.-lb.).

22. Install the rear crankcase mounting bolts. Be sure to install the engine cover bracket (**Figure 154**). Tighten the crankcase mounting bolts in a crossing pattern to 12 N•m (106 in.-lb.).

23. Rotate the transmission shafts and crankshaft to ensure there is no binding. If there is any binding,

TRANSMISSION SHIFTING CHECK

Transmission shifting can be checked with the engine mounted in the frame or with it sitting on the workbench. Always check transmission shifting after reassembling the engine cases.

1. Rotate the shift drum using the end slot (A, **Figure 158**) so the transmission is in neutral. Neutral

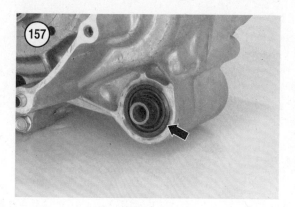

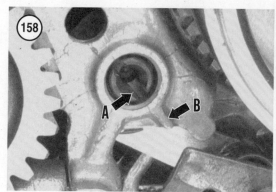

position is indicated when the end slot aligns with the boss (B, **Figure 158**) on the crankcase. When the transmission is in neutral, the countershaft and mainshaft will turn independently of each other (when one shaft is turned, the other shaft does not turn).

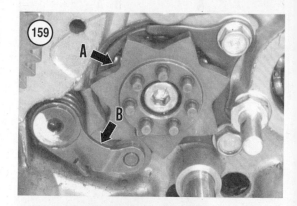

2. To check the forward gears (neutral and first through fifth gears), install the shift cam (A, **Figure 159**) and stopper arm (B) as described in *Crankcase Assembly* in this chapter. Turn the mainshaft or countershaft while turning the shifter drum counterclockwise. The transmission is in gear when the stopper arm roller seats into one of the drum shifter segment ramps. When the transmission is in gear, the countershaft and mainshaft are engaged and will turn together.

3. To check the reverse gear, move the reverse lever (**Figure 160**) down to disengage it from the shift drum and then turn the shift cam (A, **Figure 159**) clockwise. The transmission should shift into reverse.

4. If the transmission does not shift properly into each gear, disassemble the engine and check the transmission and the internal shift mechanism.

ENGINE BREAK-IN

If the piston rings or a new piston were installed, the cylinder was honed or rebored, or major lower end work was performed, break in the engine as if it were new. The performance and service life of the engine depends greatly on a careful and sensible break-in.

For the first 5-10 hours of operation, use no more than one-third throttle and vary the speed as much as possible within the one-third throttle limit. Avoid prolonged or steady running at one speed as well as hard acceleration.

Table 1 GENERAL ENGINE SPECIFICATIONS

Crankshaft type	Two main journals, unit type
Engine weight (approximate)	
FE/TE	45 kg (99 lb.)
FM/TM	44 kg (97 lb.)
Lubrication system	Wet sump, forced pressure

Table 2 STARTER DRIVEN GEAR SERVICE SPECIFICATIONS

	New mm (in.)	Service limit mm (in.)
Bearing surface outside diameter	–	45.65 (1.797)

Table 3 OIL PUMP SERVICE SPECIFICATIONS

	New mm (in.)	Service limit mm (in.)
Body clearance	0.15-0.22 (0.006-0.009)	0.25 (0.010)
Tip clearance	0.15 (0.006)	0.20 (0.008)
Side clearance	0.02-0.09 (0.001-0.004)	0.12 (0.005)

Table 4 CRANKSHAFT SERVICE SPECIFICATIONS

	New mm (in.)	Service limit mm (in.)
Crankshaft runout	–	0.05 (0.002)
Connecting rod big end radial clearance	0.006-0.018 (0.0002-0.0007)	0.05 (0.002)
Connecting rod side clearance	0.05-0.65 (0.002-0.026)	0.8 (0.03)
Connecting rod small end inside diameter	17.016-17.034 (0.6699-0.6706)	17.10 (0.673)

Table 5 ENGINE LOWER END TORQUE SPECIFICATIONS

	N•m	in.-lb.	ft.-lb.
Cooling fan shroud special bolt	18	–	13
Crankcase bolts	12	106	–
Differential mounting			
Front bracket bolt	22	–	16
Lower mounting bolt	44	–	33
Upper mounting bolt	44	–	33
Driven pulley bolt	108	–	80
Engine mounting bolts			
Lower engine mounting bolts/nuts			
Left and right side	54	–	40
Upper engine hanger bolt	32	–	24
Upper engine hanger bracket bolts	54	–	40
Gear position switch mounting bolts	12	106	–
Gearshift cam bolt	23	–	17
Gearshift stopper pin	22	–	16
Ignition pulse generator mounting bolts	6	53	–
Oil drain plug	25	–	18
Oil filter cover flange bolt	10	88	–
One-way clutch mounting bolts	23	–	17
Rear crankcase cover bolts	12	106	–
Skid plate mounting bolts	32	–	24
Stator mounting bolts	10	88	–
Stopper arm bolt	12	106	–

5

CHAPTER SIX

CLUTCH AND PRIMARY DRIVE GEAR

This chapter describes service procedures for the following subassemblies:
1. Clutch cover.
2. Clutch lever.
3. Centrifugal clutch and primary drive gear.
4. Change clutch.

The clutch cover, clutch and primary drive gear assemblies can be serviced with the engine mounted in the frame. However, because of the engine's mounting position in the frame, some of the illustrations in this chapter depict the engine removed from the frame for clarity.

Service specifications are listed in **Tables 1-3**. **Tables 1-4** are located at the end of the chapter.

ESP REDUCTION GEARS (FE AND TE MODELS)

FE and TE models are equipped with a reduction gear set that transfers shift motor rotation to the sub-gearshift spindle.

Removal/Installation/Inspection

1. Remove the angle sensor as described in Chapter Nine.
2. Remove the shift motor as described in Chapter Nine.

CAUTION
The gear cover is not secure after the shift motor is removed and may fall out.

3. Remove the gear cover (**Figure 1**).
4. Remove the sector gear (A, **Figure 2**), upper gear (B) and center gear (C).
5. Remove the O-ring (D, **Figure 2**).
6. If necessary, remove the dowel pin.
7. Clean and inspect the gears for excessive wear and damage.
8. Inspect the bearings in the clutch cover and gear cover. Replace the bearings if they are excessively worn or damaged.

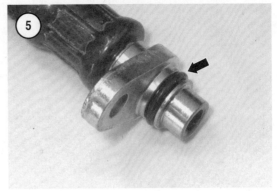

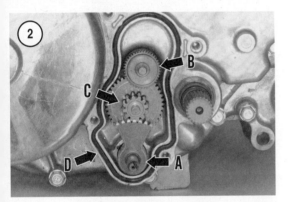

9. Install the reduction gears by reversing the preceding steps while noting the following:

6

   a. Install the sector gear so the punch mark is out (**Figure 3**).
   b. Align the master splines on the sector gear and sub-gearshift spindle.
   c. Apply 3-5 grams of N2 or N3 rated grease to the gear teeth and journals of all gears.
   d. Install a new O-ring seal.

CLUTCH COVER

Removal/Installation

1. If the engine is mounted in the frame, perform the following steps:
   a. Park the vehicle on level ground and set the parking brake.
   b. Drain the engine oil as described in Chapter Three.
   c. Remove the retaining bolt (A, **Figure 4**), then detach the oil hose (B) from each side of the engine. Cover the hose ends to prevent oil leakage and contamination.
   d. Remove the oil hose O-ring (**Figure 5**).
   e. On FE and TE models, remove the ESP reduction gears as described in this chapter.

2. On FE and FM models, proceed as follows:
   a. Remove the lower front differential mounting bolt (**Figure 6**).
   b. Remove the upper front differential mounting bolt (A, **Figure 7**) and spacer (B).
   c. Remove the front differential front mounting bracket bolts (**Figure 8**).
   d. Push the front differential forward, then push the front driveshaft forward so it disconnects from the engine output shaft (**Figure 9**).

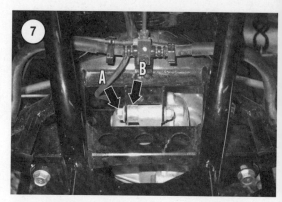

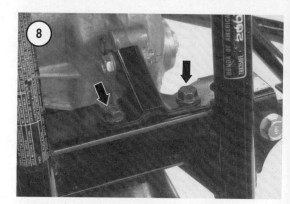

3. Remove the oil dipstick (**Figure 10**).

4. Before removing the clutch cover mounting screws, draw an outline of the cover on a piece of cardboard. Punch holes along the outline for the placement of each mounting screw.

5. Remove the clutch cover mounting screws and remove the clutch cover (A, **Figure 11**).

6. If necessary, remove the dowel pins (A, **Figure 12** and A, **Figure 13**).

7. Remove the rubber seals (B, **Figure 13**) from the oil pump dowel pins.

8. If necessary, remove the clutch lever assembly (B, **Figure 12**) as described in this chapter.

9. Remove all gasket residue from the clutch cover and crankcase mating surfaces.

10. If the clutch cover is going to be serviced and/or cleaned in solvent, perform *Clutch Cover Cleaning* in this section. Otherwise, store the clutch cover in a plastic bag until reassembly.

11. Inspect the crankshaft end bearing (**Figure 14**) as described in this section.

12. Install the clutch cover by reversing the preceding steps, while noting the following:

   a. Lubricate the crankshaft end bearing (**Figure 14**) with engine oil.

   b. Replace the oil pump rubber seals (B, **Figure 13**) if they are worn or damaged. Lubricate the rubber seals with engine oil before installing them onto the dowel pin.

   c. Install the clutch lever assembly if it was removed (B, **Figure 12**) as described in this chapter.

   d. Install the dowel pins if they were removed.

   e. Thoroughly clean the mating surfaces of the crankcase and clutch cover. Apply a bead of Yamabond No. 4 or equivalent to the clutch cover mating surface as shown in **Figure 15**.

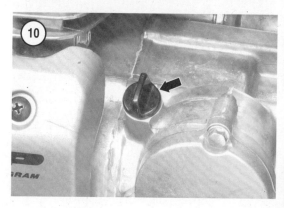

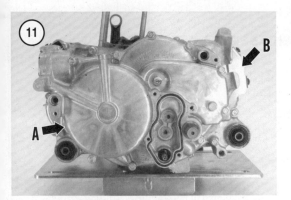

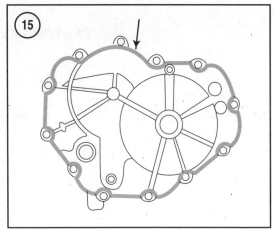

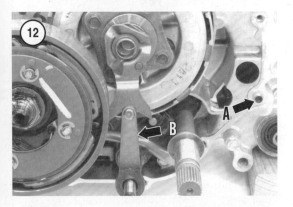

6

f. Lubricate any oil seals in the cover with engine oil.

g. Install the engine side cover bracket (B, **Figure 11**). Tighten all of the clutch cover mounting bolts to 12 N•m (106 in.-lb.).

h. Replace the oil hose O-rings if they are leaking, worn or damaged. Tighten the oil hose bracket bolts (A, **Figure 4**) to 12 N•m (106 in.-lb.).

Clutch Cover Cleaning

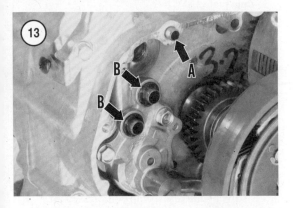

The clutch cover houses the crankshaft end bearing, oil filter, oil relief valve and a number of oil passages. Before cleaning or servicing the clutch cover, remove the oil filter and oil relief valve assemblies as follows:

1. Remove the oil filter as described in Chapter Three.

2. Clean the clutch cover and its oil passages with solvent.

3. Clean any bearings in solvent, except the sealed ESP reduction gear bearings, if so equipped. Dry the clutch cover, oil passages and bearings with compressed air.

WARNING
Do not spin bearings with compressed air. Doing so may cause the bearing to fly apart.

4. Lubricate all bearings with engine oil.

5. Install the oil filter after reinstalling the clutch cover onto the engine.

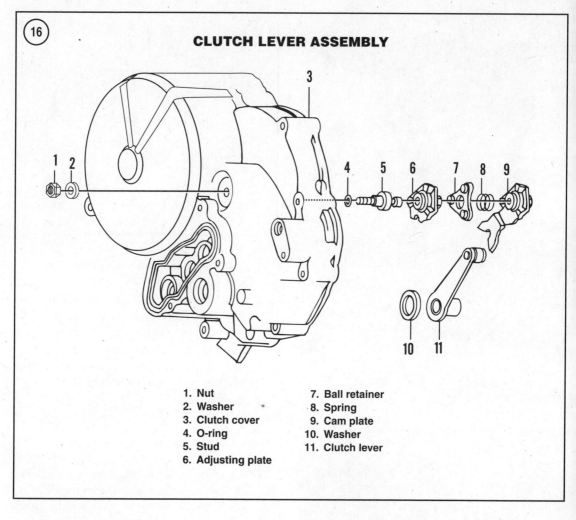

CLUTCH LEVER ASSEMBLY

1. Nut
2. Washer
3. Clutch cover
4. O-ring
5. Stud
6. Adjusting plate
7. Ball retainer
8. Spring
9. Cam plate
10. Washer
11. Clutch lever

Crankshaft End Bearing Inspection and Replacement

The bearing installed in the clutch cover supports the front crankshaft end. This bearing must be in good condition and fit tightly in its mounting bore.

1. Hold the clutch cover and slowly turn the crankshaft end bearing (**Figure 14**) inner race. Check for roughness, excessive play or noise. If the bearing feels gritty, clean the bearing as described in *Clutch Cover Cleaning* and then recheck it for wear and damage. If any of these conditions are present, the bearing is probably damaged. Replace the bearing as described in Step 3. If the bearing is good, lubricate it with engine oil.

2. Make sure the bearing outer race is a tight fit in its mounting bore. If the bearing is a loose fit, the mounting bore is probably cracked or excessively

worn. If the mounting bore is damaged, replace the clutch cover.

3. Replace the bearing as follows:

a. Remove the oil filter (Chapter Three) from the clutch cover. Clean the clutch cover in solvent and dry it with compressed air.

b. Support the clutch cover with the bearing facing up.

c. Heat the area around the bearing with a propane torch, then remove the bearing with a blind bearing remover as shown in Chapter One.

d. Heat the clutch cover again, then press the new bearing into its mounting bore until it bottoms. Install the bearing with the manufacturer's numbers facing out.

e. Install the oil filter after installing the clutch cover onto the engine.

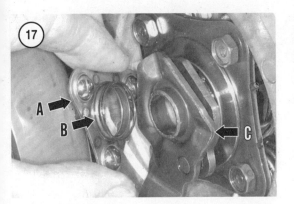

6

CLUTCH LEVER ASSEMBLY

The clutch lever assembly engages and disengages the change clutch when a gear is changed using the gearshift pedal (FM and TM models) or electric shift buttons (FE and TE models).

Refer to **Figure 16**.

Removal

1. Remove the clutch cover as described in this chapter.

2. Remove the ball retainer (A, **Figure 17**), spring (B) and cam plate (C).

3. Remove the washer (A, **Figure 18**) and clutch lever (B).

4. To remove the adjusting plate (**Figure 19**), remove the adjusting nut and washer (**Figure 20**) and then pull out the adjusting plate and O-ring (**Figure 21**) from the clutch cover.

Inspection

Replace parts that show excessive wear or damage as described in this section.

1. Clean and dry all parts.

2. Check the clutch lever for damaged splines or a cracked or severely worn lever arm.

3. Check the cam plate for damage where the arm ramps engage the clutch lever. Check the lifter cap attached to the clutch cam with a pivot pin for excessive wear or damage. Check the pivot pin for excessive wear.

4. Check the spring for stretched or damaged coils.

5. Check the ball retainer for a cracked ball cage. The balls must turn smoothly in the retainer and

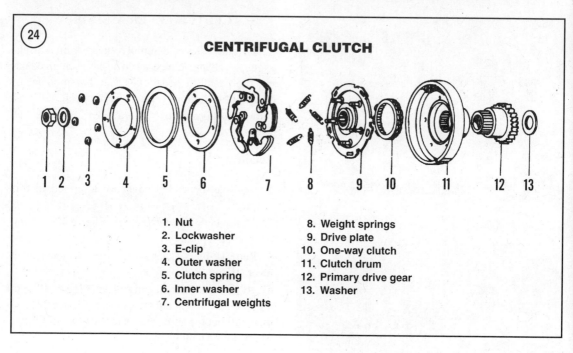

CENTRIFUGAL CLUTCH

1. Nut
2. Lockwasher
3. E-clip
4. Outer washer
5. Clutch spring
6. Inner washer
7. Centrifugal weights
8. Weight springs
9. Drive plate
10. One-way clutch
11. Clutch drum
12. Primary drive gear
13. Washer

not fall out. Check the balls for cracks or flat spots.

6. Check the adjusting plate (**Figure 19**) for stripped threads or damaged or severely worn engagement arm tabs. Replace the adjusting plate O-ring (**Figure 21**) if it is cracked or damaged.

Installation

1. Install the adjusting plate assembly as follows:

   a. Lubricate the O-ring (**Figure 21**) with engine oil, then install it into the adjusting plate bore in the clutch cover.

   b. Install the adjusting plate (**Figure 19**) by aligning the cutout with the clutch cover stopper pin.

   c. Install the washer and adjusting nut (**Figure 20**). Tighten the nut finger-tight.

2. Install the clutch lever as follows:

   a. The clutch lever and shift shaft are machined with master splines.

   b. Align the clutch lever and shift shaft master splines and install the clutch lever (B, **Figure 18**). The clutch lever roller should point toward the center of the clutch.

   c. Lubricate the clutch lever roller (C, **Figure 18**) with engine oil.

3. Install the cam plate assembly over the clutch lever and into the lifter plate as shown in **Figure 22**.

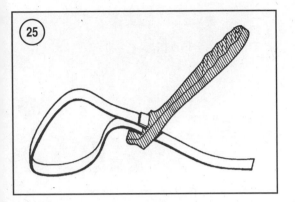

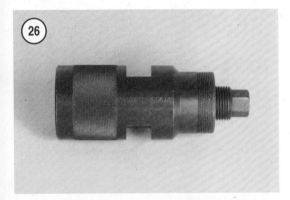

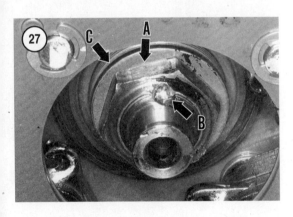

CLUTCH ASSEMBLIES

All models are equipped two clutch assemblies: centrifugal clutch (A, **Figure 23**) and the change clutch (B). The centrifugal clutch must be removed to access the change clutch.

CENTRIFUGAL CLUTCH AND PRIMARY DRIVE GEAR

The centrifugal clutch (A, **Figure 23**) can be removed with the engine installed in the frame.
Refer to **Figure 24**.

Special Tools

Before removing the clutch locknut, note the following:
1. The clutch drum must be locked in place when the clutch locknut (C, **Figure 23**) is loosened or tightened. The following tools can be used:
    a. Honda clutch holder (part No. 07GMB-HA7010B).
    b. Universal type strap wrench (**Figure 25**).

NOTE
If the engine is mounted in the frame, it may be difficult to hold the clutch drum with a strap wrench.

2. The Honda clutch puller (part No. 07933-HB3000A [**Figure 26**]) is required to pull the centrifugal clutch off the crankshaft.
3. The clutch locknut (A, **Figure 27**) is staked to a notch in the crankshaft. Purchase a new locknut for reassembly.

Removal/Installation

1. Remove the clutch cover as described in this chapter.

CAUTION
Be sure to unstake the clutch locknut where it contacts the crankshaft. This will prevent the nut from damaging the crankshaft threads as the nut is being removed.

2. Using a die grinder or other metal removal tool, unstake the clutch locknut from the groove in the

4. Install the spring (B, **Figure 17**) onto the ball retainer (A) shoulder.

5. Install the spring and ball retainer onto the lifter plate shoulder (C, **Figure 17**).

6. Make sure the clutch lever points toward the center of the change clutch.

7. Install the washer (A, **Figure 18**) onto the shift shaft.

8. Install the clutch cover as described in this chapter.

crankshaft (B, **Figure 27**). Cover nearby parts so that metal particles do not enter the clutch or engine.

3. Refer to *Change Clutch* in this chapter and secure the clutch drum with one of the tools listed. Loosen and remove the clutch locknut and washer (C, **Figure 27**). Discard the clutch locknut.

4. Thread the clutch puller (**Figure 28**) onto the drive plate threads. Hold the clutch puller body with a wrench and then turn its end bolt to pull the centrifugal clutch assembly off the mainshaft. See **Figure 29**.

5. To remove the primary drive gear, perform the following:

   a. Remove the change clutch (B, **Figure 23**) as described in this chapter.

   b. Remove the oil transfer pipe retaining bracket (A, **Figure 30**). Remove the retaining bolt (B, **Figure 30**), then remove the oil pipe (C).

   c. Remove the primary drive gear (A, **Figure 31**) and washer (B).

6. Inspect the centrifugal clutch and primary drive gear as described in this section.

7. Install the primary drive gear and centrifugal clutch by reversing the preceding removal steps while noting the following:

   a. Lubricate the mainshaft, primary drive gear bore and washer with engine oil.

   b. Lubricate the clutch weight linings (A, **Figure 32**) with engine oil.

   c. Install the centrifugal clutch by first aligning the drive plate splines with the crankshaft splines, then rotate the clutch drum and align its splines with the primary drive gear splines.

   d. Center a driver against the clutch hub and drive it onto the crankshaft until it bottoms.

   e. Lubricate the washer and the threads of a new clutch locknut (A, **Figure 27**) with engine oil and install them.

   f. Secure the clutch drum with the same tool used during removal, then tighten the centrifugal clutch locknut to 118 N•m (87 ft.-lb.). Stake the edge of the clutch locknut to the notch in the crankshaft (B, **Figure 27**).

Clutch Drum and One-Way Clutch Inspection

Refer to **Table 1** when measuring the clutch drum components (**Figure 24**) in this section. Replace parts that are out of specification or show damage.

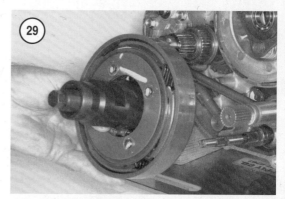

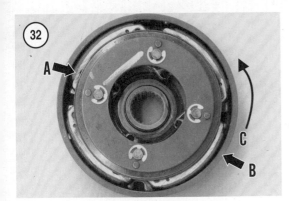

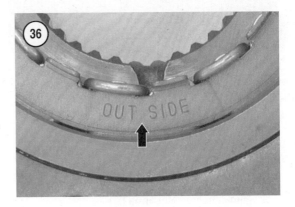

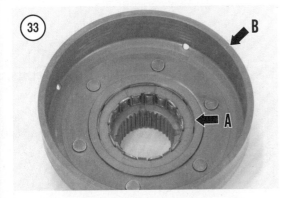

1. Check one-way clutch operation as follows:

  a. Place the assembled clutch assembly on the workbench as shown in **Figure 32**.

  b. Hold the clutch drum (B, **Figure 32**) and turn the drive plate assembly counterclockwise (C).

  c. The drive plate assembly should only turn counterclockwise (C, **Figure 32**). If the drive plate turns clockwise, the one-way clutch is faulty and must be replaced as described in this procedure.

2. Remove the drive plate assembly from the clutch drum.

3. Remove the one-way clutch (A, **Figure 33**) from the clutch drum. Inspect the one-way clutch for signs of heat damage, cracks or other damage. Replace the one-way clutch if it is damaged or if it failed to operate as described in Step 1.

4. Inspect the drive plate hub (**Figure 34**) for scoring, excessive wear or damage. Check for signs of overheating.

5. Inspect the exterior of the clutch drum (B, **Figure 33**) for cracks or damage. Check the clutch drum inside diameter for excessive wear or damage. Measure the clutch drum inside diameter (**Figure 35**) with a caliper and compare the measurement to the service limit in **Table 1**.

6. Lubricate the one-way clutch and the clutch drum bore with engine oil. Install the one-way clutch in the clutch drum with its OUTSIDE mark (**Figure 36**) facing out.

7. Inspect and service the centrifugal weight assembly as described in this section.

8. Inspect the primary drive gear as described in this section.

Centrifugal Weight Assembly
Disassembly/Inspection/Reassembly

Refer to **Table 1** when measuring the centrifugal weight components (**Figure 24**) in this section. Replace parts that are out of specification or damaged.

1. Disassemble the centrifugal weight assembly as follows:

    a. Remove the E-clips (**Figure 37**), outer washer, clutch spring and inner washer.

    b. Remove the weight springs (A, **Figure 38**) and clutch weight arms (B).

2. Measure the thickness of each weight lining at the points shown in **Figure 39**. If it is out of specification, replace all of the clutch weight arms as a set.

3. Inspect the clutch spring plate (**Figure 40**) for cracks or signs of heat damage. Measure the height of the spring plate with a vernier caliper (**Figure 40**). Replace the spring plate if the height is not as specified in **Table 1**.

4. Inspect the weight springs (A, **Figure 38**) for cracks or stretched coils. Measure the free length of each spring with a vernier caliper. If it is out of specification, replace all of the springs as a set.

5. Examine the outer and inner washers and replace them if they are cracked or damaged.

6. Inspect the drive plate for damaged splines, warp or damaged clutch weight pins. Check the E-clip groove in the end of each pin for damage.

7. Reassemble the clutch weight assembly as follows:

    a. Lubricate the drive plate pins with engine oil.

    b. Install the clutch weights and weight springs. Install the weight springs with their open ends facing down.

    c. Install the inner washer (A, **Figure 41**) with the lip facing up.

    d. Install the spring plate (B, **Figure 41**) with the cupped side facing in.

    e. Install the outer washer (A, **Figure 42**) with the locating pins facing out.

    f. Secure the drive plate in a vise by applying just enough pressure to compress the spring plate and expose the clip grooves in the end of each drive plate pin. Install the E-clips with the open end of each E-clip toward the corresponding locating pin on the outer washer (B, **Figure 42**). Make sure each E-clip seats in its groove completely.

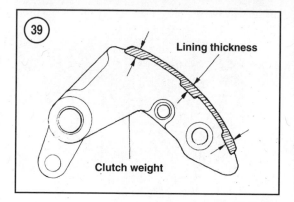

Lining thickness

Clutch weight

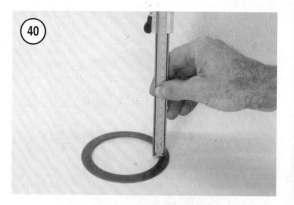

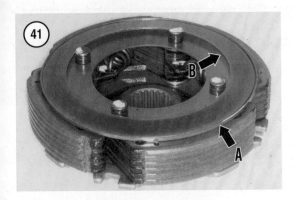

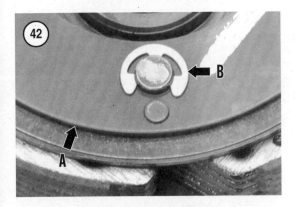

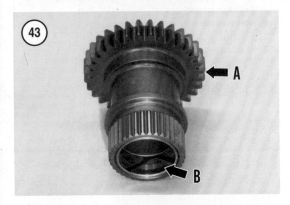

g. Remove pressure from the drive plate and Make sure the outer washer seats evenly against each E-clip.

Primary Drive Gear Inspection

Refer to **Table 2** when measuring the primary drive gear components in this section. Replace parts that are out of specification or damaged.

1. Clean and dry the primary drive gear and washer.

2. Examine the primary drive gear (A, **Figure 43**) for:

   a. Worn or damaged gear teeth or splines.

   b. Scored or damaged outer bearing surface.

   c. Worn or damaged bushings.

3. Measure the inside diameter of the bushing (B, **Figure 43**) at each end of the gear. Replace the primary drive gear if either bushing diameter is out of specification.

4. Measure the crankshaft outside diameter at the two drive gear bushing operating locations shown in **Figure 44**. Replace the crankshaft if either dimension is out of specification.

CHANGE CLUTCH

The change clutch (B, **Figure 23**) can be removed with the engine installed in the frame.

Refer to **Figure 45** when servicing the change clutch assembly.

Special Tools

Before removing the clutch locknut, note the following:

1. The clutch locknut (**Figure 46**) is staked to a notch in the mainshaft. Purchase a new locknut for reassembly.

2. When loosening and tightening the clutch locknut (**Figure 46**), some means of holding the change clutch will be required. The following list suggests methods for holding the clutch.

   a. The Honda clutch center holder (part No. 07JMB-MN50300 [**Figure 47**]) is designed to hold the clutch when the clutch locknut is loosened and tightened.

   b. Use an air impact wrench and air compressor. This tool setup can be used to loosen the clutch locknut. However, when tightening the

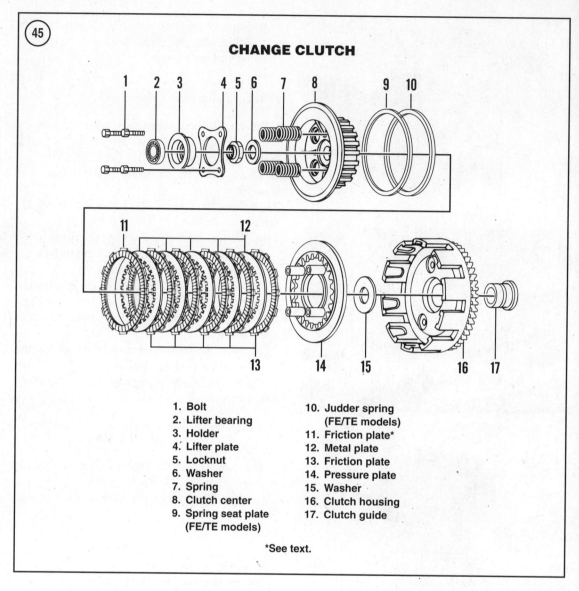

CHANGE CLUTCH

1. Bolt
2. Lifter bearing
3. Holder
4. Lifter plate
5. Locknut
6. Washer
7. Spring
8. Clutch center
9. Spring seat plate (FE/TE models)
10. Judder spring (FE/TE models)
11. Friction plate*
12. Metal plate
13. Friction plate
14. Pressure plate
15. Washer
16. Clutch housing
17. Clutch guide

*See text.

locknut during clutch assembly, a separate tool setup will be required to hold the clutch so that the clutch locknut can be tightened with a torque wrench. See substep c.

c. Use a separate gear (**Figure 48**) to lock the clutch outer gear to the primary drive gear.

Removal/Disassembly

1. Remove the clutch lever assembly as described in this chapter.

2. Remove the centrifugal clutch as described in this chapter.

3. Remove the lifter bearing and holder (A, **Figure 49**).

4. Loosen the lifter plate bolts (B, **Figure 49**) 1/4 turn at a time in a crossing pattern. Remove the bolts, lifter plate (C, **Figure 49**) and clutch springs.

NOTE
If clutch plate service is not required, keep the clutch assembled with a clutch spring, flat washer and clutch bolt as shown in A, Figure 50.

CAUTION
Be sure to unstake the clutch locknut where it contacts the mainshaft. This

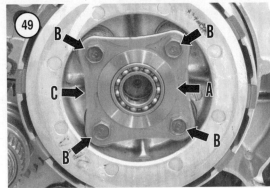

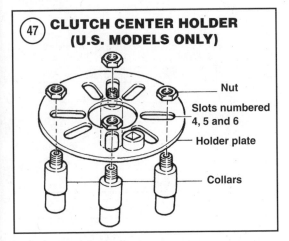

CLUTCH CENTER HOLDER (U.S. MODELS ONLY)

Nut

Slots numbered 4, 5 and 6

Holder plate

Collars

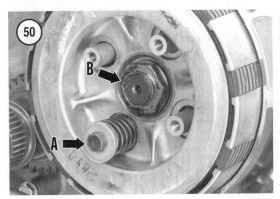

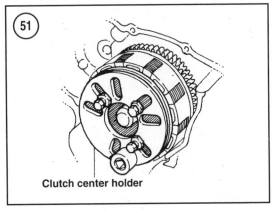

Clutch center holder

will prevent the nut from damaging the mainshaft threads as the nut is being removed.

5. Using a die grinder or other metal removal tool, unstake the clutch locknut from the groove in the mainshaft (B, **Figure 50**). Cover the parts so metal particles do not enter the clutch or engine.

6. Lock the clutch center using one of the methods listed under *Special Tools* in this section. Loosen and remove the clutch locknut and washer.

NOTE
Figure 51 *shows the Honda clutch center tool being used in a typical situation.*

7. Remove the clutch center, clutch plates and pressure plate assembly (**Figure 52**).

8. Remove the flat washer (A, **Figure 53**) and clutch housing (B).

9. Remove the clutch guide (**Figure 54**).

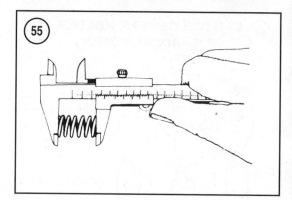

Inspection

Refer to **Table 3** when measuring the change clutch components (**Figure 45**) in this section. Replace parts that are out of specification or damaged.

1. Clean all parts in solvent and dry them with compressed air.

2. Measure the free length of each clutch spring (**Figure 55**) with a vernier caliper. Replace the springs as a set if any spring is too short.

3. Measure the thickness of each friction plate at several places around the plate (**Figure 56**). Replace all friction plates as a set if any one plate is too thin or damaged. Do not replace only one or two plates.

4. Place each clutch metal plate on a surface plate or a thick piece of glass and measure warp with a feeler gauge (**Figure 57**). Replace it if it is out of specification.

5. Examine the clutch center splines (A, **Figure 58**) and plate grooves (B) for cracks or excessive wear.

6. Examine the clutch housing outer slots (A, **Figure 59**) for grooves, steps, cracks or other damage. The slots must be smooth for proper clutch operation. Repair light damage with a fine-cut file or

oilstone. Replace the clutch housing if the damage is not repairable.

7. Examine the clutch housing bore (B, **Figure 59**) for excessive wear or damage.

8. Examine the clutch housing gear for damaged gear teeth.

9. Examine the clutch guide (C, **Figure 59**) inside and outside surfaces for cracks, deep scoring or

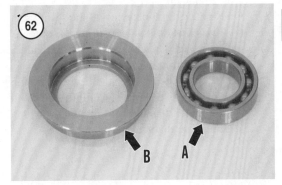

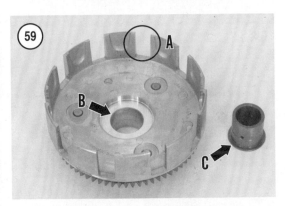

other damage. If there is no visible damage, measure the clutch guide inside and outside diameters. Replace it if either dimension is out of specification.

10. Measure the mainshaft diameter where the clutch guide operates (**Figure 60**). Replace the mainshaft if it is out of specification.

11. Examine the pressure plate (**Figure 61**) for thread damage, cracked spring towers or other damage.

12. Check the lifter bearing (A, **Figure 62**) by turning the inner race. The bearing should turn smoothly with no signs of roughness or damage. Examine the holder (B, **Figure 62**) for damage.

Assembly/Installation

Refer to **Figure 45**.

1. Lubricate the mainshaft and all clutch parts with engine oil.

> *CAUTION*
> *Never assemble the clutch without lubricating the clutch plates with oil, especially if the clutch was cleaned in solvent or new plates are being installed. Otherwise, these plates may*

grab and lock up when the engine is first started and cause clutch damage.

> **NOTE**
> *If the clutch plates were not separated from the clutch center and clutch housing, go to Step 3.*

2. Assemble the clutch plates, clutch center, and pressure plate as follows:

   a. Place the clutch center (**Figure 63**) on the workbench.

   b. Lubricate the friction and clutch metal plates with engine oil.

   c. On FE and TE models, install the spring seat (A, **Figure 64**) and judder spring (B) onto the clutch center. The cupped side of the judder spring must face out.

   d. On FE and TE models, identify the friction plates. There is one plate (A, **Figure 65**) with a larger inner diameter and five plates with a smaller inner diameter (B).

> **NOTE**
> *On FE and TE models, the friction plate must fit around the judder spring and spring seat.*

   e. On FM and TM models, install a friction plate, then install a clutch metal plate. Continue until all of the plates are installed. The last plate installed is a friction plate (**Figure 66**).

   f. On FE and TE models, install a small inner diameter friction plate (B, **Figure 65**), then install a clutch metal plate. Continue to install the plates, installing the large inner diameter plate (A, **Figure 65**) last. See **Figure 66**.

   g. Install the pressure plate (**Figure 67**) and seat it against the outer friction plate. Make sure the friction plate tabs engage with the clutch center splines and the clutch center sits flush against the friction plate as shown in **Figure 68**.

> **NOTE**
> *Substep h will align the clutch plates with the clutch center. Aligning the clutch plates now will make it easier to install the clutch plate assembly later in this procedure.*

   h. Align the friction plates with the clutch outer housing, then install the clutch plate assembly into the clutch outer housing (A, **Figure 69**).

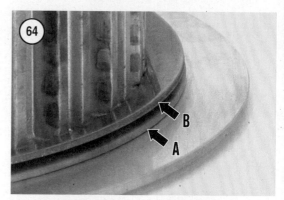

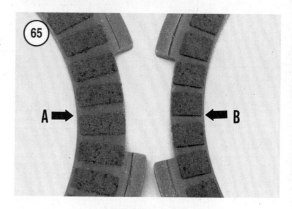

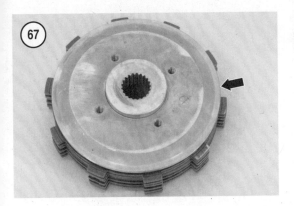

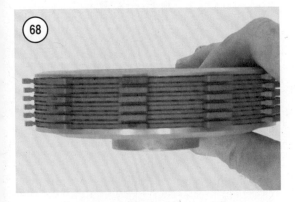

i. After properly aligning all of the friction plates, install one clutch spring, a flat washer and clutch spring bolt as shown in B, **Figure 69**. Tighten the bolt to hold the clutch plate assembly together, then remove the clutch plate assembly from the clutch outer housing.

j. Make sure all of the friction plates are properly aligned and the pressure plate seats flush against the outer friction plate (**Figure 68**).

k. Set the clutch plate assembly aside until installation.

3. Install the primary drive gear and washer as described in this chapter if they were removed.

4. Slide the clutch guide—shoulder side facing in—onto the mainshaft (**Figure 54**).

5. Install the clutch housing (B, **Figure 53**) onto the mainshaft and seat it on the clutch guide.

6. Install the large washer (A, **Figure 53**) onto the mainshaft and seat it against the clutch housing.

7. Mesh the clutch center (**Figure 52**) with the mainshaft splines and slide the clutch center into the clutch outer housing. See **Figure 50**.

8. Install the lockwasher (**Figure 70**) onto the mainshaft and seat it against the clutch center.

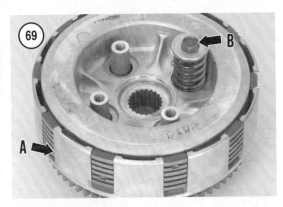

9. Using one of the methods described under *Special Tools*, lock the clutch center to the clutch housing. Note the following:

a. When using a gear to lock the clutch housing gear to the primary drive gear, install two or .more clutch springs, flat washers and bolts (A, **Figure 50**) to prevent the clutch center from slipping when the clutch locknut is tightened.

b. **Figure 71** shows typical use of the separate gear to lock the clutch housing gear to the primary drive gear.

c. When using the Honda clutch center holder tool (**Figure 51**), first remove the clutch bolt, washer and clutch spring set that were installed during Step 2.

10. Tighten the change clutch locknut (B, **Figure 50**) to 108 N•m (80 ft.-lb.).

11. Remove the tool setup installed in Step 9.

12. Using a punch, stake the locknut shoulder into the mainshaft notch. See **Figure 72**.

13. Remove the clutch spring bolts and flat washers if they were not already removed.

14. Install the clutch springs (**Figure 73**).

15. Install the lifter plate (A, **Figure 74**) with its OUT mark facing out.

16. Install the four clutch spring bolts (B, **Figure 74**) in a crossing pattern in several steps. Tighten the bolts to 12 N•m (106 in.-lb.).

17. Install the holder (A, **Figure 75**) and lifter bearing (B). Lubricate the lifter bearing with oil.

18. Install the centrifugal clutch as described in this chapter.

19. Install the clutch lever assembly as described in this chapter.

Table 1 CENTRIFUGAL CLUTCH SERVICE SPECIFICATIONS

	New mm (in.)	Service mm (in.)
Clutch drum inside diameter	126.0-126.2 (4.96-4.97)	126.4 (4.98)
Weight lining thickness	2.0 (0.08)	1.3 (0.05)
Clutch spring plate height	2.87 (0.113)	2.73 (0.107)
Clutch weight spring free length	25.8 (1.02)	26.9 (1.06)

Table 2 PRIMARY DRIVE GEAR SERVICE SPECIFICATIONS

	New mm (in.)	Service limit mm (in.)
Crankshaft outside diameter at drive gear	26.959-26.980 (1.0614-1.0622)	26.93 (1.060)
Primary drive gear bushing inside diameter	27.000-27.021 (1.0630-1.0638)	27.05 (1.065)

Table 3 CHANGE CLUTCH SERVICE SPECIFICATIONS

	New mm (in.)	Service limit mm (in.)
Clutch spring free length		
FE/TE	31.3 (1.23)	30.2 (1.19)
FM/TM	28.0 (1.10)	27.0 (1.06)
Friction plate thickness	2.62-2.78 (0.103-0.109)	2.3 (0.09)
Clutch metal plate warp	–	0.20 (0.008)
Clutch outer guide		
Outside diameter	27.959-27.980 (1.1007-1.1016)	27.92 (1.099)
Inside diameter	22.000-22.021 (0.8661-0.8670)	22.05 (0.868)
Mainshaft outside diameter at outer guide	21.967-21.980 (0.8648-0.8654)	21.93 (0.863)

6

Table 4 CLUTCH TORQUE SPECIFICATIONS

	N•m	in.-lb.	ft.-lb.
Centrifugal clutch locknut	118	–	87
Change clutch locknut	108	–	80
Clutch cover bolts	12	106	–
Oil hose bracket bolts	12	106	–

CHAPTER SEVEN

TRANSMISSION AND INTERNAL SHIFT MECHANISM

A five-speed transmission with reverse is used on all models. Transmission service requires engine removal and splitting the crankcase (Chapter Five).

Table 1 lists transmission gear ratios. **Tables 2-5** list transmission and shift fork service specifications. **Tables 1-5** are located at the end of this chapter.

TRANSMISSION/REVERSE SYSTEM IDENTIFICATION

This chapter describes service to the forward and reverse transmission assemblies identified in **Figure 1**.

1. Mainshaft (A).
2. Countershaft (B).
3. Reverse idle gear shaft (C).
4. Shift fork shaft and shift forks (D).
5. Shift drum (E).

TRANSMISSION TROUBLESHOOTING

Refer to Chapter Two.

TRANSMISSION OVERHAUL

Removal/Installation

Remove and install the transmission and internal shift assemblies as described under *Crankcase Disassembly* and *Crankcase Assembly* in Chapter Five.

Service Notes

1. Parts with two different sides, such as gears, snap rings and shift forks, can be installed backward. To maintain the correct alignment and position of the parts during disassembly, store each part in order and in a divided container.
2. The mainshaft snap ring is a tight fit on the shaft and can bend and twist during removal. Install a new snap ring during assembly.
3. To prevent bending and twisting the new snap ring during installation, use the following installation technique: open the new snap ring with a pair of snap ring pliers while holding the back of the snap ring with a pair of pliers (**Figure 2**), then slide the snap ring down the shaft and seat it into its correct transmission groove.

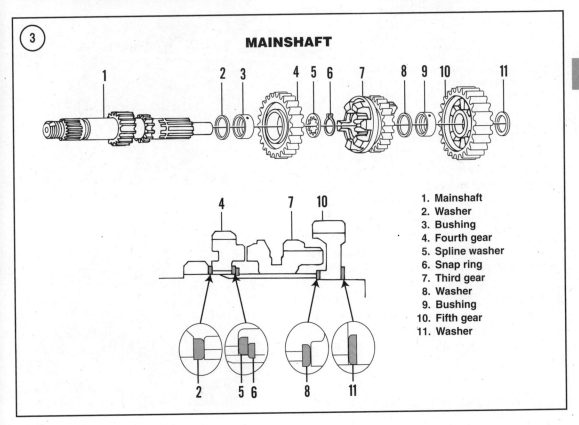

MAINSHAFT

1. Mainshaft
2. Washer
3. Bushing
4. Fourth gear
5. Spline washer
6. Snap ring
7. Third gear
8. Washer
9. Bushing
10. Fifth gear
11. Washer

Mainshaft Disassembly/Assembly

Refer to **Figure 3**.

1. Clean and dry the assembled mainshaft (**Figure 4**).

2. Remove the washer.

3. Remove fifth gear and the bushing.

4. Remove the washer.

5. Remove third gear.

6. Remove the snap ring and spline washer. Discard the snap ring.

7. Remove fourth gear and the bushing.

8. Remove the washer.

NOTE
Mainshaft second and first gears are an integral part of the mainshaft.

9. Inspect the mainshaft assembly as described under *Transmission Inspection* in this chapter.

10. Lubricate all sliding surfaces with engine oil.

11. Install the flat washer (A, **Figure 5**) and the fourth gear bushing (B).

12. Install fourth gear (A, **Figure 6**) onto the bushing. The gear dogs on fourth gear (B, **Figure 6**) must face toward the end of the shaft.

NOTE
*In Steps 13 and 14, install the spline washer and snap ring with the flat edge facing away from fourth gear as shown in **Figure 3**.*

13. Install the spline washer (C, **Figure 6**).

14. Install a new snap ring (**Figure 7**). Seat the snap ring in the groove next to fourth gear. Align the snap ring gap with the shaft groove (**Figure 8**).

15. Install third gear so the gear teeth (A, **Figure 9**) are toward the end of the shaft.

16. Install the washer (B, **Figure 9**) so the flat side faces away from the fifth gear as shown in **Figure 3**. Install the fifth gear bushing (C, **Figure 9**).

17. Install the fifth gear (A, **Figure 10**). Install the fifth gear so the flat side faces the end of the shaft. Install the washer (B, **Figure 10**) so the flat side faces away from the fifth gear as shown in **Figure 3**.

Countershaft Disassembly/Assembly

Refer to **Figure 11**.

1. Clean and dry the assembled countershaft (**Figure 12**).

2. A number of parts on the countershaft are symmetrical. This means they can be installed with either side facing in either direction. However, on a well-used transmission, a wear pattern will have developed on some of these parts. To prevent excessive wear or transmission noise after reassembling the transmission, mark the following parts with a grease pencil so they can be installed facing in their original operating positions.

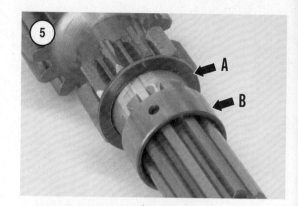

a. Spline bushing.

b. Spline collar.

c. Spline bushing.

d. Spline bushing.

e. Bushing.

3. Remove the washer and fifth gear.

4. Remove the washer, second gear and bushing.

5. Remove the reverse shifter, spline collar, reverse gear and spline bushing.

6. Disengage and remove the lockwasher and spline washer.

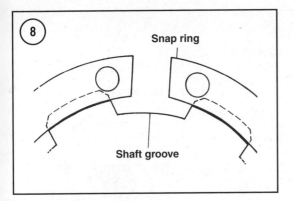

8

Snap ring

Shaft groove

9

A

C

B

10

A

B

7. Remove first gear and the spline bushing.

8. Remove the spline washer, snap ring and fourth gear.

9. Remove the snap ring, spline washer, third gear and bushing.

10. Inspect the countershaft assembly as described under *Transmission Inspection* in this chapter.

11. Lubricate all sliding surfaces with engine oil.

12. When installing the parts listed in Step 2, install them so they face in their original operating position. Refer to the marks made on the parts during disassembly.

13. Install third gear (**Figure 13**) and the bushing onto the countershaft. The dog-side of the gear must be toward the long splined end of the shaft.

NOTE
*In Step 14, install the spline washer and snap ring so the flat edge faces away from third gear as shown in **Figure 11**.*

14. Install the splined washer (A, **Figure 14**) and snap ring (B). Align the snap ring gap with the shaft groove (**Figure 8**).

15. Install the fourth gear so the gear teeth (**Figure 15**) are toward the end of the shaft.

NOTE
*In Steps 16 and 17, install the snap ring and spline washer so the flat edge faces toward fourth gear as shown in **Figure 11**.*

16. Install the snap ring into the shaft groove (**Figure 16**). Align the snap ring gap with the shaft groove (**Figure 8**).

17. Install the spline washer (A, **Figure 17**).

18. Install the spline bushing so the oil hole in the bushing (B, **Figure 17**) aligns with the oil hole in the shaft (C).

19. Install first gear (D, **Figure 17**) so the flat side is toward the end of the shaft.

20. Install the spline washer (A, **Figure 18**) so the side with the rounded edge contacts the gear as shown in **Figure 11**. Install the lockwasher (B, **Figure 18**) so the tabs (C) fit into the notches (D) in the spline washer.

21. Install the spline bushing and reverse gear (**Figure 19**). Make sure the oil hole in the bushing aligns with the oil hole in the shaft. Install the reverse gear so the flat side is toward first gear.

22. Install the spline collar (A, **Figure 20**) and shifter (B). Install the shifter so the side with eight lugs is toward the end of the shaft.

23. Install the spline bushing (C, **Figure 20**) and second gear (D). Make sure the oil hole in the bushing aligns with the oil hole in the shaft. Install the second gear so the flat side is toward the end of the shaft.

24. Install the washer so the rounded edge is toward the gear (**Figure 21**) as shown in **Figure 11**.

7

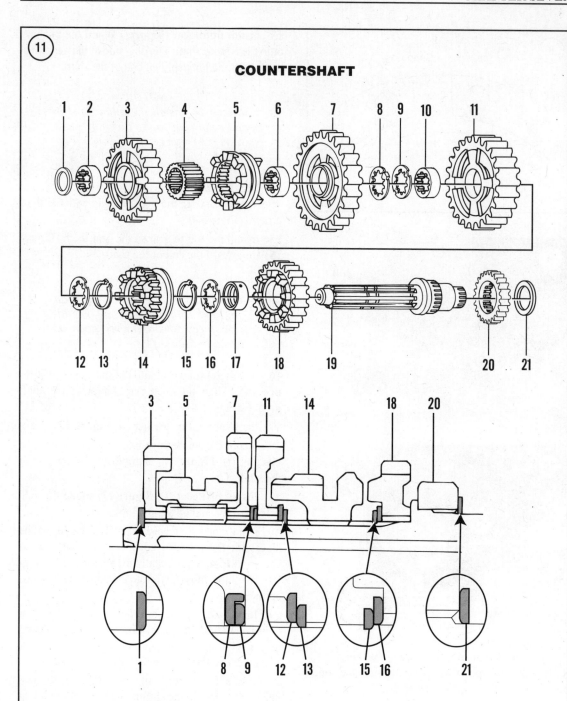

COUNTERSHAFT

1. Washer
2. Spline bushing
3. Second gear
4. Spline collar
5. Shifter
6. Spline bushing
7. Reverse gear
8. Lockwasher
9. Spline washer
10. Spline bushing
11. First gear
12. Spline washer
13. Snap ring
14. Fourth gear
15. Snap ring
16. Spline washer
17. Bushing
18. Third gear
19. Countershaft
20. Fifth gear
21. Washer

7

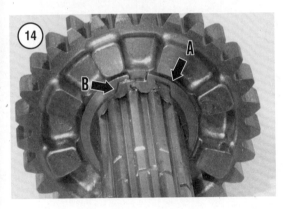

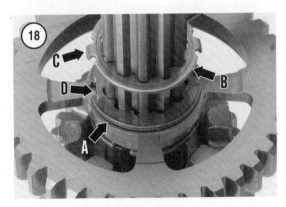

25. Install the first gear so the splined portion of the inside diameter is toward the end of the shaft (**Figure 22**).

26. Install the washer (**Figure 23**) so the rounded edge is toward the gear as shown in **Figure 11**.

27. Set the countershaft aside until transmission is installation (Chapter Five).

REVERSE IDLE GEAR ASSEMBLY

Removal/Installation/Inspection

Remove and install the reverse idle gear assembly (**Figure 24**) as described in *Crankcase and Crankshaft* in Chapter Five.

Inspect the reverse idle gear assembly as described in *Transmission Inspection* in this chapter.

TRANSMISSION INSPECTION

Mainshaft

Refer to **Table 2** when measuring the mainshaft components (**Figure 3**) in this section. Replace parts that are out of specification or damaged. When replacing a gear, also replace its mating gear, even though it may not show as much wear or damage.

1. Clean and dry the mainshaft assembly.
2. Inspect the mainshaft (**Figure 25**) for:
   a. Worn or damages splines.
   b. Missing, broken or chipped first (A, **Figure 25**) and second (B) gear teeth.
   c. Excessively worn or damaged bearing surfaces.
   d. Cracked or rounded-off snap ring groove.
3. Check each mainshaft gear for:
   a. Missing, broken or chipped teeth.
   b. Worn, damaged or rounded gear lugs.
   c. Worn or damaged splines.
   d. Cracked or scored gear bore.
4. Check each mainshaft bushing for:
   a. Excessively worn or damaged bearing surface.
   b. Worn or damaged splines.
   c. Cracked or scored gear bore.
5. Measure the mainshaft outside diameter at the fourth (C, **Figure 25**) and fifth (D) gear operating positions and record the dimensions.

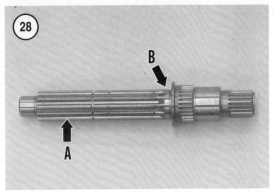

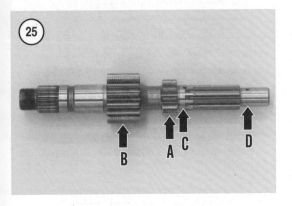

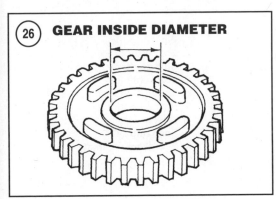

GEAR INSIDE DIAMETER

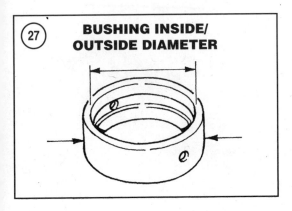

BUSHING INSIDE/
OUTSIDE DIAMETER

6. Measure the mainshaft fourth and fifth gear inside diameters (**Figure 26**) and record the dimensions.

7. Measure the mainshaft fourth and fifth gear bushing inside and outside diameters (**Figure 27**) and record the dimensions.

8. Using the dimensions recorded in Steps 5-7, determine the gear-to-bushing and bushing-to-shaft clearances.

Countershaft

Refer to **Table 3** when measuring the countershaft components (**Figure 11**) in this section. Replace parts that are out of specification or damaged. When replacing a gear, also replace its mating gear, even though it may not show as much wear or damage.

1. Clean and dry the countershaft assembly. Flush the oil holes with compressed air.

2. Inspect the countershaft (A, **Figure 28**) for:
   a. Worn or damaged splines.
   b. Worn or damaged bearing surfaces.
   c. Plugged oil holes.

3. Check each countershaft gear for:
   a. Missing, broken or chipped teeth.
   b. Worn, damaged or rounded gear lugs.
   c. Worn or damaged splines.
   d. Cracked or scored gear bore.

4. Check each countershaft bushing for:
   a. Worn or damaged bearing surface.
   b. Worn or damaged splines.
   c. Cracked or scored gear bore.

5. Measure the countershaft outside diameter at the location of the third gear (B, **Figure 28**) and record the dimension.

7

6. Inspect the reverse shifter for worn, damaged or rounded gear lugs. Check the splines for severe wear or damage.

7. Inspect the shifter collar and collar for excessive wear or damage.

8. Measure the countershaft first, second, third and reverse gear inside diameters (**Figure 26**) and record the dimensions.

9. Measure the countershaft first, second and reverse gear bushing outside diameters (**Figure 27**) and record the dimensions.

10. Using the dimensions recorded in Step 8 and Step 9, determine the gear-to-bushing clearances.

Reverse Idle Gear

Refer to **Table 4** when measuring the reverse idle gear components (**Figure 24**) in this section. Replace parts that are out of specification or damaged.

1. Clean and dry the reverse idle gear assembly.

2. Check the reverse idle gear shaft for:
   a. A loose or damaged pin.
   b. Cracked pin hole.
   c. Cracked or damaged bearing surfaces.

3. Check the reverse idle gear for:
   a. Missing, broken or chipped teeth.
   b. Cracked or scored gear bore.

4. Measure the reverse idle gear shaft outside diameter and record the dimension.

5. Measure the reverse idle gear inside diameter and record the dimension.

6. Using the dimensions recorded in Steps 4 and 5, determine the gear-to-shaft clearances.

INTERNAL SHIFT MECHANISM

Refer to **Figure 29** when performing the following procedures.

Removal/Installation

Remove and install the transmission assembly as described in *Crankcase Disassembly and Crankcase Assembly* in Chapter Five.

Shift Drum Inspection

1. Clean and dry the shift drum.

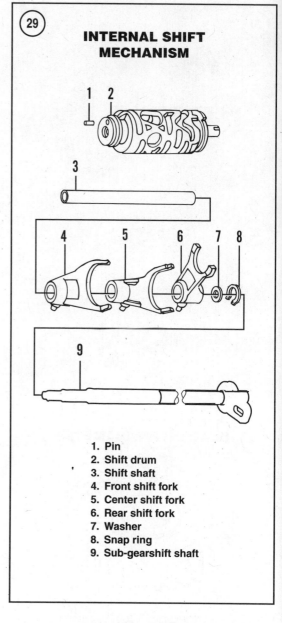

INTERNAL SHIFT MECHANISM

1. Pin
2. Shift drum
3. Shift shaft
4. Front shift fork
5. Center shift fork
6. Rear shift fork
7. Washer
8. Snap ring
9. Sub-gearshift shaft

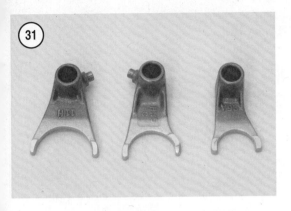

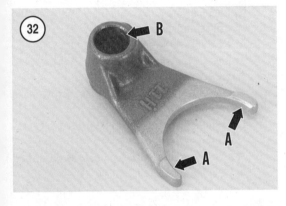

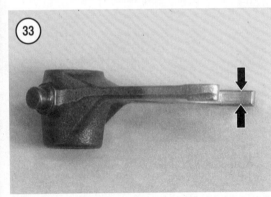

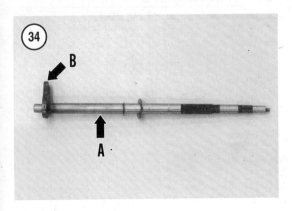

2. Check the shift drum for excessively worn or damaged cam grooves (A, **Figure 30**) or bearing surfaces (B). Replace the shift drum if necessary.

Shift Fork Inspection

Refer to **Table 5** when measuring the shift fork components in this section. Replace parts that are out of specification or damaged.

1. Inspect each shift fork (**Figure 31**) for signs of wear or damage. Examine the shift forks at the points where they contact the shifter gear (A, **Figure 32**). These surfaces must be smooth with no signs of wear, bending, cracks, heat discoloration or other damage.

2. Check each shift fork for arc-shaped wear or burn marks. These marks indicate that the shift fork has contacted the gear.

3. Check the shift fork shaft for bending or other damage. Install each shift fork on the shaft and slide it back and forth. Each shift fork should slide smoothly with no binding or tight spots. If all three shift forks bind on the shaft, check the shaft closely for bending. If only one shift fork binds on the shaft, check the shift fork closely.

4. Measure each shift fork leg thickness (**Figure 33**).

5. Measure the shift fork inside diameter (B, **Figure 32**) with a snap gauge. Then measure the snap gauge with a micrometer.

6. Measure the shift fork shaft outside diameter at three different points on the shaft.

Sub-gearshift Shaft Inspection

1. Inspect the sub-gearshift shaft and splines (A, **Figure 34**) for damage or bending.

2. Inspect the arm (B, **Figure 34**) for excessive wear or damage.

REVERSE SELECTOR CABLE REPLACEMENT

1A. On models equipped with a combination meter, remove the meter cover (Chapter Fifteen).

1B. On models not equipped with a combination meter, remove the handlebar cover (Chapter Fifteen).

2. Remove the fuel tank as described in this chapter.

3. Make a diagram of the reverse selector cable routing path from the handlebar to the engine.

4. Remove any cable guides from the reverse selector cable.

5. Loosen the reverse selector cable locknut and loosen the adjuster (**Figure 35**) to obtain as much cable free play as possible.

6. Disconnect the reverse selector cable at the handlebar.

7. Remove the rear cover screw to detach the cable bracket (**Figure 36**) from the engine.

7. Disconnect the reverse selector cable from the selector arm on the engine.

8. Remove the reverse selector cable.

9. Reverse the preceding steps to install the reverse selector cable, plus the following:

    a. Tighten the engine cover bracket screw to 12 N•m (106 in.-lb.).

    b. Lubricate the new cable as described in Chapter Three.

    c. Adjust the reverse selector cable as described in Chapter Three.

Table 1 TRANSMISSION GENERAL SPECIFICATIONS

Transmission	Constant mesh, five-speeds and reverse
Shift pattern	R-N-1-2-3-4-5
Primary reduction ratio	2.188 (70/32)
Secondary reduction ratio	1.933 (29/15)
Final reduction ratio	
Front (FE/FM)	3.769 (49/13)
Rear	3.692 (48/13)
Gear ratios	
First gear (slow)	3.455 (38/11)
Second gear	1.933 (29/15)
Third	1.333 (28/21)
Fourth	0.966 (28/29)
Fifth	0.720 (18/25)
Reverse	4.600 (39/13 × 23/15)

Table 2 MAINSHAFT SERVICE SPECIFICATIONS

	New mm (in.)	Service limit mm (in.)
Gear inside diameter		
Fourth gear	23.000-23.021 (0.9055-0.9063)	23.04 (0.907)
Fifth gear	18.000-18.021 (0.7087-0.7095)	18.05 (0.711)
Mainshaft outside diameter		
Fourth gear	19.959-19.980 (0.7858-0.7866)	19.93 (0.785)
Fifth gear	14.966-14.984 (0.5892-0.5899)	14.94 (0.588)
Gear bushings		
Fourth gear		
Inside diameter	20.000-20.021 (0.7874-0.7882)	20.04 (0.789)
Outside diameter	22.959-22.979 (0.9039-0.9047)	22.94 (0.903)
Fifth gear		
Inside diameter	15.000-15.018 (0.5906-0.5913)	15.04 (0.592)
Outside diameter	17.959-17.980 (0.7070-0.7079)	17.94 (0.706)
Gear-to-bushing clearance		
Fourth gear	0.021-0.062 (0.0008-0.0024)	0.10 (0.004)
Fifth gear	0.020-0.062 (0.0008-0.0024)	0.10 (0.004)
Bushing-to-shaft clearance		
Fourth gear	0.020-0.062 (0.0008-0.0024)	0.10 (0.004)
Fifth gear	0.016-0.052 (0.0006-0.0020)	0.10 (0.004)

Table 3 COUNTERSHAFT SERVICE SPECIFICATIONS

	New mm (in.)	Service limit mm (in.)
Gear inside diameter (all gears)	25.000-25.021 (0.9843-0.9851)	25.05 (0.986)
Gear bushing outside diameter	24.959-24.980 (0.9826-0.9835)	24.93 (0.981)
Gear-to-bushing clearance	0.020-0.062 (0.0008-0.0024)	0.10 (0.004)

Table 4 REVERSE IDLE GEAR SERVICE SPECIFICATIONS

	New mm (in.)	Service limit mm (in.)
Reverse idle gear shaft outside diameter	12.966-12.984 (0.5105-0.5112)	12.94 (0.509)
Gear inside diameter	13.000-13.018 (0.5118-0.5125)	13.04 (0.513)
Gear-to-shaft clearance	0.016-0.052 (0.0006-0.0020)	0.10 (0.004)

Table 5 SHIFT FORK SERVICE SPECIFICATIONS

	New mm (in.)	Service limit mm (in.)
Shift fork leg thickness	4.93-5.00 (0.194-0.197)	4.50 (0.177)
Shift fork inside diameter	13.000-13.018 (0.5118-0.5125)	13.04 (0.513)
Shift fork shaft outside diameter	12.966-12.984 (0.5105-0.5112)	12.96 (0.510)

7

FUEL SYSTEM

The fuel system consists of the carburetor, fuel tank, fuel shutoff valve and air filter.

This chapter includes service procedures for all parts of the fuel system, except routine air filter service which is covered in Chapter Three.

The carburetor is equipped with an air cutoff valve. The valve plunger blocks the pilot air passage when the throttle closes to prevent a lean condition afterburn in the exhaust system.

Table 1 and **Table 2** lists carburetor specifications. **Tables 1-2** are located at the end of the chapter.

CARBURETOR

Removal/Installation

1. Park the ATV on level ground and set the parking brake.
2. Remove the seat and both side covers (Chapter Fifteen).
3. Remove the air box as described in this chapter.
4. Disengage the carburetor heater wire from the clamp, then disconnect the connector (A, **Figure 1**).
5. Disconnect the breather hose (B, **Figure 1**).
6. Disconnect the fuel hose from the carburetor (A, **Figure 2**).
7. Loosen the starting enrichment (SE) valve nut (B, **Figure 2**).
8. Loosen the front carburetor hose clamp (**Figure 3**).
9. Pull the carburetor back to remove it from the intake tube.
10. Remove the SE valve (**Figure 4**) from the carburetor.
11. Disconnect the throttle cable as follows:
    a. Remove the carburetor cover screw (A, **Figure 5**) and cover (B).
    b. Slide the cover (A, **Figure 6**) away from the throttle cable adjuster (B) on the carburetor.
    c. Loosen the throttle cable locknut and unscrew the adjuster from the carburetor.
    d. Disconnect the throttle cable (C, **Figure 6**) from the throttle pulley.
12. Remove the carburetor.
13. Cover or plug all openings.
14. Install the carburetor by reversing the preceding removal steps, while noting the following:
    a. Apply a dab of grease onto the end of the throttle cable (C, **Figure 6**) before connecting it onto the throttle pulley.

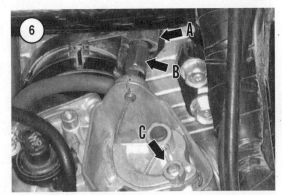

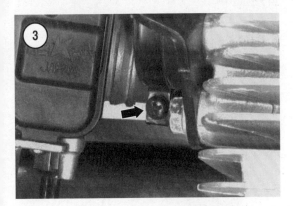

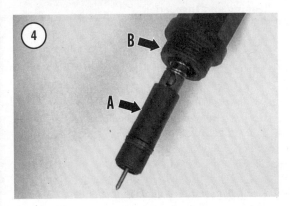

8

b. When connecting the throttle cable and threading the adjuster (B, **Figure 6**) into the carburetor, do not twist or kink the cable.

CAUTION
Do not overtighten the plastic SE valve nut.

c. Apply some multi-purpose grease into the SE valve nut at the point shown in B, **Figure 4**. Install and tighten the SE valve nut securely. Operate the choke cable by hand, making sure the SE valve moves with no binding or roughness.

CAUTION
Wipe off any grease that may contact the SE valve (A, Figure 4). Otherwise, the grease may plug the valve opening and cause the system to malfunction during engine starting.

d. When installing the carburetor, align the boss on the carburetor rim with the intake tube slot (**Figure 7**).

e. When installing the throttle cable cover, Make sure the tab at the lower end fits the slot in the carburetor (**Figure 8**).

f. Check and adjust the throttle cable adjustment (Chapter Three).

Disassembly

Refer to **Figure 9**.

1. Label, then remove any hoses from the carburetor.
2. Remove the carburetor heater (**Figure 10**).
3. Remove the screw, air cutoff valve (**Figure 11**), air jet and O-rings.
4. Remove the screws and cover (**Figure 12**).
5. Remove the spring and vacuum cylinder assembly (**Figure 13**).
6. Remove the jet needle (**Figure 14**) as follows:
   a. Turn the jet needle holder (**Figure 15**) counterclockwise to release it from the vacuum cylinder.
   b. Remove the jet needle holder, spring, jet needle and washer.

> *NOTE*
> *Before removing the jet needle, first record the clip position and compare it to the standard clip position listed in **Table 1**.*

7. Remove the screws, primer valve assembly (**Figure 16**) and spring (**Figure 17**).
8. Remove the float bowl screws (**Figure 18**), float bowl and gasket.
9. Remove the main jet baffle (**Figure 19**).
10. Remove the float pin (**Figure 20**), float and fuel valve (**Figure 21**).
11. Remove the plug (**Figure 22**).
12. Remove the starter jet (**Figure 23**).
13. Remove the slow jet (**Figure 24**).
14. Remove the main jet (A, **Figure 25**).
15. Remove the needle jet holder (B, **Figure 25**).
16. Turn the carburetor so its top side faces up and tap the body to remove the needle jet (31, **Figure 9**). If the needle jet does not fall out, gently push it out with a plastic rod.
17. While counting the number of turns, rotate the pilot screw in until it is *lightly* seated. Record the number of turns during reassembly. Back the pilot screw out and remove it from the carburetor (A, **Figure 26**).
18. Unscrew and remove the idle speed adjusting screw (A, **Figure 27**) and spring.

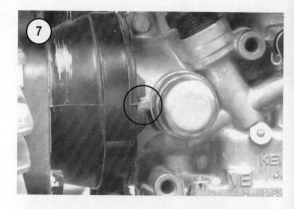

19. Remove the drain screw (**Figure 28**) and O-ring from the float bowl.

> *NOTE*
> *Further disassembly is neither necessary nor recommended. Do not remove the choke shaft or plate as these parts are not available separately.*

20. Clean and inspect all parts as described in this chapter.

Cleaning and Inspection

1. Clean and dry the carburetor parts.

> *CAUTION*
> *Do not dip the carburetor body or any of the O-rings in a carburetor cleaner or other solution that will damage the rubber parts and seals.*

> *CAUTION*
> *Do not use wire or drill bits to clean jets as minor gouges in the jet can al-*

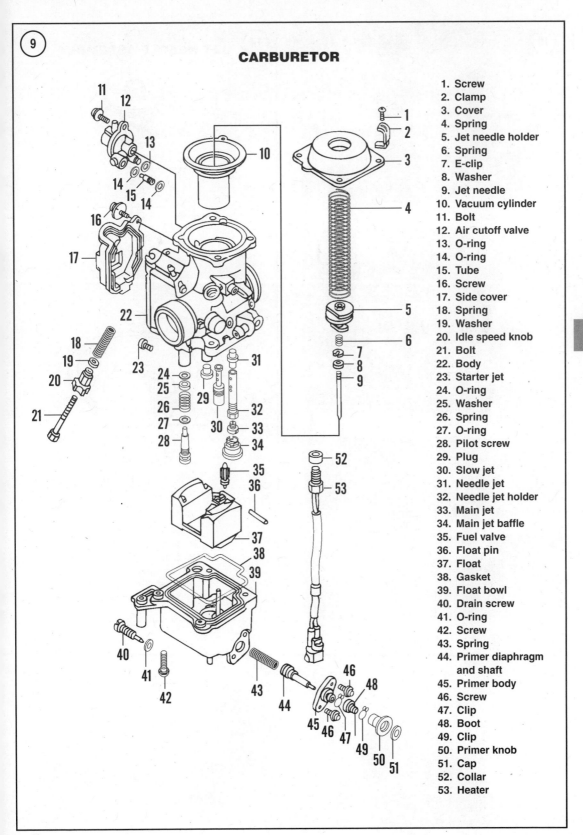

CARBURETOR

1. Screw
2. Clamp
3. Cover
4. Spring
5. Jet needle holder
6. Spring
7. E-clip
8. Washer
9. Jet needle
10. Vacuum cylinder
11. Bolt
12. Air cutoff valve
13. O-ring
14. O-ring
15. Tube
16. Screw
17. Side cover
18. Spring
19. Washer
20. Idle speed knob
21. Bolt
22. Body
23. Starter jet
24. O-ring
25. Washer
26. Spring
27. O-ring
28. Pilot screw
29. Plug
30. Slow jet
31. Needle jet
32. Needle jet holder
33. Main jet
34. Main jet baffle
35. Fuel valve
36. Float pin
37. Float
38. Gasket
39. Float bowl
40. Drain screw
41. O-ring
42. Screw
43. Spring
44. Primer diaphragm and shaft
45. Primer body
46. Screw
47. Clip
48. Boot
49. Clip
50. Primer knob
51. Cap
52. Collar
53. Heater

8

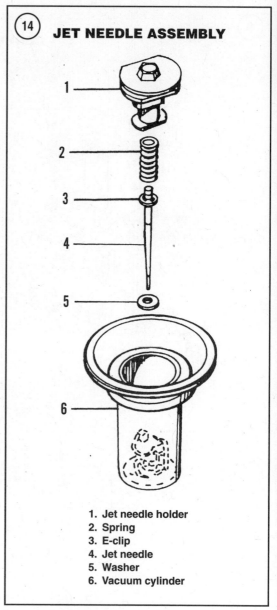

JET NEEDLE ASSEMBLY

1. Jet needle holder
2. Spring
3. E-clip
4. Jet needle
5. Washer
6. Vacuum cylinder

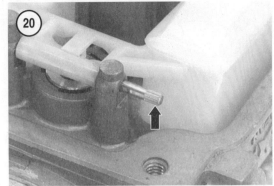

8

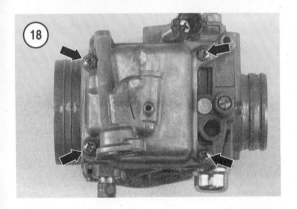

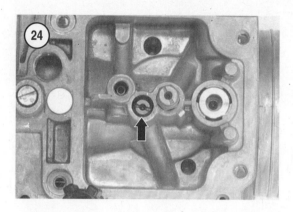

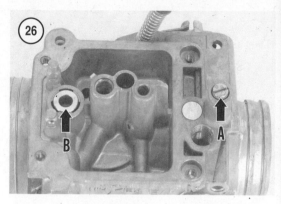

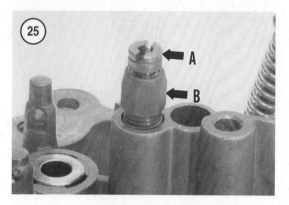

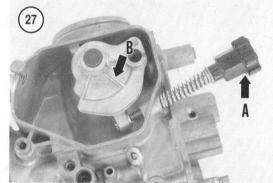

ter the flow rate and change the air/fuel mixture.

2. Clean the float bowl overflow tube with compressed air.

3. Replace the float bowl O-ring if it is leaking or damaged.

4. Inspect the fuel valve assembly as follows:

   a. Check the end of the fuel valve needle (**Figure 29**) for steps, excessive wear or damage.

   b. Inspect the fuel valve seat (B, **Figure 26**) in the carburetor for steps, uneven wear or other damage.

5. Inspect the pilot screw (**Figure 30**) and spring for damage. Replace the screw if it is damaged. Replace both pilot screw O-rings.

6. Inspect the float (**Figure 31**) for deterioration or damage. Check the float by submersing it in a container of water. If water enters the float, replace it.

7. Move the throttle pulley from stop-to-stop and check for free movement. If it does not move freely, replace the carburetor body.

8. Make sure all openings in the carburetor body are clear. Clean them with compressed air.

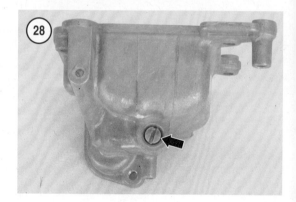

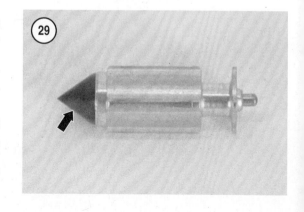

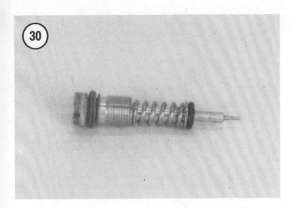

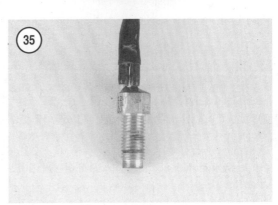

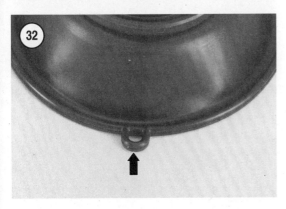

8

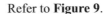

9. Check the vacuum cylinder diaphragm (**Figure 32**) for cracks, deterioration or other damage.

10. Check the primer valve assembly (**Figure 33**) for wear, damage or deterioration. Check the rubber diaphragm (**Figure 34**) for cracks or other damage.

11. Check the carburetor heater (**Figure 35**) as described in this chapter.

12. Make sure all jet openings are clear. Replace any jet that cannot be cleaned.

Assembly

Refer to **Figure 9**.

1. Install the drain screw (**Figure 28**) and O-ring into the float bowl. Tighten the drain screw securely.

2. Install the idle speed adjusting screw (A, **Figure 27**) and spring.

3. Install the two O-rings, spring and flat washer onto the pilot screw (**Figure 30**).

4. Install the pilot screw (A, **Figure 26**). Turn it in until it is *lightly* seated. Back the screw out the number of turns recorded during removal, or set it to the initial adjustment listed in **Table 1**.

5. Install the needle jet (31, **Figure 9**) with its chamfered end facing toward the needle jet holder, and install the needle jet holder. Tighten the needle jet holder (B, **Figure 25**) securely.

6. Install the main jet (A, **Figure 25**).

7. Install the slow jet (**Figure 24**).

8. Install the starter jet (**Figure 23**).

9. Install the plug (**Figure 22**).

10. Install the fuel valve onto the float, and then install the fuel valve into the fuel valve seat (**Figure 21**). Insert the float pin (**Figure 20**) through the pedestal arms and float.

11. Check the float level as described under *Carburetor Float Level Inspection* in this chapter.

12. Install the main jet baffle (**Figure 19**).

13. Install the O-ring into the float bowl groove (**Figure 36**). Then install the float bowl and secure it with its mounting screws (**Figure 18**).

14. Install the primer valve spring (**Figure 17**) and primer valve (**Figure 16**) into the float bowl. Tighten the screws securely.

15. Assemble the vacuum cylinder and install the jet needle (**Figure 14**) as follows:

    a. Install the E-clip, if it was removed, into the jet needle clip groove recorded during disassembly or refer to the clip position in **Table 1**.

    b. Install the washer onto the bottom of the jet needle and seat it against the E-clip.

    c. Install the jet needle and washer (**Figure 37**) into the vacuum cylinder.

    d. Insert the spring in the end of the jet needle holder.

    e. Insert the jet needle holder (**Figure 15**) into the vacuum cylinder and turn it 90° clockwise to lock it in place.

16. Install the vacuum cylinder into the carburetor body. Align the tab on the diaphragm (**Figure 32**) with the groove (**Figure 38**) in the carburetor body.

17. Install the spring into the vacuum cylinder (**Figure 13**).

18. Align the tab in the vacuum cylinder (A, **Figure 39**) with the raised boss (B) on the cover. Install the cover and tighten the screws securely.

19. Connect the hoses to the carburetor. Install the overflow hose so the one-way valve installed in the hose faces in the direction shown in **Figure 40**.

20. Install the air jet and O-rings, air cutoff valve (**Figure 11**) and mounting screw. Tighten the screw securely.

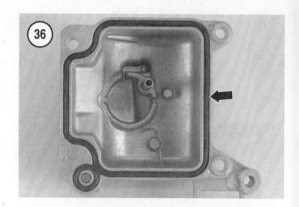

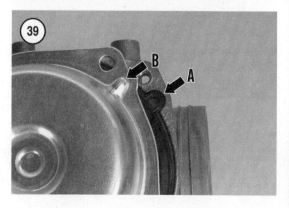

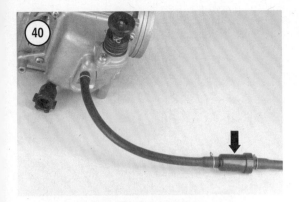

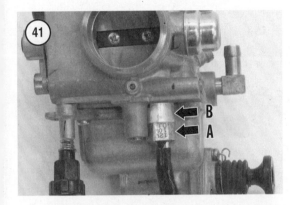

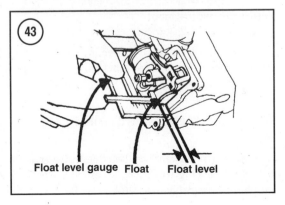

Float level gauge Float   Float level

21. Check the float level as described in this chapter.

22. Install the carburetor heater (A, **Figure 41**) and collar (B). The stepped end of the collar must be toward the carburetor.

23. Install the carburetor as described in this chapter.

24. Adjust the pilot screw as described under *Carburetor Adjustments* in this chapter.

CARBURETOR FLOAT LEVEL INSPECTION

The fuel valve and float maintain a constant fuel level in the carburetor float bowl. Because the float level affects the fuel mixture throughout the engine's operating range, the level must be within specification.

The carburetor must be removed and partially disassembled for this inspection.

1. Remove the carburetor as described in this chapter.

2. Remove the float bowl mounting screws (A, **Figure 42**) and float bowl. Do not remove the O-ring from the float bowl groove.

3. Hold the carburetor so the fuel valve just touches the float arm without pushing it down. Measure the distance from the carburetor body gasket surface to the float (**Figure 43**) using a float level gauge, ruler or vernier caliper. Refer to **Table 1** for the float level specification.

4. The float is non-adjustable. If the float level is incorrect, check the float pin and fuel valve for damage. If these parts are in good condition, replace the float and remeasure the float level.

5. Install the float bowl, O-ring and its mounting screws (A, **Figure 42**). Tighten the mounting screws securely.

6. Install the carburetor as described in this chapter.

CARBURETOR ADJUSTMENTS

Idle Speed Adjustment

Refer to Chapter Three.

Pilot Screw Adjustment

The pilot screw (A, **Figure 44**) is preset by the manufacturer. Routine adjustment is not necessary

8

unless the pilot screw was removed or replaced or the carburetor was overhauled.

> *WARNING*
> *Do not run the engine in an enclosed garage or area while adjusting the pilot screw in this procedure. Doing so will cause carbon monoxide gas to build up in the garage. Dangerous levels of carbon monoxide gas will cause loss of consciousness and death in a short time.*

1. Clean the air filter as described in Chapter Three.

2. Connect a tachometer to the engine following the manufacturer's instructions.

> *NOTE*
> *To accurately detect speed changes during this adjustment, use a tachometer with graduations of 100 rpm or smaller.*

3. Turn the pilot screw (A, **Figure 44**) clockwise until it *lightly* seats, then back it out the number of turns listed in **Table 1**.

4. Start the engine and warm it to normal operating temperature.

5. Open and release the throttle lever (**Figure 45**) a few times, making sure it returns to its closed position. If necessary, turn the engine off and adjust the throttle cable as described in Chapter Three.

6. With the engine idling, turn the idle speed screw (B, **Figure 44**) to set the engine idle speed to the rpm listed in **Table 1**.

7. Turn the pilot screw (A, **Figure 44**) in or out to obtain the highest engine idle speed.

8. Turn the idle speed screw (B, **Figure 44**) to reset the engine idle speed to the rpm listed in **Table 1**.

9. While reading the tachometer, turn the pilot screw (A, **Figure 44**) in slowly until the engine speed drops 100 rpm.

10. Open and close the throttle lever a few times while checking the idle speed reading. The engine must idle within the speed range listed in **Table 1**. If necessary, readjust the idle speed with the idle speed screw (B, **Figure 44**).

11. Turn the engine off and remove the tachometer.

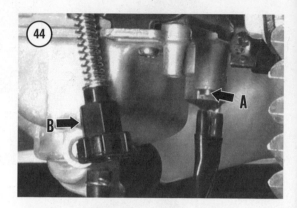

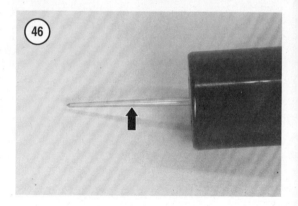

Jet Needle Adjustment

The jet needle (**Figure 46**) controls the air/fuel mixture between 1/4 and 3/4 throttle openings. The jet needle position may be changed to affect the air/fuel mixture.

1. Remove the carburetor as described in this chapter.

2. Remove the vacuum cylinder and then remove the jet needle (**Figure 37**) as described under *Carburetor Disassembly* in this chapter.

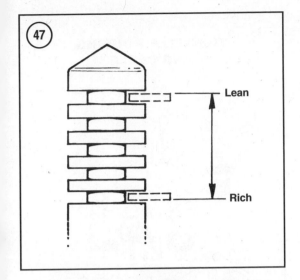

NOTE
*Record the jet needle clip position before removing it. Refer to **Table 1** for the standard jet needle clip position.*

3. Raising the needle (lowering the clip) will enrich the mixture between 1/4 and 3/4 throttle openings,

while lowering the needle (raising the clip) will lean the mixture. Refer to **Figure 47**.

4. Install the jet needle and vacuum cylinder as described under *Carburetor Assembly* in this chapter.

High Altitude Adjustment

Honda specifies two different jetting specifications for TRX350 models: standard and high altitude. Use the standard jet when operating the vehicle below 5000 ft. (1500 m). Use the high altitude jet when operating the vehicle between 3000-8000 ft. (1500-2500 m).

1. Remove the carburetor as described in this chapter.

2. Remove the float bowl mounting screws (A, **Figure 42**) and float bowl (B). Do not remove the gasket from the float bowl groove.

3. Remove the standard main jet (A, **Figure 48**) and install the high altitude main jet as listed in **Table 1**.

4. Turn the pilot screw (B, **Figure 48**) clockwise 3/4 turn.

5. Reassemble and install the carburetor.

6. Adjust the idle speed as described in Chapter Three. The idle speed is the same for standard and high altitude carburetor settings.

CAUTION
If the ATV is operated below 3000 ft. (1000 m) with the high altitude jetting, engine overheating may occur. If the ATV will be operated below this elevation, install the standard main jet and turn the pilot screw out 3/4 turn.

CARBURETOR HEATER

Carburetor Heater Testing

The carburetor heater may be tested while it is installed on the carburetor, or removed from the carburetor.

1. To test the carburetor heater while it is installed on the ATV, remove the right side cover as described in Chapter Fifteen.

2. Disconnect the electrical lead from the carburetor heater connector (**Figure 49**).

3. Connect ohmmeter leads to the two terminals of the carburetor heater connector lead. Replace the

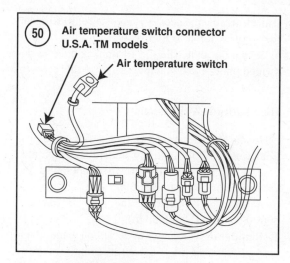

50 Air temperature switch connector
U.S.A. TM models

Air temperature switch

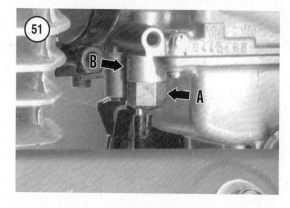

51

B →

← A

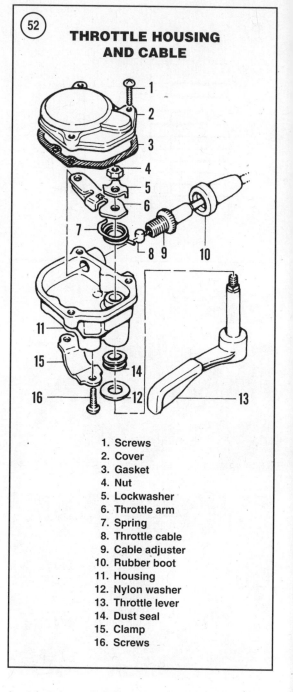

52 THROTTLE HOUSING
AND CABLE

1. Screws
2. Cover
3. Gasket
4. Nut
5. Lockwasher
6. Throttle arm
7. Spring
8. Throttle cable
9. Cable adjuster
10. Rubber boot
11. Housing
12. Nylon washer
13. Throttle lever
14. Dust seal
15. Clamp
16. Screws

heater if the resistance is outside the range specified in **Table 1**.

4. If the resistance is within specification, verify the presence of 12 volts at the wiring harness heater connector using a voltmeter. Turn the ignition switch on. Connect the positive tester lead to the brown/black wire terminal. Connect the negative tester lead to the yellow wire terminal. If the voltmeter does not indicate 12 volts, refer to Chapter Nine and determine cause.

5. On TM models, if the carburetor heater and power circuit test as specified, check the air temperature sensor as described in the following section.

Air Temperature Switch Testing

1. Unplug the air temperature switch connector (**Figure 50**) from the wiring harness.

2. Remove the air temperature switch and immerse it in a pan of ice.

3. After the switch has sat in the ice for approximately 5 minutes, check the continuity between the two terminals in the switch connector.

4. The chilled switch should have continuity (zero or very low resistance).

5. Remove the switch from the cold water. Allow the switch to warm to a temperature greater than 68°

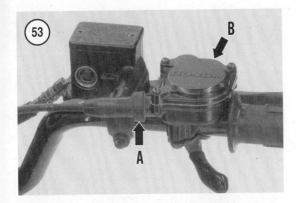

F (20° C) and recheck continuity at the switch terminals.

6. The warm switch should have no continuity.

7. Replace the air temperature switch if it fails either test.

Removal/Installation

1. Remove the right side cover as described in Chapter Fifteen.

2. Disconnect the electrical lead from the carburetor heater connector (**Figure 49**).

3. Unscrew and remove the carburetor heater (A, **Figure 51**) and collar (B) from the bottom of the float bowl.

4. Installation is the reverse of removal.

THROTTLE HOUSING AND CABLE

Throttle Housing Disassembly/Inspection/Reassembly

Refer to **Figure 52**.

1. Park the ATV on level ground and set the parking brake.

2. Slide the rubber boot (A, **Figure 53**) off the cable adjuster.

3. Remove the throttle housing cover screws and cover (B, **Figure 53**). Remove the dowel pins, if used.

4. Loosen the throttle cable adjuster locknut (A, **Figure 54**) and loosen the adjuster.

5. Pry the lockwasher tabs away from the throttle arm pivot nut (B, **Figure 54**).

6. Remove the throttle arm pivot nut (B, **Figure 54**) and lockwasher, and then remove the throttle lever and its plastic washer (**Figure 55**).

7. Disconnect the throttle cable from the throttle arm (A, **Figure 56**), and then remove the throttle arm and spring (B).

8. Clean and dry the throttle housing and all parts.

9. Replace the throttle housing dust seal (14, **Figure 52**) if it is damaged.

10. Inspect the throttle lever assembly (**Figure 57**) for:

    a. Weak or damaged spring.

    b. Damaged throttle arm.

    c. Corroded or damaged throttle arm.

    d. Worn or damaged plastic washer.

8

11. Replace the throttle housing cover gasket if it is damaged.

NOTE
Use a lithium based multipurpose grease (NLGI #2 or an equivalent) in Step 12 and Step 16.

12. Lubricate the dust seal (14, **Figure 52**) with grease.

13. Connect the throttle cable ball into the end of the throttle arm (A, **Figure 56**).

14. Connect the spring to the throttle arm. Then install the spring and throttle arm into the throttle housing. Make sure the spring engages with the throttle arm and against the throttle housing as shown in **Figure 58**.

15. Install the plastic washer (**Figure 55**) onto the throttle lever.

16. Lubricate the throttle lever shaft with grease.

17. Install the throttle lever shaft through the dust seal and throttle arm.

18. Install a new lockwasher as shown in **Figure 59**.

19. Install and tighten the throttle arm nut (B, **Figure 54**). Bend the lockwasher tab against the nut.

20. Install the throttle housing dowel pins, if they are used.

21. Install the throttle housing cover (B, **Figure 53**) and gasket, and then install and tighten the cover screws.

22. Adjust the throttle cable as described in Chapter Three.

NOTE
*After adjusting the throttle cable tighten the throttle cable adjuster locknut (A, **Figure 54**) and slide the rubber boot (A, **Figure 53**) over the adjuster.*

Throttle Cable Replacement

1. Park the ATV on level ground and set the parking brake.

2. Remove the handlebar cover (Chapter Fifteen).

3. Remove the fuel tank as described in this chapter.

4. Disconnect the throttle cable at the throttle lever as described in *Throttle Housing Disassembly/Inspection/Reassembly* in this chapter.

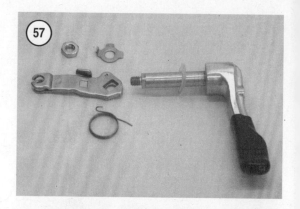

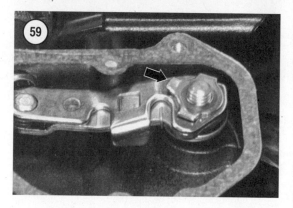

5. Disconnect the throttle cable at the carburetor as described in *Carburetor Removal* in this chapter.

6. Disconnect the throttle cable from any clips holding the cable to the frame.

7. Remove the throttle cable.

8. Install the new throttle cable through the frame, routing it from the handlebar to carburetor. Secure the cable with its frame clips.

9. Connect the throttle cable to the carburetor as described in *Carburetor Installation* in this chapter.

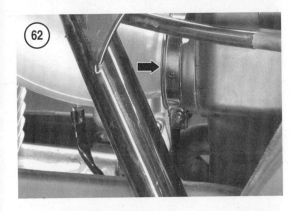

10. Reconnect the throttle cable at the throttle lever as described in *Throttle Housing Disassembly/Inspection/Reassembly* in this chapter.

11. Operate the throttle lever and make sure the carburetor throttle pulley is operating correctly. If throttle operation is sluggish, make sure the cable was attached correctly and there are no tight bends in the cable.

12. Adjust the throttle cable as described in Chapter Three.

13. Test ride the vehicle and make sure the throttle is operating correctly.

FUEL TANK

Table 2 lists fuel tank specifications.

Removal/Installation

1. Park the ATV on level ground and set the parking brake.

2. Turn off the fuel valve.

3. Remove the seat (Chapter Fifteen).

4. Disconnect the negative battery cable from the battery (Chapter Three).

5. Remove the side covers and fuel tank cover (Chapter Fifteen).

6. Disconnect the fuel hose from the carburetor (**Figure 60**).

7. Label and remove the hoses from the air intake duct (**Figure 61**).

8. Loosen the air duct clamp screw at the air box (**Figure 62**).

NOTE
Refer to Chapter Fifteen for the trim clip disengagement and engagement procedure.

9. Disengage the air duct trim clip (**Figure 63**), then remove the air duct.

10. Remove the fuel valve lever retaining screw (**Figure 64**), then remove the fuel valve lever.

11. Remove the front and rear fuel tank mounting bolts (**Figure 65**).

12. Remove the fuel tank.

13. Remove the heat guard as follows:
   a. Remove the trim clips and cable clips securing the fuel tank heat guard to the frame.

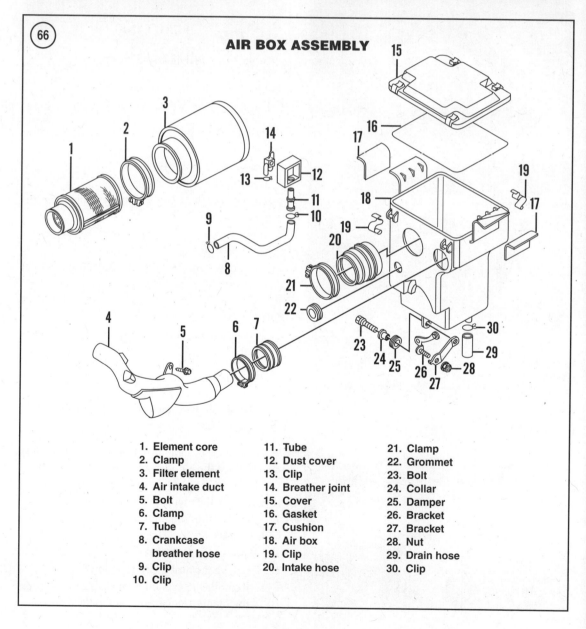

AIR BOX ASSEMBLY

1. Element core	11. Tube	21. Clamp
2. Clamp	12. Dust cover	22. Grommet
3. Filter element	13. Clip	23. Bolt
4. Air intake duct	14. Breather joint	24. Collar
5. Bolt	15. Cover	25. Damper
6. Clamp	16. Gasket	26. Bracket
7. Tube	17. Cushion	27. Bracket
8. Crankcase	18. Air box	28. Nut
breather hose	19. Clip	29. Drain hose
9. Clip	20. Intake hose	30. Clip
10. Clip		

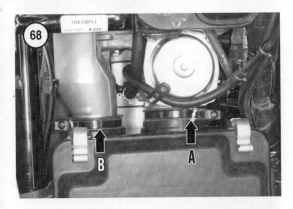

b. Push the heat guard forward to disengage the locating tabs from the frame, and remove the heat guard.

14. Install the heat guard and fuel tank by reversing the preceding removal steps while noting the following:

   a. Replace the fuel tank mounting bolt collars if they are missing or damaged.

   b. Replace missing or damaged fuel tank dampers or holder bands.

   c. After installing the fuel hose onto the fuel valve, secure the hose with a hose clamp.

   d. Tighten the fuel tank mounting bolts (**Figure 65**) securely.

   e. Turn the fuel valve on and check for leaks.

FUEL VALVE

Removal/Installation

1. Remove the fuel tank as described in this chapter.

2. Drain the fuel tank of all gas. Store the gas in a can approved for gasoline storage.

3. Remove the screws securing the fuel valve to the bottom of the fuel tank.

4. Remove the O-ring and strainer screen from the fuel valve.

5. Clean the strainer screen in a high-flash point solvent. Replace the strainer screen if it is damaged.

6. Install a new fuel valve O-ring.

7. Install the fuel valve by reversing the preceding removal steps. After installation, check the fuel valve and hose for leaks.

AIR BOX

Removal/Installation

Refer to **Figure 66**.

1. Park the ATV on level ground and set the parking brake.

2. Remove the seat and left side cover (Chapter Fifteen).

3. Disconnect the crankcase breather tube from the air box (**Figure 67**).

NOTE
Refer to Chapter Fifteen for the trim clip disengagement and engagement procedure.

4. Disengage the air duct trim clip (**Figure 63**). Move the duct forward.

5. Loosen the carburetor hose clamp at the air box (A, **Figure 68**).

7. Loosen the intake air duct clamp at the air box (B, **Figure 68**).

8. Remove the air box brace retaining nut (**Figure 69**).

9. Remove the air box assembly.

10. Cover the carburetor opening.

8

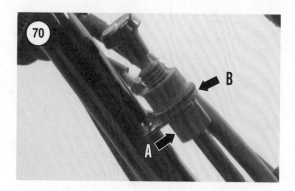

11. Installation is the reverse of the removal steps. Check the air box intake hose for loose parts or other debris before connecting it to the carburetor.

CHOKE CABLE REPLACEMENT

1. Remove the fuel tank as described in this chapter.

2. Make a diagram of the choke cable routing path from the handlebar to the carburetor.

3. Remove any cable guides from the choke cable.

4. Detach the choke cable from the left handlebar as follows:

   a. Loosen the retaining nut (A, **Figure 70**).

   b. Detach the cable from the bracket (B, **Figure 70**).

5. Loosen the starting enrichment (SE) valve nut (**Figure 71**) and remove the SE valve from the carburetor.

6. Remove the choke cable.

7. Reverse the preceding steps to install the choke cable. Position the cable so it lies in the channel in the heat guard plate. After installation, check the choke operation.

CAUTION
Do not overtighten the plastic SE valve nut.

Table 1 CARBURETOR SPECIFICATIONS

Type	Vacuum piston
Throttle bore size	32 mm (1.3 in.)
Type number	VE94A
Main jet	
Standard	130
High altitude	125
Pilot jet	42
Jet needle clip position	3rd groove from top
Idle speed	1300-1500 rpm
Pilot screw adjustment[1]	1 3/4 turns out
Float level[2]	18.5 mm (0.73 in.)
Heater resistance	13-15 ohms

1. Initial adjustment only. See text for procedure and final pilot air screw adjustment.
2. Not adjustable.

Table 2 FUEL TANK SPECIFICATIONS

	Liters	U.S. gal.
2000-2003		
Fuel tank capacity	13.0	3.43
Reserve capacity	3.2	0.85
2004-on		
Fuel tank capacity	13.9	3.67
Reserve capacity	3.1	0.82

CHAPTER NINE

ELECTRICAL SYSTEM

This chapter contains service and test procedures for all electrical and ignition components. Information regarding the battery and spark plug are covered in Chapter Three.

Models equipped with electronic shifting (FE and TE models) are also equipped with a digital combination meter that is mounted above the handlebar. Other models are equipped with standard lamp type indicator lights, but may be equipped with the digital combination meter as optional equipment.

The electrical system includes the following:

1. Charging system.
2. Ignition system.
3. Starting system
4. Lighting system.
5. Electrical components.

Tables 1-6 are located at the end of this chapter.

ELECTRICAL COMPONENT REPLACEMENT

Most ATV dealerships and parts suppliers will not accept the return of any electrical part. If you cannot determine the *exact* cause of any electrical system malfunction, have a Honda dealership retest that specific system to verify your test results. If you purchase a new electrical component(s), install it, and then find that the system still does not work

properly, you will probably be unable to return the unit for a refund.

Consider any test results carefully before replacing a component that tests only *slightly* out of specification, especially resistance. A number of variables can affect test results dramatically. These include: the testing meter's internal circuitry, ambient temperature and conditions under which the machine has been operated. All instructions and specifications have been checked for accuracy; however, successful test results depend to a great degree upon individual accuracy.

Resistance and Peak Voltage Testing

Resistance readings will vary with temperature. The resistance increases when the temperature increases and decreases when the temperature decreases.

Specifications for resistance are based on tests performed at a specific temperature (68° F [20° C]). If a component is warm or hot let it cool to room temperature. If a component is tested at a temperature that varies from the specification test temperature, a false reading may result.

To measure peak voltage, use a tester capable of measuring peak voltage or a voltmeter that has a minimum input impedance of 10M ohms/DCV and is coupled to a peak voltage adapter. An equivalent tool is the Motion Pro IgnitionMate (part No. 08-0193).

Make sure the battery of any tester being used is in good condition. The battery of an ohmmeter is the source for the current that is applied to the circuit being tested; accurate results depend on the battery having sufficient voltage.

All peak voltage specifications are minimum values. If the measured voltage meets or exceeds the specifications, the test results are acceptable.

> *NOTE*
> *When using an analog ohmmeter, always calibrate the meter between each resistance test by touching the test leads together and zeroing the meter.*

CONNECTORS

Location

Most major inline connectors are mounted on two brackets, one at the front of the frame (**Figure 1**) and the other on the right side of the frame (**Figure 2**). Refer to the following for connector identification.

1. Shift control motor on FE/TE models (A, **Figure 1**).
2. Digital combination meter models (B, **Figure 1**).
3. Handlebar switch (C, **Figure 1**).
4. Ignition switch (D, **Figure 1**).
5. Accessory socket (E, **Figure 1**).
6. Headlights (F, **Figure 1**).
7. Gear position switch on FE/TE models (A, **Figure 2**).
8. Alternator (B, **Figure 2**).
9. Speed sensor (C, **Figure 2**).
10. Carburetor heater (D, **Figure 2**).

The position of the connectors may have been changed during previous repairs. Always confirm the wire colors to and from the connector and follow the wiring harness to the various components when performing tests.

Service

> *CAUTION*
> *The internal pins are easily damaged and dislodged, which can cause a malfunction. Be careful when handling or testing the connectors.*

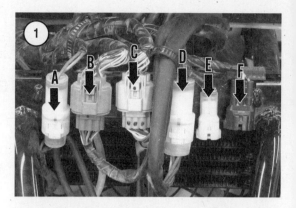

Under normal operating conditions, the connectors are weather-tight. If continuous operation in adverse conditions is expected, pack the connectors with dielectric grease to prevent the intrusion of water or other contaminants. To prevent moisture from entering into the various connectors, disconnect them, and after making sure the terminals are clean, pack the connector with dielectric grease. Do not use a substitute that may interfere with current flow. Dielectric grease is specifically formulated to seal the connector and not increase current resistance. For the best results, the compound should fill the entire inner area of the connector. Each time a connector is unplugged, clean and seal it with dielectric grease.

An often overlooked area when troubleshooting are the ground connections. Make sure they are corrosion free and tight. Apply dielectric grease to the terminals before reconnecting them.

Removal/Disassembly

To remove a connector (**Figure 1** or **Figure 2**) from the mounting bracket, use a thin screwdriver

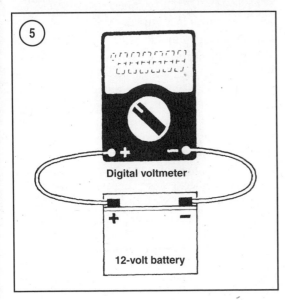

Digital voltmeter

12-volt battery

or other tool to disengage the mounting tang on the bracket from the tab on the connector.

NOTE
It is necessary to remove large rectangular connectors from the mounting

bracket for disassembly. The mounting bracket tang also locks together the connector halves. The connector must be free from the mounting bracket to disassemble or assemble the connector.

Small connectors and large round connectors may be disassembled by pulling or prying out the retaining tab at the lower end of the outer half (**Figure 3**) and pulling out the inner connector half. Large rectangular connectors are equipped with a locking tab on the outer body (**Figure 4**). Depress the tab, then pull out the inner half. It may be necessary to remove an adjacent connector from the mounting bracket to gain sufficient space to remove the desired connector. The following connectors must be removed from the mounting bracket for disassembly or assembly.

1. Combination meter connector (B, **Figure 1**).
2. Handlebar switch connector (C, **Figure 1**).
3. Gear position switch connector (A, **Figure 2**).

CHARGING SYSTEM

The charging system consists of the battery, alternator and a voltage regulator/rectifier. A 30-amp main fuse protects the circuit.

Alternating current generated by the alternator is rectified to direct current. The voltage regulator maintains the voltage to the battery and additional electrical loads at a constant voltage despite variations in engine speed and load.

Troubleshooting

Refer to Chapter Two.

Battery Voltage Check

To obtain accurate charging system test results, the battery must be fully charged.

Before testing the charging system, measure battery voltage as follows:
1. Remove the seat (Chapter Fifteen).
2. Connect a digital voltmeter between the battery negative and positive terminals (**Figure 5**) and measure the battery voltage. A fully charged battery will read between 13.0-13.2 volts. If the voltage reading

is less than this amount, recharge the battery as described in Chapter Three.

Charging System Current Draw Test

Perform this test before performing the charging voltage test.

1. Remove the seat (Chapter Fifteen).
2. Turn the ignition switch off.
3. Disconnect the negative battery cable from the battery (**Figure 6**).

> *CAUTION*
> *Before connecting the ammeter into the circuit in Step 4, set the meter to its highest amperage scale. This will prevent a large current flow from damaging the meter or blowing the meter's fuse, if so equipped.*

4. Connect an ammeter between the battery ground cable and the negative battery terminal.
5. Switch the ammeter between its highest and lowest amperage scale while reading the ammeter scale. The ammeter reading should be less than 1.0 mA.
6. A current draw higher than 1.0 mA will discharge the battery. Dirt and/or electrolyte on top of the battery or a crack in the battery case can cause this type of problem by providing a path for battery current to follow. Remove and clean the battery as described in Chapter Three. Then reinstall the battery and retest.
7. If the current draw is still excessive, consider the following probable causes.

    a. Damaged battery.

    b. Short circuit in system.

8. To find the short circuit, refer to the appropriate wiring diagram at the end of this manual. Measure the current draw while disconnecting each charging system connector one by one. When the current draw rate returns to normal, the circuit with the short circuit is identified. Test the circuit further to find the problem.
9. Disconnect the ammeter from the battery and battery cable.
10. Reconnect the negative battery cable to the battery.
11. Install the seat (Chapter Fifteen).

Charging System Voltage Test

This procedure tests charging system operation. It does not measure maximum charging system output. **Table 1** lists charging system specifications.

To obtain accurate test results, the battery must be fully charged; measure battery voltage as described in the *Battery Voltage Check* section.

1. Start and run the engine until it reaches normal operating temperature, then turn the engine off.
2. Connect a tachometer to the engine following its manufacturer's instructions.
3. Connect a 0-20 DC voltmeter to the battery terminals as shown in **Figure 5**.
4. Start the engine and allow it to run at idle speed.
5. Gradually increase engine speed from idle to 5000 rpm and read the regulated voltage reading on the voltmeter and compare it to the regulated voltage reading in **Table 1**. If the regulated voltage is higher than 15.5 volts, check for a shorted wiring harness, damaged ignition switch or a faulty regulator/rectifier; perform *Regulator/Rectifier Wiring Test* in this section. If the regulated voltage reading is correct, but there is a problem in the charging system, the battery may be faulty.
6. Disconnect the voltmeter and tachometer.
7. Install the seat (Chapter Fifteen).

Regulator/Rectifier Wiring Harness Test

1. Disconnect the regulator/rectifier electrical connector. See A, **Figure 7**, typical.

> *NOTE*
> *Make all of the tests (Steps 2-4) at the wiring harness connector, not at the regulator/rectifier.*

2. Check the battery charge lead as follows:

   a. Connect a voltmeter between the red and green connectors.

   b. With the ignition switch off, the voltmeter should read 13.0-13.2 volts (battery voltage).

   c. If the battery voltage is less than specified, check both wires for damage.

   d. Disconnect the voltmeter leads.

3. Check the ground wire as follows:

   a. Switch an ohmmeter to R × 1.

   b. Connect the ohmmeter between the green wire and a good engine ground.

   c. The ohmmeter should read continuity.

   d. If there is no continuity, check the green wire for damage.

4. Check the charge coil wires as follows:

   a. Switch an ohmmeter to R × 1.

   b. Measure resistance between each yellow wire.

   c. The ohmmeter should read 0.1-1.0 ohms at 69° F (20° C). An infinity reading indicates an open circuit. Test the stator coil resistance as described in this section.

   d. If the resistance reading is excessive, check for dirty or loose-fitting terminals or damaged wires.

5. If any regulator/rectifier measurement is out of specification, replace the regulator/rectifier as described in this chapter.

6. Reconnect the regulator/rectifier electrical connector (A, **Figure 7**).

Regulator/Rectifier Removal/Installation

1. Remove the seat.

2. Disconnect the negative battery cable from the battery (**Figure 6**).

3. Disconnect the regulator/rectifier unit electrical connector (A, **Figure 7**).

4. Remove the bolts securing the regulator/rectifier (B, **Figure 7**) to the frame and remove it.

5. Install by reversing the preceding removal steps.

ALTERNATOR

The alternator consists of the flywheel and stator coil assembly. Flywheel and stator removal and installation procedures are covered in Chapter Five.

Flywheel Testing

The flywheel is permanently magnetized and cannot be tested except by replacing it with a known good one. The rotor can loose magnetism over time or from a sharp hit, such as dropping it onto a concrete floor. Replace the flywheel if it is defective or damaged.

Stator Coil Resistance Test

NOTE
The stator coil is also referred to as the charge coil.

The stator coil (A, **Figure 8**) is mounted inside the alternator cover. The stator coil can be tested with the alternator cover mounted on the engine.

1. Disconnect the alternator/pulse generator connector (B, **Figure 2**).

2. Use an ohmmeter set at R × 1 and measure resistance between each yellow wire at the alternator end of the connector. **Table 1** lists the specified stator coil resistance.

9

3. If the resistance is as specified, the stator coil is good. If the resistance is higher than specified, the coil is damaged. Replace the stator assembly.

4. Use an ohmmeter set at R × 1 and check continuity from each yellow wire terminal in the alternator stator end of the connector and to ground. Replace the stator coil if any yellow terminal has continuity to ground. Continuity indicates a short within the stator coil winding.

> *NOTE*
> *Before replacing the stator assembly, check the electrical wires to and within the electrical connector for any open or poor connections.*

5. If the stator coil (A, **Figure 8**) fails either of these tests, replace it as described in *Alternator Cover* in Chapter Five.

6. Apply a dielectric grease to the stator coil connector before reconnecting it. This will help seal out moisture. Make sure the O-ring is mounted on the stator coil connector.

7. Reconnect the alternator/pulse generator connector.

IGNITION SYSTEM

All models are equipped with a capacitor discharge ignition system.

Servicing Precautions

1. Never disconnect any of the electrical connections while the engine is running.

2. Apply dielectric grease to all electrical connectors before reconnecting them. This will help seal out moisture.

3. The electrical connectors must be free of corrosion and properly connected.

4. The ignition control module (ICM) unit is mounted in a rubber mount. If it was removed, be sure to reinstall it into its rubber mount.

Troubleshooting

Refer to Chapter Two.

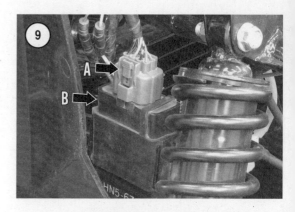

Pulse Generator

The pulse generator is mounted inside the alternator cover (B, **Figure 8**). The pulse generator may be tested with the alternator cover mounted on the engine.

Peak voltage test

The following test checks the condition of the pulse generator, wiring and connections.

1. Detach the ICM connector (A, **Figure 9**) from the ICM (B).

2. Connect the positive voltmeter lead to the blue/yellow wire terminal in the connector.

3. Connect the negative voltmeter lead to the green/white wire terminal in the connector.

4. Turn the ignition switch on.

5. Push the starter button and operate the starter while observing the voltmeter.

6. The minimum voltage reading should be at least 0.7 volts.

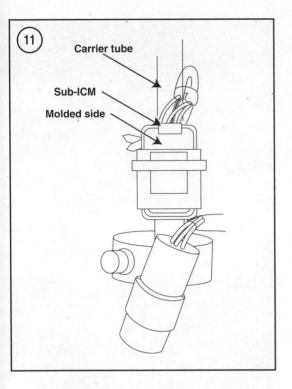

(11) Carrier tube

Sub-ICM

Molded side

NOTE
Early FE and TE models are equipped with a sub-ICM. If the tests indicate a fault, check the sub-ICM before replacing a suspected component. Refer to **Sub-ICM** *in this chapter.*

NOTE
Slow cranking speed may produce a low voltage reading. If the voltmeter indicates at least one reading that is at least 0.7 volts, then the voltmeter reading is considered acceptable.

7. If the voltage reading is less than 0.7 volts, proceed as follows:

  a. Disconnect the alternator connector (B, **Figure 2**).

  b. Connect the positive voltmeter lead to the blue/yellow wire terminal in the alternator end of the connector.

  c. Ground the negative voltmeter lead to the engine.

  d. Turn the ignition switch on.

  e. Push the starter button and operate the starter while observing the voltmeter.

  f. The minimum voltage reading should be at least 0.7 volts.

8. If the voltage reading is abnormal in Step 6, but satisfactory in Step 7, check for faulty wiring or connections.

9. If the voltage reading is abnormal in Step 6 and Step 7, the pulse generator is faulty.

Removal/installation

1. Remove the alternator cover as described in Chapter Five.

2. Remove the pulse generator mounting bolts (A, **Figure 10**) and wire clamp (B).

3. Disconnect the wire lead from the pulse generator and remove the pulse generator.

4. Reverse the removal steps to install the pulse generator. Apply threadlocker to the mounting bolts and tighten them to 6 N•m (53 in.-lb.).

Ignition Control Module

No test specifications are available for the ignition control module (ICM). The ICM should be replaced only after all other components, including wiring and connections, have been eliminated through troubleshooting as the possible cause of the malfunction. Refer to Chapter Two.

Removal/installation

The ICM (B, **Figure 9**) is mounted on the front of the ATV.

1. Remove the front fender (Chapter Fifteen).

2. Disconnect the electrical connector (A, **Figure 9**) from the ICM.

3. Remove the ICM from its rubber mount.

4. Install the ICM by reversing the removal steps.

Sub-ICM (Early FE/TE Models)

Early FE and TE models are equipped with a sub-ICM. Refer to the wiring diagrams at the back of this manual. The sub-ICM is attached to the front carrier rack under the front fender (**Figure 11**).

Removal/installation

1. Detach the connector from the sub-ICM.

2. Detach the retaining straps and remove the sub-ICM.

9

3. When installing the sub-ICM, position the molded side as shown in **Figure 11**. Route the wiring so it is secured by the upper retaining strap.

Ignition Coil

The ignition coil is mounted on the left upper frame rail (**Figure 12**). The ignition coil may be tested without removing it.

Primary peak voltage test

1. Remove the spark plug cap (**Figure 13**).
2. Connect a new spark plug to the plug cap.
3. Ground the spark plug to the crankcase.

> *WARNING*
> *High voltage is present during ignition system operation. Do not touch ignition components, wires or test leads while cranking or running the engine.*

> *NOTE*
> *All peak voltage specifications are minimum values. If the measured voltage meets or exceeds the specification, the test results are satisfactory.*

4. Check the peak voltage by performing the following:

> *NOTE*
> *Do not disconnect the wires from the ignition coil for the following test. If it is not possible to contact the coil terminal with the tester probe, pierce the wire using a needle probe.*

  a. Connect the positive test probe to the black/yellow wire or terminal on the ignition coil (**Figure 14**) and connect the negative test probe to ground.
  b. Turn the ignition switch on.
  c. Press the starter button and crank the engine for a few seconds while reading the meter. Record the highest meter reading. The minimum peak voltage is 100 volts.

5. If the peak voltage reading is less than specified, perform the troubleshooting procedure described in Chapter Two to determine the cause for low voltage reading.

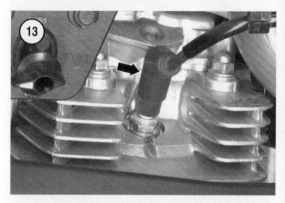

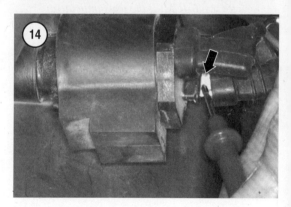

> *NOTE*
> *Before replacing an ignition coil, have it checked by a dealership on an ignition coil testing machine.*

Removal/installation

1. Remove the left side cover (Chapter Fifteen).

2. Disconnect the spark plug cap (**Figure 13**) from the spark plug and disengage the spark plug wire from the retaining clips.

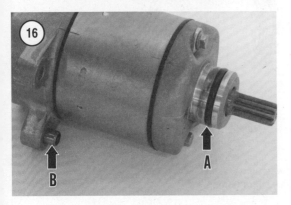

3. Disconnect the two primary wires from the ignition coil (**Figure 12**).

4. Remove the ignition coil and rubber holder from the frame.

5. Remove the rubber holder from the old ignition coil and install it onto the new coil.

6. Install the ignition coil by reversing the preceding removal steps. Make sure all electrical connections are tight and free of corrosion.

STARTER

The starting system consists of the starter, starter gears, solenoid and the starter button.

Table 3 lists starter service specifications.

The starter gears are covered in Chapter Five.

> *CAUTION*
> *Do not operate the starter for more than 5 seconds at a time. Let it cool approximately 10 seconds before operating it again.*

Troubleshooting

Refer to Chapter Two.

Removal/Installation

1. Park the ATV on level ground and set the parking brake.
2. Remove the air box (Chapter Eight).
3. Disconnect the negative battery cable from the battery.
4. Push back the rubber cap, then remove the nut and the starter cable (A, **Figure 15**) from the starter.
5. Remove the two starter mounting bolts (B. **Figure 15**) and the starter (C).
6. If necessary, service the starter as described in this chapter.
7. Install the starter by reversing the preceding removal steps, plus the following:
   a. Lubricate the starter O-ring (A, **Figure 16**) with grease.
   b. Clean any rust or corrosion from the starter cable eyelet.
   c. Be sure to install the hollow dowel pin (B, **Figure 16**) into the starter mounting leg.
   d. Tighten the starter mounting bolts securely.

Disassembly

Refer to **Figure 17**.
1. Find the alignment marks across the armature case and both end covers (**Figure 18**). If necessary, scribe new marks.
2. Remove the two case bolts (A, **Figure 19**), washers (B) and O-rings (C).

> *NOTE*
> *Record the thickness and alignment of each shim and washer removed during disassembly.*

> *NOTE*
> *The number of shims used in each starter varies. The starter may use a different number of shims than shown in the following photographs.*

3. Remove the front cover (D, **Figure 19**) and lockwasher (**Figure 20**).
4. Remove the front shims (**Figure 21**) from the armature shaft.

9

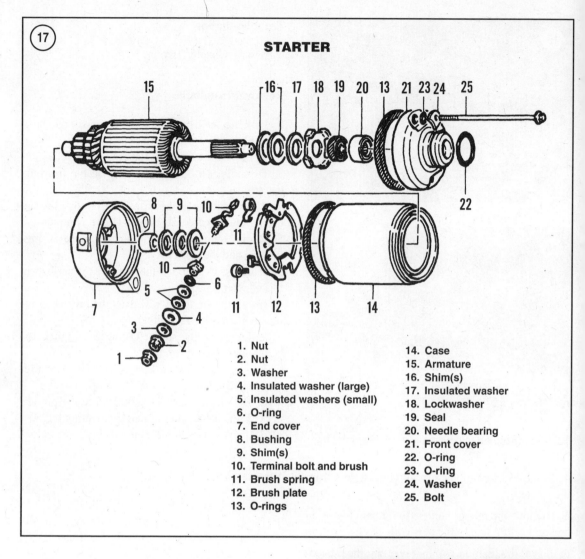

STARTER

1. Nut
2. Nut
3. Washer
4. Insulated washer (large)
5. Insulated washers (small)
6. O-ring
7. End cover
8. Bushing
9. Shim(s)
10. Terminal bolt and brush
11. Brush spring
12. Brush plate
13. O-rings
14. Case
15. Armature
16. Shim(s)
17. Insulated washer
18. Lockwasher
19. Seal
20. Needle bearing
21. Front cover
22. O-ring
23. O-ring
24. Washer
25. Bolt

5. Remove the case (**Figure 22**) and end cover (**Figure 23**).

6. Remove the rear shim set (**Figure 24**).

7. Clean all grease, dirt and carbon from the armature, case and end covers.

CAUTION
Do not immerse the wire windings in the case or the armature coil in solvent as the insulation may be damaged. Wipe the windings with a cloth lightly moistened with solvent.

Inspection

1. Pull the brush plate (A, **Figure 25**) out of the end cover.

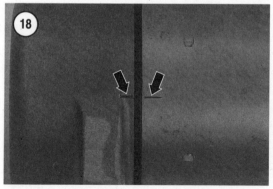

2. Pull the spring away from each brush and pull the brushes (B, **Figure 25**) out of their guides.

3. Measure the length of each brush (**Figure 26**). If the length is less than the service limit in **Table 3**,

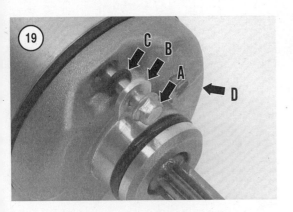

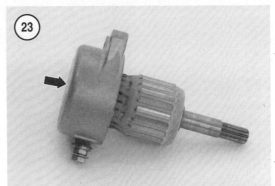

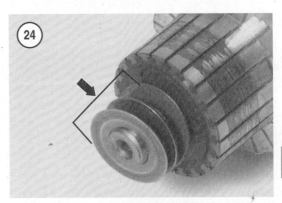

9

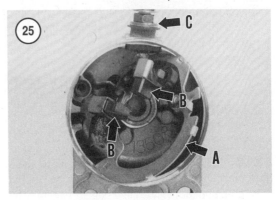

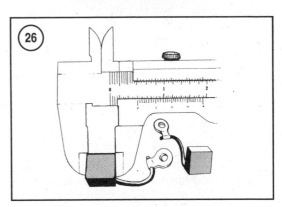

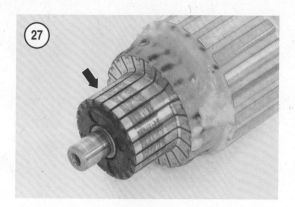

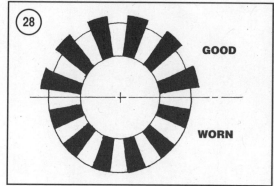

GOOD

WORN

replace both brushes as a set. When replacing the brushes, note the following:

   a. It is not necessary to solder the starter brushes when replacing them.

   b. Replace the terminal bolt and brush (C, **Figure 25**) as an assembly. Remove the terminal bolt (C, **Figure 25**) and brush, and replace them. Be sure to install the washer set in the order shown in **Figure 17**.

   c. Replace the brush plate and brush (A, **Figure 25**) as a set. Remove the brush plate and brush and replace them.

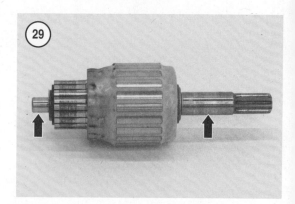

4. Inspect the brush springs and replace them if they are weak or damaged. To replace the brush springs, perform the following:

   a. Make a drawing that shows the location of the brush springs on the brush holder. Also indicate the direction in which each spring coil turns.

   b. Remove and replace both brush springs as a set.

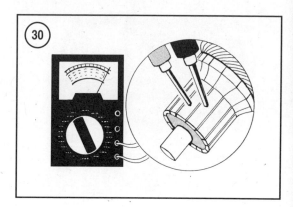

5. Inspect the commutator (**Figure 27**). The mica must be below the surface of the copper bars. On a worn commutator the mica and copper bars may be worn to the same level (**Figure 28**). If necessary, have the commutator serviced by a dealership or electrical repair shop.

6. Inspect the commutator copper bars for discoloration. A discolored pair of bars indicates grounded armature coils.

7. Inspect the armature shaft (**Figure 29**) for excessive wear, scoring or other damage.

8. Use an ohmmeter and perform the following:

   a. Check for continuity between the commutator bars (**Figure 30**). There should be continuity (low resistance) between pairs of bars.

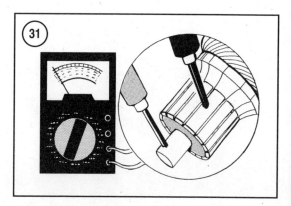

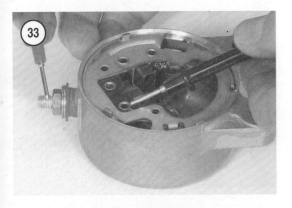

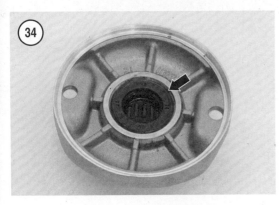

b. Check for continuity between the commutator bars and the shaft (**Figure 31**). There should be no continuity (low resistance).

c. If the armature fails either of these tests, replace the starter assembly.

9. Use an ohmmeter and perform the following:

a. Check for continuity between the starter cable terminal and the end case cover (**Figure 32**). There should be no continuity.

b. Check for continuity between the starter cable terminal and the brush black wire terminal (**Figure 33**). There should be continuity.

c. If the unit fails either of these tests, replace the starter assembly.

10. Inspect the front cover seal and needle bearing (**Figure 34**). Replace the front cover if either part is excessively worn or damaged.

11. Inspect the rear cover bushing. Replace the rear cover if the bushing is damaged.

12. Inspect the case for cracks or other damage. Then inspect it for loose, chipped or damaged magnets.

13. Inspect the O-rings and replace them if they are worn or damaged.

Assembly

1. If the brushes were removed, install them into their holders and secure them with the springs.

2. Align the brush plate arm with the notch in the end cover and install the brush plate (**Figure 35**).

3. Install the rear shims (**Figure 24**) on the armature shaft next to the commutator.

4. Insert the armature coil assembly into the rear cover (**Figure 23**). Turn the armature during installation so the brushes engage the commutator properly. Make sure the armature is not turned upside down or the shims could slide off the end of the shaft. Do not damage the brushes.

5. Install the two O-rings (**Figure 36**) onto the case. Then slide the case over the armature (**Figure 22**). Align the marks on the case and end cover (**Figure 37**).

6. Install the front shims (**Figure 21**) onto the armature shaft.

7. Install the lockwasher (**Figure 20**) onto the front cover so the lockwasher tabs engage the cover slots (**Figure 38**).

8. Install the front cover (A, **Figure 39**) over the armature shaft. Align the marks on the front cover and the case (B, **Figure 39**).

9. Lubricate the O-rings (C, **Figure 19**) with oil.

10. Install the bolts, washers and O-rings and tighten the bolts securely.

> *NOTE*
> *If one or both bolts will not pass through the starter, the end covers and/or brush plate are installed incorrectly.*

STARTER RELAY SWITCH

System Test

System testing of the starter relay switch is described in *Electric Starting System* in Chapter Two.

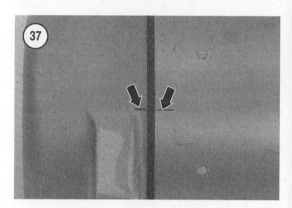

Operation Check

1. Remove the seat (Chapter Fifteen), then remove the lid above the battery.

> *NOTE*
> *To remove the lid fasteners, rotate the screw counterclockwise fully, then pull out the fastener. When turned clockwise, the screw expands the fastener body to secure it in the hole.*

2. Turn the ignition switch on and depress the starter button. The starter relay (A, **Figure 40**) should click. If the starter relay did not click, perform the *Voltage Test* in this section.

3. Turn the ignition switch off and install the seat (Chapter Fifteen).

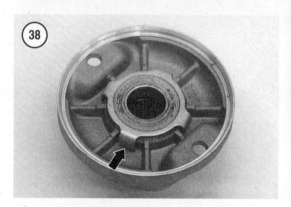

Voltage Test

1. Remove the seat (Chapter Fifteen), then remove the lid above the battery.

2. Lift the rubber cover off the starter relay.

3. Disconnect the starter relay connector (B, **Figure 40**).

4. Connect a voltmeter between the starter relay connector yellow/red (+) and green/red (–) wire terminals at the wiring harness end of the connector.

5. Shift the transmission into neutral and turn the ignition switch on, then depress the starter button.

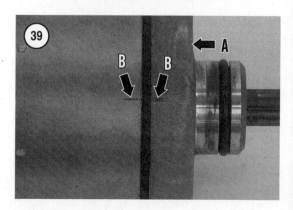

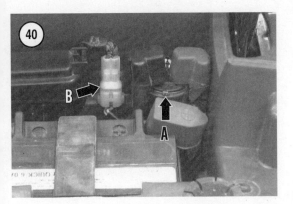

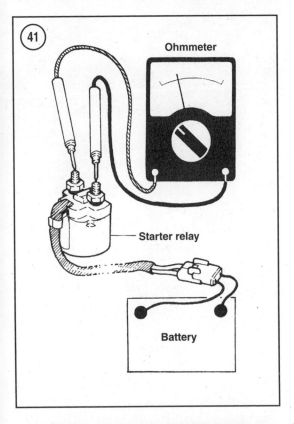

Ohmmeter

Starter relay

Battery

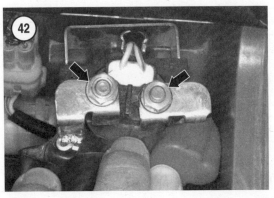

The voltmeter should read battery voltage. If the voltmeter reading is incorrect, perform the *Continuity Test* in this section.

6. Turn the ignition switch off.

7. Reverse Steps 1-3 to complete installation.

Continuity Test

1. Remove the starter relay switch as described in this chapter.

2. Connect an ohmmeter to the starter relay switch battery and starter terminals (**Figure 41**).

3. Momentarily connect a 12-volt battery to the starter relay switch terminals as shown in **Figure 41** while reading the resistance on the ohmmeter.

4. The ohmmeter should show continuity when battery voltage is applied and no continuity when the battery voltage is removed.

5. If either reading is incorrect, replace the starter relay switch and retest.

Removal/Installation

1. Remove the seat (Chapter Fifteen), then remove the lid above the battery.

2. Disconnect the negative battery cable from the battery (Chapter Three).

3. Disconnect the starter relay connector (B, **Figure 40**).

4. Slide the two covers away from the terminals on top of the starter relay switch.

5. Disconnect the battery and starter cables from the starter relay switch (**Figure 42**).

6. Remove the starter relay switch and its rubber mount from the frame.

7. Install the starter relay switch by reversing the preceding removal procedures.

DIODE

A diode is installed in the starting circuit. See the wiring diagrams at back of this manual.

Removal/Testing/Installation

1. Remove the seat (Chapter Fifteen), then remove the lid above the battery.

2. Remove the fuse box cover (**Figure 43**).

3. Pull out the diode (**Figure 44**).

9

4. Test the diode as follows:

   a. Set an ohmmeter to the R × 1 scale.

   b. Check for continuity between the middle terminal on the diode (A, **Figure 45**) and one of the end terminals (B). Reverse the ohmmeter leads and recheck for continuity between the same terminals. The ohmmeter should read continuity during one test and no continuity (infinite resistance) with the leads reversed.

   c. Repeat substep b by checking for continuity between the middle terminal and the remaining end terminal.

   d. Replace the diode if it fails the continuity tests.

5. Reverse Steps 1-3 to install the diode.

ELECTRIC SHIFT SYSTEM

FE and TE models are equipped with the electric shift system. The shift components are controlled by the electronic control unit (ECU). Input from switches and sensors prompts the ECU to operate the shift control motor, which drives a set of reduction gears to actuate the transmission shift components and the clutch. Refer to **Figure 46**.

Operation

The shift control motor (**Figure 47**) may rotate in either direction. Rotation transfers through the gear reduction assembly to the gearshift spindle. The gearshift spindle controls the transmission and change clutch similar to manually shifted models. When the control motor rotates, the gearshift spindle rotates thereby disengaging the change clutch and shifting gears.

The angle sensor converts gearshift spindle motion into electrical signals that are sent to the ECU.

The computer portion of the ECU converts the input signals from the switches and sensors into directional signals for the motor circuit, which powers the control motor. The ECU also contains a self-diagnostic circuit that stops operation of the electronic shift system if it detects an error.

NOTE
If the electronic shift system malfunctions, turn off the ignition switch, wait a short time, then turn it back on. If the electronic shift system malfunc-

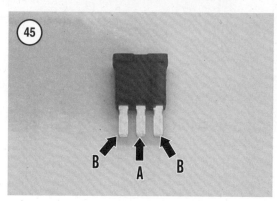

tion remains, refer to Chapter Two and follow the troubleshooting procedure.

The gearshift switches on the left handlebar assembly (A, **Figure 48**) send shift up or shift down signals to the ECU. The reverse shift button (B, **Figure 48**) engages the reverse shift cable when the rear brake lever is pulled. The reverse cable actuates the internal reverse arm, which operates the reverse switch on the rear crankcase cover. The reverse switch informs the ECU that the control motor may

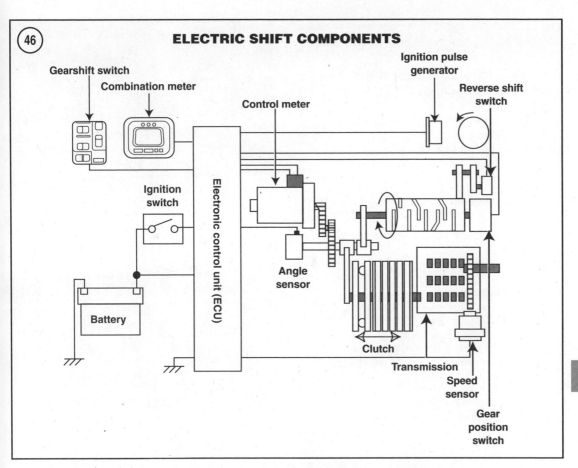

46 **ELECTRIC SHIFT COMPONENTS**

Gearshift switch
Combination meter
Control meter
Ignition pulse generator
Reverse shift switch
Ignition switch
Electronic control unit (ECU)
Angle sensor
Battery
Clutch
Transmission
Speed sensor
Gear position switch

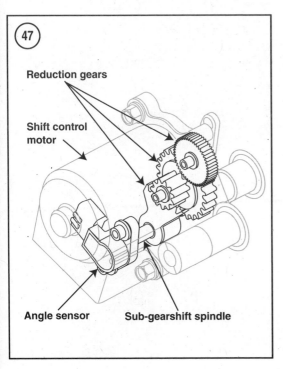

47

Reduction gears
Shift control motor
Angle sensor
Sub-gearshift spindle

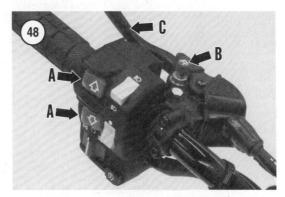

48

C
B
A
A

be operated so the transmission may be shifted into reverse.

NOTE
*The rear brake lever (C, **Figure 48**) must be pulled in to engage the reverse shift button.*

The gear position indicator switch sends a signal to the ECU to indicate the position of the shift drum.

The ECU sends a signal to the combination meter which displays a number to indicate the selected gear.

Signals from the ignition pulse generator and the speed sensor indicate to the ECU the speed of the engine and the ATV.

Electronic Control Unit (ECU)

Troubleshooting

A testing procedure is not available for the ECU. Refer to Chapter Two and determine if the ECU is faulty by eliminating other possible causes for an electric shift malfunction.

Removal/installation

> *CAUTION*
> *The ECU may be damaged by voltage surge. Make sure the ignition switch is off before detaching the electrical connectors.*

> *CAUTION*
> *The ECU may be damaged if it is dropped or struck. Use care when handling the ECU.*

1. Disconnect the electrical connectors (**Figure 49**) from the ECU.
2. Remove the ECU.
3. Inspect the mounting cushion and replace it if it is damaged.
4. Reverse the removal steps to install the ECU.

Control Motor

Testing

> *CAUTION*
> *Do not attempt the following procedure with the shift control motor in the circuit. Doing so may damage the ECU.*

Test the shift control motor as follows:
1. Remove the motor as described in the following section.
2. Connect a 12-volt battery to the terminals of the shift motor connector. Replace the motor if it does not operate. Individual parts are not available.

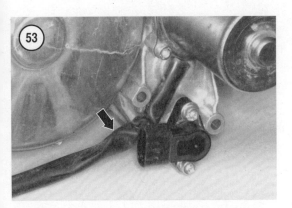

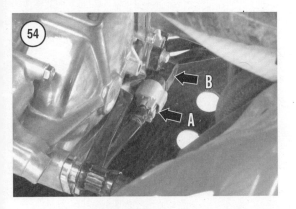

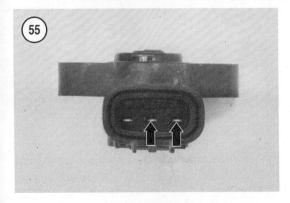

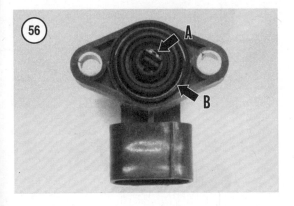

Removal/installation

1. Make sure the ignition switch is off.
2. Remove the angle sensor cover mounting bolts, then remove the cover (**Figure 50**).
3. Disconnect the control motor electrical connector (A, **Figure 1**). Detach the wire clamps securing the wire to the frame.
4. Remove the control motor mounting bolts (A, **Figure 51**), then remove the control motor (B).
5. Inspect the O-ring (**Figure 52**) and replace it if it is damaged or hard.

> *NOTE*
> *Make sure the control motor wire (Figure 53) passes under the sensor cover during assembly.*

6. Reverse the removal steps to install the control motor while noting the following:
   a. Apply engine oil to the O-ring.
   b. Install the angle sensor cover so the slot fits around the lug on the crankcase cover.
   c. Tighten the mounting bolts securely.

Angle Sensor

Testing/replacement

1. Make sure the ignition switch is off.
2. Remove the right center mud guard as described in Chapter Fifteen.
3. Remove the angle sensor cover mounting bolts, then remove the cover (**Figure 50**).
4. Disconnect the electrical connector (A, **Figure 54**) from the angle sensor.
5. Remove the angle sensor mounting bolts, then remove the angle sensor (B, **Figure 54**).
6. Connect an ohmmeter to the center and end terminals indicated in **Figure 55**.

> *CAUTION*
> *Do not damage the sensor shaft hole when turning the shaft in Step 7.*

7. Rotate the sensor shaft (A, **Figure 56**) slowly clockwise while watching the ohmmeter. The ohmmeter reading should decrease slowly when the shaft is turned clockwise, and increase slowly when the shaft is turned counterclockwise. Rotate the sensor shaft slowly counterclockwise. The ohmmeter reading should increase slowly.

8. Inspect the sensor shaft hole for damage or excessive wear.

9. Reverse the removal procedure to install the angle sensor while noting the following:

    a. Install a new O-ring onto the angle sensor (B, **Figure 56**).

    b. Align the flats on the sensor shaft (A, **Figure 56**) and the gearshift spindle (**Figure 57**) when installing the angle sensor onto the crankcase cover.

    c. Apply a threadlock to the sensor mounting bolts.

    d. Tighten the sensor mounting bolts to 6 N•m (53 in.-lb.).

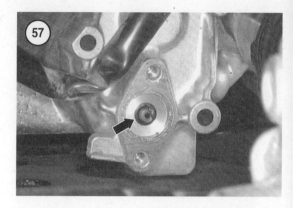

> *NOTE*
> *Make sure the control motor wire (**Figure 53**) passes under the sensor cover during assembly.*

Gear Position Switch

The gear position switch is mounted on the inside of the rear crankcase cover (A, **Figure 58**).

Testing/replacement

1. Disconnect the gear position switch connector (A, **Figure 2**).

2. Switch an ohmmeter to the R × 1 scale and connect the leads between each wire terminal and ground. The ohmmeter should show continuity when the transmission is in neutral or in gear. Refer to wiring diagram.

3. If any readings are incorrect, replace the gear position switch as follows:

    a. Remove the rear crankcase cover (Chapter Five).

    b. Remove the wire grommet from the cover (**Figure 59**).

    c. Remove the gear position switch retaining bolt (B, **Figure 58**), then remove the switch (A).

    d. Remove all threadlock residue from the bolt and bolt threads.

    e. Apply a threadlock to the bolt threads.

    f. Install the gear position switch and tighten the bolt to 12 N•m (106 in.-lb.).

    g. Apply sealant to the grommet and install it into the rear crankcase cover.

    h. Install the rear crankcase cover (Chapter Five).

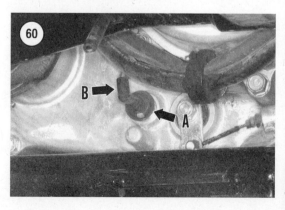

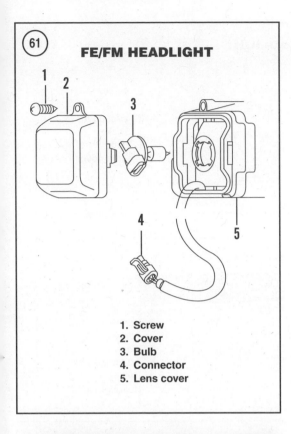

FE/FM HEADLIGHT

1. Screw
2. Cover
3. Bulb
4. Connector
5. Lens cover

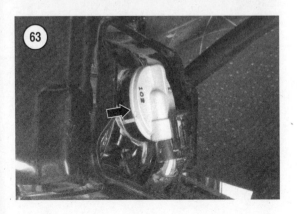

Reverse Shift Switch

Testing/replacement

The reverse shift switch (A, **Figure 60**) is mounted on the rear crankcase cover. The reverse shift switch sends a signal to the electronic control unit of the electric shift system to indicate that the transmission is in reverse gear.

1. Remove the seat as described in Chapter Fifteen.
2. Remove the alternator (B, **Figure 2**) and gear position/reverse switch (A) connectors from the frame.
3. Disconnect the gear position/reverse switch connector (A, **Figure 2**).
4. Switch an ohmmeter to the R × 1 scale and connect the leads between the gray/red wire terminal in the switch end of the connector and ground. The ohmmeter should show continuity with the reverse button depressed and infinity when the button is released.
5. If any readings are incorrect, replace the reverse shift switch as follows:
   a. Detach the switch wire (B, **Figure 60**) from the switch (A).
   b. Remove the switch. Discard the washer.
   c. Install the switch and a new washer. Tighten the switch to 13 N•m (115 in.-lb.).

LIGHTING SYSTEM

The lighting system consists of a headlight, assist headlight, taillight and indicator lights. **Table 4** lists replacement bulbs for these components.

Always use the correct wattage bulb. Using the wrong size bulb will produce a dim light or cause the bulb to burn out prematurely.

Headlight Bulb Replacement (FE/FM Models)

> *WARNING*
> *If the headlight just burned out or was just turned off, it will be hot! Do not touch the bulb until it cools.*

Refer to **Figure 61**.

1. Remove the screw and the headlight bulb cover (**Figure 62**).
2. Turn the bulb (**Figure 63**) counterclockwise and remove it.

9

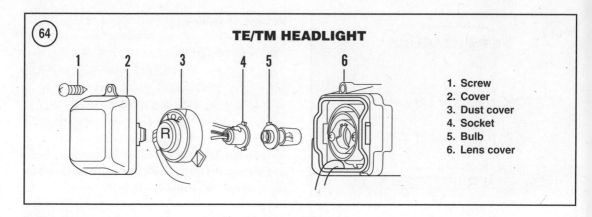

TE/TM HEADLIGHT

1. Screw
2. Cover
3. Dust cover
4. Socket
5. Bulb
6. Lens cover

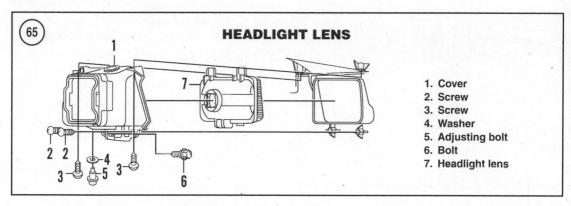

HEADLIGHT LENS

1. Cover
2. Screw
3. Screw
4. Washer
5. Adjusting bolt
6. Bolt
7. Headlight lens

3. Disconnect the electrical lead from the bulb.

4. Install the new bulb by reversing the removal procedure. Make sure the rubber seal ring on the electrical connector is in good condition.

5. Check headlight operation.

Headlight Bulb Replacement (TE/TM Models)

WARNING
If the headlight just burned out or was just turned off, it will be hot! Do not touch the bulb until it cools.

Refer to **Figure 64**.

1. Remove the screw and the headlight bulb cover.

2. Remove the dust cover.

3. Turn the bulb socket counterclockwise and remove it.

4. Remove the bulb.

5. Install the new bulb by aligning the bulb tab with the groove in the bulb housing.

6. Install the bulb socket. Turn and lock it in place.

7. Install the dust cover with the TOP mark facing up. Make sure the dust cover seats completely against the headlight housing.

8. Install the headlight bulb cover by aligning the tab with the groove in the headlight housing.

9. Check headlight operation.

Headlight Lens Removal/Installation

Refer to **Figure 65**.

1. Remove the headlight bulb as described in this chapter.

2. Remove the headlight aim adjusting screw (A, **Figure 66**).

3. Remove the lower mounting bolt (B, **Figure 66**).

4. Remove the four retaining screws (C, **Figure 66**), then remove the headlight.

5. Disengage the lens tabs from the headlight housing slots and separate the lens from the housing (**Figure 67**).

6. Install the headlight lens and housing by reversing the preceding removal steps. Check headlight operation. Adjust the headlight as described in this chapter.

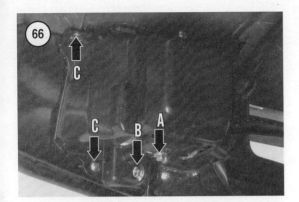

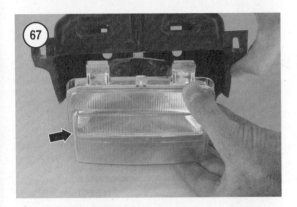

Headlight Adjustment

The headlight is equipped with only a vertical aiming adjust screw located at the bottom of the headlight (A, **Figure 66**).

To adjust the headlight vertically, turn the screw clockwise to aim the light lower and counterclockwise to direct the light up.

Taillight Bulb Replacement

1. Open the tool box cover.

2. Push the taillight studs (**Figure 68**) out of the grommets and remove the taillight housing.

3. Turn the bulb holder (**Figure 69**) counterclockwise and remove it from the lens housing.

4. Remove the old bulb from the bulb holder.

5. Reverse the preceding steps to install a new bulb. Note the UP mark on the taillight housing when installing it into the tool box cover. Check taillight operation.

Indicator Bulb Replacement

U.S. FM and TM models are equipped with individual indicator bulbs for oil pressure, reverse gear and neutral. FE and TE models, as well as Canadian FM and TM models, are equipped with LED indicator lights that are part of the digital display in the combination meter. Refer to the following procedure to remove individual indicator bulbs.

NOTE
The digital display combination meter, which includes LED indicator lights, is optional on U.S. FM and TM models.

1. Remove the handlebar cover as described in Chapter Fifteen.

2. Pull the socket out of the handlebar cover, then remove the bulb.

3. Reverse the preceding steps to install the new bulb.

4. When installing the socket, align the tab on the socket with the groove in the handlebar cover.

5. Start the engine and check bulb operation.

COMBINATION METER

All models except U.S. FM and TM models are equipped with a digital display combination meter (**Figure 70**). The combination meter is also offered as optional equipment on U.S. FM and TM models.

Troubleshooting

Refer to Chapter Two.

Removal/Installation

1. Disconnect the ignition switch connector (D, **Figure 1**) and meter connector (B).
2. Detach the wiring retaining clips on the steering shaft holder and the frame.
3. Remove the three meter cover retaining screws (A, **Figure 71**).
4. Remove the meter cover (B, **Figure 71**) while also pulling out the fuel tank breather hose (C).
5. Remove the meter bracket mounting bolts (**Figure 72**), then remove the meter and bracket.
6. Remove the meter retaining nuts (**Figure 73**) and separate the meter from the bracket.
7. Install the combination meter by reversing the preceding removal steps.
8. Start the engine and check the meter operation.

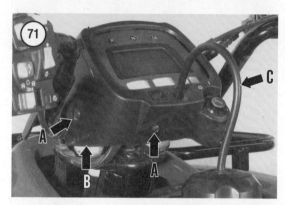

SWITCHES

Testing

Test switches for continuity using an ohmmeter (Chapter One) or a self-powered test light. Test at the switch connector by operating the switch in each of its operating positions and comparing the results with the switch continuity diagram. For example, **Figure 74** shows the ignition switch continuity diagram.

When the ignition switch key is turned to the on position, there will be continuity between the red/black and pink wire terminals, and between the red and black wire terminals. The line joining the terminals shows continuity (**Figure 74**). An ohmmeter connected between these terminals will show no resistance or a test light will light. When the ignition switch is turned off, there will be no continuity between the same terminals.

When testing switches, note the following:

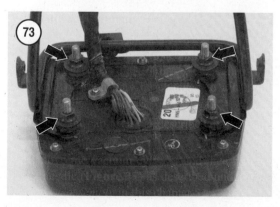

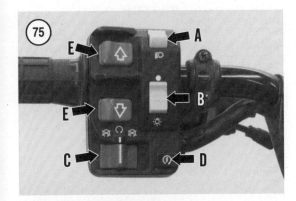

74	IGNITION SWITCH			
	BAT2	**DC**	**BAT1**	**BAT**
On	●———●		●———●	
Off				
Color	R/B	P	R	B

R = Red
B = Black
P = Pink

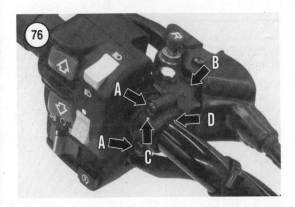

1. Check the fuses as described in *Fuses* in this chapter.

2. Check the battery as described in *Battery* in Chapter Three. Charge the battery to the correct state of charge, if required.

3. Before testing the switches, disconnect the negative battery cable from the battery (Chapter Three) and disconnect the switch electrical connector.

CAUTION
Do not attempt to start the engine with the negative battery cable disconnected.

4. When separating two connectors, pull on the connector housings and not the wires.

5. After finding a defective circuit, check the connectors to make sure they are clean and properly connected. Check all wires going into a connector housing for loose connections or damage.

6. When joining two connectors, push them until they click or snap into place.

7. If a switch or button does not perform properly, replace the switch as described in this section.

Left Handlebar Switch Housing Replacement

FE and TE models

FE and TE models are equipped with the left handlebar switch housing shown in **Figure 75**. The left handlebar switch is equipped with the following switches.

1. Lighting switch (A).
2. Dimmer switch (B).
3. Engine stop switch (C).
4. Starter switch (D).
5. Gearshift switches (E).

NOTE
The switches mounted in the left handlebar switch housing are not available separately. If one switch is damaged, replace the switch housing assembly.

6. Remove the three meter cover retaining screws (A, **Figure 71**).

7. Remove the meter cover (B, **Figure 71**) while also pulling out the fuel tank breather hose (C).

8. Disconnect the green handlebar switch connector (C, **Figure 1**). The connector has ten pins.

9. Detach the wiring retaining clips on the steering shaft holder and the frame.

10. Remove the rear (parking) brake lever clamp screws (A, **Figure 76**), remove the clamp and move the brake lever assembly (B) out of the way.

11. Remove the switch housing screws and separate the switch halves. Remove the switch and its wiring harness from the frame.

12. Install the switch housing by reversing the preceding removal steps, while noting the following:

9

a. Install the switch housing, but do not tighten the screws.

b. Install the brake lever assembly while inserting the tab on the brake lever (A, **Figure 77**) into the slot (B) in the switch housing.

c. Install the brake lever clamp so the punch mark is up (C, **Figure 76**). Position the clamp so the inner edge aligns with the punch mark (D, **Figure 76**) on the handlebar. Tighten the upper clamp screw first, then tighten the lower clamp screw.

d. Tighten the upper switch housing screw first, then the lower screws.

13. Start the engine and check the switch in each of its operating positions.

FM and TM models

FM and TM models are equipped with the left handlebar switch housing shown in **Figure 78**. The left handlebar switch is equipped with the following switches.

1. Lighting switch (A).
2. Dimmer switch (B).
3. Engine stop switch (C).
4. Starter switch (D).

> *NOTE*
> *The switches mounted in the left handlebar switch housing are not available separately. If one switch is damaged, replace the switch housing assembly.*

5. Remove the handlebar cover (Chapter Fifteen).

6. Disconnect the green handlebar switch connector (C, **Figure 1**, typical). The connector has eight pins.

7. Detach the wiring retaining clips on the steering shaft holder and the frame.

8. Remove the switch housing screws and separate the switch halves. Remove the switch and its wiring harness from the frame.

9. Install the switch housing by reversing the preceding removal steps, while noting the following:

a. Align the rear switch housing pin with the hole in the handlebar (**Figure 79**), then install the housing.

b. Tighten the upper switch housing screw first, then the lower screw.

10. Start the engine and check the switch in each of its operating positions.

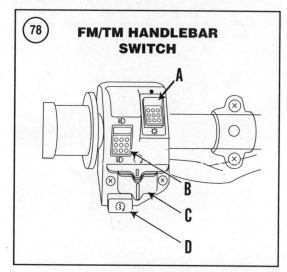

78   **FM/TM HANDLEBAR SWITCH**

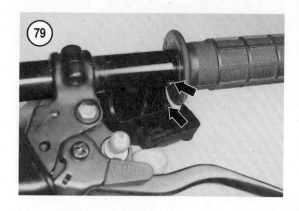

Ignition Switch Replacement

The ignition switch is mounted in the handlebar cover or combination meter cover (**Figure 80**, typical).

1. Disconnect the white ignition switch connector (D, **Figure 1**, typical).

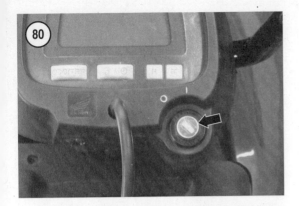

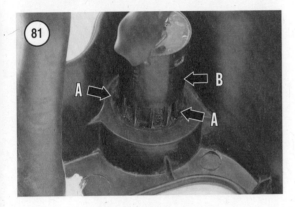

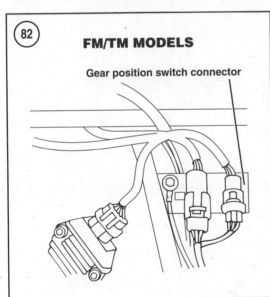

FM/TM MODELS

Gear position switch connector

2. Detach the wiring retaining clips on the steering shaft holder and the frame.

3A. On FE/TE models:

a. Remove the three meter cover retaining screws (A, **Figure 71**).

b. Remove the meter cover (B, **Figure 71**) while also pulling out the fuel tank breather hose (C).

3B. On FM/TM models, remove the handlebar cover (Chapter Fifteen).

4. Depress the ignition switch tabs (A, **Figure 81**), then remove the ignition switch (B) by pushing it from the bottom side.

5. Install the ignition switch by reversing the preceding steps while noting the following:

a. Install the new switch by aligning the two plastic guide strips on the switch housing with the notch in the switch mounting hole. Push the switch into place.

b. Turn the ignition switch on and check operation.

Gear Position Switch

Testing (FM/TM models)

> *NOTE*
> *Refer to Chapter Two for testing the gear position switch on FE and TE models.*

1. Disconnect the gear position switch connector (**Figure 82**).

2. Switch an ohmmeter to the R × 1 scale and connect the leads between the light green/red wire terminal and ground. The ohmmeter should show continuity when the transmission is in neutral and infinity when the transmission is in gear.

3. Connect the ohmmeter leads between the gray wire and ground. The ohmmeter should show continuity when the transmission is in reverse and infinity when the transmission is in any other gear or neutral.

4. If any readings are incorrect, replace the gear position switch.

Removal

The gear position switch (A, **Figure 83**) is mounted inside the rear crankcase cover.

1. Remove the rear crankcase cover (Chapter Five).

2. Remove the wire grommet from the cover (**Figure 84**).

3. Remove the switch retaining bolt (B, **Figure 82**), then remove the switch (A).

4. Remove all threadlock residue from the bolt and bolt threads.

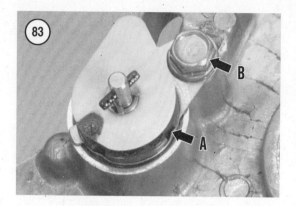

5. Apply a threadlock to the bolt threads.

6. Install the switch and tighten the bolt to 12 N•m (106 in.-lb.).

7. Apply sealant to the grommet and install it into the rear crankcase cover.

8. Install the rear crankcase cover (Chapter Five).

OIL THERMOSENSOR

The oil thermosensor (**Figure 85**) is located on the left side of the crankcase.

Testing

1. Remove the oil thermosensor as described in this section.

> *WARNING*
> *Wear safety glasses and gloves during this test. Keep all flammable materials away from the burner.*

2. Use an ohmmeter with an alligator clip on one test lead end. Attach one of the alligator clips to the electrical connector on the sensor.

3. Suspend the thermosensor in a small container filled with engine oil (A, **Figure 86**).

4. Place a thermometer in the pan of oil (B, **Figure 86**). Do not let the sensor or the thermometer touch the pan as it will give false readings.

5. Heat the oil and place the remaining ohmmeter test lead against the threads on the thermosensor body.

6. Check the resistance readings at the temperatures listed below:

    a. At 302° F (150° C), the ohmmeter should read 306-340 ohms.

    b. At 338° F (170° C), the ohmmeter should read 209-231 ohms.

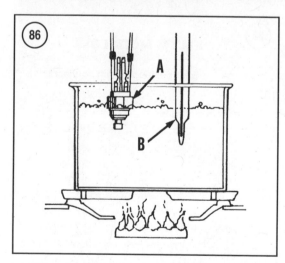

7. If the resistance readings are incorrect, replace the thermosensor.

8. Install the oil thermosensor as described in this section.

Removal/Installation

1. Drain the engine oil (Chapter Three).

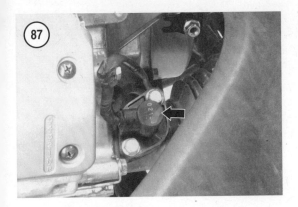

2. Disconnect the connector from the thermosensor and remove the thermosensor (**Figure 85**).

3. Reverse Steps 1 and 2 to install the thermosensor while noting the following:

   a. Install a new sealing washer.

   b. Tighten the oil thermosensor to 18 N•m (13 ft.-lb.).

   c. After starting the engine, check for oil leaks.

SPEED SENSOR UNIT

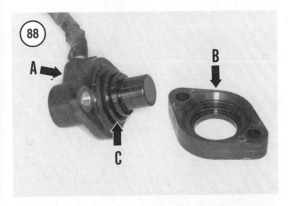

All FE and TE models, as well as FM and TM models equipped with a combination meter, are equipped with a speed sensor unit. The speed sensor unit is mounted in the rear crankcase cover (**Figure 87**).

Testing

Refer to *Combination Meter* in Chapter Two.

Removal/Installation

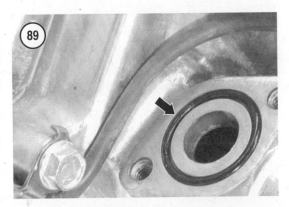

1. Remove the rear crankcase cover as described in Chapter Fifteen.

2. Disconnect the speed sensor electrical connector (C, **Figure 2**).

3. Remove the bolts, speed sensor unit (A, **Figure 88**) and insulator (B).

4. Replace the O-ring on the speed sensor (C, **Figure 88**) and crankcase cover (**Figure 89**) if it is leaking or damaged.

5. Installation is the reverse of the preceding removal steps while noting the following:

   a. Lubricate the two O-rings with engine oil.

   b. Tighten the mounting bolts securely.

FUSES

Whenever the fuse blows, determine the reason for the failure before replacing the fuse. Usually, the trouble is a short circuit in the wiring, which may be caused by worn-through insulation or a disconnected wire touching ground.

All fuses are contained in the fuse box located next to the battery (**Figure 90**).

See **Table 5** for fuse ratings.

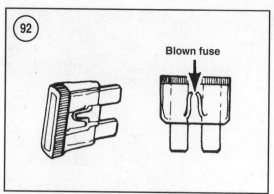

Blown fuse

Removal/Installation

1. Remove the seat (Chapter Fifteen), then remove the lid above the battery.

> *NOTE*
> *To remove the lid fasteners, rotate the screw counterclockwise fully, then pull out the fastener. When turned clockwise, the screw expands the fastener body to secure it in the hole.*

2. Make sure the ignition switch is turned off.

> *CAUTION*
> *If the fuse is replaced with the ignition switch turned on, an accidental short circuit could damage the electrical system.*

3. Remove the fuse box cover. Remove the fuse (**Figure 91**). Replace the fuse if it is blown (**Figure 92**).

> *NOTE*
> *The size and function of each fuse is labeled inside the fuse box cover (Figure 93).*

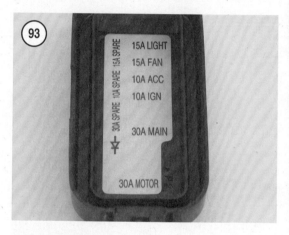

> *NOTE*
> *Always carry spare fuses.*

4. Installation is the reverse of the preceding removal steps.

WIRING DIAGRAMS

Wiring diagrams for all models are located at the end of this manual.

Table 1 CHARGING SYSTEM SPECIFICATIONS

Alternator	
Capacity	0.245 kW at 5000 rpm
Stator coil resistance*	0.1-1.0 ohms
Regulator/rectifier	
Type	Three phase/full-wave rectification
Regulated voltage	Battery voltage-15.5 volts at 5000 rpm

*Perform tests at 68° F (20° C). Do not test if the engine or component is hot.

Table 2 IGNITION SYSTEM PEAK VOLTAGE SPECIFICATIONS*

Ignition coil peak voltage	100 volts minimum
Ignition pulse generator peak voltage	0.7 volts minimum

*The Honda peak voltage adapter (part No. 07HGJ-0020100) and a digital multimeter with an impedance of 10M ohms/DVC minimum are required.

Table 3 STARTER SERVICE SPECIFICATIONS

	New mm (in.)	Service limit mm (In.)
Brush length	12.5 (0.49)	9.0 (0.35)

Table 4 REPLACEMENT BULBS

	Voltage-wattage
Headlight	12V-30W
Neutral indicator	12V-1.7W
Oil light indicator	12V-1.7W
Reverse indicator	12V-1.7W
Taillight	12V-5W

Table 5 FUSES

	Fuse rating
Main fuse	30 amp
Sub-fuses located in fuse box	
Accessories	10 amp
Fan motor/horn	15 amp
Ignition	10 amp
Lights	15 amp

Table 6 ELECTRICAL SYSTEM TORQUE SPECIFICATIONS

	N•m	in.-lb.	ft-lb.
Angle sensor (FE/TE)	6	53	–
Gear position switch	12	106	–
Ignition pulse generator Allen bolts	6	53	–
Oil thermosensor	18	–	13
Recoil pulley flange bolt (rotor bolt)	108	–	80
Reverse shift switch bolt	13	115	–
Starter one-way clutch Allen bolts	23	–	17
Stator Allen bolts	10	88	–
Timing hole cap	10	88	–

9

FRONT SUSPENSION AND STEERING

This chapter describes repair and maintenance of the front wheels, suspension arms and steering components.

Refer to **Table 1** for general front suspension and steering specifications. **Tables 2-5** list service specifications and torque specifications. **Tables 1-5** are located at the end of this chapter.

WARNING
Self-locking nuts are used to secure some of the front suspension components. Honda recommends that all self-locking nuts be discarded once they have been removed. The self-locking portion of the nut is weakened once the nut has been removed and will no longer properly lock onto the mating threads. Always install new self-locking nuts. Never reinstall a used nut once it has been removed.

FRONT WHEEL

Removal/Installation

1. Park the ATV on level ground and set the parking brake.

NOTE
Mark the tires for location and direction before removing them.

2. Loosen the front wheel lug nuts (**Figure 1**).
3. Support the ATV with the front wheels off the ground.
4. Place wooden blocks(s) under the frame to support the vehicle securely with the front wheels off the ground.
5. Remove the wheel nuts and front wheel.
6. Inspect the nuts and replace them if they are damaged.

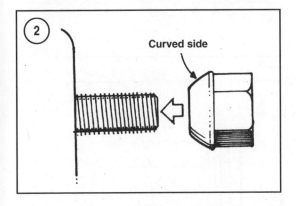

Curved side

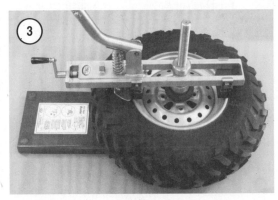

7. Inspect the wheels and replace them if they are damaged. Refer to the *Tires and Wheels* in this chapter.

8. Install the front wheel by reversing these removal steps, plus the following:

   a. Install the wheel nuts (**Figure 2**) with their curved side facing toward the wheel. First install the wheel nuts finger-tight and make sure the wheel sits squarely against the front hub.

   b. Lower the ATV so both front wheels are on the ground.

   c. Tighten the wheel nuts in a crossing pattern to a torque of 64 N•m (47 ft.-lb.).

   d. Support the ATV again so both front wheels are off the ground.

   e. Rotate the wheels and then apply the front brake. Repeat this step several times to make sure each wheel rotates freely and that its brake is working properly.

TIRES AND WHEELS

The TRX350 is equipped with tubeless, low pressure tires designed specifically for off-road use. Rapid tire wear will occur if the ATV is ridden on paved surfaces.

Tire Changing

A bead breaker tool, tire irons and rim protectors are required to change a tire. K & L Supply Co. (1-800-727-6767) offers a heavy-duty tire breakdown removal tool (**Figure 3**) that is available through motorcycle dealerships.

> *CAUTION*
> *If the tire is difficult to remove or install using the proper tools, do not take a chance on damaging the tire or rim sealing surface. Take the tire and rim to a dealership and have them service the tire.*

1. Remove the valve stem cap and core, and deflate the tire. Do not reinstall the core at this time.

2. Lubricate the tire bead and rim flanges with a rubber tire lubricant. Press the tire sidewall/bead down to allow the lubricant to run into and around the bead area. Also apply lubricant to the area where the bead breaker arm will contact the tire sidewall.

3. Position the wheel in the bead breaker tool (**Figure 4**).

4. Slowly work the bead breaker tool, making sure the tool arm seats against the inside of the rim, and break the tire bead away from the rim.

5. Apply hand pressure against the tire on either side of the tool to break the rest of the bead free from the rim.

6. If the rest of the tire bead cannot be broken loose, raise the tool, rotate the tire/rim assembly and repeat Steps 4 and 5 until the entire bead is broken loose from the rim.

10

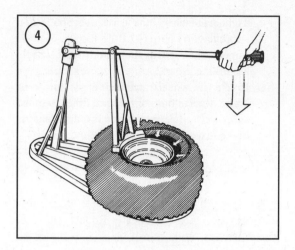

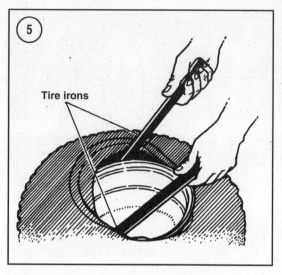

7. Turn the wheel over and repeat the preceding steps to break the opposite side loose.

> *CAUTION*
> *When using tire irons in the following steps, work carefully so the tire or rim sealing surfaces are not damaged. Damage to these areas may cause an air leak and require replacement of the tire or rim.*

8. Lubricate the tire beads and rim flanges as described in Step 2. Pry the bead over the rim with two tire irons (**Figure 5**). Take small bites with the tire irons. Place rim protectors between the tire irons and the rim.

9. When the upper tire bead is free, lift the second bead up into the center rim well and remove it as described in Step 8.

10. Clean and dry the rim.

11. Inspect the sealing surface on both sides of the rim (**Figure 6**). If the rim is bent, it may leak air.

12. Replace the air valve as follows:
    a. Support the rim and pull the valve stem out of the rim. Discard the valve stem.
    b. Lubricate the new valve stem with a tire lubricant.
    c. Pull a new valve stem into the rim, from the inside out, until it snaps into place.

> *NOTE*
> *Special tools are available for installing this type of valve stem.*

13. Inspect the tire for cuts, tears, abrasions or any other defects.

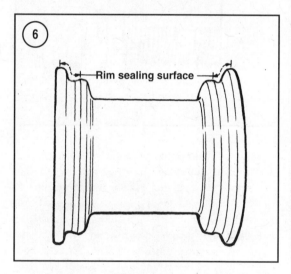

14. Clean the tire and rim of any lubricant used during removal.

> *WARNING*
> *When mounting the tire, use only clean water as a tire lubricant. Other lubricants may leave a slippery residue on the tire that would allow the tire to slip on the rim, causing a loss of air pressure.*

> *NOTE*
> *The tire tread pattern on the orignial equipment tires is directional. Position the tire on the rim so the rotation arrow on the tire sidewall (**Figure 7**) faces in the correct direction of wheel rotation.*

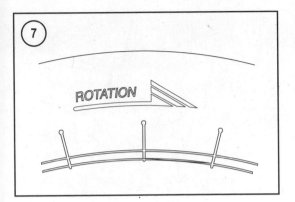

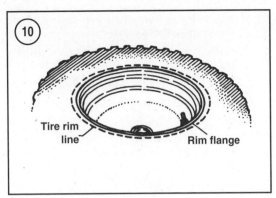

rim flange. Force the bead into the center of the rim to help installation (**Figure 8**).

16. Install the rest of the bead with tire irons (**Figure 9**).

17. Repeat the preceding steps to install the second bead onto the rim.

18. Install the valve stem core, if necessary.

19. Apply water to the tire bead and inflate the tire to seat the tire onto the rim. Make sure the rim lines on both sides of the tire are parallel with the rim flanges as shown in **Figure 10**. If the rim flanges are not parallel, deflate the tire and break the bead. Then lubricate the tire with water again and re-inflate the tire.

20. When the tire is properly seated, remove the air valve (**Figure 11**) to deflate the tire and wait 1 hour before putting the tire into service. After 1 hour, inflate the tire to the operating pressure listed in **Table 4**.

21. Check for air leaks and install the valve cap.

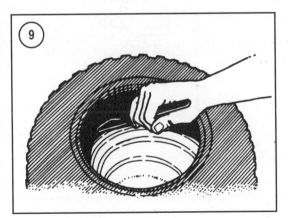

Cold Patch Repair

Use the manufacturer's instructions for the tire repair kit. If there are no instructions, use the following procedure.

1. Remove the tire as described in this chapter.

2. Prior to removing the object that punctured the tire, mark the puncture location with chalk or crayon. Remove the object.

3. Working on the inside of the tire, roughen the area around the hole larger than the patch (**Figure 12**). Use the cap from the tire repair kit or a pocket knife. Do not scrape too vigorously or additional damage may occur.

4. Clean the area with a non-flammable solvent. Do not use an oil based solvent as it will leave a residue rendering the patch useless.

NOTE
If the tire is difficult to install, place the tire outside in the sun (or in the trunk of a car). The higher temperatures will soften the tire and help with installation.

15. Install the tire onto the rim starting with the side opposite the valve stem. Push the first bead over the

5. Apply a small amount of special cement to the puncture and spread it evenly.

6. Allow the cement to dry until it is tacky; usually 30 seconds is sufficient.

7. Remove the backing from the patch.

> *CAUTION*
> *Do not touch the newly exposed rubber or the patch will not stick firmly.*

8. Center the patch over the hole. Hold the patch firmly in place for about 30 seconds to allow the cement to dry. Use a roller, if available, to press the patch into place (**Figure 13**).

9. Dust the area with talcum powder.

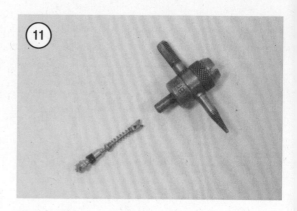

FRONT HUB/BRAKE DRUM (TWO-WHEEL DRIVE)

Refer to **Figure 14**.

Removal/Installation

1. Remove the front wheel as described in this chapter.

> *WARNING*
> *Do not inhale brake dust. It may contain asbestos, which can cause lung injury and cancer.*

2. Remove the cotter pin and axle nut (**Figure 15**, typical) securing the front hub/brake drum assembly. Remove the front hub/brake drum.

3. Remove the outer spacer (A, **Figure 16**, typical).

4. Remove the seal (B, **Figure 16**, typical).

5. Turn the inner and outer bearings. Both bearing races should turn freely and without any sign of roughness, catching or excessive noise. Replace damaged bearings as follows:
   a. Insert a drift into one side of the hub. Push the inner spacer over to one side and place the drift on the inner race of the outer bearing. Tap the bearing out of the hub, working around the perimeter of the inner race.
   b. Remove the inner spacer, then tap out the remaining bearing.
   c. Clean the inside of the hub.
   d. Drive in a new inner bearing (brake drum side) so the marked side of the bearing is out. Drive in the bearing until it is seated.

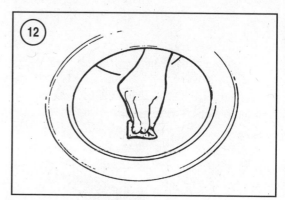

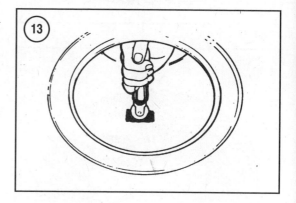

   e. Install the inner spacer.

   f. Drive in a new outer bearing so the marked side of the bearing is out. Drive in the bearing until it is seated.

6. Install a new seal (B, **Figure 16**, typical). Apply a light coat of grease to the seal lips.

7. Install the outer spacer (A, **Figure 16**, typical).

8. Inspect the O-ring on the axle spindle (**Figure 17**) and replace it if it is damaged. Apply grease to the O-ring.

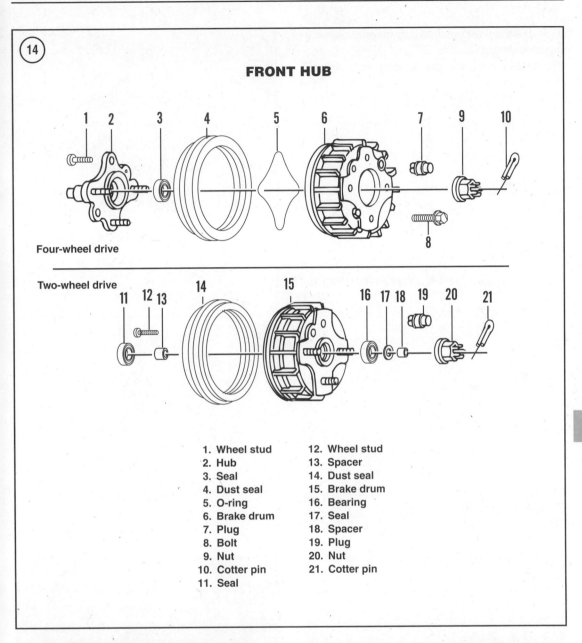

FRONT HUB

14

1. 2. 3. 4. 5. 6. 7. 9. 10.

Four-wheel drive

8.

Two-wheel drive

11. 12. 13. 14. 15. 16. 17. 18. 19. 20. 21.

1. Wheel stud
2. Hub
3. Seal
4. Dust seal
5. O-ring
6. Brake drum
7. Plug
8. Bolt
9. Nut
10. Cotter pin
11. Seal

12. Wheel stud
13. Spacer
14. Dust seal
15. Brake drum
16. Bearing
17. Seal
18. Spacer
19. Plug
20. Nut
21. Cotter pin

10

9. Install the front hub/brake drum onto the steering knuckle.

10. Install the axle nut and tighten it to 78 N•m (58 ft.-lb.).

> *WARNING*
> *Always install a new cotter pin. If necessary, tighten the axle nut to align it with the cotter pin hole in the axle. Do not loosen the axle nut to align it with the hole.*

11. Install a new cotter pin through the nut groove and axle hole, and then spread the ends to lock it in place (**Figure 18**).

FRONT HUB (FOUR-WHEEL DRIVE)

Refer to **Figure 14**.

Removal/Installation

1. Remove the front wheel as described in this chapter.

> *WARNING*
> *Do not inhale brake dust. It may contain asbestos, which can cause lung injury and cancer.*

2A. To remove the brake drum only, remove the bolts (A, **Figure 19**) and brake drum.

2B. To remove the brake drum and front hub at the same time, perform the following:
    a. Remove and discard the axle nut cotter pin (B, **Figure 19**).
    b. Remove the axle nut and front hub assembly (C, **Figure 19**).

3. Inspect the front hub as described in this chapter.

4. Refer to Chapter Thirteen to service the brake drum and brake drum seal (A, **Figure 20**).

5. Install the front hub by reversing the preceding removal steps while noting the following:
    a. If the brake drum was removed from the front hub, install the O-ring (B, **Figure 20**) into the brake drum groove.
    b. If the brake drum was removed from the front hub, install the brake drum and tighten the mounting bolts (A, **Figure 19**) to 10 N•m (88 in.-lb.).
    c. Install and tighten the axle nut (B, **Figure 19**) to 78 N•m (58 ft.-lb.).

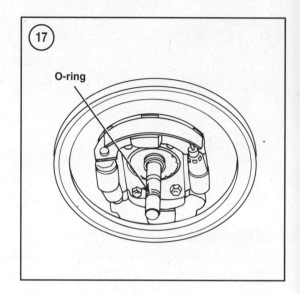

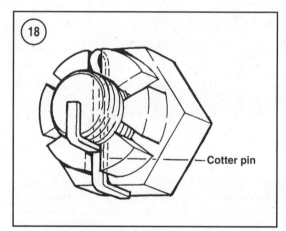

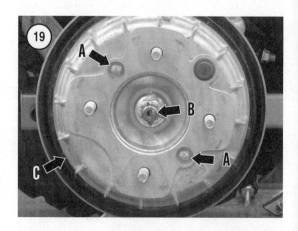

> *WARNING*
> *Always install a new cotter pin. If necessary, tighten the axle nut to align it with the cotter pin hole in the axle. Do*

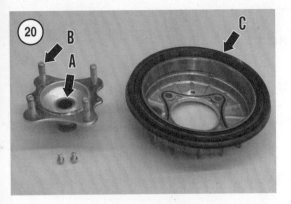

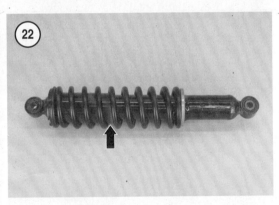

not loosen the axle nut to align it with the hole.

   c. Install a new cotter pin through the nut groove and axle hole, and then spread the ends to lock it in place (**Figure 18**).

Inspection

1. Inspect the seal (A, **Figure 20**) and replace it if it is damaged.
2. Inspect the studs (B, **Figure 20**) and replace them if they are damaged.
3. Clean and dry the hub splines.
4. Check the hub for cracks or other damage.
5. Service the dust seal (C, **Figure 20**) and brake drum as described in *Brake Drum* in Chapter Thirteen.

SHOCK ABSORBERS

Removal/Installation

1. Support the ATV with the front wheels off the ground.
2. Remove the upper and lower shock absorber locknuts and bolts, and remove the shock absorber (**Figure 21**). Discard the locknuts.
3. Inspect the shock absorber as described in this chapter.
4. Install the shock absorber by reversing the preceding removal steps, while noting the following:
   a. Note that the upper bolt is shorter than the lower bolt.
   b. Install new shock locknuts.
   c. Tighten the upper and lower shock absorber locknuts to 30 N•m (22 ft.-lb.).

Inspection

1. Clean and dry the shock absorber (**Figure 22**).
2. Check the damper unit for leaks or other damage. Inspect the damper rod for bending.
3. Inspect the upper and lower rubber bushings (**Figure 23**). Replace severely worn or damaged bushings as described in this section.
4. Inspect the spring for damage.
5. If the damper unit or spring is damaged, replace the entire shock absorber unit. Other than end

10

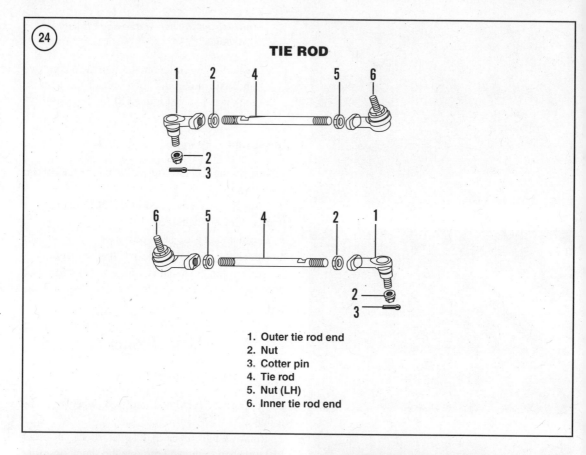

TIE ROD

1. Outer tie rod end
2. Nut
3. Cotter pin
4. Tie rod
5. Nut (LH)
6. Inner tie rod end

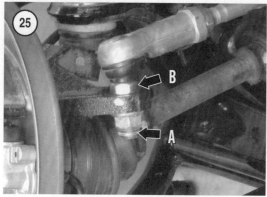

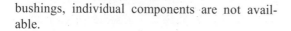

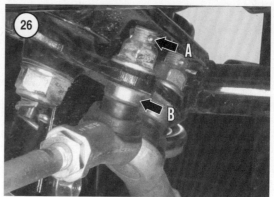

bushings, individual components are not available.

Shock Bushing Replacement

1. Support the damper unit in a press and press out one of the bushings (**Figure 23**).

2. Clean the shock bushing bore.

3. Press in the new bushing, being sure to center it in the bushing bore.

4. Repeat for the other bushing.

TIE RODS

The tie rods consist of an inner end and outer end. Individual parts that make up the tie rod assembly (**Figure 24**) are available.

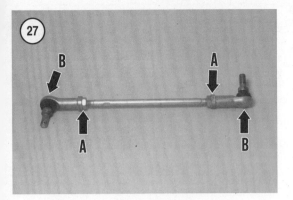

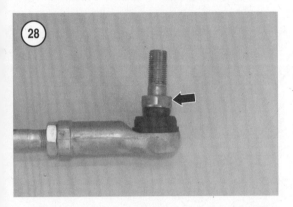

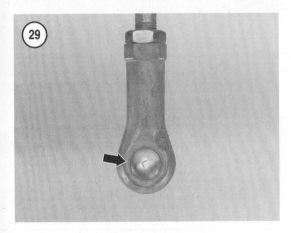

Removal

1. Support the ATV with the front wheels off the ground.

2. Remove the cotter pins from both tie rod ends. See A, **Figure 25** and A, **Figure 26**.

3. Hold the flat on each tie rod stud with a wrench, (B, **Figure 25** or B, **Figure 26**) and remove the tie rod nuts, then remove the tie rod.

Inspection

NOTE
When cleaning the tie rods, do not immerse the ball joints in any type of chemical that could contaminate the grease and/or damage the rubber boots.

1. Inspect the tie rod shaft (**Figure 27**) and replace it if it is damaged.

2. Inspect the rubber boot at each end of the tie rod end swivel joint (**Figure 28**). The swivel joints are permanently packed with grease. Replace the ball joint if it is severely worn or if the rubber boot is damaged. Refer to *Disassembly/Reassembly* in this section.

3. Pivot the tie rod end (**Figure 28**) back and forth by hand. If the tie rod end moves roughly or has excessive play, replace it as described in the following procedure.

Disassembly/Reassembly

If the tie rod ends need to be replaced, refer to **Figure 24** and perform the following:

1. Loosen the locknuts (A, **Figure 27**) securing the tie rod ends. The locknut securing the outside tie rod has left-hand threads.

2. Unscrew the damaged tie rod end(s) (B, **Figure 27**).

3. Clean the mating shaft and tie rod end threads with contact cleaner.

4. The inner tie rod is marked with an L (**Figure 29**). Install this tie rod onto the end of the tie rod without the flat on it. This tie rod has a silver colored nut.

5. The outer tie rod end is not marked, but uses a gold colored nut.

6. Position the rod ends and nuts as shown in **Figure 30**. Refer to **Table 1** for the specified tie rod length. The maximum difference allowable for the locknut positions is 3 mm (0.12 in.). The tie rod end studs must be 180° from each other. Turn the locknuts up against the tie rod end but do not tighten them at this time. They will be tightened when the wheel alignment is checked in Chapter Three.

10

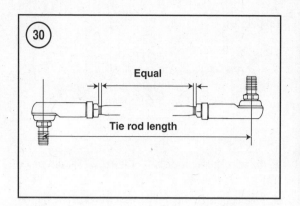

Equal

Tie rod length

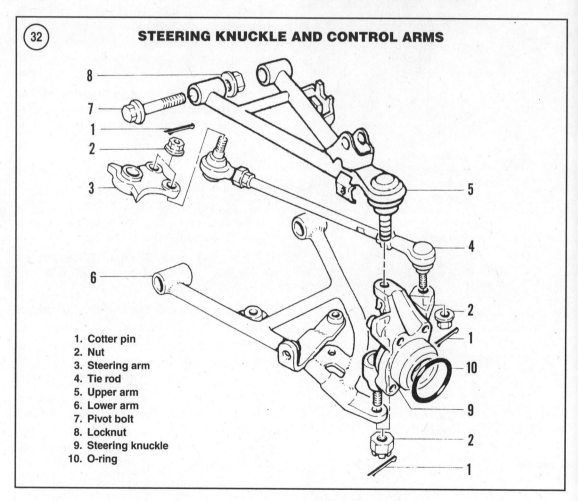

STEERING KNUCKLE AND CONTROL ARMS

8
7
1
2
3
5
4
6
2
1
10
9
2
1

1. Cotter pin
2. Nut
3. Steering arm
4. Tie rod
5. Upper arm
6. Lower arm
7. Pivot bolt
8. Locknut
9. Steering knuckle
10. O-ring

Installation

1. Install the tie rod with the flat on the shaft (**Figure 31**) closer to the steering knuckle.

2. Attach the tie rod assembly to the steering shaft and steering knuckle. See **Figure 25** and **Figure 26**.

3. Thread the nut onto each ball joint stud.

4. Hold the flat on each tie rod stud with a wrench and tighten the tie rod nuts to 54 N•m (40 ft.-lb.). Tighten the nut(s), if necessary, to align the cotter pin hole with the nut slot. Do not loosen the nut to align the hole and slot.

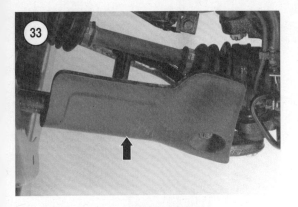

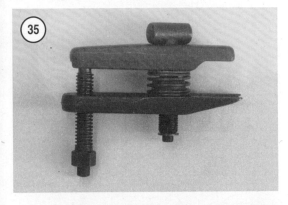

5. Install new cotter pins through all ball joint studs. Spread the cotter pin arms to lock them in place.

6. Check the toe-in adjustment as described in *Toe-in Adjustment* in Chapter Three. If the tie rod ends were replaced, their locknuts will be tightened during the adjustment procedure.

STEERING KNUCKLE

Removal/Installation

Refer to **Figure 32**.

> *NOTE*
> *In this procedure, illustrations depict a four-wheel drive model. The only major difference between the two-wheel and four-wheel drive versions is the presence of the front drive axle and other minor items that are unique to the four-wheel drive system. Where differences occur that relate to the procedure, they are identified.*

1. Remove the front hub as described in this chapter.

2. Remove the boot protector (**Figure 33**).

3. Detach the brake vent hose and brake hose from the mounting brackets on the upper suspension arm.

> *CAUTION*
> *It is not necessary to disconnect the brake hose in Step 3. Do not allow the brake panel to hang from the brake hose.*

4. Remove the brake panel (Chapter Thirteen) and hang the panel so it is out of the way.

5. Disconnect the tie rod from the steering knuckle as described in this chapter.

6. Remove the cotter pins and nuts (**Figure 34**) from the upper and lower control arm ball joints.

7. Disconnect the upper and lower control arm ball joints using the Honda ball joint remover (part No. 07MAC-SL00200 [**Figure 35**]) or an equivalent. Perform the following:

> *CAUTION*
> *Do not strike the ball joint or its stud when removing it; otherwise, the ball joint may be damaged.*

    a. Mount the ball joint remover between the ball joint upper arm as shown in **Figure 36**.

10

b. Operate the tool and break the upper ball joint loose from the upper arm.

c. Repeat for the lower control arm.

8A. On two-wheel drives, remove the steering knuckle.

8B. On four-wheel drives, remove the steering knuckle (**Figure 37**) while being careful not to damage the axle splines or boots.

9. Inspect the steering knuckle as described in this chapter.

10. Install the steering knuckle by reversing these removal steps, plus the following:

   a. On four-wheel drives, lubricate the steering knuckle seal lips with a waterproof grease, then insert the axle into the steering knuckle (**Figure 37**).

   b. Install the steering knuckle onto the upper and lower control arms. Install the ball joint nuts and tighten them to 29 N•m (22 ft.-lb.).

   c. Install new cotter pins and bend the ends over completely.

   d. Check front brake operation before riding the ATV.

   e. Install the brake hose clamps and tighten them to 12 N•m (106 in.-lb.).

Inspection

CAUTION
When cleaning the steering knuckle, do not wash the ball joint in solvent. The ball joint cover may be damaged or the grease may be contaminated.

1. Clean and dry the steering knuckle assembly (**Figure 38**).

2. Inspect the steering knuckle and replace it if it is damaged.

3. Examine the holes (A, **Figure 38**) where the tie rod and upper control arm attach. Check for elongation and fractures.

4. Inspect the ball joint and rubber boot (B, **Figure 38**). Pivot the ball joint by hand. It should move freely. The ball joint is permanently packed with grease. If the rubber boot is damaged, dirt and moisture can enter the ball joint and damage it. If the ball joint or boot is damaged, replace the steering knuckle assembly. The ball joint is not available separately.

5. Check the hole at the end of the ball joint where the cotter pin fits. Make sure there are no fractures or cracks leading out toward the end of the ball

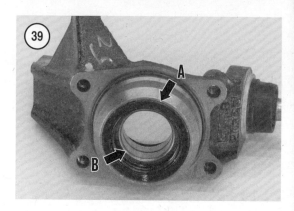

joint. If any are present, replace the steering knuckle.

6A. On four-wheel drive models, perform the following:

   a. Check the inner (C, **Figure 38**) and outer (A, **Figure 39**) dust seals for wear or damage. If necessary, replace the seals as described in this section.

   b. Turn the inner and outer bearings (B, **Figure 39**) by hand. Both bearing races should turn freely and without any sign of roughness,

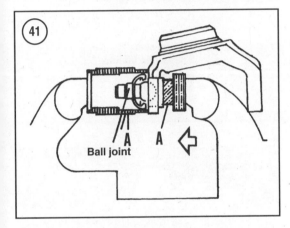

Ball joint

A A

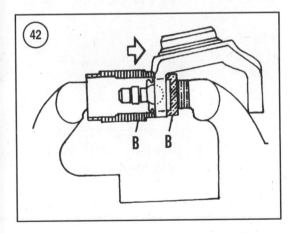

B B

catching or excessive noise. Replace the damaged bearings as described in this section.

6B. On two-wheel drive models, perform the following:

a. Inspect the spindle portion where the front wheel bearings ride for wear or damage. If the spindle is damaged in any way, replace the steering knuckle.

b. Examine the cotter pin hole in the end of the spindle. Replace the steering knuckle if it is fractured or cracked.

Lower Ball Joint Replacement

> *CAUTION*
> *Ball joint removal and installation require special tools. Do not try to replace the ball joints without these tools as the steering knuckle may be damaged.*

1. Remove the snap ring (**Figure 40**) securing the lower ball joint to the steering knuckle.
2. Position the special tools (Honda part No. 07JMF-HC50110) or equivalents, with the A mark facing the ball joint and install the special tools and the steering knuckle in a vise (**Figure 41**).
3. Slowly tighten the vise and press the ball joint out of the steering knuckle.
4. Remove the special tools, steering knuckle and ball joint from the vise.
5. Clean the ball joint receptacle in the steering knuckle with solvent and thoroughly dry it.
6. Correctly position the new ball joint in the steering knuckle and use the same special tools used for removal. Position the special tools with the B mark facing toward the ball joint.
7. Install the special tools and the steering knuckle in a vise (**Figure 42**).

> *CAUTION*
> *While tightening the vise, if there is a strong resistance or if the vise stops moving, stop immediately. There probably is an alignment problem with either the ball joint or the special tool. Realign the ball joint and special tools and try again. The ball joint should press in with a minimum amount of resistance.*

8. Slowly tighten the vise and press the ball joint straight into the steering knuckle. Press the ball joint in until it bottoms.
9. Remove the special tools and the steering knuckle from the vise.
10. Make sure the snap ring groove is completely visible in order to accept the snap ring . Press the ball joint in farther if necessary.
11. Install the snap ring so the flat side is out. Make sure the snap ring seats correctly.

10

Steering Knuckle Dust Seal and
Bearing Replacement (Four-Wheel Drive)

Refer to **Figure 43**.

1. Remove the inner (C, **Figure 38**) and outer (A, **Figure 39**) dust seals. Discard both dust seals.

NOTE
When only replacing the dust seals, go to Step 10.

2. Remove the snap ring (4, **Figure 43**).

3. Support the steering knuckle and press or drive out the bearing.

4. If the bearing was a loose fit in the steering knuckle, check the bearing bore for cracks or severe wear.

5. Clean the bearing bore.

6. Check the snap ring groove for cracks or other damage.

7. Pack the new bearing with grease.

8. Press or drive the new bearing into the steering knuckle. Press or drive against the marked side of the bearing. Force the bearing in until it is fully seated. See *Bearings* in Chapter One for bearing installation information.

9. Install a new snap ring (4, **Figure 43**) with the flat side out. Make sure it seats in the groove completely.

10. Install the dust seals as follows:

    a. Pack the lip of each dust seal with grease.

    b. Install both dust seals with the closed side facing out.

    c. Press both dust seals into the steering knuckle.

CONTROL ARMS

Refer to **Figure 32**.

Removal/Installation

NOTE
In this procedure, illustrations depict a four-wheel drive model. The only major difference between the two-wheel and four-wheel drive versions is the presence of the front drive axle and other minor items that are unique to the four-wheel drive system. Where differences occur that relate to the procedure, they are identified.

1. Remove the steering knuckle as described in this chapter.

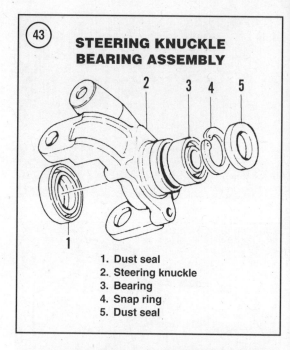

43

STEERING KNUCKLE BEARING ASSEMBLY

1. Dust seal
2. Steering knuckle
3. Bearing
4. Snap ring
5. Dust seal

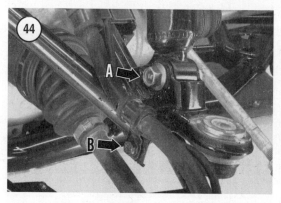

44

2. Remove the upper control arm as follows:

    a. Remove the locknut and bolt (A, **Figure 44**) securing the shock absorber to the upper control arm.

    b. Remove the brake hose and breather tube clamp bolt (B, **Figure 44**) from the upper control arm.

    c. Remove locknuts and bolts and the upper control arm (A, **Figure 45**).

3. Remove the locknuts and bolts and the lower control arm (B, **Figure 45**).

4. Discard all of the control arm and lower shock absorber locknuts removed in Step 2 and Step 3.

5. Inspect the upper and lower control arms as described in this section.

NOTE
Install the locknuts in Step 6 and Step 7 hand-tight. These locknuts will be tightened to their final torque specification after the front wheels are installed and with the ATV resting on the ground.

NOTE
Install all control arm mounting bolts so the bolt head is facing toward the front of the ATV.

6. Install the lower control arm (B, **Figure 45**) onto the frame and secure it with bolts and new locknuts.

7. Install the upper control arm (A, **Figure 45**) and secure it with bolts and new locknuts.

8. Install the shock absorber lower mounting bolt and a new locknut (A, **Figure 44**). Tighten the locknut to 30 N•m (22 ft.-lb.).

9. Install the brake hose and breather tube clamp bolt (B, **Figure 44**).

10. Install the steering knuckle as described in this chapter.

11. Install the front wheels as described in this chapter.

12. Lower the ATV so all four wheels are on the ground.

13. Tighten the upper control arm locknuts to 44 N•m (33 ft.-lb.).

14. Tighten the lower control arm locknuts to 44 N•m (33 ft.-lb.).

Inspection

CAUTION
*When cleaning the upper control arm, do not wash the ball joint in solvent. The ball joint cover (**Figure 46**) may be damaged or the grease contaminated.*

1. Clean and dry the control arms.

2. Examine both control arms for bending, cracks or other damage. Replace them if necessary.

3. Inspect the upper control arm ball joint and rubber boot (**Figure 46**). Pivot the ball joint by hand. It should move freely. The ball joint is permanently packed with grease. If the rubber boot is damaged, dirt and moisture can enter the ball joint and destroy it. If the ball joint or boot is damaged, replace the ball joint as described in this chapter.

4. Inspect the pivot bolts and replace them if they are excessively worn or damaged.

5. Inspect the pivot bushings (**Figure 47**) for excessive wear, separation or other damage. If they are damaged, replace the control arm as the bushings cannot be replaced separately.

Upper Control Arm Ball Joint Replacement

CAUTION
Ball joint removal and installation require special tools. Do not try to re-

10

place the ball joints without these tools as the control arm may be damaged.

NOTE
The lower ball joint is installed on the steering knuckle.

1. Remove the upper control arm as described in this chapter.

2. Remove the snap ring (**Figure 48**) securing the upper ball joint to the upper control arm.

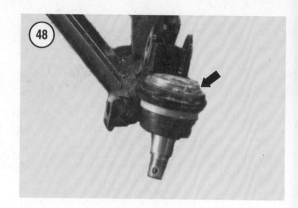

3. Position the special tools (Honda part No. 07WMF-HN00100) or equivalents, with the A mark facing the ball joint and install the special tools and the control arm in a vise (**Figure 49**) or press.

4. Slowly press the ball joint out of the control arm.

5. Remove the special tools, control arm and ball joint from the vise.

6. Clean the ball joint receptacle in the control arm with solvent and thoroughly dry it.

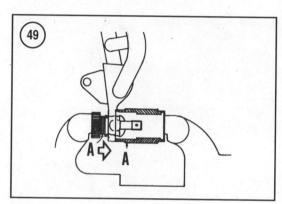

7. Correctly position the new ball joint into the control arm and use the same special tools used for removal. Position the special tools with the B mark facing toward the ball joint.

8. Install the special tools and the control arm in a vise (**Figure 50**) or press.

CAUTION
While tightening the vise, if there is a strong resistance or if the vise stops moving, stop immediately. There probably is an alignment problem with either the ball joint or the special tool. Realign the ball joint and special tools and try again. The ball joint should press in with a minimum amount of resistance.

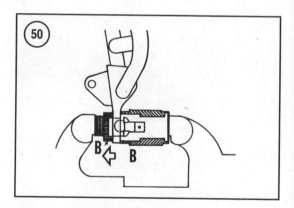

9. Slowly press the ball joint straight into the control arm. Press the ball joint in until it bottoms.

10. Remove the special tools and the control arm from the vise.

11. Make sure the snap ring groove is completely visible in order to accept the snap ring. Press the ball joint in farther if necessary.

12. Install the snap ring so the flat side is out. Make sure the circlip seats correctly.

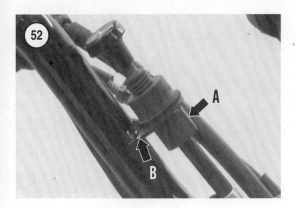

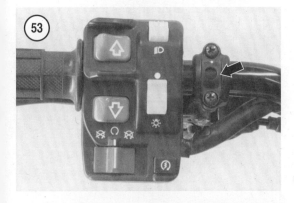

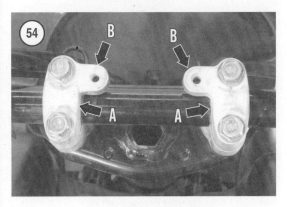

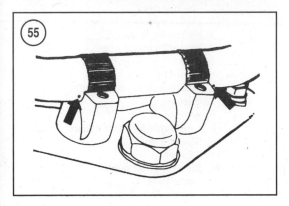

HANDLEBAR

Removal

1A. Remove the digital combination meter, if equipped, as described in Chapter Fifteen.

1B. If the ATV is not equipped with the digital combination meter, remove the handlebar cover (Chapter Fifteen).

2. Remove the wire retaining bands securing the wiring harness to the handlebar.

3. Remove the throttle housing screws, clamp and throttle housing (**Figure 51**).

4. Remove the front master cylinder as described in Chapter Thirteen.

5. Detach the choke cable from the left handlebar as follows:

    a. Loosen the retaining nut (A, **Figure 52**).

    b. Detach the cable from the bracket (B, **Figure 52**).

6. Remove the screws and the rear brake lever clamp (**Figure 53**).

7. Remove the switch housing as described in *Left Handlebar Switch Housing Replacement* in Chapter Nine.

8. Remove the upper handlebar holder mounting bolts, holders (A, **Figure 54**) and handlebar.

Installation

1. Position the handlebar on the lower handlebar holders and hold it in place.

2. Install the upper handlebar holders with the meter or cover bolt holes (B, **Figure 54**) toward the front.

3. Align the punch mark on the handlebar with the top surface of the lower holders (**Figure 55**).

4. Install the handlebar holder bolts. Tighten the forward bolts first and then the rear bolts. Tighten each bolt securely.

5. Install the choke cable in the bracket (B, **Figure 52**) and tighten the retaining nut (A).

6A. On FE and TE models, install the switch housing and rear brake lever assembly as described in *Left Handlebar Switch Housing Replacement* in Chapter Nine.

6B. On FM and TM models, install the switch housing as described in *Left Handlebar Switch Housing Replacement* in Chapter Nine, then install the rear brake lever bracket as follows:

10

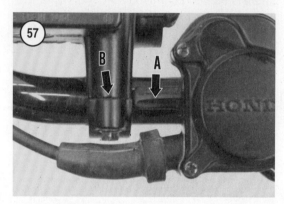

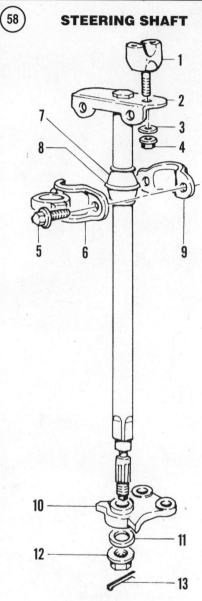

STEERING SHAFT

a. Install the rear brake lever bracket, clamp and mounting screws. Install the clamp so the punch mark (A, **Figure 56**) faces up.

b. Align the end of the bracket with the punch mark (B, **Figure 56**) on the handlebar.

c. Install the clamp screws. Tighten the upper screw first, then the lower screw.

7. Install the master cylinder as described in Chapter Thirteen.

8. Install the throttle housing by aligning the lug on the throttle housing (A, **Figure 57**) with the mating surfaces of the master cylinder and clamp (B). Install the clamp and screws (**Figure 51**) and tighten them securely.

9. Secure the wiring harness to the handlebar with the wire bands.

10. Check all cable adjustments as described in Chapter Three.

11. Make sure the front brake works properly.

12. Make sure each handlebar switch works properly.

13. Install the combination meter or handlebar cover (Chapter Fifteen).

1. Handlebar lower holders
2. Steering shaft
3. Lock washers
4. Handlebar lower holder locknuts
5. Steering shaft holder mounting bolts
6. Steering shaft outer holder
7. Bushing
8. Set ring
9. Steering shaft inner holder
10. Steering arm
11. Washer
12. Steering shaft nut
13. Cotter pin

STEERING SHAFT

Refer to **Figure 58**.

Removal

1. Remove the front fender and inner fender panels (Chapter Fifteen).

2. Remove both front wheels as described in this chapter.

3. Remove the lower handlebar holder nuts and washers (**Figure 59**). Disengage the wires and cables from the retaining guides and clamps. Move the handlebar assembly out of the way while being careful not to damage the brake hose, cables or wiring harness.

4. Detach both inner tie rod ends (A, **Figure 60**) from the steering shaft as described in *Tie Rods* in this chapter.

5. Remove the cotter pin and nut at the bottom of the steering shaft (B, **Figure 60**).

6. Remove the steering shaft holder bolts (A, **Figure 61**) and holder assembly (B).

7. Remove the steering shaft and steering arm assembly from the frame.

Inspection

Replace parts that are excessively worn or damaged as described in this section.

1. Clean and dry all parts.

2. Remove the set ring (**Figure 62**) and the steering shaft bushing from the steering shaft. Check both parts for excessive wear or damage.

3. Check the steering shaft for bending and spline or thread damage.

4. Examine the cotter pin hole at the end of the steering shaft. Make sure there are no fractures or cracks leading out toward the end of the steering shaft. If any cracks are present, replace the steering shaft.

5. Inspect the steering arm for cracks, spline damage or other damage.

6. Check the bushing for severe wear or damage.

7. Inspect the steering bearing (A, **Figure 63**) by turning the inner race by hand. Replace the bearing if it turns roughly or has excessive play.

8. Inspect the dust seals (B, **Figure 63**) for severe wear or other damage.

10

9. Replace the dust seals and bearing as described in the following procedure.

Steering Shaft Dust Seal and Bearing Replacement

The steering shaft bearing is pressed into the frame. Do not remove the bearing unless it requires replacement.

1. Remove the dust seals from both sides of the bearing.

> *NOTE*
> *When only replacing the dust seals, go to Step 9.*

2. Remove the snap ring (**Figure 64**) from the bearing bore groove.

3. Before removing the bearing, make sure its outer race is a tight fit in the bearing bore. If the bearing is loose, check the bearing bore for cracks or other damage.

4. Pull the bearing up and out of the frame with a bearing removal tool (**Figure 65**).

5. Clean the bearing bore and check it for cracks or other damage.

6. Install the new bearing so the marked side faces up.

7. Tap the bearing squarely into place; tap on the outer race only. Use a socket or bearing driver that matches the outer race diameter. Do not tap on the inner race or the bearing might be damaged. Install the bearing so it is fully seated below the snap ring groove in the bearing bore.

8. Install the snap ring into the bearing bore groove. Make sure the snap ring seats in the groove completely.

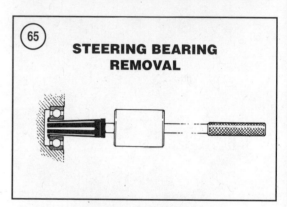

STEERING BEARING REMOVAL

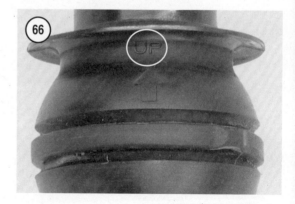

9. Pack the lips of the new dust seals with grease, then install each dust seal so its closed side faces out.

Installation

1. Lubricate the steering shaft bushing with grease and install it onto the steering shaft so the UP mark (**Figure 66**) faces toward the handlebar. Install the set ring (**Figure 62**) into the bushing groove.

2. Install the steering shaft into the frame

3. Install the inner (C, **Figure 61**) and outer (B) steering shaft holders around the bushing and install the bolts (A). Tighten the steering shaft holder bolts to 32 N•m (24 ft.-lb.).

4. Lubricate the steering shaft splines with grease.

5. Align the master spline on the steering shaft (**Figure 67**) with the master spline on the steering arm splines (**Figure 68**).

6. Lubricate the steering shaft nut flange and threads with grease. Install the steering shaft nut (B, **Figure 60**) and washer, and tighten to 108 N•m (80 ft.-lb.). Secure the nut with a new cotter pin and bend the ends over completely.

7. Reattach both inner tie rod ends to the steering shaft (A, **Figure 60**) as described in *Tie Rods* in this chapter.

8. Install the handlebar assembly onto the steering shaft. Check the routing of the brake hose, cables and wiring harness.

9. Install new handlebar lower holder locknuts (**Figure 59**) and tighten them to 39 N•m (29 ft.-lb.).

10. Install both front wheels as described in this chapter.

11. Install the front fender and inner fender panels (Chapter Fifteen).

12. Make sure the handlebar turns properly and that the throttle returns to its closed position after releasing it.

10

Table 1 STEERING AND FRONT SUSPENSION SPECIFICATIONS

Front suspension type	Double wish-bone
Front wheel travel	150 mm (5.90 in.)
Front damper type	Double tube
Toe-in/out (TE/TM)	*
Toe-out (FE/FM)	3-33 mm (0.12-1.30 in.)
Caster angle	
FE/FM	4°
TE/TM	7°
Camber angle	
FE/FM	0.1°
TE/TM	0°
Trail length	
FE/FM	17 mm (0.7 in.)
TE/TM	31 mm (1.2 in.)
Tie rod distance between ball joints	
FE/FM	345-347 mm (13.58-13.66 in.)
TE/TM	354-356 mm (13.94-14.02 in.)

*Toe-in/out on models TE and TM may range from 18 mm (0.71 in.) toe-in to 12 mm (0.47 in.) toe-out.

Table 2 TIRE AND WHEEL SPECIFICATIONS (FE/FM)

Tires	
Type	Bridgestone Dirt Hook
Size	
Front	AT24 × 8-12
Rear	AT24 × 9-11
Wheels	
Front rim size	12 × 6.0 AT
Rear rim size	11 × 7.0 AT

Table 3 TIRE AND WHEEL SPECIFICATIONS (TE/TM)

Tires	
Type	Goodyear Tracker CL
Size	
Front	AT24 × 8-12
Rear	AT25 × 11-10
Wheels	
Front rim size	12 × 6.0 AT
Rear rim size	10 × 8.5 AT

Table 4 TIRE INFLATION PRESSURE

	Front and rear tires psi (kPa)
TRX350TE/TM	
Normal pressure	2.9 (20)
Minimum pressure	2.5 (17)
Maximum pressure	3.3 (23)
TRX350FE/FM	
Normal pressure	3.6 (24.8)
Minimum pressure	3.2 (22)
Maximum pressure	4.0 (27.6)

Table 5 FRONT SUSPENSION AND STEERING TORQUE SPECIFICATIONS

	N•m	in.-lb.	ft.-lb.
Axle nut	78	–	58
Ball joint nuts	29	–	22
Brake drum mounting bolts	10	88	–
Brake hose clamp	12	106	–
Control arm locknuts	44	–	33
Damper rod locknut	38	–	28
Handlebar lower holder locknuts	39	–	29
Shock absorber locknuts	30	–	22
Steering shaft holder bolts	32	–	24
Steering shaft nut	108	–	80
Throttle case cover screws	2	18	–
Tie rod nuts	54	–	40
Wheel nuts	64	–	47

CHAPTER ELEVEN

FRONT DRIVE MECHANISM
(FOUR-WHEEL DRIVE)

This chapter describes repair and replacement procedures for the front drive mechanism used on four-wheel drive FE and FM models. This includes the front drive axles, front driveshaft and front differential gearcase.

Refer to **Table 1** for front drive specifications. . **Table 2** lists torque specifications for the front drive mechanism assembly. **Tables 1-2** are located at the end of this chapter.

FRONT DRIVE AXLES

Removal/Installation

1. Detach the lower end of the shock absorber for the side being serviced (Chapter Ten). Raise the shock absorber out of the way.

NOTE
It is not necessary to remove the brake panel when performing Step 2.

2. Separate the lower ball joint from the steering knuckle (Chapter Ten) for the side being serviced.

3. Raise the steering knuckle assembly and remove the outer axle end from the steering knuckle (**Figure 1**). Support the steering knuckle assembly so it is out of the way.

CAUTION
When removing the front axle, be careful not to damage the rubber boots.

CAUTION
To avoid damage to the front differential oil seal and splines, pull the inboard joint straight out of the front differential.

4. Hold the inboard joint and pull the driveshaft (**Figure 2**) out of the differential. It may be necessary to use a screwdriver to pry the axle loose.

5. Perform the inspection procedures described in this section.

6. Install the front axle by reversing the preceding removal steps while noting the following:

11

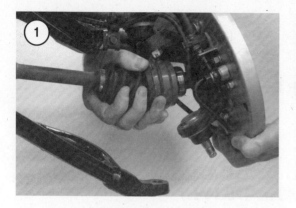

a. Install a new stopper ring (A, **Figure 3**) in the groove in the inboard joint. Make sure it is properly seated in the axle groove.

b. Lubricate the front axle seal (**Figure 4**) and inner splines (B, **Figure 3**) with molybdenum disulfide grease.

c. Carefully guide the front axle into the gearcase (**Figure 1**). Push it in all the way until it bottoms. Pull the inboard joint a little to make sure the stopper ring locks into the front differential side gear groove.

d. Install the steering knuckle and shock absorber (Chapter Ten).

Inspection

> *NOTE*
> *The axle boots encounter much abuse. Damaged boots allow dirt, mud and moisture to enter the boot, contaminate the grease and damage the bearing.*

1. Inspect the rubber boots (A, **Figure 5**) for wear, cuts or damage. Replace them if necessary as described in *Disassembly* in this section.

2. Move each end of the front axle (B, **Figure 5**) in a circular motion and check the constant velocity joints for excessive wear or play.

Disassembly

Refer to **Figure 6**.

> *NOTE*
> *The outboard joint cannot be disassembled or repaired. If it is damaged*

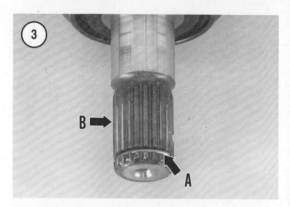

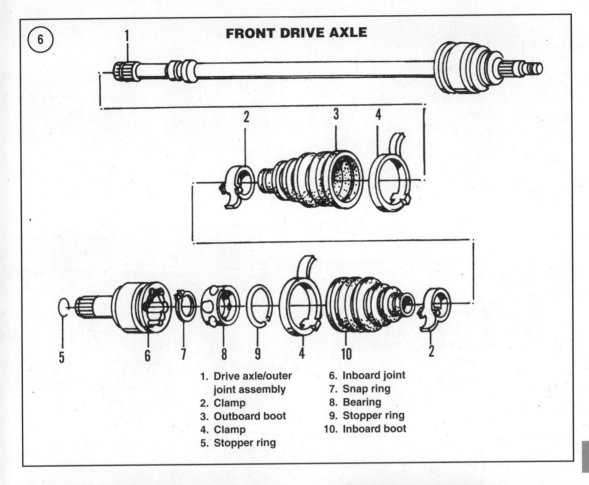

FRONT DRIVE AXLE

1. Drive axle/outer joint assembly
2. Clamp
3. Outboard boot
4. Clamp
5. Stopper ring
6. Inboard joint
7. Snap ring
8. Bearing
9. Stopper ring
10. Inboard boot

11

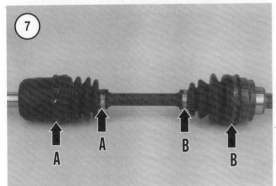

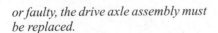

or faulty, the drive axle assembly must be replaced.

1. Open the clamps (A, **Figure 7**) on the inboard joint, then remove the clamps. Discard the clamps because they cannot be reused.

2. Carefully slide the boot (A, **Figure 8**) onto the front axle and off the inboard joint.

3. Wipe all of the grease from the inboard joint cavity (B, **Figure 8**).

4. Remove the stopper ring (**Figure 9**) from the inboard joint.

5. Remove the inboard joint (**Figure 10**).

6. Remove the snap ring (**Figure 11**) and slide off the bearing assembly (**Figure 12**). Be careful not to drop any of the steel balls from the bearing cage.

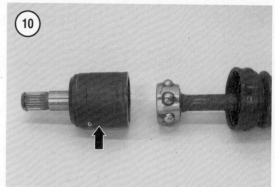

7. Slide the inboard boot off the front axle and discard the clamp. It cannot be reused.

8. If the outboard boot requires replacement, perform the following:

    a. Open the clamps (B, **Figure 7**) on the outboard joint, then remove and discard the clamps.

    b. Slide the outboard boot off the drive axle and discard the clamp.

9. Inspect the drive axle as described in this procedure.

Inspection

Refer to **Figure 6**.

> *CAUTION*
> *Before cleaning the rubber boots, make sure the cleaning solvent will not damage rubber products.*

1. Clean and dry the bearing assembly.

2. Inspect the steel balls (A, **Figure 13**), bearing cage (B) and bearing race (C) for excessive wear or damage.

3. Check the bearing race inner splines (D, **Figure 13**) for wear or damage.

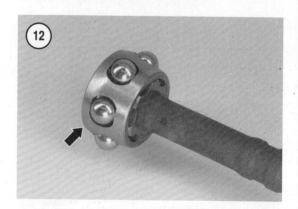

4. If necessary, disassemble the bearing assembly for further inspection. Carefully remove the steel balls from the bearing cage then remove the bearing race from the bearing cage.

5. If any of the bearing components are damaged, replace the entire assembly. Individual replacement parts are not available.

6. Clean and dry the inboard joint.

7. Inspect the inboard joint ball guides (A, **Figure 14**) for excessive wear or damage.

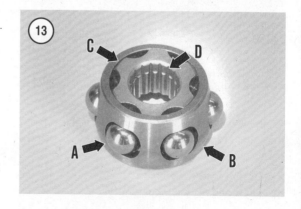

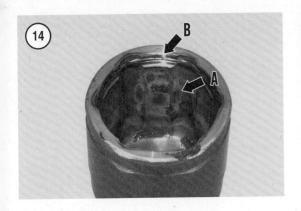

8. Inspect the inboard joint stopper ring groove (B, **Figure 14**) for wear or damage.

9. Check the stopper ring groove (A, **Figure 3**) in the inboard joint shaft for cracks or other damage.

10. Inspect the axle and inboard joint splines (B, **Figure 3**) for excessive wear or damage.

11. Inspect the inboard joint (**Figure 15**) for cracks or damage.

12. Move the outboard joint axle through its range of motion and check for excessive play or noise.

13. Inspect the front drive axle for bending, wear or damage.

14. Inspect the inner end splines (**Figure 16**), the outer end splines (A, **Figure 17**) and the front hub cotter pin hole (B) for wear or damage.

15. Inspect the rubber boots for cracks, age deterioration or other damage.

16. Replace the front drive axle assembly if any of the components are excessively worn or damaged. Individual replacement parts for the front drive axle, other than the rubber boots and clamps, are not available.

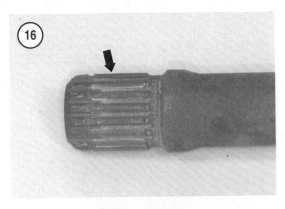

Assembly

Refer to **Figure 6**.

1. The rubber boots are not identical and must be installed on the correct joint. Original equipment replacement boots are marked with an identifying number (**Figure 18**) as follows:

    a. Inboard joint—68.

    b. Outboard joint—68L.

2. If the outboard boot was removed, install a new boot on the front axle at this time.

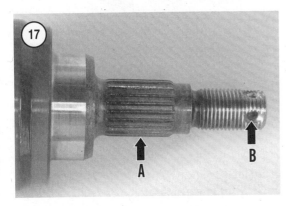

NOTE
Install the new boot clamps with their tabs facing in the direction shown in **Figure 19**.

11

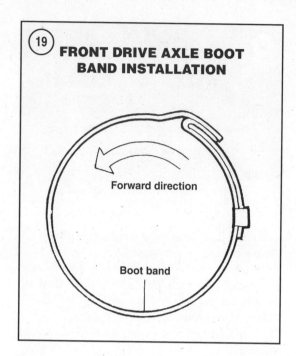

FRONT DRIVE AXLE BOOT
BAND INSTALLATION

Forward direction

Boot band

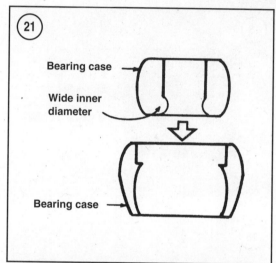

Bearing case

Wide inner
diameter

Bearing case

3. Install two new small boot clamps onto the front axle.

4. Install the inboard boot and move the small boot clamp onto the boot (**Figure 20**). Do not lock the clamp at this time.

5. If the bearing assembly was disassembled, assemble the bearing as follows:

    a. Position the bearing race with the wide inner diameter going on first and install the race (**Figure 21**) into the bearing case. Align the steel ball receptacles in both parts.

    b. Install the steel balls into their receptacles in the bearing case.

    c. Pack the bearing assembly with grease included in the boot replacement kit. Grease will help hold the steel balls in place.

6. Position the bearing assembly with the small end of the bearing going on first and install the bearing onto the drive axle (**Figure 12**).

7. Push the bearing assembly on until it stops, then install a new snap ring (**Figure 22**) into the groove in the shaft. Make sure the snap ring seats in the groove completely.

8. Apply a liberal amount of grease to the bearing assembly (**Figure 23**). Work the grease between the balls, race and case. Check for voids and fill them with grease. .

9. Lubricate the inboard joint inner surface with grease.

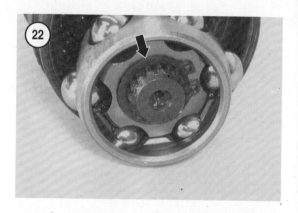

10. Install the inboard joint onto the bearing assembly (**Figure 24**) and install the stopper ring (**Figure 25**). Make sure the stopper ring seats in the groove completely.

11. After the stopper ring is in place, fill the inboard joint cavity behind the bearing assembly with grease (B, **Figure 8**).

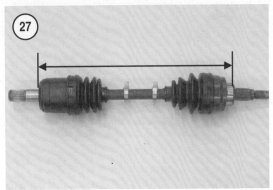

12. Pack each boot with the following amounts of molybdenum disulfide grease:

   a. Inboard boot—40-60 g (1.4-2.1 oz.).

   b. Outboard boot—30-50 g (1.1-1.8 oz.).

13. Move the inboard boot onto the inboard joint (**Figure 26**).

14. Move the inboard joint on the drive axle until the distance between the ends of the inboard and outboard joints are as specified in **Table 1** (**Figure 27**).

15. Move the small boot clamp onto each boot (**Figure 28**). Bend down the tab on the boot clamp and secure the tab with the locking clips and tap them with a plastic hammer. Make sure the tab is locked in place (**Figure 29**). Repeat for the opposite boot.

NOTE
Install the new boot clamps with their tabs facing in the direction shown in **Figure 19**.

16. Install the large boot clamps onto each boot. Make sure the boots are not twisted on the axle.

CAUTION
Make sure the inboard joint does not move while installing the boot

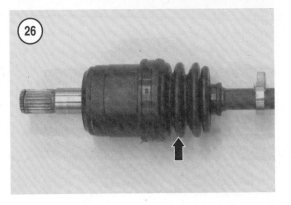

clamps. The dimension achieved in Step 14 must be maintained at all times. This dimension is critical to avoid undue stress on the rubber boots during vehicle operation.

17. Refer to **Figure 30** and secure all large boot clamps. Bend down the tab (**Figure 31**) on the boot clamp and secure the tab with the locking clips and tap them with a plastic hammer. Make sure they are locked in place (**Figure 29**).

18. Install a new stopper ring (A, **Figure 3**) if it was removed. Make sure the stopper ring is seated correctly in the drive axle groove.

19. Apply molybdenum disulfide grease to the drive axle splines.

DRIVESHAFT

The driveshaft **Figure 32** can be removed without removing the front differential or front drive axles.

Removal

1. Support the ATV with the front wheels off the ground.

2. Remove the center mud guard and inner front fender panel on the left side of the vehicle as described in Chapter Fifteen.

3. Remove the lower front differential mounting bolt (**Figure 33**).

4. Remove the upper front differential mounting bolt (A, **Figure 34**) and spacer (B).

5. Remove the front differential front mounting bracket bolts (**Figure 35**).

6. Push the front differential forward, then push the front driveshaft forward so it disconnects from the engine output shaft (**Figure 36**).

7. Remove the front boot band (A, **Figure 37**).

8. Push the boot (B, **Figure 37**) off the differential pinion joint while pulling the driveshaft rearward and removing it.

9. Remove the driveshaft joint and spring from the driveshaft.

10. Inspect the driveshaft as described in this section.

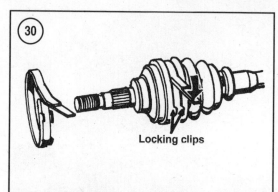

Locking clips

Inspection

1. Inspect the driveshaft for bending or other damage.

2. Examine the splines in each end for damage.

3. Examine the seals for excessive wear or damage. Install a new seal using the following procedure:

CAUTION
The seal is a tight fit when passing over the shaft splines. Lubricate the

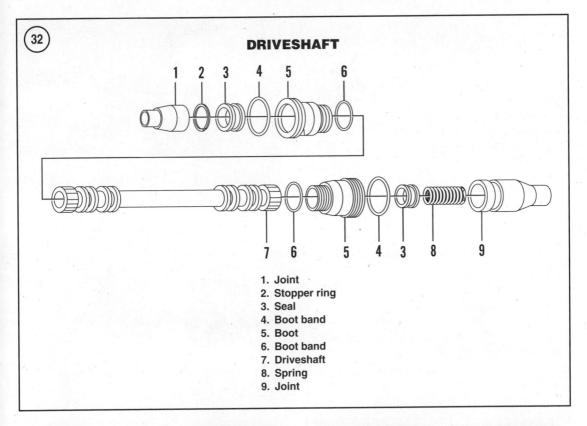

DRIVESHAFT

1. Joint
2. Stopper ring
3. Seal
4. Boot band
5. Boot
6. Boot band
7. Driveshaft
8. Spring
9. Joint

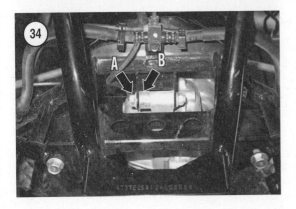

11

splines and seal, and be careful not to cut the seal.

a. Place a seal protector sleeve or plastic cone against the shaft end (A, **Figure 38**).
b. Place the lubricated seal on the cone (B, **Figure 38**). The open side must be toward the shaft as shown in **Figure 38**.
c. Push the seal onto the shaft, then work the seal into place on the seal seat as shown in **Figure 39**.

Installation

1. Lubricate the driveshaft splines and dust seals with molybdenum disulfide grease.
2. Push the front differential assembly forward in the frame.
3. Apply 5-8 g (0.18-0.28 oz.) of molybdenum disulfide grease onto the shaft splines at the differential end of the shaft.
4. Install the driveshaft into the differential pinion joint (**Figure 40**).
5. Insert a piece of wire between the driveshaft and boot to release air from the pinion joint. Leave the wire in place until Step 16.
6. Install the O-ring (**Figure 41**) onto the final driveshaft, if it was removed.
7. Apply 5-8 g (0.18-0.28 oz.) of molybdenum disulfide grease onto the rear driveshaft splines. Also apply grease to the O-ring (**Figure 41**).
8. Install the spring into the front shaft joint.
9. Install the spring and front shaft joint onto the driveshaft and under the boot.
10. Push the driveshaft forward, then connect the driveshaft to the engine (**Figure 36**). If necessary, rotate the driveshaft to align the splines.
11. Move the front differential rearward and align the mounting holes with the frame.

> *NOTE*
> *Do not tighten the differential housing mounting bolts until all of the fasteners have been installed.*

12. Install the two bolts and the front mounting bracket (**Figure 35**).
13. Install the upper mounting bolt, nut and spacer. Install the spacer as shown in B, **Figure 34**.
14. Install the lower mounting bolt (**Figure 33**).

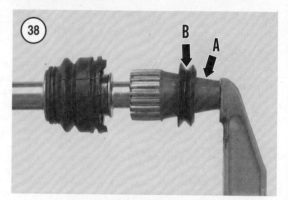

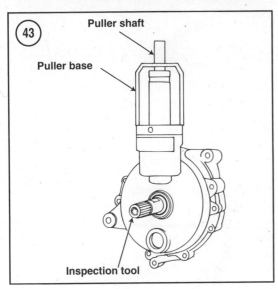

Puller shaft

Puller base

Inspection tool

15. Tighten the differential mounting bolts to the following torque specifications:

   a. Tighten the front differential mounting bracket bolts to 22 N•m (16 ft.-lb.).

   b. Tighten the lower mounting bolt to 44 N•m (33 ft.-lb.).

   c. Tighten the upper mounting bolt to 44 N•m (33 ft.-lb.).

16. Remove the piece of wire.installed in Step 5.

17. Install the inner front fender panel and center mudguard.

FRONT DIFFERENTIAL

The front differential gearcase can be removed with one front drive axle still attached to the steering knuckle. The front driveshaft may be removed before the differential, or removed with the differential. If it is only necessary to remove the driveshaft, refer to *Driveshaft* in this chapter.

Removal

1. Remove the front wheels.

2. Remove the center mud guard and inner front fender panel on the left side of the vehicle as described in Chapter Fifteen.

3. Remove one or both front drive axles as described in this chapter.

4. Disconnect the vent hose (A, **Figure 42**) from the differential gearcase.

5. Remove the lower front differential mounting bolt (B, **Figure 42**).

6. Remove the upper front differential mounting bolt (C, **Figure 42**) and spacer (D).

7. Remove the front differential front mounting bracket bolts (**Figure 35**).

8. Push the front differential forward, then push the front driveshaft forward so it disconnects from the engine output shaft (**Figure 36**).

9. If necessary, remove the front driveshaft as described in this chapter.

10. Remove the front differential gearcase (**Figure 42**) from the frame.

11. Remove the front mounting bracket.

Backlash Measurement/Adjustment

Perform gear backlash measurement prior to disassembly to determine gear wear and whether the internal shim thicknesses must be adjusted. Measuring gear backlash is also necessary after overhaul.

1. Install the pinion puller base, puller shaft, adapter and special nut as shown in **Figure 43** so

11

any pinion end play is removed and the pinion cannot rotate.

2. Place the differential in a soft-jawed vise.

3. Insert the differential inspection tool (Honda part No. 07KMK-HC5010A) into the right side of the differential so it engages the internal splines.

4. Remove the oil fill cap.

5. Position a dial indicator so the tip rests against a gear tooth (**Figure 44**).

6. To determine the gear backlash, gently rotate the differential inspection tool while reading the dial indicator. Refer to **Table 1** for the specified backlash.

7. Remove the dial indicator, then rotate the ring gear using the inspection tool and take two additional backlash readings 120° from the original measuring point. If the difference between any two readings exceeds 0.2 mm (0.01 in.), note the following:

   a. The differential assembly is not square in the case, which may be due to the incorrect seating of a bearing.

   b. The housing may be deformed.

8. To correct the gear backlash, refer to **Figure 45** and note the following:

   a. If gear backlash is less than the desired specification, reduce the thickness of the right shim and increase the thickness of the left shim.

   b. If gear backlash is greater than the desired specification, reduce the thickness of the left shim and increase the thickness of the right shim.

> *NOTE*
> *When adjusting shim thickness, adjust the sides equally. For instance, if the right shim is increased 0.10 mm (0.004 in.), decrease the left shim 0.10 mm (0.004 in.). Changing a shim thickness by 0.10 mm (0.004 in.) will change backlash 0.06 mm (0.002 in.).*

Disassembly

The front differential gearcase requires a number of special tools for disassembly, inspection and reassembly. The price of these tools could be more than the cost of most repairs performed at a dealership. Read the procedure and determine the cost before undertaking the repair.

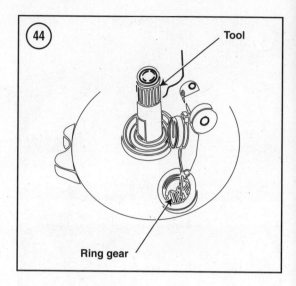

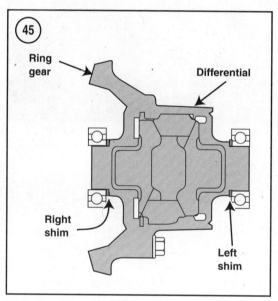

The face cams, differential housing and cover are available only as a unit assembly.

If the pinion gear, ring gear, gearcase, case cover, side bearings or pinion shaft bearing are replaced, perform the backlash and gear mesh pattern adjustments described in the following sections.

Refer to **Figure 46**.

1. Remove the front mounting bracket from the gearcase.

2. Remove the cover retaining bolts in a crossing pattern (**Figure 47**).

3. Insert a prying tool in the gap between the gearcase and cover (**Figure 48**), and pry the cover off the gearcase.

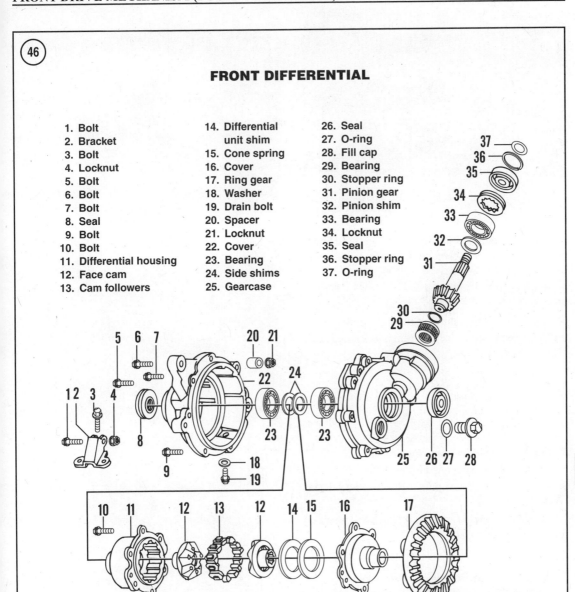

FRONT DIFFERENTIAL

1. Bolt
2. Bracket
3. Bolt
4. Locknut
5. Bolt
6. Bolt
7. Bolt
8. Seal
9. Bolt
10. Bolt
11. Differential housing
12. Face cam
13. Cam followers

14. Differential unit shim
15. Cone spring
16. Cover
17. Ring gear
18. Washer
19. Drain bolt
20. Spacer
21. Locknut
22. Cover
23. Bearing
24. Side shims
25. Gearcase

26. Seal
27. O-ring
28. Fill cap
29. Bearing
30. Stopper ring
31. Pinion gear
32. Pinion shim
33. Bearing
34. Locknut
35. Seal
36. Stopper ring
37. O-ring

11

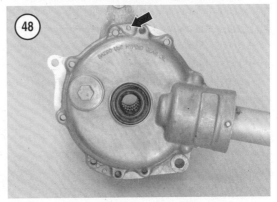

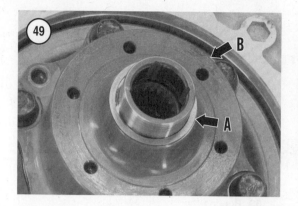

4. Note the right-side shim on the differential housing (A, **Figure 49**). Remove the shim, label it and set it aside.

5. Remove the differential assembly (B, **Figure 49**).

6. Note the left-side shim on the differential housing (**Figure 50**). Remove the shim, label it and set it aside.

> *NOTE*
> *The pinion joint is retained by a wire ring on the pinion shaft that fits in a groove in the pinion joint.*

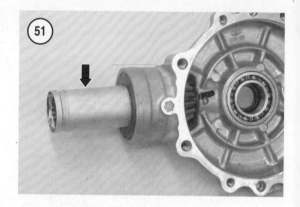

7. Pull out the pinion joint (**Figure 51**).

8. Remove the O-ring (A, **Figure 52**).

9. Using a suitable seal puller, remove the oil seal (B, **Figure 52**).

10. Rotate the pinion shaft and check for noisy or rough pinion bearings.

> *NOTE*
> *Cover the internal parts when unstaking the locknut in Step 11 to prevent the entry of metal debris.*

11. Using a grinder or metal removal tool, remove the staked portion of the locknut (A, **Figure 53**).

12. Using the locknut wrench (Honda part No. 07916-ME50001) or an equivalent, remove the locknut (B, **Figure 53**).

13. Assemble the following tools as shown in **Figure 54**, and remove the pinion and bearing assembly.

    a. Pinion puller base (Honda part No. 07HMC-MM8011A).

    b. Puller shaft (Honda part No. 07931-ME4010B).

    c. Adapter (Honda part No. 07YMF-HN4010A).

    d. Special nut (Honda part No. 07931-HB3020A).

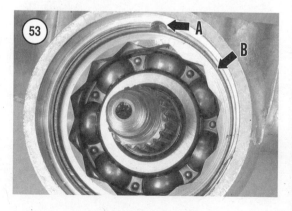

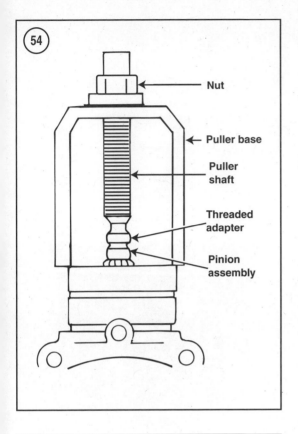

Nut

Puller base

Puller shaft

Threaded adapter

Pinion assembly

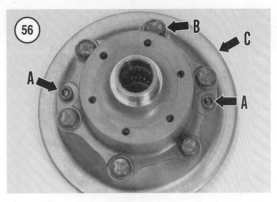

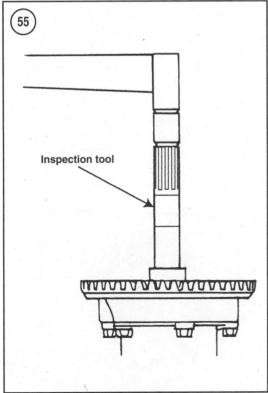

Inspection tool

14. Before disassembling the differential unit, check the slip torque to determine its operating condition as follows:

    a. Install the differential inspection tool (Honda part No. 07KMK-HC5010A) into both face cams.

    b. Secure the flat surface of the tool in a vise.

    c. Rotate the tool with a torque wrench (**Figure 55**). Refer to **Table 1** for the specified torque reading.

    d. Disassemble, inspect and, if necessary, repair the differential unit if the torque reading is below specification.

15. Install two short 6 mm socket-head bolts into the differential housing (A, **Figure 56**) to hold the cap to the housing while removing the ring gear bolts.

16. Remove the ring gear mounting bolts (B, **Figure 56**) and remove the ring gear (C).

17. Remove the two temporary bolts and remove the differential cap (**Figure 57**).

18. Remove the cone spring (A, **Figure 58**) and shim (B).

11

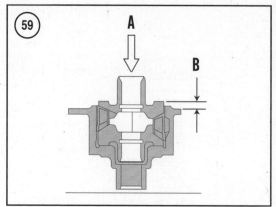

19. Check the differential unit for excessive wear as follows:

    a. Using a press or other means, apply 1.47 kN (330 lb.) to the face cam hub (A, **Figure 59**).

    b. Measure the distance from the face cam to the differential housing mating surface (B, **Figure 59**).

    c. If the distance exceeds the specification in **Table 1**, the differential unit is excessively worn and should be replaced.

20. Remove the left face cam (C, **Figure 58**).

21. Remove the cam followers (A, **Figure 60**).

22. Remove the right face cam (B, **Figure 60**).

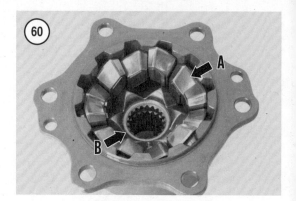

Inspection

1. Clean, then inspect, all components for excessive wear and damage. Carefully remove gasket material from the mating surfaces on the differential cover and gearcase.

2. Measure the depth of the spring seating surface in the differential cap (**Figure 61**). Replace the cap if the depth exceeds the specification in **Table 1**.

3. Inspect the grooves and sliding surfaces in the differential housing (**Figure 62**).

4. Measure the height of the cone spring. Replace the spring if the height is less than the specification in **Table 1**.

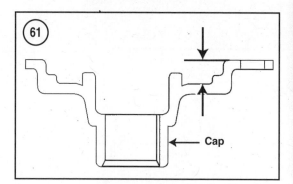

> *NOTE*
> *If bearing replacement is required, install new oil seals after bearing installation.*

5. Remove the oil seals in the differential gearcase and cover using a suitable seal removal tool. Install a new oil seal so the flanged side is out (**Figure 63**).

6. Turn the bearings in the differential gearcase and cover by hand. The bearings should turn freely and

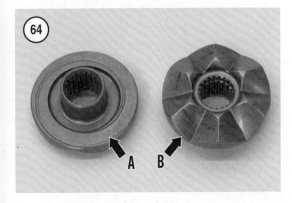

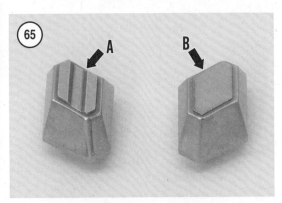

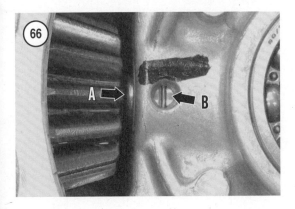

without any sign of roughness, catching or excessive noise. Replace the damaged bearings as described in *Basic Service Methods* in Chapter One. The bearing must bottom in the gearcase or cover bore.

7. Examine the face cam sliding surface (A, **Figure 64**) and cam surfaces (B).

8. Examine the sliding surfaces of the cam followers (**Figure 65**). The cam followers must be replaced as a set.

9. Inspect the pinion needle bearing (A, **Figure 66**) in the gearcase. If it is damaged, replace the bearing using the following procedure:

   a. Using needlenose pliers, extract the wire retainer ring (B, **Figure 66**) through the access hole. Rotate the ring so the end is accessible, pry out the end and pull out the ring.

> *CAUTION*
> *Do not use a flame to heat the gearcase; it can warp the gearcase.*

   b. Heat the gearcase in an oven to 176° F (80° C) and extract the bearing.

   c. Install a new wire ring into the groove on the outside of the new bearing.

   d. Install the bearing into the ring compressor tool (Honda part No. 07YME-HN4010A).

   e. Place the compressor tool with the bearing into a freezer for at least 30 minutes.

   f. Heat the gearcase in an oven to 176° F (80° C).

   g. Position the compressor in the gearcase and drive the bearing into the gearcase. Only one blow should be required. Multiple blows may dislodge the wire ring, which will require the installation of a new ring and bearing. Make sure the wire ring is properly positioned as viewed in the access hole (B, **Figure 66**).

10. Inspect the pinion gear and bearing. If the bearing must be replaced, replace it as follows:

   a. Using a press or puller, remove the bearing from the pinion shaft.

   b. If only the bearing is being replaced, use the original shim on the pinion shaft. If the differential cover or housing, ring and pinion gears or the side bearings are being replaced, install a 2.0 mm (0.79 in.) thick shim as a starting point for the gear position adjustments.

   c. Press or drive the new bearing onto the pinion shaft so the marked side of the bearing is toward the threaded end of the shaft.

11

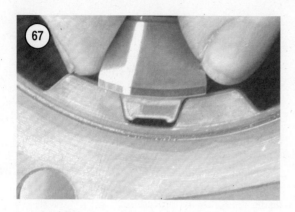

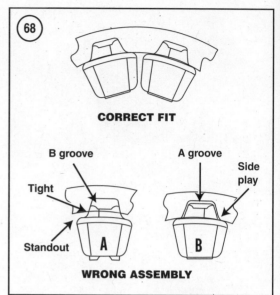

Assembly

Refer to **Figure 46** when performing the following procedure. Install the bearings and oil seals as described in *Inspection*.

> *NOTE*
> *Lubricate all moving parts with SAE 80 hypoid gear oil.*

1. Install the face cam into the differential housing.

2. Note that there are two types of cam followers. Type A followers are ribbed while type B followers are flat. Refer to **Figure 65**. Each type of cam follower must fit into a corresponding groove in the differential housing (**Figure 67**). The cam follower must engage the groove fully, to its maximum depth without excessive side play. A type A follower in a B groove will result in a tight fit and it will standout. A type B follower in an A groove will have excessive side play. Refer to **Figure 68**.

3. Install the cam followers in pairs as shown in **Figure 69**.

4. Install the face cam onto the cam followers (**Figure 70**).

5. Determine the thickness of the differential unit shim (14, **Figure 46**) as follows:

   a. Measure the distance from the face cam to the differential housing mating surface (**Figure 71**).

   b. Measure the depth of the spring seating surface in the differential cap (**Figure 61**).

   c. Subtract the face cam height (**Figure 71**) from the cap depth (**Figure 61**). From the result, subtract 1.7 mm. That result is the desired shim thickness. Select a shim closest in thickness to the calculated desired thickness.

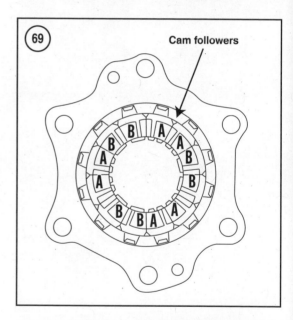

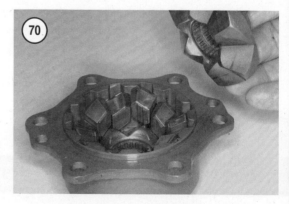

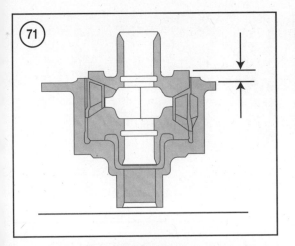

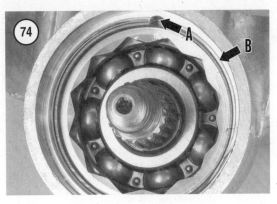

10. Install the pinion gear and bearing into the gearcase.

NOTE
The torque wrench attachment point on the Honda tool specified in Step 11 increases wrench leverage. The actual tightening torque is 98 N•m (72 ft.-lb.).

11. Install the locknut (B, **Figure 74**). Using the locknut wrench (Honda part No. 07916-ME50001) tighten the locknut to 89 N•m (66 ft.-lb.) as indi-cated on the torque wrench.

NOTE
Do not stake the locknut when per-forming the gear mesh pattern check in Step 12.

12. If the pinion, ring gear, bearings, gearcase or cover have been replaced, check the gear mesh pat-tern as follows:

    a. Apply Prussian Blue or other gear marking compound onto the ring gear teeth.
    b. Install the side shims (24, **Figure 46**) onto the differential unit, then install the ring gear/dif-ferential unit assembly into the gearcase.
    c. Install the cover onto the gearcase.

NOTE
While tightening the cover bolts in substep d, rotate the pinion shaft.

    d. Install the cover bolts. Install the two 10 mm bolts in the locations shown in **Figure 75**. Tighten the bolts evenly in a crossing pattern in several steps until the cover is seated on the gearcase. Tighten the 8 mm bolts to 25 N•m (19 ft.-lb.). Tighten the 10 mm bolts to 49 N•m (36 ft.-lb.).

6. Install the shim (A, **Figure 72**) and cone spring (B). The cone side of the spring must be out.

7. Install the cap. Secure the cap by installing short 6 mm socket-head screws (A, **Figure 73**).

8. Install the differential unit onto the ring gear (B, **Figure 73**). Tighten new bolts to 49 N•m (36 ft.-lb.).

9. Remove the temporary socket-head bolts (A, **Figure 73**).

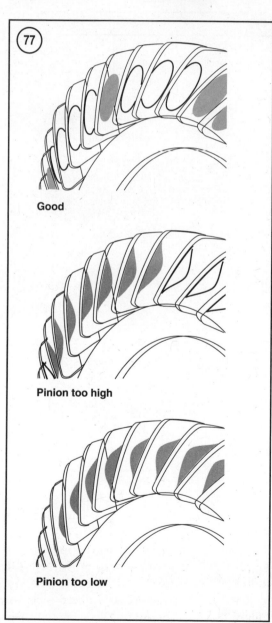

e. Remove the oil fill cap.

f. Rotate the pinion shaft several rotations so a pattern is evident on the ring gear teeth. View the ring gear teeth through the gearcase oil fill hole (**Figure 76**).

g. Refer to the typical gear patterns in **Figure 77**. If the pinion is low, install a thinner pinion shim (32, **Figure 46**). If the pinion is high, install a thicker shim. Remove the pinion and bearing to replace the shim. Changing shim thickness 0.12 mm (0.005 in.) moves the contact pattern approximately 0.5-1.0 mm (0.02-0.04 in.).

h. Reinstall the pinion gear and bearing, if they were removed, as described in Steps 10 and 11.

i. After obtaining a satisfactory gear contact pattern, check the gear backlash.

j. Remove the cover and differential unit and continue with the final assembly procedure.

13. Stake the pinion locknut (B, **Figure 74**) into the notch in the gearcase (A).

14. Install the stopper ring (A, **Figure 78**) onto the pinion shaft.

15. Install the oil seal (B, **Figure 78**) so it is bottomed. Lubricate the oil seal lips with grease.

16. Apply grease to a new O-ring and install it onto the pinion shaft (C, **Figure 78**).

17. Lubricate the pinion shaft splines with molybdenum disulfide grease, then install the pinion joint (**Figure 79**). The joint groove must engage the stopper ring on the shaft. Pull lightly on the joint to ensure it is properly installed.

18. Install the side shims (24, **Figure 46**) onto the differential unit.

19. Install the ring gear/differential unit assembly into the gearcase.

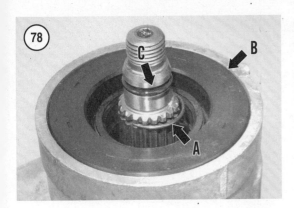

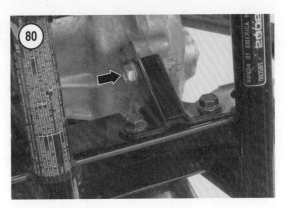

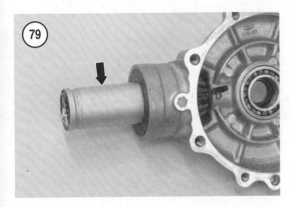

22. Make sure the gears rotate freely without binding.

20. Apply a liquid sealant such as Yamabond No. 4 to the mating surface of the differential cover, then install the cover onto the gearcase.

NOTE
While tightening the cover bolts in Step 21, rotate the pinion shaft.

21. Install the cover bolts. Install the two 10 mm bolts in the locations shown in **Figure 75**. Tighten the bolts evenly in a crossing pattern in several steps until the cover is seated on the gearcase. Tighten the 8 mm bolts to 25 N•m (19 ft.-lb.). Tighten the 10 mm bolts to 49 N•m (36 ft.-lb.).

Installation

1. Install the front mounting bracket on the gearcase, if it was removed, but do not tighten the bolt.

2. If a front axle remains installed, lubricate the axle splines with grease and insert the axle while installing the front differential.

3. Install the front differential and position it as far forward as possible.

4. Install the driveshaft as described in this chapter.

5. After tightening the upper and lower differential mounting bolts, and the two front bracket bolts, tighten the front gearcase mounting bolt (**Figure 80**) to 22 N•m (16 ft.-lb.).

6. Install the front axle(s) as described in this chapter.

7. Connect the vent hose (A, **Figure 42**) to the differential gearcase and secure it with the clamp.

8. Fill the front differential with the correct amount and type of oil (Chapter Three).

11

Table 1 FRONT DRIVE SPECIFICATIONS

	New	Service limit
Cone spring free height	2.8 mm (0.11 in.)	2.6 mm (0.10 mm)
Differential housing cap depth	9.55-9.65 mm (0.376-0.380 in.)	9.55 mm (0.376 in.)
Differential slip torque	14-17 N•m (10-12.5 ft.-lb.)	12 N•m (9 ft.-lb.)
Driveshaft length between		
axle joints	344.8-354.8 mm (13.57-13.97 in.)	–
	(continued)	

Table 1 FRONT DRIVE SPECIFICATIONS (continued)

	New	Service limit
Face cam-to-housing distance		
2000-2003	6.3-6.7 mm (0.25-0.26 in.)	6.3 mm (0.25 in.)
2004-on	3.3-3.7 mm (0.13-0.15 in.)	3.3 mm (0.13 in.)
Gear backlash	0.05-0.25 mm (0.002-0.010 in.)	0.4 mm (0.016 in.)

Table 2 FRONT DRIVE TORQUE SPECIFICATIONS

	N•m	in.-lb.	ft.-lb.
Differential bolts			
8 mm	25	–	19
10 mm	49	–	36
Differential mounting bolts			
Front mounting bolt	22	–	16
Lower mounting bolt	44	–	33
Upper mounting bolt	44	–	33
Mounting bracket bolts	22	–	16
Pinion locknut*	89	–	66
Ring gear bolts	49	–	36

*Torque wrench reading using Honda tool.

CHAPTER TWELVE

REAR AXLE, SUSPENSION AND FINAL DRIVE

This chapter contains repair and replacement procedures for the rear wheels, rear axle, suspension and final drive unit.

Rear suspension specifications are listed in **Table 1** and torque specifications in **Table 2**. **Table 1** and **Table 2** are at the end of this chapter.

> *WARNING*
> *Self-locking nuts are used to secure some of the rear suspension components. Honda recommends discarding all self-locking nuts once they have been removed. The self-locking portion of the nut is weakened once the nut has been removed and will no longer properly lock onto the mating threads. Always install new self-locking nuts. Never reinstall a used nut once it has been removed.*

REAR WHEELS

Refer to **Figure 1**.

Removal/Installation

> *NOTE*
> *The tire tread on the original-equipment tires is directional and must be installed on the correct side of the ATV. The tire is marked with an arrow to indicate forward rotation (**Figure 2**).*

1. Park the ATV on level ground and set the parking brake. Block the front wheels so the ATV cannot roll in either direction.

2. If the tires are not equipped with a mark to indicate forward rotation, identify the rear tires with an L (left side) or R (right side) mark. Refer to these marks to install the wheels on the correct side.

3. Loosen the wheel nuts (**Figure 3**) securing the wheel to the hub/brake drum.

4. Jack up the rear of the ATV so the rear wheel(s) is off the ground. Support the vehicle with safety stands or wooden blocks in the event the jack fails.

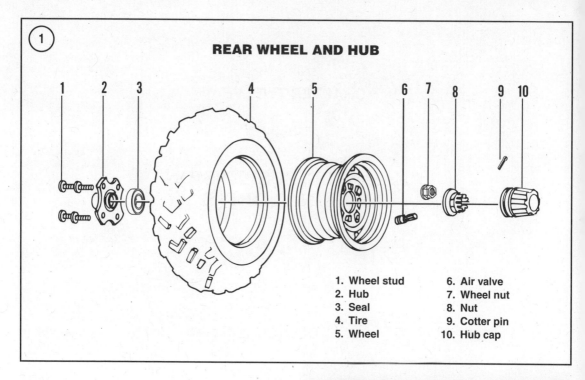

REAR WHEEL AND HUB

1. Wheel stud
2. Hub
3. Seal
4. Tire
5. Wheel
6. Air valve
7. Wheel nut
8. Nut
9. Cotter pin
10. Hub cap

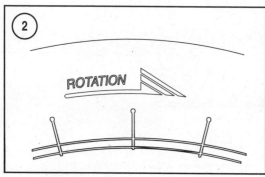

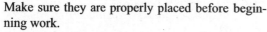

ROTATION

Make sure they are properly placed before beginning work.

5. Remove the wheel nuts and remove the rear wheel.

6. Clean the wheel nuts in solvent and dry them thoroughly.

7. Inspect the wheel for cracks, bending or other damage. If necessary, replace the wheel as described in *Tires and Wheels* in Chapter Ten.

8. Install the wheel onto its original side.

9. Install the wheel nuts with their curved end (**Figure 4**) facing toward the wheel. Tighten the nuts finger-tight to center the wheel squarely against the brake drum or hub.

10. Tighten the wheel nuts (**Figure 3**) to 64 N•m (47 ft.-lb.).

11. After the wheel is installed completely, rotate it and then apply the rear brake several times to make sure the wheel rotates freely and the brake is operating correctly.

12. Jack up the rear of the vehicle and remove the safety stands or wooden blocks.

13. Lower the ATV so both rear wheels are on the ground and remove the jack.

SHOCK ABSORBER

Removal/Installation

1. Support the rear of the ATV so the rear wheels are off the ground.

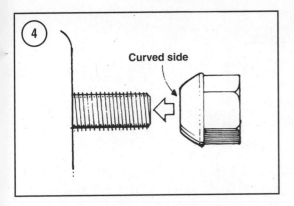

Curved side

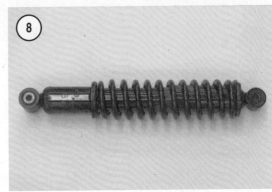

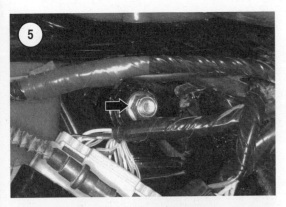

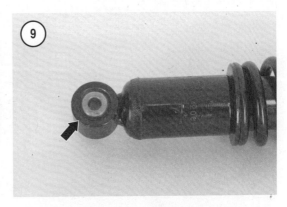

2. Place a support under the final drive to support the rear axle assembly.

3. Remove the shock absorber upper mounting locknut (**Figure 5**). Discard the locknut.

4. Remove the shock absorber lower mounting bolt (**Figure 6**).

5. Remove the shock absorber (**Figure 7**).

6. Inspect the shock absorber as described in this chapter.

7. Install the shock absorber by reversing the removal steps, while noting the following:

   a. Install a new locknut on the upper mounting bolt.

   b. Tighten the upper and lower shock absorber bolts to 44 N•m (33 ft.-lb.).

Inspection

1. Clean and dry the shock absorber (**Figure 8**).

2. Check the damper unit for leaks or other damage. Inspect the damper rod for bending.

3. Inspect the upper and lower rubber bushings (**Figure 9**). Replace a severely worn or damaged lower bushing. The upper bushing is not replaceable.

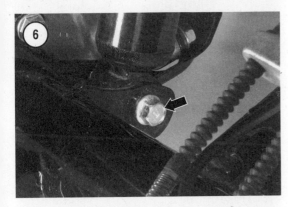

12

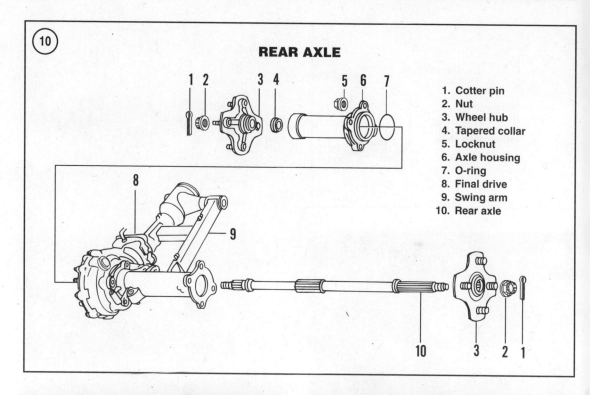

REAR AXLE

1. Cotter pin
2. Nut
3. Wheel hub
4. Tapered collar
5. Locknut
6. Axle housing
7. O-ring
8. Final drive
9. Swing arm
10. Rear axle

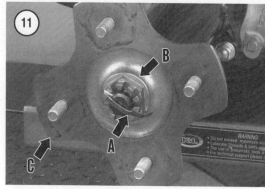

4. Inspect the spring for damage.

5. If the damper unit or spring is damaged, replace the entire shock absorber unit. Other than the lower end bushing and seals, individual components are not available.

REAR AXLE

Refer to **Figure 10**.

Removal

1. Remove both rear wheels as described in this chapter.

2. Remove the left rear axle nut cotter pin (A, **Figure 11**) and discard it.

3. Remove the left rear axle nut (B, **Figure 11**) and rear hub (C).

4. Remove the skid plate (A, **Figure 12**).

5. Remove the locknuts (B, **Figure 12**) and the left rear axle housing (C). Discard the locknuts.

6. Remove the tapered collar (**Figure 13**).

7. Remove the rear brake panel assembly (Chapter Thirteen).

8. Remove the axle (**Figure 14**) from the right side. If necessary, drive out the axle with a rubber hammer.

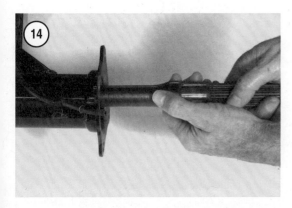

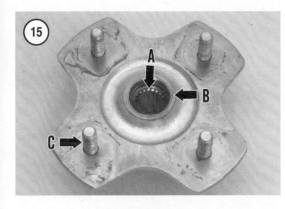

9. Inspect the rear hubs and axle as described in this chapter.

Wheel Hubs Inspection

1. Inspect the hub inner splines (A, **Figure 15**) for wear or damage. Replace the hub if necessary.
2. Replace the dust seal (B, **Figure 15**) if it is worn or damaged.
3. Examine the studs (C, **Figure 15**) for damaged threads. Replace damaged studs with a press.
4. Inspect the seal contact surface (A, **Figure 16**) and bearing contact surface (B). Replace the hub if it is damaged.

Rear Axle Inspection

1. Clean and dry the rear axle.
2. Inspect the axle splines for twisting or other damage.
3. Check the axle cotter pin holes. Replace the axle if either hole is cracked or damaged and cannot hold the cotter pin.
4. Place the rear axle on a set of V-blocks and measure runout with a dial indicator (**Figure 17**). Replace the rear axle if the runout exceeds the service limit in **Table 1**.

Left Final Drive Housing Axle Seal and Bearing Inspection and Replacement

1. Inspect the axle seal (A, **Figure 18**) for damage.
2. Check the bearing (B, **Figure 18**) by turning the inner race by hand. The bearing should turn without roughness, catching, binding or excessive noise. If the bearing is damaged, replace it as described in this procedure.

12

3. Support the final drive housing and pry the axle seal out with a seal removal tool.

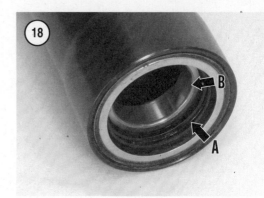

NOTE
If only seal replacement is required, go to Step 8.

4. Remove the bearing by driving it out of the housing with a long drift or bearing driver.

5. Clean and dry the final drive housing.

6. Check the bearing bore for cracks or other damage.

7. Install the new bearing as follows:

    a. Install the bearing with its closed side facing out.

    b. Install the bearing with a bearing driver to the depth shown in **Figure 19**. Press on the bearing outer race only.

8. Install the new axle seal as follows:

    a. Pack the oil seal lips with a waterproof grease.

    b. Install the new oil seal into the housing in the direction shown in **Figure 19**. Install the new oil seal so it seats against the bearing.

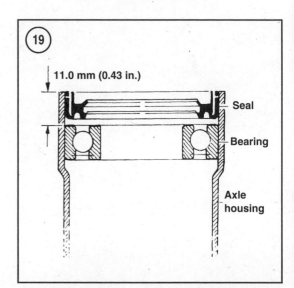

Installation

1. Apply molybdenum disulfide grease to the center axle splines.

2. Install the rear axle (**Figure 14**) from the right side. At the same time, align the rear axle and final drive housing splines. Insert the axle until it is fully seated.

3. Install the rear brake panel, brake drum and brake drum cover (Chapter Thirteen).

4. Clean the rear hubs where they contact the brake drum (right side) or bearing (left axle housing).

5. Lubricate the axle shaft splines on the right end with molybdenum disulfide grease.

6. Install the right rear hub (A, **Figure 20**) and axle nut (B). Tighten the axle nut hand-tight at this time.

7. Install the tapered axle collar so the taper is inward as shown in **Figure 13**.

8. Replace the final drive case O-ring (**Figure 21**) if it is damaged. Lubricate the O-ring with grease.

9. Install the left rear axle housing (C, **Figure 12**) so the skid plate (A) mounting hole is down. Install new axle housing locknuts (B, **Figure 12**) and tighten them to 44 N•m (33 ft.-lb.).

10. Install the skid plate (A, **Figure 12**). Tighten the bolts to 32 N•m (24 ft.-lb.).

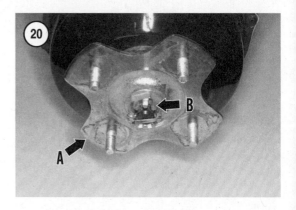

11. Lubricate the axle shaft splines on the left end with molybdenum disulfide grease. Also apply grease to the rear hub seal.

12. Install the left rear hub (C, **Figure 11**). Install the left rear axle nut (B) and tighten it hand-tight.

13. Tighten the left side axle nut (B, **Figure 11**) to 137 N•m (101 ft.-lb.).

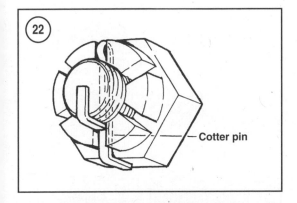

Cotter pin

14. Tighten the right side axle nut (B, **Figure 20**) to 137 N•m (101 ft.-lb.).

> *WARNING*
> *Always install a new cotter pin. If the cotter pin hole(s) in the axle does not align with the castellations on the nut, tighten the nut further until hole alignment is correct. Never loosen the axle nut to achieve hole alignment.*

15. Secure each axle nut with a new cotter pin. Spread the cotter pin ends to lock it in place. See **Figure 22**.

16. Install both rear wheels as described in this chapter.

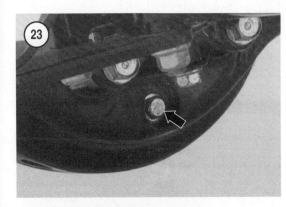

FINAL DRIVE UNIT

Removal

1. Remove the drain bolt (**Figure 23**) and drain the final drive oil.

2. Remove the rear axle as described in this chapter.

3. Disconnect the vent hose (A, **Figure 24**) from the final drive housing tube.

4. Remove the right axle housing bolts (**Figure 25**).

> *NOTE*
> *The lower final drive housing retaining bolts also secure the skid plate bracket.*

5. Remove the final drive housing bolts (B, **Figure 24**) and skid plate bracket (C).

6. Remove the final drive unit.

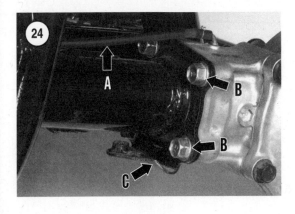

12

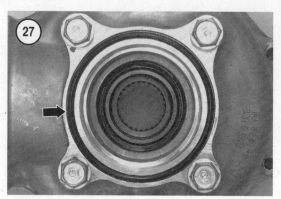

7. Remove the spring (**Figure 26**) from the driveshaft.

8. Remove the O-rings from the front and sides of the final drive housing.

9. Refer to *Disassembly, Inspection and Assembly* for further information.

Installation

1. Lubricate new O-rings with grease and install them into the grooves at the front and sides of the final drive housing (**Figure 27**).

2. Lubricate the spring with grease and install it into the end of the driveshaft (**Figure 26**).

3. Lubricate the shaft splines with molybdenum disulfide grease.

> *NOTE*
> *Make sure the driveshaft is properly engaged in the universal joint in the swing arm.*

4. Install the final drive unit onto the swing arm, making sure the pinion shaft engages the driveshaft and spring.

5. Install the front bolts (B, **Figure 24**) and skid plate bracket (C). Tighten the bolts to 54 N•m (40 ft.-lb.).

6. Install the side bolts (**Figure 25**). Tighten the bolts to 54 N•m (40 ft.-lb.).

7. Reconnect the vent hose (A, **Figure 24**) to the vent tube.

8. Install the rear axle as described in this chapter.

9. Refill the final drive unit with the recommended type and quantity of oil as described in Chapter Three.

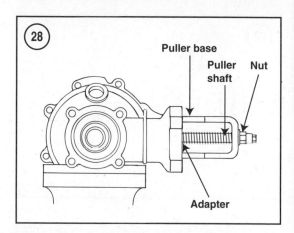

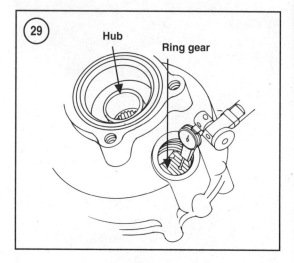

Backlash Measurement/Adjustment

Perform gear backlash measurement prior to disassembly to determine gear wear and whether the internal shim thicknesses must be adjusted. Measuring gear backlash is also necessary after overhaul.

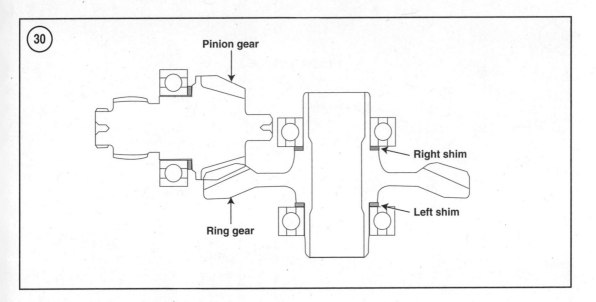

1. Install the pinion puller base, puller shaft, adapter and special nut as shown in **Figure 28** so any pinion end play is removed and the pinion cannot rotate.

2. Place the final drive in a soft-jawed vise.

3. Remove the oil fill cap.

4. Insert a tool into the center splines of the ring gear hub so the ring gear can be rotated.

5. Position a dial indicator so the tip rests against a gear tooth (**Figure 29**).

6. To determine the gear backlash, gently rotate the ring gear while reading the dial indicator. Refer to **Table 1** for the specified backlash.

7. Remove the dial indicator, then rotate the ring gear and take two additional backlash readings 120° from the original measuring point. If the difference between any two readings exceeds 0.2 mm (0.01 in.), note the following:

   a. The gear assembly is not square in the case, which may be due to the incorrect seating of a bearing.

   b. The housing may be deformed.

8. To correct the gear backlash, refer to **Figure 30** and note the following:

   a. If gear backlash is less than the desired specification, reduce the thickness of the left shim and increase the thickness of the right shim.

   b. If gear backlash is greater than the desired specification, reduce the thickness of the right shim and increase the thickness of the left shim.

NOTE
When adjusting shim thickness, adjust the sides equally. For instance, if the right shim is increased 0.10 mm (0.004 in.), decrease the left shim 0.10 mm (0.004 in.). Changing a shim thickness by 0.12 mm (0.005 in.) will change backlash 0.06 mm (0.002 in.).

Disassembly

The rear final drive unit requires a number of special tools for disassembly, inspection and reassembly. The price of these tools could be more than the cost of most repairs performed at a dealership. Read the procedure and determine the cost before undertaking the repair.

If the pinion gear, ring gear, gearcase, case cover, side bearings or pinion shaft bearing are replaced, perform the backlash and gear mesh pattern adjustments prior to disassembly.

Refer to **Figure 31**.

1. Remove the cover retaining bolts in a crossing pattern (A, **Figure 32**).

3. Insert a prying tool in the gaps between the gearcase and cover (B, **Figure 32**), and pry the cover off the gearcase.

4. Note the left-side shim on the ring gear (A, **Figure 33**). Remove the shim, label it and set it aside.

5. Remove the ring gear (B, **Figure 33**).

12

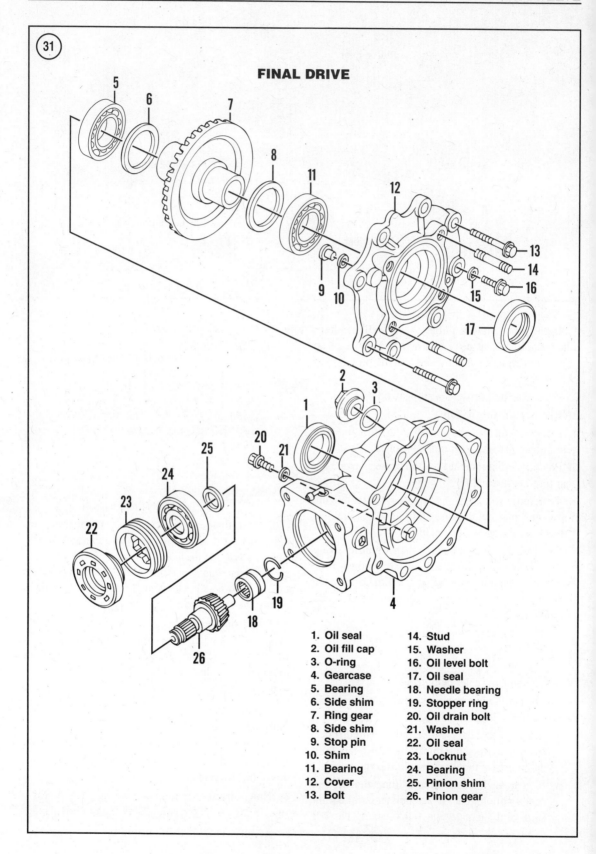

FINAL DRIVE

1. Oil seal
2. Oil fill cap
3. O-ring
4. Gearcase
5. Bearing
6. Side shim
7. Ring gear
8. Side shim
9. Stop pin
10. Shim
11. Bearing
12. Cover
13. Bolt
14. Stud
15. Washer
16. Oil level bolt
17. Oil seal
18. Needle bearing
19. Stopper ring
20. Oil drain bolt
21. Washer
22. Oil seal
23. Locknut
24. Bearing
25. Pinion shim
26. Pinion gear

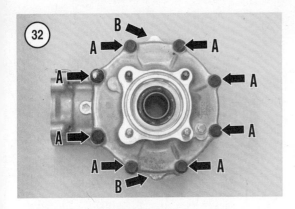

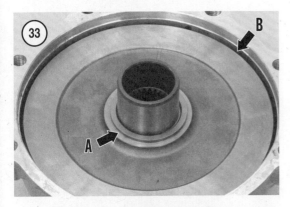

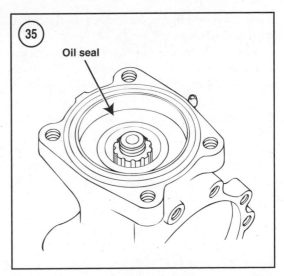

Oil seal

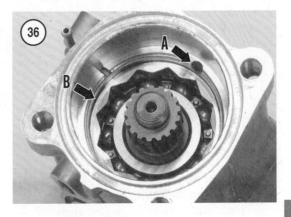

6. Note the right-side shim on the ring gear (**Figure 34**). Remove the shim, label it and set it aside.

7. Using a suitable seal puller, remove the oil seal (**Figure 35**).

8. Rotate the pinion shaft and check for noisy or rough pinion bearings.

> *NOTE*
> *Cover the internal parts when unstaking the locknut in Step 9 to prevent the entry of metal debris.*

9. Using a grinder or metal removal tool, remove the staked portion of the locknut (A, **Figure 36**).

10. Using the locknut wrench (Honda part No. 07916-MB00002) or an equivalent, remove the locknut (B, **Figure 36**).

11. Assemble the following tools as shown in **Figure 37**, and remove the pinion and bearing assembly.

   a. Pinion puller base (Honda part No. 07HMC-MM80011A).

   b. Puller shaft (Honda part No. 07931-ME4010B).

   c. Adapter (Honda part No. 07YMF-HN4010A).

   d. Special nut (Honda part No. 07931-HB3020A).

Inspection

1. Clean, then inspect, all components for excessive wear and damage. Carefully remove gasket

12

material from the mating surfaces on the final drive cover and gearcase.

2. Remove the oil seals in the final drive gearcase and cover using a suitable seal removal tool. Install a new oil seal so the closed side is out (**Figure 38**).

3. Turn the bearings (A, **Figure 39**) in the final drive gearcase and cover by hand. The bearings should turn freely and without any sign of roughness, catching or excessive noise. Replace the damaged bearings as described in *Basic Service Methods* in Chapter One. The bearing must bottom in the gearcase or cover bore.

4. Inspect the ring gear and hub (**Figure 40**). Inspect the gear teeth, splines and seal running surfaces on the hub. Replace them if they are excessively worn or damaged.

5. Inspect the pinion needle bearing (A, **Figure 41**) in the gearcase. If it is damaged, replace the bearing using the following procedure:

   a. Using needlenose pliers, extract the wire retainer ring (B, **Figure 41**) through the access hole. Rotate the ring so the end is accessible, pry out the end and pull out the ring.

CAUTION
Do not use a flame to heat the gearcase; it can warp the gearcase.

   b. Heat the gearcase in an oven to 176° F (80° C) and extract the bearing.

   c. Install a new wire ring into the groove on the outside of the new bearing.

   d. Install the bearing into the ring compressor tool (Honda part No. 07YME-HN4010A).

   e. Place the compressor tool with the bearing into a freezer for at least 30 minutes.

   f. Heat the gearcase in an oven to 176° F (80° C).

   g. Position the compressor in the gearcase and drive the bearing into the gearcase. Only one blow should be required. Multiple blows may dislodge the wire ring, which will require the installation of a new ring and bearing. Make sure the wire ring is properly positioned as viewed in the access hole (B, **Figure 41**).

6. Inspect the pinion gear and bearing. If the bearing must be replaced, replace it as follows:

   a. Using a press or puller, remove the bearing from the pinion shaft.

   b. If only the bearing is being replaced, use the original shim on the pinion shaft. If the final

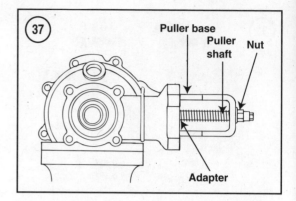

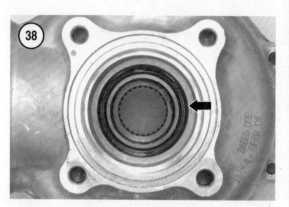

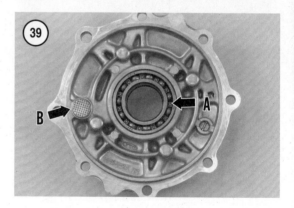

drive cover or housing, ring and pinion gears, or the side bearings are being replaced, install a 2.0 mm (0.79 in.) thick shim as a starting point for the gear position adjustments.

   c. Press or drive the new bearing onto the pinion shaft so the marked side of the bearing is toward the threaded end of the shaft.

7. Check the ring gear side clearance using the following procedure:

   a. Install the ring gear and side shim into the cover.

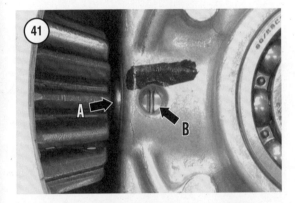

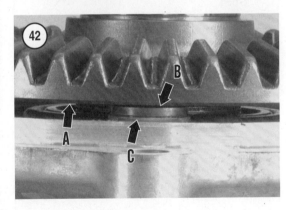

b. Using a feeler gauge, measure the clearance between the ring gear (A, **Figure 42**) and the stop pin (B). Refer to **Table 1** for the recommended clearance. The shim (C, **Figure 42**) under the stop pin is used to adjust the clearance.

c. To adjust the clearance, heat the cover in an oven to 176° F (80° C). Remove the stop pin (B, **Figure 39**).

d. Install or remove shims as necessary to obtain the desired clearance.

e. Drive the stop pin into the cover and recheck the clearance.

Assembly

Refer to **Figure 31**. Install the bearings and oil seals as described in *Inspection*.

> NOTE
> *Lubricate all moving parts with SAE 80 hypoid gear oil.*

1. Install the pinion gear and bearing into the gearcase.

> NOTE
> *The torque wrench attachment point on the Honda tool specified in Step 2 increases wrench leverage. The actual tightening torque is 98 N•m (72 ft.-lb.).*

2. Install the locknut (B, **Figure 36**). Using the locknut wrench (Honda part No. 07916-MB00002), tighten the locknut to 89 N•m (66 ft.-lb.) as indicated on the torque wrench.

> NOTE
> *Do not stake the locknut when performing the gear mesh pattern check in Step 3.*

3. If the pinion, ring gear, bearings, gearcase or cover have been replaced, check gear mesh pattern using the following procedure:

   a. Apply Prussian Blue or another gear marking compound to the ring gear teeth.

   b. Install the side shims (6 and 8, **Figure 31**) onto the ring gear, then install the ring gear into the gearcase.

   c. Install the cover onto the gearcase.

> NOTE
> *While tightening the cover bolts in substep d, rotate the pinion shaft.*

   d. Install the cover bolts. Install the two 10 mm bolts in the locations shown in **Figure 43**. Tighten the bolts evenly in a crossing pattern in several steps until the cover is seated on the gearcase. Tighten the 8 mm bolts to 25 N•m (19 ft.-lb.). Tighten the 10 mm bolts to 49 N•m (36 ft.-lb.).

   e. Remove the oil fill cap.

12

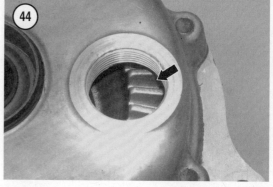

f. Rotate the pinion shaft several rotations so a pattern is evident on the ring gear teeth. View the ring gear teeth through the gearcase oil fill hole (**Figure 44**).

g. Refer to the typical gear patterns in **Figure 45**. If the pinion is low, install a thinner pinion shim (25, **Figure 31**). If the pinion is high, install a thicker shim. The pinion and bearing must be removed to replace the shim. Changing shim thickness 0.12 mm (0.005 in.) moves the contact pattern approximately 0.5-1.0 mm (0.02-0.04 in.).

h. Reinstall the pinion gear and bearing, if they were removed, as described in Steps 10 and 11.

i. After obtaining a satisfactory gear contact pattern, check the gear backlash.

j. Remove the cover and continue with the final assembly procedure.

4. Stake the pinion locknut (A, **Figure 36**) into the notch in the gearcase.

5. Install the oil seal (**Figure 35**) so it is bottomed. Lubricate the oil seal lips with grease.

6. Install the side shims (6 and 8, **Figure 31**) onto the ring gear.

7. Install the ring gear into the gearcase.

8. Apply a liquid sealant, such as Yamabond No. 4, to the mating surface of the final drive cover, then install the cover onto the gearcase.

NOTE
While tightening the cover bolts in Step 9, rotate the pinion shaft.

9. Install the cover bolts. Install the two 10 mm bolts in the locations shown in **Figure 43**. Tighten the bolts evenly in a crossing pattern in several steps until the cover is seated on the gearcase. Tighten the

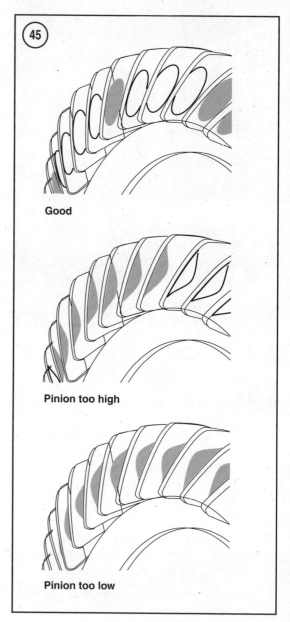

Good

Pinion too high

Pinion too low

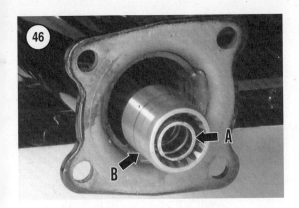

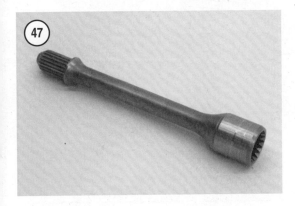

8 mm bolts to 25 N•m (19 ft.-lb.). Tighten the 10 mm bolts to 49 N•m (36 ft.-lb.).

10. Make sure the gears rotate freely without binding.

DRIVESHAFT

Removal/Inspection/Installation

1. Remove the final drive unit as described in this chapter.

2. Remove the spring in the end of the driveshaft (A, **Figure 46**).

3. Remove the driveshaft (B, **Figure 46**).

4. Inspect the splines and seal contact surface on the driveshaft (**Figure 47**). Replace the driveshaft if it is excessively worn or damaged.

5. Before installation, apply molybdenum disulfide grease to the splines of the driveshaft.

6. Insert the driveshaft into the splines of the universal joint. Make sure the driveshaft is fully seated in the universal joint.

7. Install the spring into the end of the driveshaft (A, **Figure 46**).

8. Install the final drive unit as described in this chapter.

SWING ARM

Bearings are pressed into both sides of the swing arm. Seals are installed on the outside of each bearing to prevent dirt and moisture from entering the bearings. Refer to **Figure 48**.

Special Tools

The Honda swing arm locknut wrench (part No. 07908-4690003 [A, **Figure 49**]) and a 17 mm hex socket (B) are required to remove and install the swing arm.

Removal

1. Remove the rear fender (Chapter Fifteen).

2. Remove the final drive unit and driveshaft as described in this chapter.

3. Remove the breather tubes from their clamps on the swing arm.

4. Support the rear of the swing arm, then remove the lower shock absorber mounting bolt (**Figure 50**).

5. Grasp the rear end of the swing arm and try to move it from side to side in a horizontal arc. There should be no noticeable side play. If play is evident and the pivot bolts are tightened correctly, replace the swing arm bearings.

6. Loosen the swing arm boot clamp (A, **Figure 51**) and work the boot off the swing arm.

NOTE
It may be helpful to remove the rear brake pedal for greater tool access.

7. Remove the pivot cap (B, **Figure 51**) from each side of the swing arm.

8. Loosen and remove the right pivot locknut using the locknut wrench (**Figure 52**).

9. Using the 17 mm hex socket, remove the pivot bolts (**Figure 53**) on both sides.

10. Remove the swing arm.

11. Remove the universal joint (A, **Figure 54**) if it did not come off with the swing arm.

12. If necessary, loosen the remaining clamp and remove the boot (B, **Figure 54**).

12

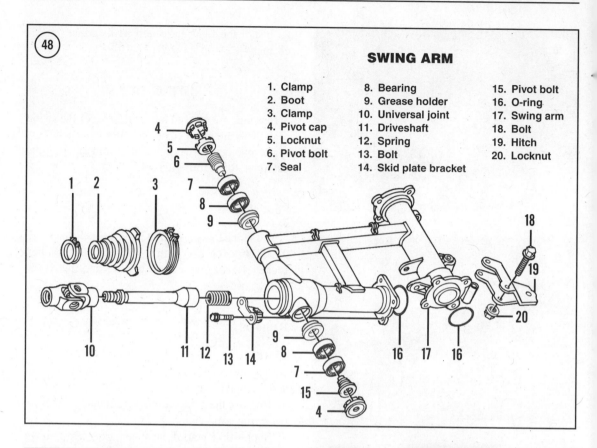

SWING ARM

1. Clamp
2. Boot
3. Clamp
4. Pivot cap
5. Locknut
6. Pivot bolt
7. Seal

8. Bearing
9. Grease holder
10. Universal joint
11. Driveshaft
12. Spring
13. Bolt
14. Skid plate bracket

15. Pivot bolt
16. O-ring
17. Swing arm
18. Bolt
19. Hitch
20. Locknut

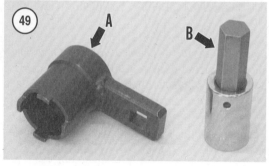

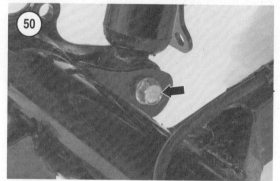

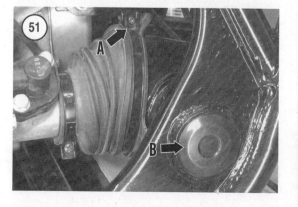

Inspection

1. Clean and dry the swing arm and its components.

2. Inspect the welded sections on the swing arm for cracks or other damage.

3. Remove the seals (**Figure 55**) with a seal removal tool or screwdriver.

4. Inspect each bearing (A, **Figure 56**) for severe wear, pitting or other damage. If necessary, replace the bearings as described in *Bearing Replacement* in this section.

5. Make sure each grease holder (B, **Figure 56**) fits tightly in its swing arm bore.

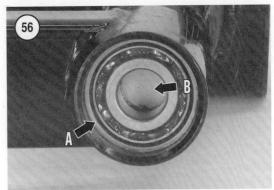

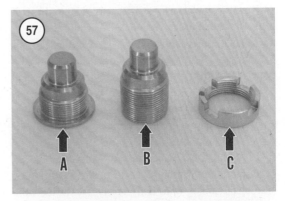

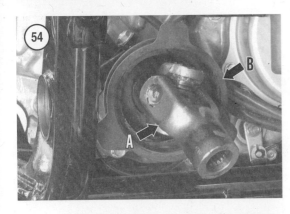

6. Inspect the pivot bolts (**Figure 57**) for excessive wear, thread damage or corrosion. Make sure the machined end on each pivot bolt is smooth. Replace if necessary.

7. Check the threaded holes in the frame (**Figure 58**) for corrosion or damage.

8. Replace the boot if it is damaged.

Universal Joint Inspection

1. Make sure the universal joint (**Figure 59**) pivots smoothly with no binding or roughness.

12

2. Inspect both universal joint spline ends for damage. If these splines are damaged, inspect the driveshaft and engine output shaft splines for damage.

Bearing Replacement

Replace the left and right side bearings (**Figure 48**) at the same time.
1. Support the swing arm in a vise with soft jaws.
2. Remove the seals (**Figure 55**) with a seal removal tool or screwdriver.
3. Remove the bearings with a blind bearing remover (**Figure 60**).
4. Check the grease holders (B, **Figure 56**) for looseness or damage. If necessary, replace the plates as follows:
   a. Drive the existing grease retainer plate inward, then remove it.
   b. Drive a new grease retainer into each side of the swing arm.
5. Lubricate the new bearings with grease.
6. Drive a new bearing (A, **Figure 56**) into each side of the swing arm. Only apply pressure on the outer race of each bearing. Install both bearings so the manufacturer's marks face out.
7. Lubricate each bearing by packing 3 grams (0.1 oz.) of No. 2 multipurpose grease into the bearing.
8. Lubricate the new dust seal lips with grease and install them into the swing arm with the closed side facing out (**Figure 55**).

Installation

1. Install the boot (B, **Figure 54**) onto the engine if it was removed.
2. Lubricate the universal joint and driveshaft splines with molybdenum disulfide grease.
3. Install the universal joint (A, **Figure 54**).

> *NOTE*
> *Refer to **Figure 57** to identify the pivot bolts when installing them in the following steps. Note that the left pivot bolt (A, **Figure 57**) is flanged.*

4. Install the swing arm into the frame, while noting the following:
   b. Install the right pivot bolt (A, **Figure 61**) and tighten it finger-tight.

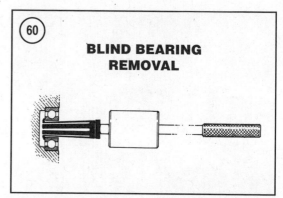

BLIND BEARING REMOVAL

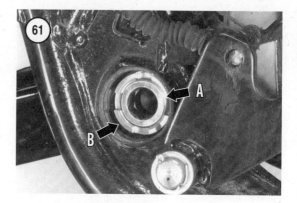

   c. Install the left pivot bolt (**Figure 53**) and tighten it finger-tight.
   d. Swing the swing arm up and down, making sure it pivots smoothly with no binding or roughness.

5. Tighten the left pivot bolt (**Figure 53**) to 118 N•m (87 ft.-lb.).

6. Tighten the right pivot bolt (A, **Figure 61**) to 4 N•m (36 in.-lb.).

7. Pivot the swing arm up and down several times to help seat the bearings.

8. Retighten both pivot bolts to the specified torque.

NOTE
The torque wrench attachment point on the Honda tool specified in Step 9 increases wrench leverage.

9. Install the right pivot bolt locknut (B, **Figure 61**) and tighten it with the locknut wrench as follows:

a. Hold the right pivot bolt with a 17 mm hex socket wrench (**Figure 62**).

b. Tighten the right pivot bolt locknut with the locknut wrench and a torque wrench (**Figure 62**) to 107 N•m (79 ft.-lb.) as indicated on the torque wrench. The actual locknut tightening torque is 118 N•m (87 ft.-lb.).

10. Install the left and right side swing arm pivot caps (B, **Figure 51**).

11. Reattach the shock absorber by installing the lower mount bolt (**Figure 50**). Tighten the bolt to 44 N•m (33 ft.-lb.).

12. Reinstall the boot onto the swing arm and tighten the swing arm boot clamp (A, **Figure 51**).

13. Secure the breather tubes in the clamps on the swing arm.

14. Install the final drive unit as described in this chapter.

15. Install the rear brake pedal (Chapter Thirteen) if it was removed.

16. Install the rear fender (Chapter Fifteen).

Table 1 REAR SUSPENSION AND FINAL DRIVE SPECIFICATIONS

Gear backlash	0.05-0.25 mm (0.002-0.010 in.)
Service limit	0.4 mm (0.016 in.)
Rear axle runout service limit	3.0 mm (0.12 in.)
Rear damper type	Double tube
Rear suspension type	Swing arm
Rear wheel travel	150 mm (5.90 in.)
Ring gear stop pin clearance	0.3-0.6 mm (0.01-0.02 in.)

Table 2 REAR DRIVE TORQUE SPECIFICATIONS

	N•m	in.-lb.	ft.-lb.
Axle nuts	137	–	101
Final drive bolts			
8 mm	25	–	19
10 mm	49	–	36
Final drive mounting bolts			
Front	54	–	40
Side	54	–	40
Left axle housing locknuts	44	–	33
Pinion locknut*	89	–	66
Right pivot bolt locknut*	107	–	79
Shock absorber bolt	44	–	33
Skid plate bolt	32	–	24
Swing arm pivot bolts			
Left pivot bolt	118	–	87
Right pivot bolt	4	36	–
Wheel nuts	64	–	47

*Torque wrench reading using Honda tool.

12

CHAPTER THIRTEEN

BRAKES

This chapter includes service procedures for the front and rear brake systems.

The front brakes are actuated by the hand lever on the right end of the handlebar. The rear brake is actuated by the brake pedal and the brake lever on the left end of the handlebar. The left end brake lever is also equipped with a lock which allows it to be used as a parking brake.

Brake specifications are listed in **Table 1** and **Table 2**. **Tables 1-3** are located at the end of the chapter.

BRAKE SERVICE

When working on hydraulic brake systems, the work area and tools must be clean. Place the parts on clean lint-free cloths and wipe all oil and other chemical residues off of the tools. Tiny particles of foreign matter and grit in the master cylinder or wheel cylinders can damage the components. If there is any doubt about your ability to correctly and safely carry out major service on the brake components, take the job to a Honda dealership.

Consider the following when servicing the front drum brake:

1. When adding brake fluid, use only a brake fluid clearly marked or DOT 4 and from a sealed container. Other types may vaporize and cause brake failure. Try to use the same brand name. Before intermixing brake fluid, make sure the two fluids are compatible. Brake fluid will draw moisture which greatly reduces its ability to perform correctly. It is a good idea to purchase brake fluid in small containers and discard any small left-over quantities properly. Do not store a container of brake fluid with less than 1/4 of the fluid remaining as this small amount will draw moisture very rapidly.

WARNING
Do not intermix silicone based (DOT 5) brake fluid as it can cause brake component damage leading to brake system failure.

WARNING
Never reuse brake fluid, such as fluid expelled during brake bleeding. Con-

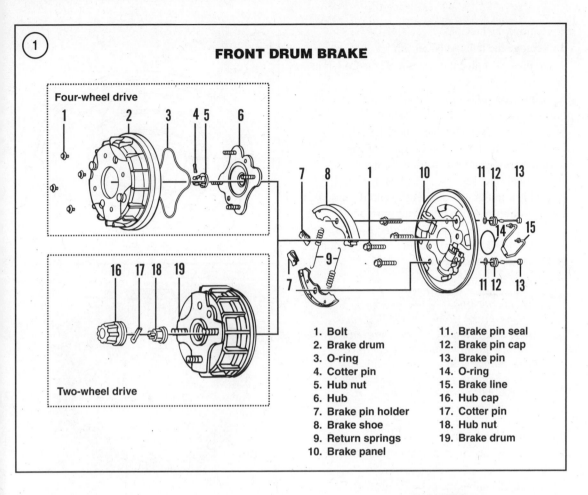

FRONT DRUM BRAKE

Four-wheel drive

Two-wheel drive

1. Bolt
2. Brake drum
3. O-ring
4. Cotter pin
5. Hub nut
6. Hub
7. Brake pin holder
8. Brake shoe
9. Return springs
10. Brake panel
11. Brake pin seal
12. Brake pin cap
13. Brake pin
14. O-ring
15. Brake line
16. Hub cap
17. Cotter pin
18. Hub nut
19. Brake drum

taminated brake fluid can cause brake failure.

2. Do not allow brake fluid to contact any plastic parts or painted surfaces as damage will result.

3. Always keep the master cylinder reservoir and spare cans of brake fluid closed to prevent dust or moisture from entering. Brake fluid contamination and will cause brake problems.

4. Use only new or DOT 4 brake fluid to wash parts. Never clean any internal brake components with solvent or any other petroleum based cleaners as these cleaners will cause the rubber components to swell, resulting in distorted and damaged parts.

5. When any component has been removed from the brake system, the system is considered opened and must be bled to remove air bubbles. Also, if the brake feels spongy, there are usually air bubbles in the system and it must be bled. For safe brake operation, refer to *Brake Bleeding* in this chapter for complete details.

WARNING
When working on the brake system, never blow off brake components or use compressed air. Do not inhale any airborne brake dust as it may contain asbestos, which can cause lung injury and cancer. As an added precaution, wear an OSHA approved filtering face mask and thoroughly wash your hands and forearms with warm water and soap after completing any brake work.

FRONT BRAKE DRUM

The front brake drum can be removed without having to remove the front hub.

Removal/Installation (Two-Wheel Drive)

Refer to **Figure 1**.

1. Remove the front wheels (Chapter Ten).

2. Remove the hub cap.

3. Remove the hub nut cotter pin.

4. Remove the hub nut, then remove the front brake drum.

5. Inspect the brake drum and service the waterproof seal as described in this section.

6. Inspect the O-ring on the end of the axle (**Figure 2**). Replace it if necessary. Apply grease to the O-ring before installing the brake drum.

7. Lubricate the waterproof seal (B, **Figure 3**, typical) with a multipurpose grease (NLGI No. 3) as shown in **Figure 4**. If a new waterproof seal was installed, refer to *Brake Drum Waterproof Seal Inspection and Replacement* for the correct amount of grease to apply to the seal.

> *WARNING*
> *Do not get grease on the inner surface of the brake drum where the brake shoe linings make contact. The grease will contaminate the lining surfaces and reduce braking performance. If grease does get onto the brake drum, thoroughly clean off all grease residue with lacquer thinner.*

8. Install the brake drum.

9. Install the hub nut and tighten it to 78 N•m (58 ft.-lb.).

10. Rotate the hub nut clockwise just until the cotter pin can be inserted through the holes in the hub nut and axle. Spread the cotter pin ends to lock it in place.

> *NOTE*
> *After installing the cotter pin, make sure the pin ends will not contact the hub cap.*

11. Install the hub cap.

12. Install the front wheels (Chapter Ten).

Removal/Installation (Four-Wheel Drive)

Refer to **Figure 1**.

> *NOTE*
> *To remove the brake drum and front hub at the same time, refer to **Front Hub** in Chapter Ten.*

1. Remove the front wheels (Chapter Ten).

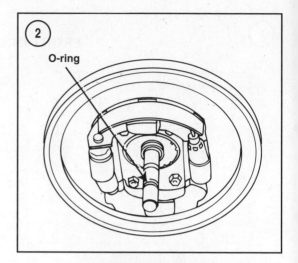

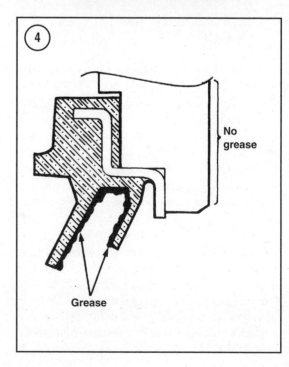

2. Remove the bolts (A, **Figure 5**) and the front brake drum (B).

3. Remove the O-ring (A, **Figure 3**), if necessary.

4. Inspect the brake drum and service the waterproof seal as described in this section.

5. Install the O-ring (A, **Figure 3**), if it was removed.

6. Lubricate the waterproof seal (B, **Figure 3**) with a multipurpose grease (NLGI No. 3) as shown in **Figure 4**. If a new waterproof seal was installed, refer to *Brake Drum Waterproof Seal Inspection and Replacement* for the correct amount of grease to apply to the seal.

> *WARNING*
> *Do not get grease on the inner surface of the brake drum where the brake shoe linings make contact, as this will contaminate the lining surfaces and reduce braking performance. If grease does get onto the brake drum, thoroughly clean off all grease residue with lacquer thinner.*

7. Install the brake drum (B, **Figure 5**) onto the wheel hub and brake linings.

8. Install the brake drum mounting bolts (A, **Figure 5**) and tighten them to 12 N•m (106 in.-lb.).

9. Install the front wheels (Chapter Ten).

Brake Drum Inspection

1. Inspect the brake drum (**Figure 3**, typical) for cracks, excessive wear or other damage.

2. On four-wheel drives, replace the O-ring (A, **Figure 3**) if it is excessively worn or damaged.

3. Inspect and service the waterproof seal (B, **Figure 3**, typical) as described later in this section.

4. Check the brake drum contact surface for grease residue, scoring, cracks or other damage.

> *WARNING*
> *If oil or grease is on the drum surface, clean it off with a clean rag soaked in lacquer thinner—do not use any solvent that may leave an oil residue. Keep the cleaning solution away from the waterproof seal.*

5. Measure the brake drum inside diameter (**Figure 6**) and compare it to the service limit in **Table 1**. Measure it at several points around the brake drum. Replace the brake drum if it is out of specification.

Brake Drum Waterproof Seal Inspection and Replacement

The brake drum waterproof seal keeps water out of the brake drum. Inspect this seal and replace it when necessary to prevent excessive brake drum and lining wear from water and other debris.

1. Remove the brake drum as described in this section.

2. Inspect the waterproof seal (B, **Figure 3**) for excessive wear, damage, hardness or deterioration.

3. Measure the waterproof seal lip length (**Figure 7**). Measure at several different points around the seal. See **Table 1** for service specifications. Replace the seal if it is out of specification.

> *NOTE*
> *The following dimensions must be calculated because the inner portion of the waterproof seal cannot be seen when the seal is installed in the brake drum.*

4. Perform the following:

13

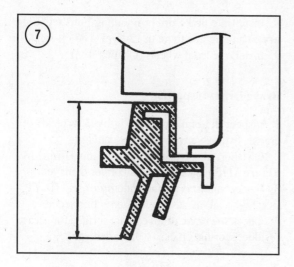

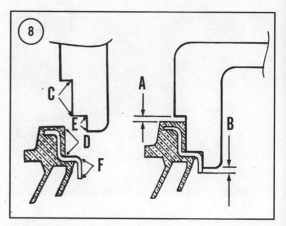

a. Measure the brake drum and seal as shown in **Figure 8**.

b. Calculate the clearance A and B between the brake drum and the seal. A = C - D and B = E - F.

c. When the new waterproof seal is installed correctly, dimension A will equal B.

5. Apply clean water to all surfaces of the new waterproof seal (**Figure 9**) and to the surface plate.

> *CAUTION*
> *The brake drum must be backed up with a round steel plate to prevent it from being warped or damaged. Place a steel plate about 140 mm (5.5 in.) in diameter and more than 10 mm (0.4 in.) thick on the brake drum during Step 6.*

> *CAUTION*
> *Do not exert too much pressure on the seal during installation or the seal lip may be damaged as shown in* **Figure 10**.

6. Place the new seal on a clean surface plate, then slowly and squarely press the brake drum (and steel backup plate) onto the new seal. Continue to press on the brake drum and frequently check the clearance between the seal and the drum. Refer to the dimensions calculated in Step 4. This dimension must be the same all around the perimeter of the brake drum. If the clearance is not equal, the seal will either not seal properly or wear prematurely.

7. After the seal has been installed correctly with uniform clearance all around the perimeter, wipe all water from the seal with a lint-free cloth.

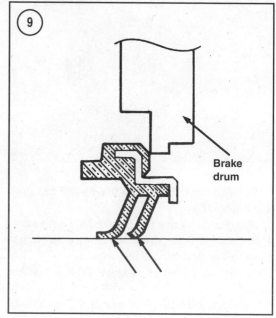

Brake drum

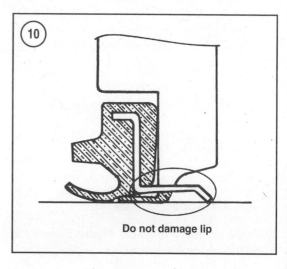

Do not damage lip

WARNING
Do not get grease on the inner surface of the brake drum where the brake shoe linings make contact, as this will contaminate the lining surfaces and reduce braking performance. If grease does get onto the brake drum, thoroughly clean off all grease residue with lacquer thinner.

8. Uniformly pack the sealing lip cavity (**Figure 11**) with multipurpose grease (NLGI No. 3) as shown in **Figure 4**. Apply 14-16 grams (0.5-0.6 oz.) of grease.

9. Install the brake drum as described in this chapter.

FRONT BRAKE SHOE REPLACEMENT

There is no recommended mileage interval for changing the front brake shoes. Lining wear depends on riding habits and conditions.

Refer to **Figure 1**.

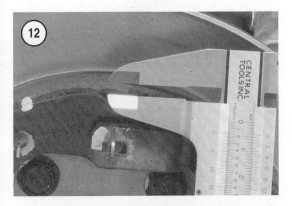

NOTE
Service one set of brake shoes at a time. Leave the other set intact so it may be used as a reference for the proper location of the brake components.

NOTE
The following illustrations depict a four-wheel drive model. Two-wheel drive models are similar.

1. Remove the brake drum as described in this chapter.

2. Measure the brake shoe lining thickness with a vernier caliper (**Figure 12**) and compare the measurement to the specifications in **Table 1**. Replace the brake shoes if they are out of specification.

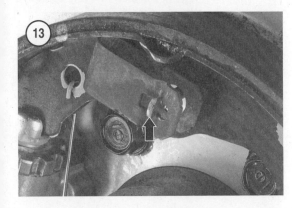

NOTE
If brake shoe replacement is necessary, continue with Step 3.

3. On four-wheel drives, remove the wheel hub as described in Chapter Ten.

4. Rotate the brake pins 90° (**Figure 13**) and remove the brake pin holders (**Figure 14**).

NOTE
If the brake shoes are going to be reused, mark them so they can be reinstalled in their original position.

13

5. Remove the brake shoes and springs (**Figure 15**).

6. If necessary, remove the brake pins (A, **Figure 16**), seals and caps.

7. Inspect the return springs for damaged or stretched coils. Replace both return springs at the same time.

8. Inspect the brake pins and pin holders, and replace them if they are excessively worn or damaged.

9. Inspect the wheel cylinders (B, **Figure 16**) for damaged boots or leaking brake fluid. If necessary, service the wheel cylinders as described in this chapter.

> *WARNING*
> *Silicone brake grease, used in the following steps, is not the same as a silicone sealant (RTV) used on engine gaskets. Make sure the lubricant is specified for brake use. For example, Permatex Ultra Disc Brake Caliper Lube (part No. 20356) is designed specifically for use on brake systems. Do not apply too much grease because it may fall onto the brake linings and cause brake slippage.*

10. Apply a light coat of silicone brake grease to the brake shoe locating notches in the wheel cylinders and the brake shoe anchor (A, **Figure 17**).

11. Apply a light coat of silicone brake grease to the raised pads on the backside of the brake shoes metal plates where the brake shoes ride on the brake panel. Avoid getting any grease on the brake linings.

> *NOTE*
> *Install the original brake shoes in their original mounting positions.*

12. Install the new brake shoes and attach the springs (B, **Figure 17**). Be sure to offset the spring coils as shown in **Figure 17**. Install the brake shoes with their flatter edges facing toward the wheel cylinders.

13. Install the upper brake shoe into the upper wheel cylinder notches (**Figure 18**).

14. Hold the upper brake shoe in place, then pull on the lower brake shoe and install it into the lower wheel cylinder notches (**Figure 18**). If a spring popped out of its shoe slot, reinstall it with a pair of

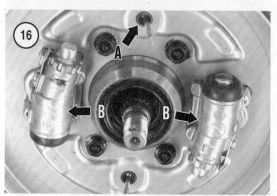

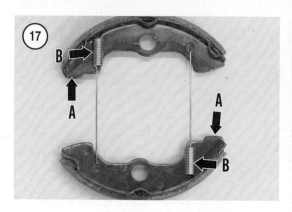

locking pliers. Make sure both spring ends are hooked securely into the brake shoe holes and slots.

15. Install the brake pins and holders as follows:

   a. Insert the pins, seals and cap into the brake panel.

   b. Insert a flat blade screwdriver behind the wheel cylinder to hold the pin in place.

   c. Install the holder (**Figure 14**) and secure it with a pair of pliers.

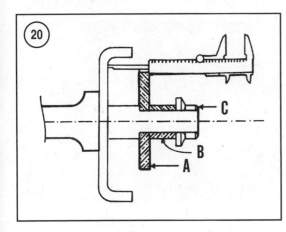

d. While holding the pin in place with a screwdriver, compress the holder with the pliers, then rotate the pin 90° (**Figure 13**) to lock the pin in place.

e. Remove the pliers and screwdriver and repeat for the other retainer and pin assembly.

f. Make sure both retainers and pins are properly locked in place. See **Figure 19**.

16. Repeat the preceding steps to replace the brake shoes on the opposite side of the vehicle.

17. Install the front brake drums as described in this chapter.

18. Adjust the brake shoes as described in Chapter Three.

FRONT BRAKE PANEL

Refer to **Figure 1**.

Warp Inspection (Two-Wheel Drive)

Before removing the brake panel, check it for warp as follows. A dial indicator and magnetic stand will be required.

1. Remove the brake drum and brake shoes as described in this chapter.

2. Clean off any grease from the brake panel where the brake drum seal rides.

3. Install a suitable size flat metal plate (A, **Figure 20**) and collar (B) onto the steering knuckle. Secure both parts with the hub nut (C, **Figure 20**). Tighten the nut securely.

4. Use the depth gauge portion of a vernier caliper and measure the distance from the attached plate to the brake panel surface at several points. If there is a variation of 0.4 mm (0.02 in.) or more, the brake panel is warped and must be replaced.

5. Remove the temporary plate and collar.

Warp Inspection (Four-Wheel Drive)

Before removing the brake panel, check it for warp as follows. A dial indicator and magnetic stand will be required.

1. Remove the brake drum and brake shoes as described in this chapter.

2. Clean off any grease from the brake panel where the brake drum seal rides.

3. Install a metal plate (A, **Figure 21**) onto the wheel hub and secure it with a wheel nut. This plate provides a mounting location for the magnetic stand.

4. Attach a dial indicator and magnetic stand (B, **Figure 21**) to the metal plate and place the pointer in the area where the brake drum seal rides (**Figure 21**).

5. Slowly rotate the wheel hub and check for warp. A variation of 0.4 mm (0.02 in.) or more indicates the brake panel is warped and must be replaced.

6. Remove the dial indicator and metal plate.

13

Removal/Installation

NOTE
The following illustrations depict a four-wheel drive model. Two-wheel drive models are similar.

1. Drain the brake fluid as described in *Brake Fluid Draining* in this chapter.
2. Remove the brake shoes as described in this section.
3. Remove the brake hose banjo bolt and sealing washers (A, **Figure 22**) at the back of the brake panel. Place the loose end of the brake hose in a thick plastic bag or container to prevent the entry of dirt and foreign matter, and to prevent brake fluid from leaking out onto the suspension and brake components. Tie the brake hose up out of the way.

CAUTION
Wash brake fluid off any painted or plated surfaces immediately as it will destroy the finish. Use soapy water and rinse completely.

4. Disconnect the vent hose (B, **Figure 22**) from the brake panel.
5. Remove the bolts (**Figure 23**) that hold the brake panel to the steering knuckle and remove the brake panel. Discard these bolts.
6. Remove the O-ring (**Figure 24**) from the steering knuckle.
7. To service the wheel cylinders, refer to *Wheel Cylinders* in this chapter.
8. Perform the inspection procedure in this section.
9. Install the brake panel by reversing these removal steps, plus the following:
   a. Install a new O-ring onto the steering knuckle (**Figure 24**).

CAUTION
Always install new brake panel mounting bolts. The bolts are treated with a special dry-coated material that is necessary for waterproofing.

   b. Install the brake panel and new mounting bolts. Tighten the brake panel mounting bolts (**Figure 23**) to 29 N•m (22 ft.-lb.).
   c. Position the brake hose end between the stoppers on the backside of the brake panel. See C, **Figure 22**, typical.

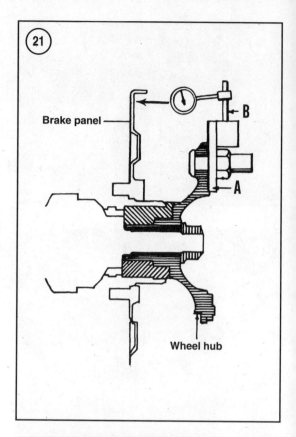

Brake panel

B

A

Wheel hub

   d. Install a new sealing washer on each side of the brake hose. Tighten the banjo bolt to 34 N•m (25 ft.-lb.).
10. Repeat the previous steps to service the other brake panel assembly.
11. Turn the handlebar from side to side while observing the movement of the brake and vent hoses. Make sure these parts are not kinked or pulled incorrectly.
12. Bleed the front brakes as described in this chapter.

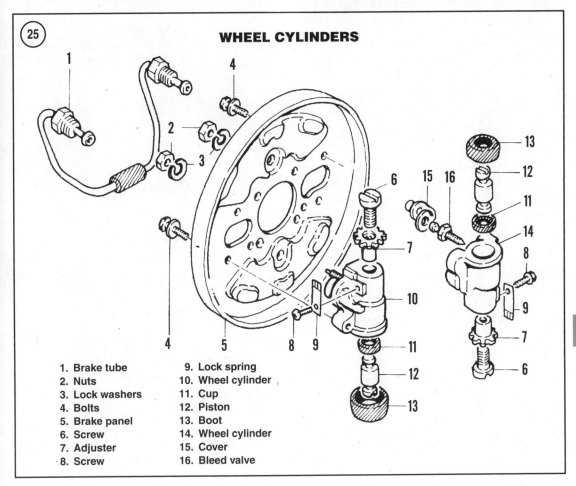

WHEEL CYLINDERS

1. Brake tube
2. Nuts
3. Lock washers
4. Bolts
5. Brake panel
6. Screw
7. Adjuster
8. Screw
9. Lock spring
10. Wheel cylinder
11. Cup
12. Piston
13. Boot
14. Wheel cylinder
15. Cover
16. Bleed valve

13

Inspection

1. Remove all sealer residue from the brake panel and steering knuckle mounting surfaces.

2. Wipe off all old grease from all of the brake panel parts.

3. Inspect the brake panel for damage.

4. Inspect the metal wheel cylinder brake tube. If necessary, replace it as described in *Wheel Cylinders* in this chapter.

WHEEL CYLINDERS

Refer to **Figure 25**.

Removal

1. Remove the brake panel from the steering knuckle as described in this chapter.
2. Remove the brake shoes (A, **Figure 26**) if they were not already removed.

> *CAUTION*
> *Do not bend the brake tube when re-*
> *moving it in Step 3. Doing so can*
> *damage the brake tube and cause mis-*
> *alignment during installation.*

3. Loosen the brake tube fittings (A, **Figure 27**) and remove the brake tube (B). Store the brake tube in a sealed plastic bag.

> *NOTE*
> *Identify each wheel cylinder so it can*
> *be installed in its original mounting*
> *position.*

4. Remove the wheel cylinder mounting nuts, bolts and washers (C, **Figure 27**), and remove the wheel cylinder. If the wheel cylinder is not going to be serviced, store it in a sealed plastic bag until installation.
5. Repeat Step 4 for the opposite wheel cylinder.
6. If necessary, service the wheel cylinders as described in this chapter.

Disassembly

Refer to **Figure 25**.
1. Remove the screw, lockspring and adjuster from the cylinder body.
2. Remove the bleed screw and its cover.
3. Remove the boot from the groove in the piston and cylinder.
4. Push the piston and piston cup out of the cylinder bore.
5. Remove the screw from the adjuster body.

Wheel Cylinder Inspection

Refer to **Table 1** when inspecting and measuring the wheel cylinder components in this section. Replace parts that are out of specification or show damage.

> *NOTE*
> *It is a good idea to replace the boots*
> *and piston cups whenever the wheel*

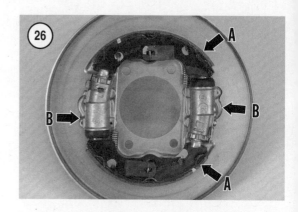

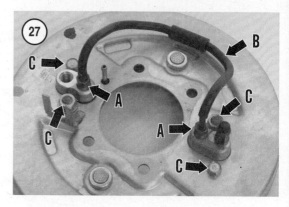

cylinders are disassembled, even though they might not appear worn.

1. Remove all sealer residue from the wheel cylinders where they mount on the brake panel.
2. Clean all the parts, except the outer boot, with or DOT 4 brake fluid.
3. Clean the cylinder passages with compressed air.
4. Check the boot for damage.
5. Check the piston cup for excessive wear, cracks or other damage.
6. Check the cylinder bore for deep pits, scratches and other damage. Check the part of the cylinder bore that contacts the piston cup. If the cylinder bore is severely damaged, replace the wheel cylinder assembly. The wheel cylinder housing is not available separately.
7. Check the piston for scratches, flat spots, cracks or other damage. If the damage is severe, replace the piston.
8. Measure the wheel cylinder inside diameter and compare it to the service specification in **Table 1**. If it is out of specification, replace the wheel cylinder assembly.

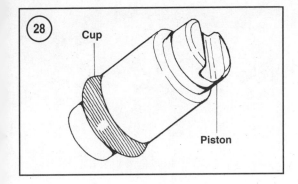

28 Cup
Piston

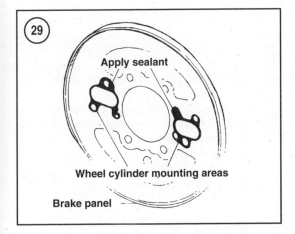

29 Apply sealant
Wheel cylinder mounting areas
Brake panel

9. Measure the piston outside diameter and compare it to the service specification in **Table 1**. Replace the piston if it is out of specification.
10. Inspect the lockspring for cracks, fatigue or other damage.
11. Inspect the screw and adjuster body for corrosion. Check the adjuster body for excessively worn or damaged adjuster arms.

Brake Panel Inspection

1. Remove all sealer residue from the brake panel where the wheel cylinders mount.
2. Check the brake panel for warp, cracks or other damage. Replace it if necessary.

Brake Tube Inspection

1. Clean the brake tube with compressed air.
2. Inspect the brake tube for bending, cracks and corrosion. Check the two end nuts for damage.
3. Check the tube's flared ends for cracks or other damage. If these ends are damaged, do not try to re-

pair them as this may distort or burr the ends and cause the tube to leak. If the tube is damaged in any way, replace it.
4. Store the brake tube in a sealed plastic bag until reassembly.

Assembly

Use new or DOT 4 brake fluid when brake fluid is called out in the following steps. Do not use DOT 5 (silicone based) brake fluid.

> *CAUTION*
> *Do not allow grease or oil to contact the boots or piston cups when assembling the wheel cylinders. Grease or oil will destroy the rubber parts.*

1. When installing a new piston cup, perform the following:
   a. Soak the new piston cup in brake fluid for approximately 5-10 minutes.
   b. Lubricate the piston with brake fluid.
   c. Install the piston cup onto the piston and seat it into its groove as shown in **Figure 28**.
2. Coat the piston cup, piston and cylinder bore with brake fluid.
3. Install the piston into the cylinder as shown in **Figure 25**. Make sure the piston cup does not turn inside out. The cup should be compressed when installed inside the cylinder.
4. Install a new boot over the piston. Make sure it is seated in the piston and cylinder body grooves.
5. Apply a light coat of silicone brake grease onto the screw threads, then install the screw into the adjuster body.
6. Apply silicone brake grease onto the adjuster threads and install the adjuster into the wheel cylinder.

Installation

1. Apply sealant to the brake panel where the wheel cylinders mount. See **Figure 29**.
2. Install the wheel cylinders as follows:
   a. Install the wheel cylinders (A, **Figure 30**) in their original mounting positions.
   b. Secure each wheel cylinder with its nut, lockwasher (B, **Figure 30**) and bolt (C).
   c. Tighten the wheel cylinder nut and bolt as specified in **Table 3**.
3. Repeat Step 2 to install the other wheel cylinder.

13

4. Install the brake tube (D, **Figure 30**) onto the wheel cylinders, then thread the nuts into the wheel cylinders and tighten them as specified in **Table 3**.
5. Install the brake panel as described in this chapter.

FRONT MASTER CYLINDER

Refer to **Figure 31**.

Removal/Installation

1. Park the ATV on level ground and set the parking brake.
2. Drain the brake fluid as described in this chapter.
3. Cover the area under the master cylinder to prevent brake fluid from damaging any component that it might contact.

> *CAUTION*
> *If brake fluid should contact any surface, wash the area immediately with soapy water and rinse completely. Brake fluid will damage plastic, painted and plated surfaces.*

4. Remove the banjo bolt (**Figure 32**) and the sealing washers securing the upper brake hose to the master cylinder. Place the loose end of the brake hose in a plastic bag to prevent the entry of dirt and foreign matter, and to prevent residual brake fluid from leaking out onto the frame components. Tie the brake hose to the handlebar.
5. Unbolt and remove the master cylinder and its clamp (**Figure 33**) from the handlebar.
6. If necessary, service the master cylinder as described in this chapter.
7. Clean the handlebar, master cylinder and clamp mating surfaces.
8. Install the master cylinder, clamp and mounting bolts onto the handlebar. Install the clamp with its UP mark and arrow facing up (**Figure 33**). Tighten the upper master cylinder mounting bolt to 12 N•m (106 in.-lb.).
9. Turn the master cylinder to align its clamp surfaces with the punch mark on the handlebar (**Figure 34**), then tighten the lower master cylinder mounting bolt (**Figure 33**) to 12 N•m (106 in.-lb.).
10. Connect the brake hose onto the master cylinder using the banjo bolt and two new washers. Install a washer on each side of the hose fitting. Tighten the banjo bolt (**Figure 32**) to 34 N•m (25 ft.-lb.).

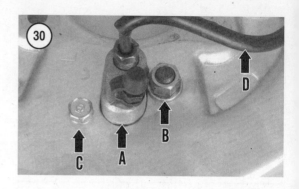

11. Refill the master cylinder with DOT 3 or DOT 4 brake fluid and bleed the brake as described in this chapter.

> *WARNING*
> *Do not ride the ATV until the front brakes are working properly. Make sure the brake lever travel is not excessive and the lever does not feel spongy. Either condition indicates that repeating the bleeding procedure is necessary.*

12. Install the handlebar cover (Chapter Fifteen).

Disassembly

Refer to **Figure 31**.
1. Remove the master cylinder as described in this chapter.
2. Remove the nut, bolt and front brake lever.
3. Remove the screws, top cover, diaphragm plate, diaphragm and float.
4. Pour out any brake fluid and discard it properly. Never reuse brake fluid.
5. Remove the dust boot (**Figure 35**) from the end of the piston and piston bore.

> *NOTE*
> *If brake fluid leaks from the piston bore, the piston cups are worn or damaged. Replace the piston assembly.*

> *NOTE*
> *To hold the master cylinder when removing and installing the snap ring, thread a bolt with a nut into the master cylinder. Tighten the nut against the master cylinder to lock the bolt in place, then clamp the bolt and nut in a vise as shown in **Figure 36**.*

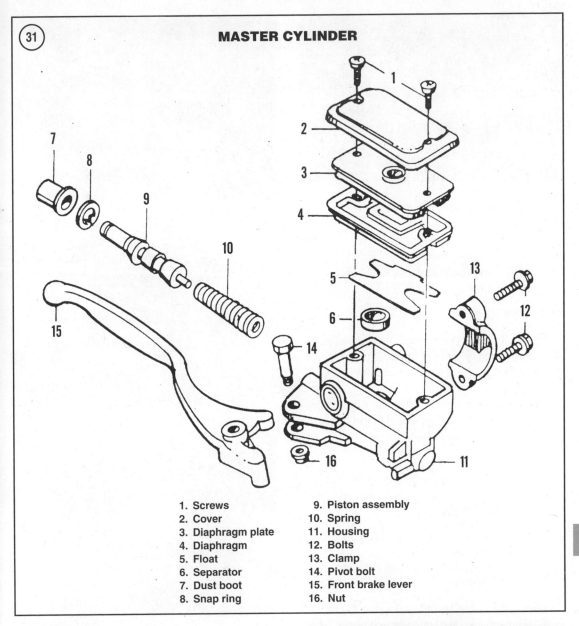

MASTER CYLINDER

1. Screws
2. Cover
3. Diaphragm plate
4. Diaphragm
5. Float
6. Separator
7. Dust boot
8. Snap ring
9. Piston assembly
10. Spring
11. Housing
12. Bolts
13. Clamp
14. Pivot bolt
15. Front brake lever
16. Nut

13

6. Compress the piston and remove the snap ring (**Figure 37**) from the bore groove.

7. Remove the piston and spring assembly (**Figure 38**).

8. Remove the oil seal from inside the reservoir.

Inspection

Refer to **Table 1** when inspecting and measuring the front master cylinder (**Figure 31**) components in this section. Replace parts that are out of specification or damaged.

1. Clean the diaphragm, reservoir housing (inside) and piston assembly with new brake fluid. Place the parts on a clean lint-free cloth.

> *NOTE*
> *Do not remove the secondary cup (C, Figure 39) from the piston when inspecting it in Step 2. If the secondary cup is damaged, replace the entire piston assembly. Leave the secondary cup in place so it can serve as a reference when installing the new cup onto the new piston.*

2. Inspect the piston assembly (**Figure 39**) for:
   a. A broken, distorted or collapsed piston return spring (A, **Figure 39**).
   b. A worn, cracked, damaged or swollen primary (B, **Figure 39**) and secondary cup (C).
   c. A scratched, scored or damaged piston (D, **Figure 39**).

If any of these parts are worn or damaged, replace the piston assembly. Individual parts are not available separately from Honda.

3. Inspect the snap ring (E, **Figure 39**) for corrosion, rust, weakness or other damage. Replace it if necessary.

4. Inspect the boot (F, **Figure 39**) and replace it if it is damaged.

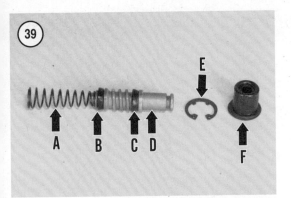

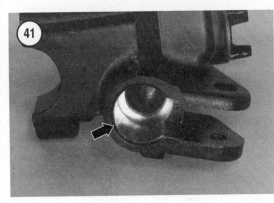

5. Measure the piston outside diameter (**Figure 40**) and replace it if it is out of specification.

6. Inspect the cylinder bore (**Figure 41**) for scratches, pitting, excessive wear, corrosion or other damage. Do not hone the bore to remove nicks, scratches or other damage.

7. Measure the cylinder bore diameter (**Figure 42**). Replace the master cylinder assembly if the bore diameter is out of specification.

8. Check for plugged supply and relief ports in the master cylinder. Clean them with compressed air.

NOTE
A plugged relief port will cause the brake linings to drag on the drum.

9. Check the entire master cylinder body for wear or damage.

10. Check the cover and diaphragm assembly for damage.

11. Inspect the banjo bolt threads in the master cylinder body bore. Repair minor damage with the correct size metric tap, or replace the master cylinder assembly.

12. Check the hand lever pivot holes and mounting lugs on the master cylinder body for elongation or cracks. If damaged, replace the master cylinder assembly.

13. Inspect the hand lever and pivot bolt and replace if damaged.

Assembly

1. Use new DOT 4 brake fluid when brake fluid is called for in the following steps. Do not use DOT 5 (silicone based) brake fluid.

2A. When installing a new piston assembly, perform the following:

    a. Soak the new secondary cup in new brake fluid for at least 15 minutes to make it pliable.

    b. Lubricate the new piston with brake fluid.

    c. After soaking the secondary cup in brake fluid, install it onto the piston as shown in C, **Figure 39**.

    d. Install the new primary cup onto the end of the new spring as shown in B, **Figure 39**.

2B. When reusing the original piston, lubricate the piston assembly with brake fluid.

CAUTION
When installing the piston assembly into the master cylinder bore, do not

13

allow the cups to turn inside out as this damages them and allows brake fluid to leak out of the bore.

3. Install the spring and piston assembly into the master cylinder bore in the direction shown in **Figure 38**. Make sure the cups did not turn inside out.

4. Push the piston in and hold it in place, then install the snap ring (**Figure 37**) into the cylinder bore groove. Install the snap ring with its flat edge facing out (away from the piston). Make sure the snap ring is fully seated in the bore groove. Push and release the piston a few times. It should move smoothly and return under spring pressure.

5. Install the dust boot into the end of the cylinder bore. Seat the large boot end against the snap ring. Seat the small boot end into the groove in the end of the piston (**Figure 43**). Make sure it is correctly seated in the cylinder bore (**Figure 35**).

6. Install the brake lever as follows:
  a. Install the brake lever and its pivot bolt. Tighten the pivot bolt to 6 N•m (53 in.-lb.). Operate the brake lever, making sure it moves smoothly.
  b. Install the brake lever nut. Then hold the pivot bolt and tighten the nut to 6 N•m (53 in.-lb.). Operate the brake lever again, making sure it moves smoothly with no roughness or binding.

7. Temporarily install the master cylinder cover assembly.

8. Install the master cylinder as described in this chapter.

BRAKE FLUID DRAINING

Drain the brake fluid before disconnecting any of the front brake hoses or lines. To drain the front brake system, obtain an empty bottle, a length of clear hose that fits tightly onto the wheel cylinder bleed valve, and a wrench to open and close the bleed valve (**Figure 44** and **Figure 45**). A vacuum pump (**Figure 46**) can also be used to drain the brake system.

1. Turn the handlebar so the front master cylinder (**Figure 32**) is level with the ground.

2. Remove the reservoir cover and diaphragm assembly.

3. Connect a hose to one of the wheel cylinder bleed valves. Insert the other end of the hose into a clean bottle. See **Figure 44**.

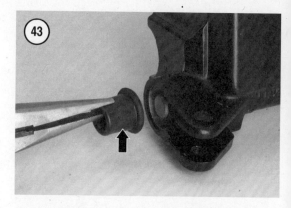

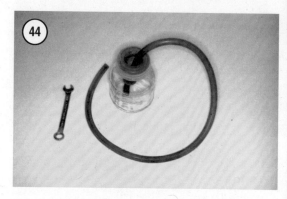

4. Loosen the bleed valve and pump the brake lever to drain part of the brake system.

5. Close the bleed valve when fluid stops flowing through the valve.

6. Repeat Steps 4-6 for the other side. Because air has entered the brake lines, not all of the brake fluid will drain out.

NOTE
Because some residual brake fluid will remain in the lines, be careful when disconnecting and removing the brake hoses in Step 9.

7. Reinstall the diaphragm assembly and reservoir cover.

8. Perform the required service to the front brake system as described in this chapter.

9. After servicing the brake system, bleed the front brakes as described in this chapter.

BRAKE BLEEDING

Bleed the front brakes when they feel spongy, after repairing a leak or replacing parts in the system, or when replacing the brake fluid.

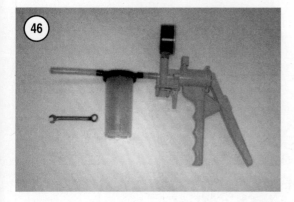

This section describes two methods for bleeding the brake system. The first requires a vacuum pump (**Figure 46**), and the second requires a container and a piece of clear tubing (**Figure 44**).

1. Remove the dust cap from the bleed valve on the wheel cylinder.

2A. When using a vacuum pump, assemble the pump by following the manufacturer's instructions. Connect the vacuum pump hose to the wheel cylinder bleed valve.

2B. When a vacuum pump is not being used, perform the following:

   a. Connect a piece of clear tubing onto the bleed valve (**Figure 45**).

   b. Insert the other end of the tube into a container partially filled with new brake fluid. Tie the tube in place so it cannot slip out of the container.

3. Clean the master cylinder cover of all dirt and foreign matter.

4. Turn the front wheels so the master cylinder (**Figure 32**) is level with the ground.

5. Cover the area underneath the master cylinder with a heavy cloth to protect the parts from accidentally spilled of brake fluid.

> *CAUTION*
> *Wash spilled brake fluid from any plastic, painted or plated surface immediately as it will destroy the finish. Clean with soapy water and rinse completely.*

6. Unscrew and remove the master cylinder cover and diaphragm assembly.

7. Fill the master cylinder with DOT 4 brake fluid.

> *WARNING*
> *Use DOT 3 or DOT 4 brake fluid from a sealed container. Do not intermix different brands of fluid. Do not use a silicone based DOT 5 brake fluid as it can damage the brake components, leading to brake system failure.*

> *NOTE*
> *When bleeding the front brake, frequently check the fluid level in the master cylinder. If the reservoir runs dry, air will enter the system. If this occurs, the entire procedure must be repeated.*

8A. When using a vacuum pump, perform the following:

   a. Operate the vacuum pump several times to create a vacuum in the attached hose.

   b. Open the bleed valve 1/4 turn to allow extraction of air and fluid through the line. When the flow of air and fluid starts to slow down, close the bleed valve.

   c. Operate the brake lever several times and release it.

   d. Refill the master cylinder reservoir as necessary.

   e. Repeat Step 8A for the opposite brake line.

   f. Repeat Step 8A until there is a solid feel when the brake lever is operated and there are no bubbles being released from the system.

8B. When a vacuum pump is not being used, perform the following:

   a. Operate the brake lever several times until resistance is felt, then hold it in its applied position. If the system was opened or drained

13

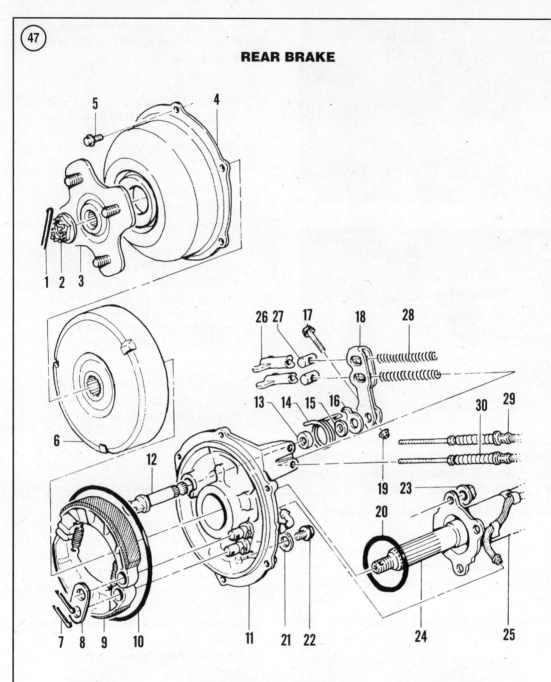

REAR BRAKE

1. Cotter pin
2. Axle nut
3. Wheel hub
4. Drum cover
5. Bolt
6. Brake drum
7. Cotter pins
8. Washer
9. Brake shoes
10. O-ring
11. Brake panel
12. Brake cam
13. Dust seal
14. Return spring
15. Felt washer
16. Indicator plate
17. Bolt
18. Brake arm
19. Nut
20. O-ring
21. Washer
22. Drain plug
23. Locknuts
24. Rear axle
25. Axle housing
26. Brake cable adjusters
27. Collars
28. Springs
29. Rear brake/parking brake cable
30. Rear brake pedal cable

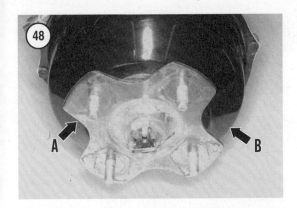

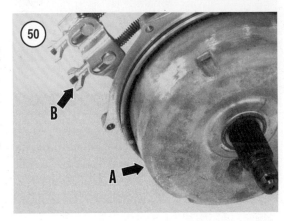

completely, there will be no initial resistance at the brake lever.

b. Open the bleed valve 1/4 turn and allow the lever to travel to its limit, then close the bleed valve and release the brake lever.

c. Operate the brake lever several times and release it.

d. Refill the master cylinder reservoir as necessary.

e. Repeat Step 8B for the opposite brake line.

f. Repeat Step 8B until there is a solid feel when the brake lever is operated and there are no bubbles being released from the system.

> *NOTE*
> *When flushing the system, continue with Step 8A or 8B until the fluid expelled from the system is clean.*

9. Remove the vacuum pump or container and hose from the system. Snap the bleed valve dust cap onto the bleed valve.

10. If necessary, add fluid to correct the level in the reservoir. It should be to the upper level line inside the master cylinder reservoir.

11. Install the diaphragm and cover. Tighten the screws securely.

12. Recheck the feel of the brake lever. It should be firm and offer the same resistance each time it's operated. If the lever feels spongy, check all of the hoses for leaks and bleed the system again.

REAR DRUM BRAKE

Removal

Refer to **Figure 47**.

1. Remove the right side rear wheel (Chapter Twelve).

2. Remove the right rear hub (A, **Figure 48**) as described in Chapter Twelve.

3. Remove the bolts and the brake drum cover (B, **Figure 48**).

4. Remove the brake drum cover O-ring (**Figure 49**), if necessary.

5. Remove the brake drum (A, **Figure 50**). If the brake drum is tight, loosen the brake cable adjusters (B, **Figure 50**) to withdraw the brake shoes away from the brake drum, then remove the brake drum.

6. Clean and inspect the brake drum cover and brake drum as described in this section.

Inspection

When measuring the brake drum in this section, compare the actual measurement to the new and service limit specification in **Table 1**. Replace the brake drum if it is out of specification or if it shows damage as described in this section.

1. Inspect the brake drum cover for cracks, warp or other damage.

13

2. Inspect the brake drum cover dust seal (**Figure 51**) for excessive wear or damage. If necessary, replace the dust seal as follows:

    a. Support the brake drum cover and drive the dust seal out of the cover.

    b. Clean the dust seal mounting bore.

    c. Install a new dust seal by driving or pressing it into the brake drum cover. Apply pressure against the outer dust seal surface with a suitable bearing driver.

    d. Pack the dust seal lip with grease.

3. Check the brake drum surface (A, **Figure 52**) for oil or grease and clean it with a rag soaked in lacquer thinner. Check the brake shoe linings for contamination.

> *WARNING*
> *Do not clean the brake drum with any type of solvent that may leave an oil residue.*

4. Clean the brake drum in a detergent solution, then dry it thoroughly to prevent rust from forming on the drum surface.

> *WARNING*
> *Discard the detergent solution and wash your hands.*

5. Check the drum contact surface (A, **Figure 52**) for scoring or other damage.

6. Inspect the brake drum for cracks or damage.

7. Inspect the drum splines (B, **Figure 52**) for twisting or damage.

8. Measure the brake drum inside diameter (**Figure 53**) and compare the measurement to the service limit in **Table 2**.

Installation

1. Apply grease to the brake drum cover dust seal lips (**Figure 51**).

2. Lubricate the brake drum splines (B, **Figure 52**) with grease.

3. Lightly lubricate the brake drum cover O-ring (**Figure 49**) with oil before installing it into the brake panel.

4. Slide the brake drum (A, **Figure 50**) over the rear axle and brake shoes.

5. Install the brake drum cover (B, **Figure 48**) and its mounting bolts. Tighten the brake drum cover mounting bolts securely.

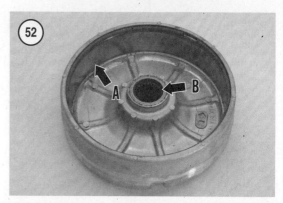

6. Install the right rear hub (A, **Figure 48**) as described in Chapter Twelve.

7. Install the right side rear wheel (Chapter Twelve).

8. Adjust the rear brake as described in Chapter Three.

REAR BRAKE SHOE REPLACEMENT

There is no recommended mileage interval for changing the rear brake shoes. Lining wear depends on riding habits and conditions.

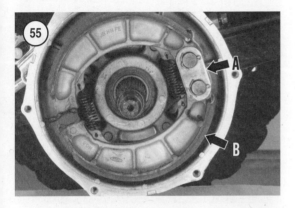

Refer to **Figure 47**.

1. Remove the rear brake drum as described in this chapter.

2. Determine rear brake shoe lining wear using the procedure in *Rear Brake Lining Check* in Chapter Three. However, always measure the brake lining thickness (**Table 2**) with a vernier caliper (**Figure 54**) after removing the brake drum to check for uneven wear. Replace both brake shoes at the same time.

CAUTION
To protect brake shoes suitable for re-installation from oil and grease, place

a clean shop cloth on the linings during removal.

NOTE
When reusing the brake shoes, mark them so they can be installed in their original mounting positions.

3. Remove the cotter pins and washer (A, **Figure 55**) and brake shoes (B).
4. Disconnect the brake shoe springs and separate the brake shoes.
5. Inspect the springs and replace them if there are any bent or unequally spaced coils.

NOTE
Always replace both springs at the same time.

6. Remove old grease from the camshaft and anchor pin surfaces.
7. Apply a light coat of high-temperature brake grease to the camshaft and anchor pins. Avoid getting any grease on the brake panel where the brake linings can make contact.
8. Install the springs onto the brake shoes.
9. Install the brake shoes onto the brake cam and anchor pins.
10. Install the washer (**Figure 56**) with its chamfered side facing toward the brake shoes.
11. Install two new cotter pins and bend their ends over to lock into place.
12. Install the rear brake drum as described in this chapter.
13. Adjust the rear brake (Chapter Three).

REAR BRAKE PANEL

The brake panel can be removed with the brake shoes attached. When servicing the brake panel, remove the brake shoes before removing the brake panel.
Refer to **Figure 47**.

Removal/Installation

1. Remove the rear brake drum as described in this chapter.

NOTE
Brake cables can be left attached to the brake panel if brake panel service is not required.

13

2. Unscrew the parking brake (A, **Figure 57**) and rear brake (B) adjusters from the end of the brake cables. Remove the collars and springs. Remove the brake cables from the brake panel.

3. Disconnect the vent hose from the brake panel fitting.

4. Remove the locknuts (A, **Figure 58**) and the brake panel (B). Discard the locknuts.

5. Inspect the brake panel assembly as described in this chapter.

6. Install the brake panel by reversing these removal steps, plus the following:

    a. Lubricate the dust seal lip (A, **Figure 59**) and O-ring (B) with grease.

    b. Secure the brake panel to the rear axle housing using new locknuts (A, **Figure 58**). Tighten the brake panel locknuts to 44 N•m (33 ft.-lb.).

    c. Adjust the rear brake as described in Chapter Three.

Brake Panel Inspection

1. Service and inspect the brake cam assembly as described in this section.

2. Inspect the dust seal (A, **Figure 59**) for excessive wear or damage. Replace the dust seal as described in *Rear Axle/Brake Panel Bearing Replacement*.

3. Turn the inner race of the rear axle/brake panel bearings (C, **Figure 59**) by hand. Both bearings must turn smoothly with no roughness or binding. Also make sure the outer race of each bearing fits tightly in the brake panel. Replace both bearings as described in *Rear Axle/Brake Panel Bearing Replacement*.

4. Inspect the O-ring (B, **Figure 59**) for excessive wear or damage. Replace the O-ring if necessary.

5. Check the brake panel for cracks or other damage.

Brake Cam Removal/Inspection/Installation

The brake cam can be removed with or without the brake panel mounted on the vehicle. Refer to **Figure 47** for this procedure.

1. If the brake panel is mounted on the vehicle, disconnect the brake cables (**Figure 57**) from the brake arm.

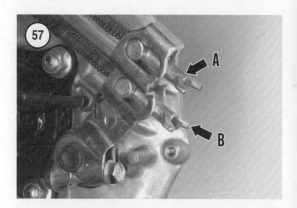

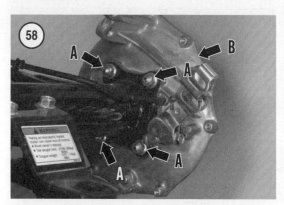

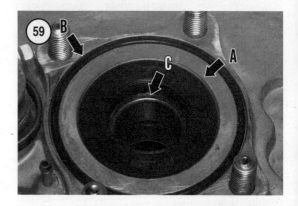

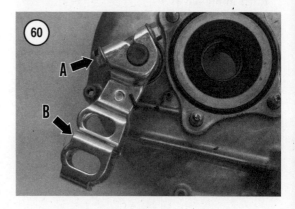

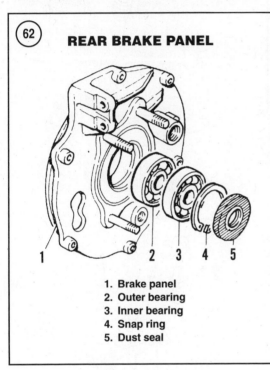

REAR BRAKE PANEL

1. Brake panel
2. Outer bearing
3. Inner bearing
4. Snap ring
5. Dust seal

2. Remove the brake shoes as described in this chapter.

3. Remove the brake arm nut and bolt (A, **Figure 60**).

4. Make punch marks on the brake cam and brake arm (**Figure 61**), if they are not already marked, so they can be installed in the same position.

5. Remove the brake arm (B, **Figure 60**), return spring, indicator plate and brake cam.

6. Remove the felt washer and dust seal from the brake panel.

7. Inspect the brake cam for excessive wear or damage.

8. Replace the felt washer and dust seal if it is excessively worn or damaged.

9. Inspect the return spring for cracks and other damage.

10. Apply grease to the dust seal before installing it.

11. Apply oil to the felt washer before installing it.

12. Install the dust seal and then the felt washer.

13. Lubricate the brake cam with grease and install it through the brake panel.

14. Install the return spring by hooking its end into the hole in the brake panel.

15. Install the indicator plate by aligning its wide tooth with the wide groove on the brake cam.

16. Install the brake arm (B, **Figure 60**) by aligning its punch mark with the punch mark on the brake cam (**Figure 61**). Hook the return spring onto the brake arm as shown in **Figure 60**.

17. Install the brake arm bolt and nut (A, **Figure 60**) and tighten them to 20 N•m (15 ft.-lb.). Move the brake arm by hand to make sure it moves smoothly. If there is any binding or roughness, remove and inspect the brake cam assembly.

18. Install the brake shoes as described in this chapter.

19. Reconnect the parking brake (A, **Figure 57**) and rear brake (B) cables at the brake arm.

20. Adjust the rear brake as described in Chapter Three.

Rear Axle/Brake Panel Bearing Replacement

The brake panel is equipped with a dust seal and two bearings (**Figure 62**). The bearings are identical (same part number).

1. Remove the brake shoes and brake panel as described in this chapter.

2. Remove the dust seal (A, **Figure 59**) with a wide blade screwdriver.

NOTE
If only replacing the dust seal, go to Step 8.

3. Remove the snap ring.

4. Support the brake panel in a press and press out both bearings. Discard both bearings.

5. Inspect the mounting bore for cracks, galling or other damage. Clean the mounting bore thoroughly.

6. Inspect the snap ring groove for cracks or other damage.

13

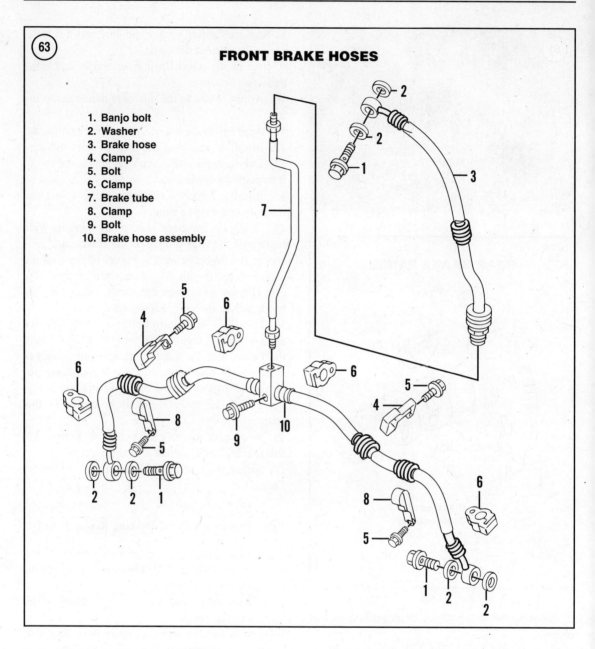

63

FRONT BRAKE HOSES

1. Banjo bolt
2. Washer
3. Brake hose
4. Clamp
5. Bolt
6. Clamp
7. Brake tube
8. Clamp
9. Bolt
10. Brake hose assembly

7. Install the new bearings as follows:

a. Install both bearings with a bearing driver placed on the outer bearing race. Use a press or drive the bearings into the mounting bore. Make sure each bearing turns smoothly after installing it.

b. Install the outer bearing (2, **Figure 62**) so its sealed side faces toward the brake shoes. Install the outer bearing until it bottoms in the mounting bore.

c. Install the inner bearing so its sealed side faces toward the snap ring and dust seal. Install the inner bearing until it bottoms against the outer bearing and the snap ring groove is accessible.

d. Install the snap ring into the mounting bore groove. Make sure the snap ring seats in the groove completely.

8. Install the new dust seal (5, **Figure 62**) as follows:

a. Pack the new dust seal lip with grease.

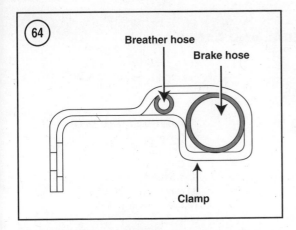

64

Breather hose

Brake hose

Clamp

67

65

66

b. Align the dust seal with the mounting bore so its closed side (A, **Figure 59**) faces out.

c. Tap the dust seal into place until it seats against the snap ring.

FRONT BRAKE HOSE REPLACEMENT

The upper brake hose can be replaced separately from the lower brake hoses. The lower brake hoses

must be replaced as an assembly with the three-way joint (**Figure 63**).

1. Remove the front fender (Chapter Fifteen).

2. Remove both front wheels (Chapter Ten).

3. Note the path and attachment points for the brake hoses. Note that the clamps secure both the brake hoses and the breather hoses (**Figure 64**, typical).

4. Drain the front brake fluid as described in this chapter. Because air has entered the brake lines, not all of the brake fluid will drain out.

NOTE
Because some residual brake fluid will remain in the lines, be careful when disconnecting and removing the brake hoses in the following steps.

5. To remove the upper brake hose, remove the banjo bolt and sealing washers from the brake master cylinder (**Figure 65**). Unscrew the lower end of the brake hose from the brake tube and remove the brake hose.

6. Remove the lower brake hose assembly as follows:

    a. Remove the banjo bolt and sealing washers (**Figure 66**) at the back of a wheel cylinder. Hold the open hose end in a container to catch any residual brake fluid. Repeat for the other side.

    b. Unscrew the lower end of the brake tube from the three-way fitting (A, **Figure 67**)

    c. Remove the bolt securing the three-way fitting to the frame (B, **Figure 67**).

    d. Remove the lower brake hose assembly.

7. Install new brake hose(s) in the reverse order of removal. Install new sealing washers.

8. Tighten the banjo bolts to 34 N•m (25 ft.-lb.).

13

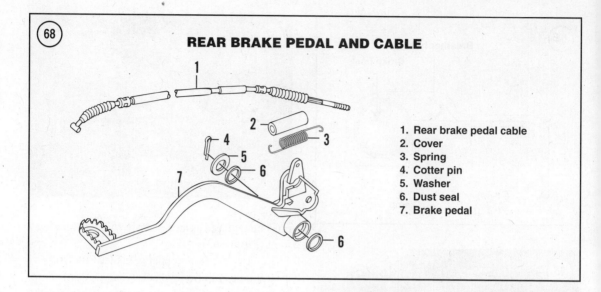

REAR BRAKE PEDAL AND CABLE

1. Rear brake pedal cable
2. Cover
3. Spring
4. Cotter pin
5. Washer
6. Dust seal
7. Brake pedal

9. Refill the master cylinder with fresh brake fluid clearly marked DOT 4. Bleed both front brakes as described in this chapter.

WARNING
Do not ride the vehicle before making sure the brakes operate properly.

REAR BRAKE PEDAL AND CABLE

This section describes service to the rear brake pedal and cable (**Figure 68**). To service the rear brake lever/parking brake cable, refer to *Rear Brake Lever/Parking Brake Cable* in this chapter.

1. Loosen and remove the rear brake pedal cable adjusting nut (A, **Figure 69**), collar and spring from the brake arm.

2. Disconnect the brake cable from the bracket on the brake panel.

3. Disconnect the brake return spring (A, **Figure 70**) from the brake pedal assembly.

4. Remove the cotter pin and washer (B, **Figure 70**), and remove the brake pedal assembly (C).

5. Disconnect the brake cable from the brake pedal.

6. When replacing the rear brake pedal cable, perform the following:

  a. Remove the rear brake cable from the frame, noting any cable guides or brackets.

  b. Lubricate the new brake cable as described in Chapter Three.

  c. Route the new rear brake pedal cable along the frame and through any cable guides or brackets.

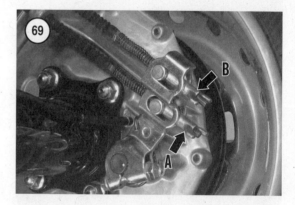

7. Remove all old grease from the brake pedal pivot shaft.

8. Check the brake pedal dust seals and replace them if they are excessively worn or damaged.

9. Pack the dust seal lips with grease.

10. Apply grease to the brake pedal pivot shaft and brake cable end (brake pedal side).

11. Reconnect the brake cable to the brake pedal, then install the brake pedal (C, **Figure 70**) onto its pivot shaft.

12. Install the washer and secure it with a new cotter pin (B, **Figure 70**). Bend the cotter pin ends over to lock it in place. Operate the brake pedal by hand, making sure it moves without any binding or roughness.

13. Reconnect the brake return spring (A, **Figure 70**) to the brake pedal.

14. Reconnect the rear brake pedal to the brake panel. Install the spring, collar and adjusting nut (A, **Figure 69**).

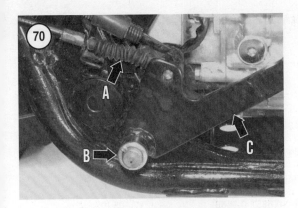

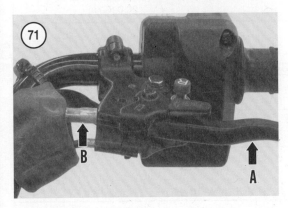

15. Adjust the rear brake as described in Chapter Three.

> *WARNING*
> *Do not ride the ATV before making*
> *sure the brakes operate properly.*

REAR BRAKE LEVER/PARKING BRAKE CABLE

The handlebar mounted rear brake lever (A, **Figure 71**) operates the rear brake and is also equipped with a lock which allows it to be used as a parking brake.

1. Remove the front fender (Chapter Fifteen).

2. Loosen and remove the rear brake lever/parking brake cable adjusting nut (B, **Figure 69**), collar and spring at the brake arm.

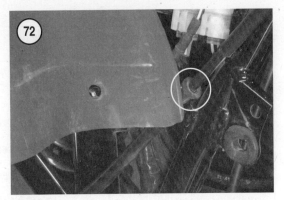

3. Disconnect the brake cable from the bracket on the brake panel.

4. Disconnect the brake cable (B, **Figure 71**) from the brake lever.

5. Tie a long piece of heavy string to one end of the brake cable. While removing the brake cable, the string will follow the cable's original path, allowing the new cable to be installed correctly.

6. Remove any clamps or cable guides (**Figure 72**, typical) securing the brake cable to the frame.

7. Remove the brake cable, making sure the string follows its original path.

8. Lubricate the new brake cable as described in Chapter Three.

9. Cut the string and tie it to the end of the new brake cable. Then pull the string and install the new brake cable along its original path.

10. Reconnect the brake cable to the brake lever (B, **Figure 71**).

11. Secure the brake cable with clamps or cable guides (**Figure 72**, typical).

12. Reconnect the rear brake lever/parking brake cable to the brake panel. Install the spring, collar and adjusting nut (B, **Figure 69**).

13. Adjust the rear brake as described in Chapter Three.

> *WARNING*
> *Do not ride the ATV before making*
> *sure the brakes operate correctly.*

13

Tables 1-3 are on the following page.

Table 1 FRONT BRAKE SERVICE SPECIFICATIONS

	New mm (in.)	Service limit mm (in.)
Brake drum inside diameter	160.0 (6.30)	161.0 (6.34)
Brake shoe lining thickness	4.0 (0.16)	1.0 (0.04)
Brake panel seal lip length	22 (0.9)	20 (0.8)
Brake panel warp	–	0.4 (0.02)
Master cylinder bore diameter	12.700-12.743 (0.5080-0.5017)	12.755 (0.5022)
Master cylinder piston outside diameter	12.657-12.684 (0.4983-0.4994)	12.645 (0.4978)
Wheel cylinder inside diameter	17.460-17.503 (0.6874-0.6891)	17.515 (0.6896)
Wheel cylinder piston outside diameter	17.417-17.444 (0.6857-0.6868)	17.405 (0.6852)
Waterproof seal lip length	22.0 (0.87)	20.0 (0.79)

Table 2 REAR BRAKE SERVICE SPECIFICATIONS

	New mm (in.)	Service limit mm (in.)
Brake drum inside diameter	160.0 (6.30)	161.0 (6.34)
Brake lining thickness	5.0 (0.20)	See text

Table 3 BRAKE TORQUE SPECIFICATIONS

	N•m	in.-lb.	ft.-lb.
Brake bleeder valve	6	53	–
Brake drum bolts	12	106	–
Brake hose clamp	12	106	–
Brake hose three-way joint nut	17	–	13
Brake hose banjo bolt	34	–	25
Front brake panel mounting bolts	29	–	22
Front hub nut	78	–	58
Master cylinder brake lever			
Pivot bolt	6	53	–
Nut	6	53	–
Master cylinder mounting bolts	12	106	–
Master cylinder reservoir cap screw	2	17.7	–
Rear brake arm bolt and nut	20	–	15
Rear brake panel drain plug	12	106	–
Rear brake panel locknuts	44	–	33
Wheel cylinder			
Bolt	8	71	–
Nut	17	–	13
Brake line nuts	16	–	12

CHAPTER FOURTEEN

OIL COOLER AND COOLING FAN

TRX350FE, TRX350FM and TRX350TE models are equipped with an oil cooler and cooling fan. TRX350TM model is equipped with an oil cooler, but not a cooling fan.

This chapter describes information for servicing the oil cooler and cooling fan assembly. These components can be left in place when servicing the engine and suspension components.

OIL HOSES

Replacement

Refer to **Figure 1**.
1. Label the hoses before disconnecting them from the oil cooler.
2A. On the right hose, remove the right center mud guard, front mud flap and inner fender panel as described in Chapter Fifteen.
2B. One the left hose, remove the left center mud guard, front mud flap and inner fender panel as described in Chapter Fifteen.

3. Remove the lower mounting bolts (**Figure 2**).
4. Remove the upper mounting bolts (A, **Figure 3**), then remove the oil hose.
5. Replace the O-rings (**Figure 4**) if they are leaking, chafing or damaged.
6. Lubricate the O-rings with engine oil.
7. Install the new hoses as shown in **Figure 1**. Tighten the mounting bolts securely.

OIL COOLER

Refer to **Figure 1**.

Removal/Installation

1. Drain the engine oil (Chapter Three).
2. Remove the oil cooler hoses as described in this chapter.
3. Remove the bolts and the oil cooler mounting brackets (B, **Figure 3**).
4. Remove the oil cooler (C, **Figure 3**) from the frame.

14

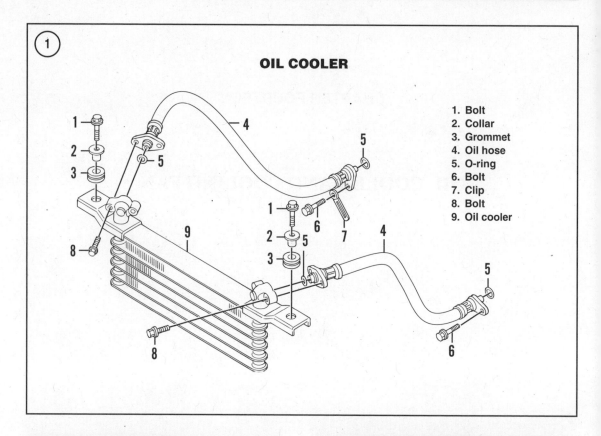

OIL COOLER

1. Bolt
2. Collar
3. Grommet
4. Oil hose
5. O-ring
6. Bolt
7. Clip
8. Bolt
9. Oil cooler

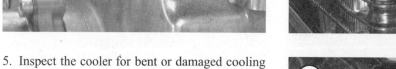

5. Inspect the cooler for bent or damaged cooling fins.

6. Install the oil cooler by reversing the preceding removal steps. Tighten all of the mounting bolts securely.

COOLING FAN
(EXCEPT TRX350TM)

Refer to **Figure 5**.

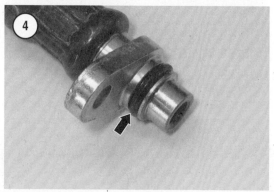

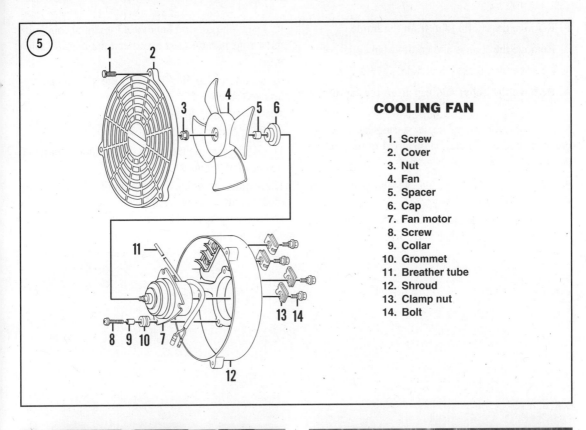

COOLING FAN

1. Screw
2. Cover
3. Nut
4. Fan
5. Spacer
6. Cap
7. Fan motor
8. Screw
9. Collar
10. Grommet
11. Breather tube
12. Shroud
13. Clamp nut
14. Bolt

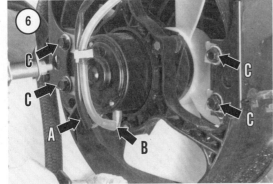

Removal/Installation

1. Remove the right side cover (Chapter Fifteen).

2. Remove the right inner fender (Chapter Fifteen).

3. Disconnect the electrical connectors of the fan motor power lead (A, **Figure 6**).

4. Disconnect the upper end of the breather tube (B, **Figure 6**).

6. Loosen, but do not remove, the cooling fan bracket bolts (C, **Figure 6**).

7. Remove the upper bracket bolts on the right mounting bracket (**Figure 7**).

8. Remove the fan bracket bolts (C, **Figure 6**) on both sides, then remove the fan assembly from the right side of the vehicle.

9. Install the cooling fan by reversing the preceding removal steps while noting the following:

   a. Check the breather tube for any obstructions.

   b. Tighten the cooling fan bracket bolts to 18 N•m (13 ft.-lb.).

Shroud Disassembly/Reassembly

Refer to **Figure 5** for this procedure.

14

1. Remove the cooling fan from the frame.

2. Remove the screws and cooling fan cover.

3. Remove the nut and fan blade.

4. Remove the collar and cap from the fan motor shaft.

5. Mark the fan motor so its wiring harness and breather tube clamp can be installed in its original position.

6. Remove the screws, fan motor, collars and grommets from the shroud.

7. Inspect all of the parts for excessive wear or damage. Check the fan blade for cracks or other damage.

8. Install the cooling fan motor into the shroud with its wiring harness and breather tube clamp facing up.

9. Secure the cooling fan with the grommets, collars and screws. Tighten the screws securely.

10. Install the cap and collar over the fan motor shaft.

11. Align the fan blade with the fan motor shaft and install the fan blade.

12. Apply threadlocking compound onto the fan motor shaft threads, then install the fan motor nut and tighten it securely.

13. Install the cooling fan cover and mounting screws.

CHAPTER FIFTEEN

BODY

This chapter contains removal and installation procedures for the seat, body panels, tool box and handlebar cover (FM and TM models).

Reinstall mounting hardware (such as small brackets, bolts, nuts, rubber bushings, metal collars, etc.) onto the removed part to prevent its loss or misidentification. Honda makes frequent changes during the model year, so the part and the way it is attached to the frame may differ slightly from the one used in the service procedures in this chapter.

RETAINING CLIPS

The TRX350 uses a plastic retaining clip assembly to secure many body components to the frame or other parts. Refer to **Figure 1** for steps on how to remove and install the retaining clips.

RETAINING TABS

Some panels are equipped with directional tabs (**Figure 2**). The tab fits into a slot in the adjoining panel. Be sure to move the panel properly to disengage or engage the tab in the slot.

SEAT

Removal/Installation

1. Park the ATV on level ground and set the parking brake.

2. Pull the lever (A, **Figure 3**) to release the seat lock and remove the seat (B).
3. Slide the seat hook underneath the frame brace, then push the seat down until it locks in place.
4. Make sure the seat is firmly locked in place.

> *WARNING*
> *Do not ride the ATV unless the seat is secured in place.*

RECOIL STARTER COVER

Removal/Installation

1. Pull out the upper end of the cover (**Figure 4**) to disengage the mounting stud from the frame grommet.
2. Move the cover up to disengage the tabs and remove the cover.
3. Reverse the removal steps to install the recoil starter cover.

SIDE COVERS

Removal/Installation

Refer to **Figure 5**.
1. Park the ATV on level ground and set the parking brake.
2. Remove the seat as described in this chapter.
3. Detach the air vent tube retainer (**Figure 6**) from the side cover being removed.
4. Remove the retaining clips.

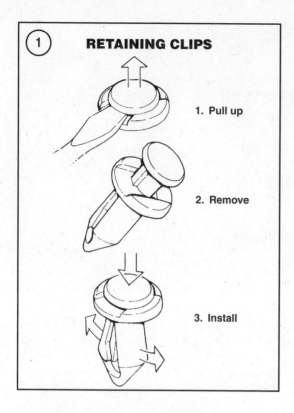

RETAINING CLIPS

1. Pull up

2. Remove

3. Install

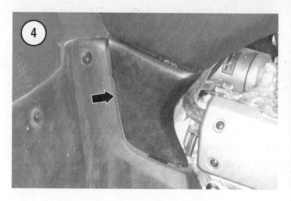

5. Push the side cover forward to disengage the upper tabs, then remove the side cover.

6. Install the side cover by reversing the preceding removal steps.

FUEL TANK COVER

Removal/Installation

Refer to **Figure 5**.

1. Park the ATV on level ground and set the parking brake.

2. Remove the seat as described in this chapter.

> *WARNING*
> *Fuel vapor is present when the fuel tank cap is removed. Because gasoline is extremely flammable and explosive, perform this procedure away from all open flames (including pilot lights) and sparks. Do not smoke or allow someone who is smoking in the work area as an explosion and fire may occur. Always work in a well-ventilated area. Wipe up any spills immediately.*

3. Remove the fuel tank cap and breather tube.

4. Remove the retaining clips securing the fuel tank cover.

5. Move the cover rearward to disengage the retaining tabs (**Figure 7**), then remove the cover.

6. Install the fuel tank cover by reversing the preceding removal steps.

FRONT CARRIER

Removal/Installation

1. Park the ATV on level ground and set the parking brake.

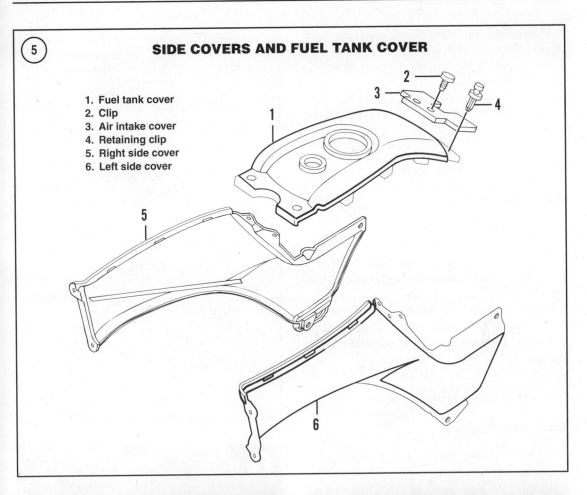

SIDE COVERS AND FUEL TANK COVER

1. Fuel tank cover
2. Clip
3. Air intake cover
4. Retaining clip
5. Right side cover
6. Left side cover

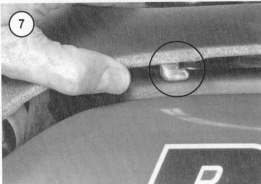

2. On early FE/TE models, remove the straps securing the sub-ICM module to the front carrier strut (**Figure 8**).

3. Remove the bolts securing the front carrier to the frame and front bumper.

4. Remove the front carrier (A, **Figure 9**).

5. Install the front cover by reversing the preceding removal steps.

FRONT BUMPER

Removal/Installation

1. Park the ATV on level ground and set the parking brake.

2. Remove the front carrier as described in this chapter.

15

3. Remove the headlight lower mounting bolts (**Figure 10**).

4. Remove the bolts securing the front bumper to the frame.

5. Remove the front bumper (B, **Figure 9**).

6. Install by reversing the preceding removal steps.

CENTER MUD GUARDS
(FE AND TE MODELS)

Removal/Installation

1. Remove the recoil starter cover as described in this chapter.

2. Remove the footpeg (A, **Figure 11**).

3. On the right side, remove the socket bolt (B, **Figure 11**).

4. Remove the retaining clips.

5. Remove the center mud guard (C, **Figure 11**).

6. Reverse the removal steps to install the center mud guard.

FRONT MUD GUARDS

Removal/Installation

1. On FE/TE models, remove the center mud guard as described in this chapter.

2. Remove the retaining clips at the front of the mud guard (**Figure 12**).

3. Remove the socket bolt (A, **Figure 13**).

4. Remove the remaining retaining clips, then remove the front mud guard (B, **Figure 13**).

5. Reverse the removal steps to install the front mud guard.

REAR MUD GUARDS
(FM AND TM MODELS)

Removal/Installation

1. Remove the recoil starter cover as described in this chapter.

2. On the right side, remove the socket bolts at the inner corner and at the center of the mud guard.

3. On the left side, remove the socket bolt.

4. Remove the retaining clips, then remove the rear mud guard.

5. Reverse the removal steps to install the rear mud guard.

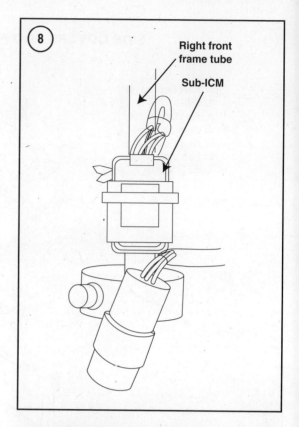

Right front frame tube

Sub-ICM

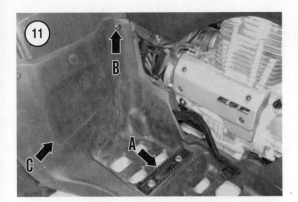

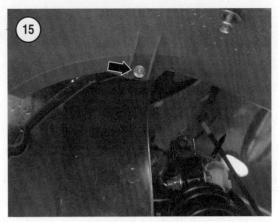

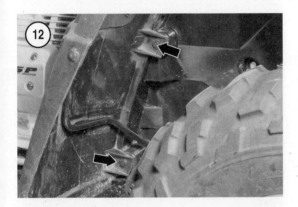

FRONT FENDER

Removal/Installation

1. Park the ATV on level ground and set the parking brake.

2. Remove the side covers and fuel tank cover assembly as described in this chapter.

3. Remove the front carrier and front bumper as described in this chapter.

4. On FE/TE models, remove the front mud guards as described in this chapter.

5. Detach the wire retaining band.

6. Disconnect the headlight connector (A, **Figure 14**) and accessory socket connector (B).

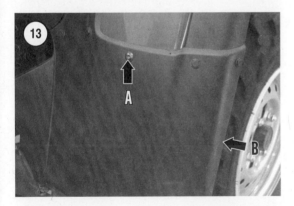

> *NOTE*
> *To unlock the connector, depress the tab on the front of the connector using a thin-blade screwdriver.*

7. Remove the self-tapping screw under the fender on both sides (**Figure 15**).

8. On FM/TM models, remove the socket bolt securing each side of the fender to the lower brace (**Figure 16**).

9. On FM/TM models, remove the retaining clips at the front of the mud guard (**Figure 17**, typical).

10. Remove the front fender mounting bolts.

11. Spread the front fender around the steering shaft and remove the front fender.

12. Remove the inner fender mounting bolt (A, **Figure 18**) and remove each inner fender (B).

13. Remove the mud guard brace mounting bolt (C, **Figure 18**) and remove the guard braces.

15

14. Reverse the removal steps to install the front fender.

HEADLIGHT GRILL

Removal/Installation

1. Remove the headlight housings as described in the *Headlight Lens* section in Chapter Nine.
2. Remove the mounting screws and retaining clips.
3. Remove the headlight grill.
4. Reverse the removal procedure to install the headlight grill.

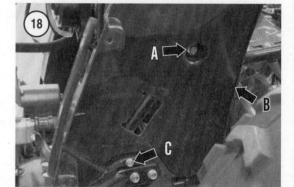

REAR CARRIER

Removal/Installation

1. Park the ATV on level ground and set the parking brake.
2. Remove the bolts (A, **Figure 19**) securing the rear fender to the carrier on each side.
3. Remove the bolts (B, **Figure 19**) securing the rear carrier to the frame on each side.
4. Remove the rear carrier (**Figure 20**).
5. Install the rear carrier by reversing the preceding removal steps.

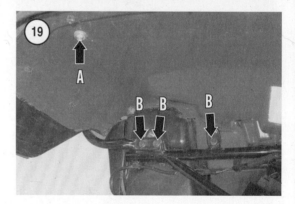

REAR FENDER

Removal/Installation

1. Park the ATV on level ground and set the parking brake.
2. Remove the rear carrier as described in this chapter.
3. Remove the battery (Chapter Three).

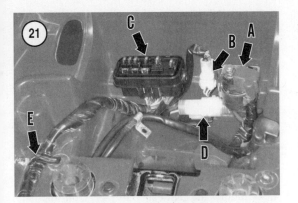

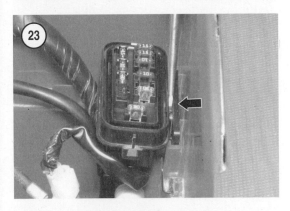

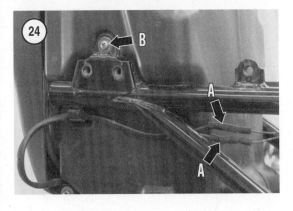

4. Pull off the black rubber boot on the starter relay, then disconnect the starter motor lead from the starter relay terminal (A, **Figure 21**). With the starter relay in place, remove the mounting bracket screw and remove the relay and bracket.

5. Remove the upper connector (B, **Figure 21**) from the mounting bracket. Use a thin-blade screwdriver and push forward the tab on the connector (**Figure 22**) to disengage it from the mounting bracket.

6. Disengage the fuse box (C, **Figure 21**) from the mounting bracket by pushing forward the retaining tab with a thin-blade screwdriver (**Figure 23**). Lift the fuse box off the bracket.

7. Remove the lower connector (D, **Figure 21**) from the mounting bracket. Use a thin-blade screwdriver and push up the tab on the connector to disengage it from the mounting bracket.

8. Detach the wiring harness clamp (E, **Figure 21**).

9. On FM/TM models, remove the rear mud guards as described in this chapter.

10. On FE/TE models, remove the center mud guards as described in this chapter.

CAUTION
If the muffler is hot, do not allow the
rear fender to contact it.

11. Remove the retaining clips.

12. Remove the rear fender while directing the electrical wires through the opening in the rear fender.

13. Reverse the removal procedure to install the rear fender.

TOOL BOX

Removal/Installation

1. Remove the rear fender as described in this chapter.

2. Disconnect the taillight connectors (A, **Figure 24**).

3. Remove the mounting screws (B, **Figure 24**) on each side, then remove the tool box.

4. Reverse the removal procedure to install the rear fender. Be sure to install the collars on the mounting screws.

15

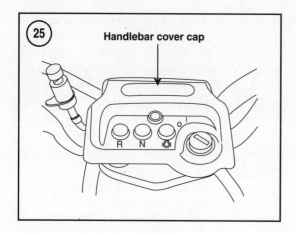

Handlebar cover cap

HANDLEBAR COVER

Refer to the following section for information concerning the handlebar cover on FM and TM models. Refer to Chapter Nine for information concerning the combination meter and cover used on FE and TE models, or FM and TM models so equipped.

Removal/Installation

1. Park the ATV on level ground and set the parking brake.

2. Remove the front fender as described in this chapter.

3. Disconnect the ignition switch connector (four wires) and indicator light connector (six wires) located on the front wiring connector bracket under the front fender.

4. Withdraw the fuel cap vent hose from the handlebar cover.

5. Remove the handlebar cover cap (**Figure 25**).

6. Remove the handlebar cover mounting screws.

7. Release both ends of the handlebar cover from the handlebar, then remove the handlebar cover assembly.

8. Install the handlebar cover by reversing the preceding removal steps. Check indicator light operation after starting the engine.

INDEX

16

16

NOTES

NOTES

WIRING
DIAGRAMS

TRX350 FE/TE USA AND CANADA
(2000-2002 MODELS)

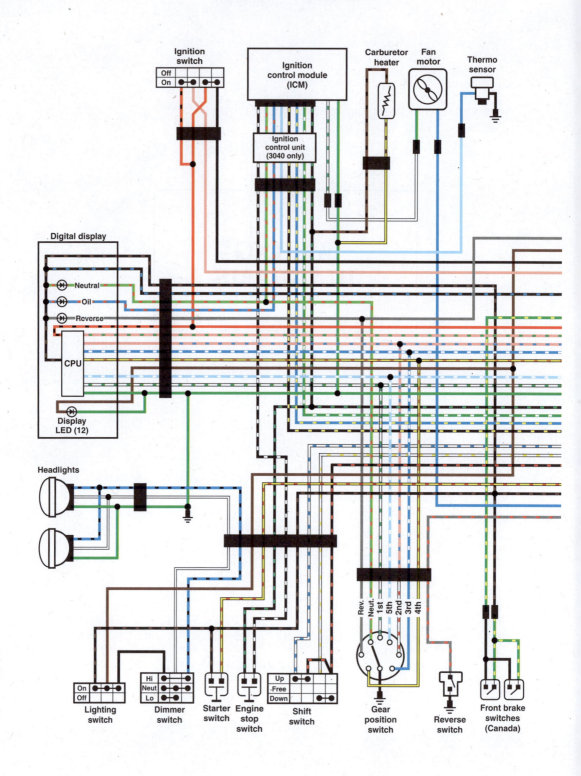

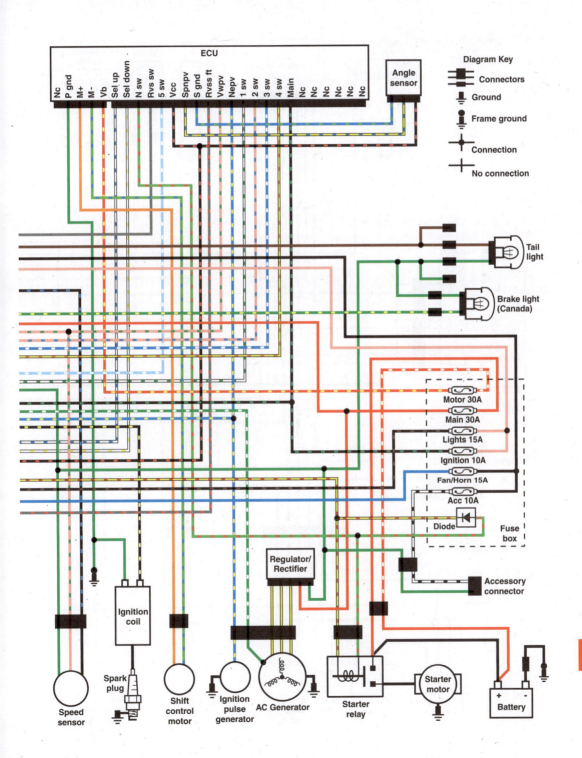

ECU

Nc | P gnd | M+ | M- | Vb | Sel up | Sel down | N sw | Rvs sw | 5 sw | Vcc | Spnpv | S gnd | Rvss ft | Vwpv | Nepv | 1 sw | 2 sw | 3 sw | 4 sw | Main | Nc | Nc | Nc | Nc | Nc | Nc | Nc

Angle sensor

Diagram Key

Connectors

Ground

Frame ground

Connection

No connection

Tail light

Brake light (Canada)

Motor 30A

Main 30A

Lights 15A

Ignition 10A

Fan/Horn 15A

Acc 10A

Diode

Fuse box

Regulator/ Rectifier

Accessory connector

Ignition coil

Speed sensor

Spark plug

Shift control motor

Ignition pulse generator

AC Generator

Starter relay

Starter motor

Battery

17

TRX350TM USA (2000-2006 MODELS)

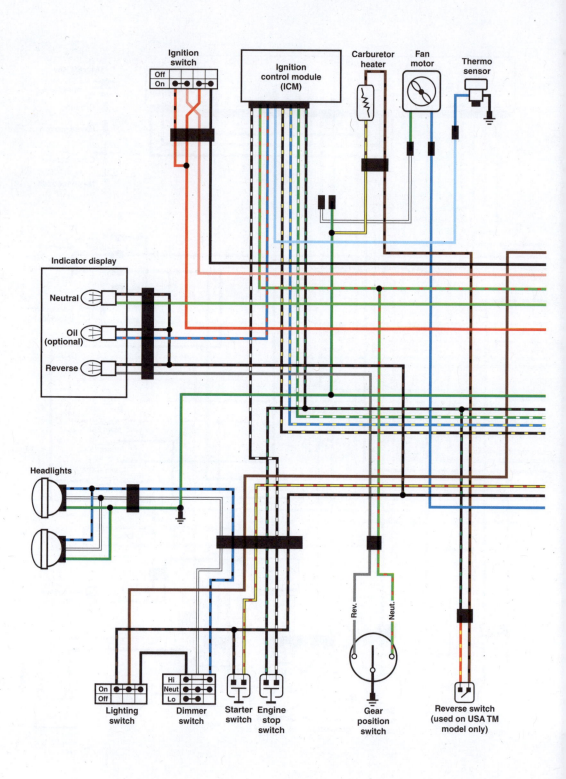

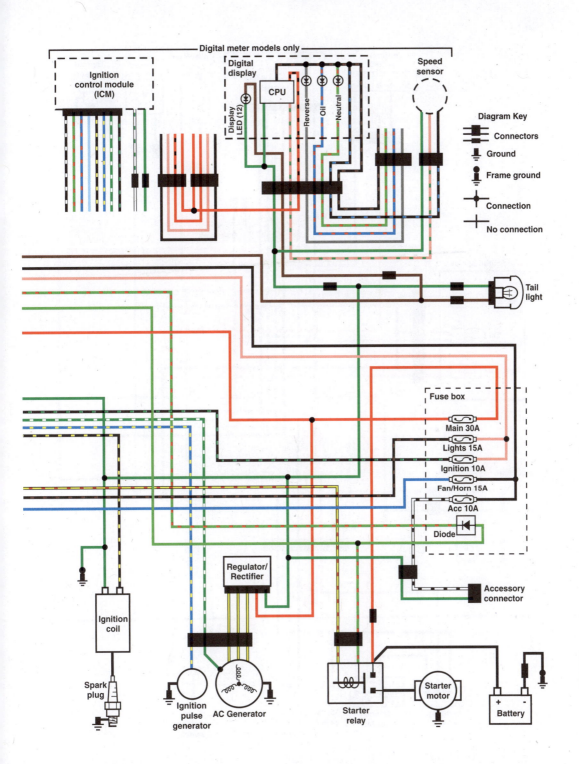

TRX350FM USA (2000-2006 MODELS)

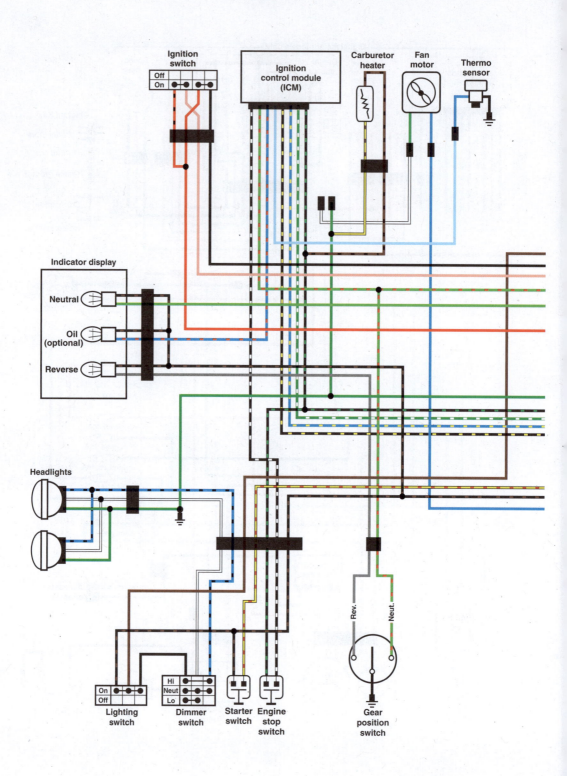

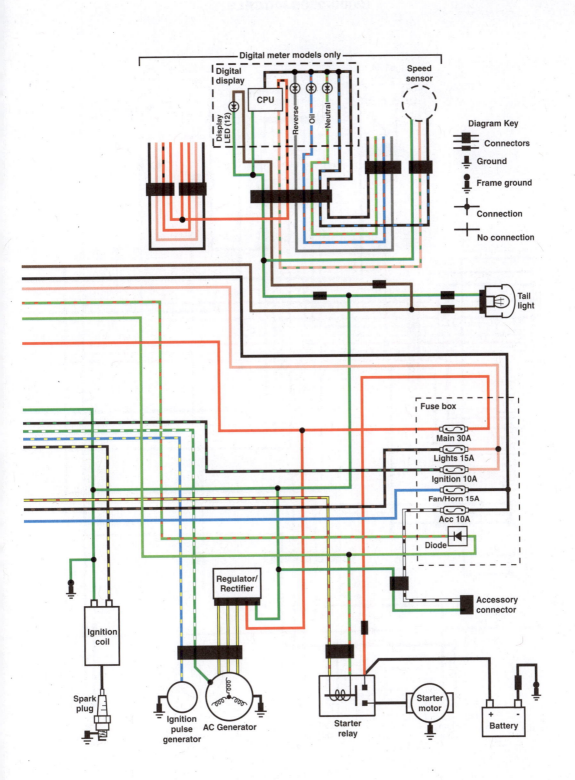

TRX350 FM/TM CANADA
(2000-2006 MODELS)

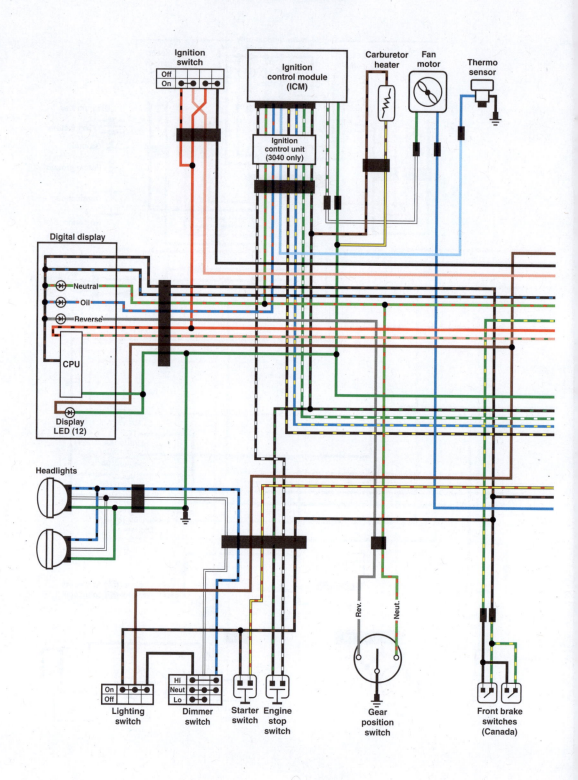

Ignition switch

Ignition control module (ICM)

Ignition control unit (3040 only)

Carburetor heater

Fan motor

Thermo sensor

Digital display

Neutral

Oil

Reverse

CPU

Display LED (12)

Headlights

Lighting switch

Dimmer switch

Starter switch

Engine stop switch

Gear position switch

Rev.

Neut.

Front brake switches (Canada)

On / Off

Hi / Neut / Lo

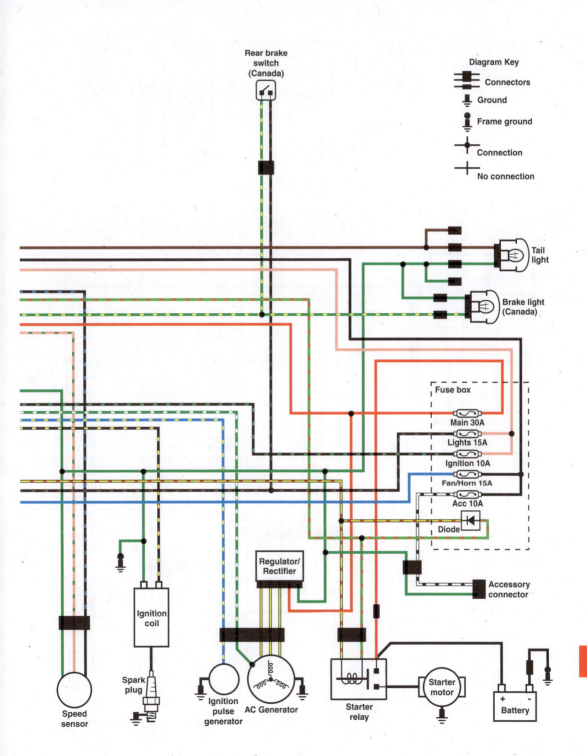

Rear brake
switch
(Canada)

Diagram Key

Connectors
Ground
Frame ground
Connection
No connection

Tail
light

Brake light
(Canada)

Fuse box

Main 30A
Lights 15A
Ignition 10A
Fan/Horn 15A
Acc 10A

Diode

Regulator/
Rectifier

Accessory
connector

Ignition
coil

Spark
plug

Speed
sensor

Ignition
pulse
generator

AC Generator

Starter
relay

Starter
motor

Battery

17

TRX350 FE/TE (2003-2006 MODELS)

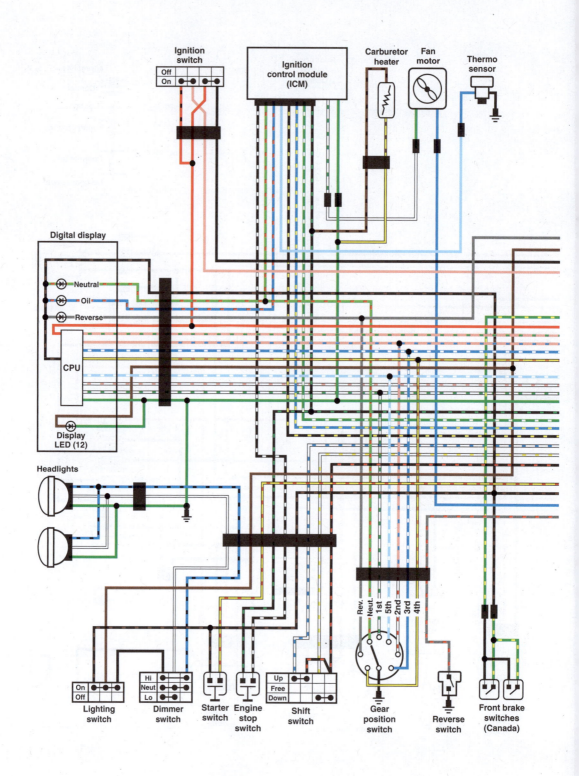

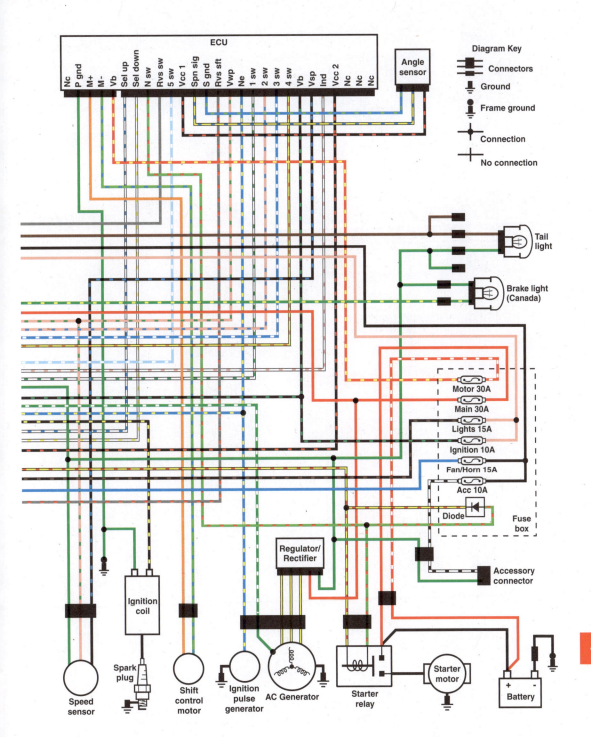

NOTES

NOTES

MAINTENANCE LOG

Date	Miles	Type of Service

MAINTENANCE LOG

Date	Miles	Type of Service